In the Margins
Special Populations
and American Justice

❖

Edited by

REID C. TOTH, Ph.D.

GORDON A. CREWS, Ph.D.

CATHERINE E. BURTON, Ph.D.

PEARSON
Prentice
Hall

Upper Saddle River, New Jersey 07458

Library of Congress Cataloging-in-Publication Data

In the margins: special populations and American justice / edited by Reid C. Toth,
Gordon A. Crews, Catherine E. Burton.
   p. cm.
Includes bibliographical references and index.
ISBN-13: 978-0-13-028431-0 (alk. paper)
ISBN-10:   0-13-028431-9 (alk. paper)
  1. Discrimination in criminal justice administration—United States. 2. Criminal justice, Administration of —
United States. 3. Discrimination—Law and legislation—United States. 4. Marginality, Social—United States.
I. Toth,Reid C. II. Crews, Gordon A. III. Burton, Catherine E.
  KF9223.I56 2008
  345.73'05—dc22

2007031491

Editor-in-Chief: Vernon R. Anthony
Senior Acquisitions Editor: Tim Peyton
Associate Editor: Jillian Allison
Editorial Assistant: Alicia Kelly
Marketing Manager: Adam Kloza
Production Liaison: Joanne Riker
Cover Design Director: Jayne Conte

Cover Design: Kiwi Design
Cover Illustration: Christian Pierre, 1962-American,
   "All Sorts" 1996, Private Collection/Christian
   Pierre/SuperStock
Full-Service Project Management/
   Composition: Integra Software Services, Ltd.
Printer/Binder: King Printing Co., Inc.

Credits and acknowledgments borrowed from other sources and reproduced, with permission, in this textbook
appear on appropriate page within text.

Pearson Education LTD.
Pearson Education Singapore, Pte. Ltd
Pearson Education, Canada, Ltd
Pearson Education–Japan

Pearson Education Australia PTY, Limited
Pearson Education North Asia Ltd
Pearson Educación de Mexico, S.A. de C.V.
Pearson Education Malaysia, Pte. Ltd

4 5 6 7 8 9 10 VOCR 15 14 13 12 11
ISBN-13: 978-0-13-028431-0
ISBN-10:   0-13-028431-9

The editors would like to dedicate this book to

My grandparents, Mr. Edward W. and Mrs. Frances R. Counts,
Mrs. Jetta Y. Dearman, Mrs. Myrtle Jacobsen, and Mrs. Eula Chalk;
and in memory of Rev. Harry Chalk and Mr. Joe R. Dearman.—*RCT*

My beautiful wife, Dr. Angela D. Crews, and our wonderful children,
Brandon, Konnor, Garrison, and Samantha.—*GAC*

My parents, Obie and Lucille Burton.—*CEB*

Contents

❖

Contents xiii

Preface

The purpose of *In the Margins: Special Populations and American Justice* is to examine the myriad issues relating to the concept of marginalized groups and their various roles in the American criminal justice system. Taken from criminological, anthropological, and sociological perspectives, this text presents discussions of historical development, societal issues, crime and punishment, discrimination, employment, and other serious problems that can be considered by readers interested in the topic of marginalization and its effects.

In a world living in the aftermath of the September 11, 2001, terrorist attacks on the United States, Americans are more aware than ever of cultural differences that exist among the nation's citizens. The results, in some cases, have been increases in discriminatory attitudes and behaviors toward groups that had already experienced a history of marginalization. The focus of this work is an appreciation of the need for information relating to the treatment of minorities and other marginalized groups by the current system of justice in America. Inherent in this focus is an attempt to provide the most comprehensive examination possible, while still not simply relying on "numbers and statistics" to serve as the foundation for the subjects discussed. This focus also attempts to cover not only the traditional groups (e.g. racial minorities), but also discusses in depth other special groups that tend to be ignored by the standard texts (e.g. religious groups, the physically impaired, gender, etc.). Again, this text does not rely on an overabundance of statistics that, while providing an accurate picture of the current state, have no longevity and are difficult to understand and recall. Instead, the issues in this book are presented in reference to general trends (information that will not be substantially different in a year or two) and will rely on documented, anecdotal discussions (both historical and contemporary) to illustrate significant points. It is believed by the authors that this approach is more interesting to the reader, and therefore will facilitate learning by holding one's attention. It is said that those who do not remember the past are condemned to repeat it.

Excluding the first and last chapters, the remaining chapters each concentrate on a separate cultural, racial, or ethnic group that has experienced a definitive history of marginalization in the United States. Efforts were made to consistently address topics relevant to the primary elements of the criminal justice system such as those individuals employed by the system, those involved in the commission of crime such as offenders and victims, those processed through the court system, and those under correctional control. The reader will notice that the marginalized populations covered in this comprehensive book include ones that are traditionally ignored by other texts such as the disabled, the elderly, and those subscribing to religious beliefs that differ from those of the dominant culture. Also included, of course, are discussions of the more commonly recognized special populations such as prominent racial minorities.

The editors originally conceived the idea for this book in 1999 when lead co-editor Reid C. Toth was teaching a course on Minorities in the Criminal Justice system at the University of Nebraska–Kearney. Dr. Toth found that of the available texts at that time, none was comprehensive enough in coverage. Having conducted research on discrimination in various forms in the justice system, Dr. Toth noticed the glaring omissions in the literature of that time that dealt with special populations. For example, despite the passage of the *Americans With Disabilities Act* in 1990, very few state criminal justice agencies were fully compliant with the architectural barriers requirement of the ADA by 1999. Dr. Toth recruited co-editors Dr. Gordon A. Crews and Dr. Catherine E. Burton to participate in the project. After many years of revisiting the topic since the original conception, the editors have put together a superb team of authors to construct this inclusive book on the topic of special populations in criminal justice.

The editors would like to acknowledge the support and tremendous patience of the staff at Prentice Hall publishing. A special thanks to Margaret Lannamann, Sarah Holle, and Tim Peyton for their guidance and assistance throughout this process. Dr. Toth would especially like to thank her husband, Frederick M. Toth IV, for his unwavering support and devotion. Dr. Crews would like to thank his beautiful wife, Dr. Angela W. Crews, for her loving support and contribution to the manuscript as well as their children Brandon, Garrison, Konnor, and Samantha for their support. Dr. Burton would like to thank her parents, Obie and Lucille Burton, who made all things possible for her. Finally the editors would like to extend their sincere appreciation to the additional contributors who wrote chapters for this book: Drs. Marjie Britz, Angela Crews, John Falconer, Lynne Snowden, and Skip Grubb.

About the Contributors

Marjie T. Britz, Ph.D., is an Associate Professor of Sociology in the Department of Sociology at Clemson University in Clemson, SC. She has authored numerous books and articles on topics ranging from organized crime to computer forensics. Her most recent works focus on the intersection of technology and international criminal syndicates. She is a member of a variety of professional and academic organizations, including the Academy of Criminal Justice Sciences, the Southern Criminal Justice Association, the International Association of Chiefs of Police, and the High Technology Crime Investigation Association.

Catherine E. Burton, Ph.D., is an Assistant Professor of Criminal Justice in the Department of Political Science and Criminal Justice at The Citadel in Charleston, South Carolina. Her research interests include examining the relationship between race, ethnicity, and gender as it relates to crime and the criminal justice system.

Angela W. Crews, Ph.D., is an Associate Professor of Criminal Justice in the Department of Criminal Justice at Washburn University in Topeka, Kansas. Dr. Crews' current research interests relate to policy analysis and program evaluation in all areas of the criminal justice system, particularly in corrections and law enforcement.

Gordon A. Crews, Ph.D., is an Associate Professor of Criminal Justice in the Department of Criminal Justice at Washburn University in Topeka, Kansas. Dr. Crews' current research interests focus on an international comparison of police and societal responses to individuals involved in alternative belief systems and practices (e.g. Goth, Wicca, Satanism).

John Falconer, Ph.D., is Director of Sponsored Programs at the University of Nebraska at Kearney. He works with faculty to develop grants and contracts to support their scholarly work, and he conducts a multi-disciplinary undergraduate research program. His research includes policy work on issues of access and diversity in higher education, as well as economic development. Dr. Falconer holds a Ph.D. in Educational Administration from the University of Nebraska–Lincoln, and an M.A. in Foreign Affairs from the University of Virginia.

Skip Grubb, Ph.D., is the Program Director of Criminal Justice Technology at Columbia State Community College in Columbia, TN. After retiring from the Roanoke City Police Department he earned his doctorate from the University of Southern Mississippi. Dr. Grubb taught at Marshall University for approximately 10 years prior to his current position at Columbia State Community College.

Lynne L. Snowden, Ph.D., is an Associate Professor at the University of North Carolina–Wilmington. She has published four books, including *Collective Violence* (2000) and *Terrorism: Research, Readings, and Realities* (2005), as well as numerous journal articles on violence, policing, and other related topics. Currently she is working on a second edition of *Collective Violence*. In 1993, she developed a course on terrorism which she continues to teach every year. Last year, her work broadened to include the study of Homeland Security since the topic combines her lifelong research topics. In her service activities, Dr. Snowden has worked with Latino social service agencies for almost 20 years teaching ESL, developing education and healthcare programs, and serving on their Boards of Directors.

Reid C. Toth, Ph.D., is an Assistant Professor in the Department of Sociology, Criminal Justice, and Women's Studies at the University of South Carolina Upstate. She has authored and co-authored articles relating to hate crimes, minorities, criminal justice history, administration, and juvenile justice. She has previously co-authored a book with Gordon A. Crews on the history of school violence. Dr. Toth is a member of the Academy of Criminal Justice Sciences, the American Society of Criminology, the Southern Criminal Justice Association, the North Carolina Criminal Justice Association, and the National Association of Scholars. She is a graduate of the University of South Carolina.

1

America's Intolerant History

Reid C. Toth

❖

CHAPTER OUTLINE

A HISTORICAL OVERVIEW OF AMERICAN INTOLERANCE

In this first chapter, a discussion of the various manifestations of intolerance throughout American history is presented. Social groups such as homosexuals and religious organizations as well as racial minorities are given a brief examination as to their place in America's history of discrimination. To cover each group exhaustively is beyond the scope of this chapter. It is intended to provide a brief insight into the major themes facing each class of citizens. Subsequent chapters specific to the individual groups offer a complete discussion of their plight in modern day America. The discussion begins with a focus on the White Anglo-Saxon Protestants who first settled the continent and later developed the majority culture known today. The chapter ends with a detailed discussion of the most significant act of defiance against intolerance—the Civil Rights Movement of the twentieth century.

WASPs

In the early days of the United States, the most significant portion of the population was made up of White Anglo-Saxon Protestants (WASPs) who had four main values that defined their ethnicity: (1) a belief in democracy that promoted equality, freedom and individualism; (2) a belief in private economic enterprise and success; (3) a belief in the Protestant branch of the Judeo-Christian religion; and (4) a belief in secularism defined by rationality, progress, and scientific advancement. The WASPs were so grounded in these principles that any diversion from them was considered deviant and held in reproach. Eventually, a social class system was developed that centered on traditional WASP values. By the 1830s, the physical differences of Native Americans, Mexicans, and African Americans from those of the homogeneous WASP culture relegated these groups to the bottom of the social hierarchy. Groups who were less physically distinct from the WASPs, such as Germans, Dutch, and Irish, were received with greater acceptance by the predominantly British society (Purpura 2001).

The WASPs established the early economic, political, social, and religious foundations of America. Pressure was put on non-WASPs to conform to the traditional culture by learning English and abandoning opposing cultural values. Laws were even passed that established quotas for immigration, which resulted in discrimination against individuals who were least like the WASPs in appearance (Purpura 2001).

Nativism

Once European Protestants established themselves as the "native core" of the United States, they were openly hostile to the cultural influences of other immigrant groups. While they found the cheap labor provided by immigrants to be useful, they saw themselves as the only true "Americans." Immigrants who did not embrace Protestantism were ostracized and reminded of their inferiority by the actions of nativist mobs. These mobs were fiercely protective of all cultural values that they considered to be truly American and included anti-immigrant leagues, the various manifestations of the Ku Klux Klan, and political parties such as the Know Nothings (Perry 2000a).

It was not long after the Revolutionary War that *nativism*, or the practice of protecting the indigenous culture through conscious effort, began to take hold. Programs and policies were developed that were supposed to encourage non-WASPs to adopt WASP values and traditions. The WASP belief in secular progressivism allowed for prejudices that they believed were based on logic and science. The 1800s saw the onset of supposed scientifically justified racial ideologies that further supported the WASP-held negative perceptions of immigrants. WASPS believed themselves to be inherently superior physically, culturally, intellectually, and politically (Perry 2000a).

The 1820s saw the beginning of a broad WASP-based political movement centered on a hatred of Catholics, Jews, and other recent immigrants, including Irish, Italians, and Germans. This nativist movement extended into the twentieth century. Leaders were not confined to the fringes of American politics but were elected to prominent political office and published widely read anti-immigrant newspapers. The movement eventually became the Know Nothing Party and by the late nineteenth century had evolved into the American Protective Association. The nativists encouraged expression of hatred through church burnings, riots, and mob attacks against priests and immigrants. In the 1840s, Philadelphia alone saw three consecutive months of rioting that resulted in thirty deaths, hundreds of injuries, and dozens of burned homes (Jacobs and Henry 1996).

Anti-Jewish rhetoric became the focus of the nativists in the twentieth century as Jews were openly denied employment, housing, and rentals. The National Union for Social Justice (NUSJ), founded in the 1930s by Father Charles Coughlin, used radio broadcasts to launch anti-Jewish attacks and praise Nazi Germany. In addition to the Catholics, it was not unusual to see other groups such as the Irish and Germans who had previously been victims of nativism become active participants in anti-Jewish activities. It was even present at the highest levels of the federal government. Breckenridge Long, an anti-Jewish nativist, was appointed assistant secretary of state under President Roosevelt. He publicly declared that the "large number of Jews from Russia and Poland are entirely unfit to become citizens of this country . . . They are lawless, scheming, defiant . . . just the same as the criminal Jews who crowd our police court dockets in New York" (Jacobs and Henry 1996, 367).

The Eugenics Movement

By the turn of the century, the WASP pseudo-scientific practice of justifying their treatment of groups deemed inferior took a decidedly sinister turn. Between the years of 1907 and 1937, thirty-one states enacted legislation that permitted the involuntary sterilization of certain predefined classes of individuals. Known as *eugenics*, this practice was generally restricted to mentally ill, mentally deficient, and epileptic individuals. Currently, there are still a few states where forced sterilization of these groups is a legal option. Historically, over 70,000 individuals were involuntarily sterilized and countless others incarcerated because their intellect, behavior, or backgrounds were considered undesirable. In Lynchburg, Virginia, over 8,000 individuals were sterilized between 1924 and 1972. The practice was so common, in fact, that the system adopted the rather routine method of sterilizing men on Tuesdays and women on Thursdays. The eugenics movement even had support on the U.S. Supreme Court where, in a 1927 case, Justice Oliver Wendell Holmes quipped, "Three generations of imbeciles is enough." Even as late as 1980, the state of Texas was advocating forced sterilization of welfare recipients (McCaghy et al. 2000).

Women

Belief in the WASP culture and its superiority was held by both men and women. However, while WASP women were not specifically targeted by the nativists, they also were not viewed with the same level of respect as WASP men. In colonial America, women were not seen as independent persons and were therefore not subject to legal prosecution nor afforded legal protection. Prior to the twentieth century, women were not permitted to vote, file civil complaints, serve on juries, or enter into contracts. They did not have any legal rights concerning their children and generally could not own property. If they were single, then they were the property of their fathers; if married, they were considered the property of their husbands.

Until the 1970s, the United States subscribed to the English doctrine of *coverture* that asserted that the husband and wife were a single legal entity and that the husband had legal control of that entity. This meant that the wives were legally obligated to be submissive to their husbands and the husbands had the legal right to use "domestic chastisement" or physical force if necessary to ensure submission. It was not until 1971 that the U.S. Supreme Court, in the case of *Reed v. Reed*, finally recognized women as "persons" (Hackstaff 2000).

Witch Hunts and Religion

Religious persecution was present in the American colonies from the earliest settlements. The Puritans had fled England to avoid persecution for their fanatical practices, yet they were equally intolerant of anyone who did not strictly subscribe to Puritan practices. Typical religious-oriented offenses in Puritan society of the Massachusetts Bay Colony included heresy, blasphemy, Quakerism, and violation of the Sabbath. Given that women were expected to live an existence of servitude and compliance, it is not surprising that they were often singled out for prosecution of these offenses. One of the most significant cases surrounded the trials of Anne Hutchison in 1637 and 1638. She was accused of heresy and failing to heed the standard expectations of women by holding religious meetings in her home. In the first trial she was found guilty and sentenced to a period of confinement followed by banishment. During her incarceration however, she continued espousing her progressive views, and therefore was tried and convicted again, this time by the church. She was excommunicated and banished. She was later killed by Indians during her banishment. By 1692, hysteria created by the intense religious persecution resulted in two hundred people being tried for witchcraft in Salem, Massachusetts (Sheldon 2001).

It is ironic that the Puritans were fueling such persecution given that they had left England to escape precisely this type of harassment. In fact, trials for witchcraft were not an invention of the Puritans but had been practiced for centuries in England (Sheldon 2001). Such English traditions and ideologies became grounded in colonial culture. Historically, religious communities have been compared to the standard of Anglo-Saxon Protestantism. Religious difference has served as the basis for much hostility and violence in the United States. Mormons, for example, were forced to leave New York, Ohio, Missouri, and Illinois to escape victimization (Perry 2000d).

Anglo-Saxon Protestants were particularly intolerant of Catholics because it was feared that the Pope desired to be head not only of the Catholic Church but of the United

States government as well. Protestants also viewed the practice of celibacy as deviant and one that gave rise to "unnatural" sexual practices within the church. As a result, New York banned priests and other Catholic clergy in 1700, threatening them with imprisonment as well as death. Catholics saw legislation passed that drastically restricted their political rights, and anti-Catholic sentiment frequently resulted in violence (Perry 2000d).

Religious intolerance has continued through the twentieth century into the twenty-first. Modern anti-Semitism was epitomized by the Nazi-instigated Holocaust. The result of the Nazi persecution was emigration of European Jews to the United States. Christian anti-Jewish rhetoric in the United States has resulted from the idea that Jewish beliefs concerning their own faith are simply inaccurate. It has been believed that Jews practice Old Testament rituals of child sacrifice and blood drinking. Such stereotypes also led to a general belief that the perceived economic success of Jews was a result of deceit and conspiracy (Perry 2000d).

The Islamic faith has been a relatively new arrival to the United States. Many Americans continue to associate the fundamentalism of Muslims with violence, believing that most followers will do anything for their faith. Muslims therefore are often targeted as suspects of terrorism. This is further compounded by the fact that most Westerners lump all Muslims and Arabs into one group without distinction for other cultural variations (Perry 2000d).

Other forms of non-mainstream religion have also been targeted throughout the twentieth century. During the 1960s, many members of the "peace and love" hippie scene drifted toward fringe religious groups. The parents of such individuals, already opposed to their children's involvement in the peace movement, launched a crusade against these religious groups. It became known as the Anti-Cult Movement (ACM). Individuals from the ACM acting as "deprogrammers" would at times forcibly abduct persons from fringe religious groups, take them to a hotel room or other suitable facility, and batter them with anti-cult messages until the person relented their religious affiliation. Ironically, by using this tactic the ACM was engaging in virtually the same techniques that had been used on the indoctrinated individual by the cult in the first place. ACM groups such as the Cult Awareness Network continued to grow in response to tragedies like the mass suicides at Jonestown, Guyana, in the late 1970s and the clash between law enforcement and the Branch Davidians in Waco, Texas, during the 1990s (Barkan and Snowden 2001).

Homosexuals

Religious intolerance in Colonial America and the United States has not been limited to practitioners of alternative faiths. Individuals engaging in acts such as homosexuality that were deemed unacceptable by the doctrine of the mainstream religion were often perse-cuted. Colonial Americans took the view, based on English common law, that if the church forbade it, then the state should forbid it as well. Because sodomy and buggery were con-sidered sinful by the church, they were subsequently outlawed in most colonies. In the Massachusetts Bay Colony in 1646, William Paine was executed for the crime of homo-sexuality. Jan Creoli in the New Netherland Colony was choked to death and burned in the same year for being a gay man. Death was the sentence for any woman that "went against nature" in New Haven Colony of 1655 (Perry 2000c). Thomas Jefferson, in an effort to soften the harshness of such laws, recommended that Virginia change the penalty for sodomy from death to castration. After the American Revolution, Pennsylvania was at the vanguard by abolishing the death penalty for sodomy. Laws against homosexuality remained on the books in most states, but were punished by long prison sentences rather than death or physical harm (Perry 2000c).

The "sin" view of homosexuality eventually gave way to the "illness" view, where homosexuality was still considered wrong and deviant, but as a symptom of disease, rather than a symptom of immorality. Because this view still attached the label of "deviant," same-sex relations continued to be criminalized. From the 1800s to the 1900s public figures such as British legal scholar William Blackstone still referred to sodomy as "the infamous crime against nature; a crime not fit to be named" (Perry 2000c). As a result of being defined as deviant, homosexuals were frequently the victims of violence. Comstock (1991) stated that in the 1930s lesbians were "often the subject of police brutality. Using a rule of thumb that required women to wear at least three articles of women's clothing, policemen often beat and obscenely manhandled those who preferred to dress in . . . drag" (Perry 2000c, 18). Much of the police abuse aimed at homosexuals was both verbal and physical. Gay bars were frequently raided and patrons randomly arrested without being informed of the charges or legal rights.

The police were not the only group targeting homosexuals for violence. Groups of teenage males often considered them easy prey, as described in the following passage by Comstock (1991):

> Seedy characters haunted male homosexual cruising areas in order to beat and rob their victims. "Pickups" suddenly metamorphosed into thieves, seizing the valuables in one's home, secure in the knowledge that the incident would not be reported. Gangs of men stalked lesbian bars to attack women who rebuffed their sexual overtures. The police, if they intervened, were more likely to arrest the women than their male assailants (p. 13).

While assaults of homosexuals were not legal, the officials tended to side with the perpetrators, especially when the offender was a police officer. Without legal protection, homosexuals were subjected to increased levels of violence as their places in society became more visible. Homosexuals often experienced abuse at the hands of their families well before they were accessible to street gangs and police. It was not uncommon for lesbians to be locked in their homes when they disclosed their sexual orientation. The fact that violence was considered a virtue when used against homosexuals demonstrates the universal hatred of the group by the American mainstream culture (Perry 2000c).

In the 1950s, homosexuality was believed by some to be an epidemic that was spread by communists in an effort to deteriorate the moral fiber of the country. President Eisenhower declared that homosexuality would void a person's eligibility for federal jobs. Senator Joseph McCarthy, and the infamous House Un-American Activities Committee, implied that homosexuality was synonymous with being a traitor. As a result, the military became more aggressive in expelling lesbians and gay men. Police forces were given blanket permission to invade homes and meeting places with purpose of harassing and arresting homosexuals. Sodomy, at one time a capitol offense, was no longer punished by the death penalty beginning in the early nineteenth century. However, in 1950, two states still considered it a felony that was only surpassed in seriousness by murder, kidnapping, and rape. After World War II, state legislatures, with the support of the medical community, began passing sexual psychopath laws that included homosexuality. This allowed for a wide range of legally sanctioned medical experiments on institutionalized homosexuals including psychotherapy, hypnosis, castration, hysterectomy, lobotomy, electroshock, aversion therapy, and untested drugs.

It was not until the 1960s that homosexuals in the United States began to empower themselves on the social and political fronts (Perry 2000c).

Hate Groups

Since colonial times, Americans have used hatred as a common bond. Many groups target individuals with whom they do not identify for discrimination, violence, and neglect. When these groups formally organize themselves around the rally cry of hate, we consider them to be *hate groups*. Barkan and Snowden (2001) note that ironically, the American Revolution may have established a culture and destiny of intolerance in the United States by providing a model for the use of violence to support any cause that seems honorable. This fact has not escaped leaders of many hate groups, who often declare themselves to be intensely patriotic. A detailed discussion of hate groups will be provided in Chapter 11. For the purposes of this brief historical overview, we will concentrate this discussion on the development of America's most recognized hate group, the Ku Klux Klan.

The evolution of the Ku Klux Klan can be divided into three eras, during each of which the Klan transformed into three distinct groups. The Klan was developed originally in the former Confederate states after the Civil War. Members included former Confederate Army officers and vigilantes who sought to protect the white community. At the hands of the Klan, blacks experienced violence that was rarely punished by law. The second era of the Klan began in 1915 and continued until the 1930s. By this time the Klan had nationwide support and membership. The group had gathered support through coalitions of religious fundamentalist groups in addition to the traditional racist groups. Members of this Klan were able to win gubernatorial elections and other state and local government positions. During this time it broadened its scope beyond hatred of blacks to opposition to socialism, communism, and sexual liberalism. This era demonstrates the height of Klan power. By 1930, however, the Klan's influence began to decline. By the 1970s, the Klan had seen a steep decline in membership due largely to government crackdowns and sustained litigation by interest groups such as Klanwatch and the Southern Poverty Law Center. In addition to the declining membership, the Klan's weakening power after World War II can be attributed to a lack of cohesion between smaller factions (Maguire 1995).

The Ku Klux Klan and organized hate groups cannot be fingered as the sole perpetrators of organized discriminatory behavior. In addition to the social groups already discussed in this chapter, racial groups that did not fit into the WASP category have historically been targeted by hate groups, the general citizenry, and most significantly by the federal as well as state governments. In the following discussion, we examine the major racial groups present in the United States and the historical manifestations of discrimination that they faced at the hands of the WASP society.

Native Americans

Nielson (2000) discusses three "ages" of Native American and European American relations. The first age extended from colonial settlement by Europeans through the Revolutionary War and was characterized by relative harmony between the two groups. The Europeans recognized the Native Americans as the dominant group and were dependent upon them for resources. Colonial discrimination against the Native Americans characterized the second age, which lasted through World War II. Military campaigns, massacres, epidemics of foreign disease, and social disorganization immobilized any effort the Native Americans made to resist colonial invasion. During this time period it is estimated that the Native American population dropped from a high of twelve million prior to European contact to a low of 250,000 at the turn of the twentieth century.

Initially the Europeans viewed the Native Americans as savages, heathens, and pagans who were often dirty, drunken, or violent. This allowed the colonists to justify inhuman treatment and denial of basic rights. This ideology of pure hatred eventually evolved into one of paternalism in which Native Americans were seen as naïve children who needed the Europeans' protection and help in running their own lives (Nielson 2000).

Nativism was evident in schools, where Native American children were punished physically for speaking their language, trying to see families, or refusing to learn European culture. "Indian Agents had the right to determine who married, who could work, who got farming tools and medicines, and were not above using starvation and violence to make them obey" (Nielson 2000, 49). Eugenics was also practiced against the Native Americans. According to Jacobs and Henry (1996), documents from the War Department in the early nineteenth century demonstrate that an organized effort by the United States was made to exterminate the Native Americans through tactics such as distributing to them smallpox infested blankets (Jacobs and Henry 1996).

In 1830, Native Americans who lived in the southern region of the United States were forced by the Indian Removal Law to be moved to what would eventually become the states of Oklahoma, Arkansas, and Kansas. All of these lands were west of the Mississippi river and were often referred to as "the Great American Desert." At that point in American history it was not believed that anyone of white ethnicity would ever want to live there. In 1836, the Cherokee nation was forcibly moved by federal troops from Georgia to Oklahoma. Because this trek took six months during the middle of winter and resulted in a loss of one-quarter of the Cherokee people, it became known as "the Trail of Tears." When it was found that the lands of eastern Oklahoma were rich in fossil fuels, Congress was quick to act. In 1902, they dissolved the land governance of the Cherokee, Creek, Choctaw, Chickasaw, and Seminole tribes. An allotment system was used to break up communal tribal lands for individual ownership, and surplus lands were sold. Since it was required that a person be on the tribal register to receive benefits from the allotments, many whites took this opportunity to enroll themselves as part of the tribes (Ogawa 1999).

Navajo tribes in Arizona and New Mexico were harassed by members of the Catholic Church. Navajo women and children were abducted and used as slaves. Just prior to the Civil War, the U.S. military participated in a planned effort to kill the Navajos. Many surrendered after their orchards and crops were burned. Like the Cherokee in the Southeast, the Navajos were forced to march "the Long Walk" to a military outpost in New Mexico called Bosque Redondo. Those who were feeble or otherwise unable to endure the journey were shot. After four years of imprisonment at Bosque Redondo, virtually half of the Navajo population had died. By the end of the century, premiums were being paid for Indian scalps in Arizona and New Mexico. A male scalp could garner as much as $500 and women and children $250 (Jacobs and Henry 1996).

By the mid-twentieth century, it was believed by whites that the best way to "deal" with Native Americans was to assimilate them into mainstream society. A process known as "termination" was developed, whereby thirteen tribes lost federal protections and services. President Kennedy, in agreement with the National Congress of American Indians, believed the termination to be a great threat to Indian survival and outlawed the practice in 1962 (Ogawa 1999). However, even as late as 1974, Native Americans were still being removed from their lands. Supposedly as an effort to settle a land dispute between the Hopi and Navajo tribes, Congress passed the *Hopi Land Settlement Act,* which forced the relocation of 12,000 Navajo members. This was the largest act of Indian removal since the 1800s. Despite claims of dispute settlement, it should not be overlooked that the relocated Navajo members were living over large amounts of coal deposits that were desperately wanted by the largest producer of coal in the United States, the Peabody Coal Company (Ogawa 1999).

The third age characterizes present day society in which Native Americans struggle to survive as a culturally distinct people. Many of the earlier cultural practices were either eradicated by law or lost through population decimation. Today, the Native Americans are marginalized from the dominant society and are immersed in a criminogenic subculture of poverty. High rates of suicide, family violence, alcoholism, and drug abuse are common (Nielson 2000).

Latinos

It is ironic that Latinos have historically been discriminated against in the same fashion experienced by other "immigrant" groups. The irony lies in the fact that Mexican Americans and Puerto Ricans did not initially immigrate, but were naturalized as U.S. citizens when the borders changed. In 1847, Mexico lost the Mexican-American war and was coerced into the Treaty of Guadalupe Hidalgo. The treaty resulted in Mexico losing 50 of its territory to the U.S., and the 80,000 Mexicans inhabiting the land became U.S. citizens virtually overnight. Puerto Ricans became citizens after the United States defeated Spain in the Spanish-American war. Despite the fact that these groups preceded the Anglo-Saxon presence in North America, they were treated as second-class citizens and deprived of their land and wealth. Tax laws and land-use laws were passed in the territory that eventually became the states of Texas, New Mexico, California, Arizona, Nevada, Utah, and half of Colorado. These laws stripped ranches away from rich Californians and took modest homes from the poor. Once deprived of their economic base, Mexican Americans were relegated to the economic subclass where they remain today (Alvarez 2000).

Asians

Asian immigration to the United States began in the 1840s and 1850s. The Chinese arrived first, on Hawaii and the West Coast. Laborers were the first to arrive, finding work on sugar plantations and in gold mines, and later in the building of the transcontinental railroad. By the twentieth century, these same employment opportunities resulted in the immigration of Japanese, Filipinos, Koreans, and Indians. As their numbers grew, anti-Asian sentiments erupted based on stereotypes regarding the perceived threats to employment through wage deflation, to morality through opium use, and to hygiene through prostitution (Perry 2000b).

The Chinese immigrated during the California gold-rush era and were the first non-white group to do so. They were looked upon primarily as cheap labor. As their number increased, new anti-Chinese laws were designed to limit their rights such as testifying in court, attending white schools, mining, running laundries, and gaining employment. They were the first group to receive restricted entry into the United States with the Chinese Exclusion Act of 1882. Similar laws further reducing their numbers were subsequently enacted, and it was not until 1965 that a normal quota of Chinese immigration was permitted (Flowers 1988).

In 1872, a violent outbreak between some Chinese and police left a white person dead. In retaliation, a white mob killed eighteen Chinese and looted and burned their homes and stores. Eight of the rioters were eventually convicted, but within a year all of them had been freed. Such episodes of violent, brutal, and other harsh forms of treatment towards Chinese were not unusual in the decades following the 1850s. They routinely experienced crime, poverty, and disease, along with other social ills and cruelties. As the Chinese became urbanized, they formed "Chinatowns" across the country in an effort to preserve their traditional culture and protect themselves from persecution. This was partly a result of being barred from white neighborhoods and suffering mass discrimination in other walks of life (Flowers 1988).

Years of systematic hatred toward the Chinese provided fertile ground for Japanese discrimination once Chinese immigration declined. Like the Chinese, the Japanese were considered a source of cheap labor and were often used on plantations. By the early 1900s, legislation was created to exclude the Japanese in much the same fashion as earlier policies had excluded the Chinese. In 1924, the *Oriental Exclusion Act* was passed, stopping almost all Japanese immigration (Flowers 1988).

The Japanese hold the distinction of being the only ethnic group in American history to be systematically removed and placed in concentration camps. With West Coast hostilities toward the Japanese already intense, the Japanese attack on Pearl Harbor in 1941 fueled panic, hysteria, and irresponsibility. Beginning in 1942, people of Japanese ethnicity, including many who were U.S. citizens, were systematically removed from the Pacific Coast military zone and relocated to internment camps. Such relocation caused the Japanese to suffer deprivation and hardship, given that in some cases as little as two days' notice was given before relocation. The Japanese had no time to dissolve property or assets in a fair manner, and many buyers were more than willing to exploit the desperate situation of this perceived enemy. After the dissolution of the internment camps, many of the dislocated Japanese resettled in areas away from the Pacific coast (Flowers 1988).

African Americans

The history of African Americans in the United States is long and battle-scarred. Like the Latinos, they did not voluntarily immigrate to the U.S., but were forced here through the slave trade. Because there was no legal precedent in England for enslavement, the first blacks to arrive in the American colonies performed labor as indentured servants. By the 1660s, lifetime enslavement was instituted. Even prior to the legalization of slavery, blacks were viewed by whites as inferior and received differential treatment based on their physical characteristics. As the plantation system developed in the agricultural South, the growth and acceptance of slavery intensified. Because there was a significant labor shortage, blacks were imported from Africa. This was the most significant source of slaves until 1720 when native-born blacks exceeded importation in terms of population growth (Flowers 1988).

Blacks suffered obvious cruelties during enslavement. Aside from being owned as property, there was forced servitude, beatings, murder and rape. However, the most intense cruelty may have come through the doctrine of black inferiority, whereby white oppressors firmly believed that blacks were beneath whites. This ideology was used to justify slavery and racism. Slave codes allowed plantation owners to police and control their slaves using cruel and inhumane methods. For example, a slave caught off of the plantation could be killed simply for refusing to answer questions. Dismembered body parts from slaves were publicly displayed as a deterrent. It was also illegal for whites to openly oppose the institution of slavery (Smith 2000) and teaching a slave to read was punishable by death. Slave codes stigmatized blacks as inferior, branded them as unequal human beings, and allowed for exploitation of their labor (Smith 2000).

The doctrine of black inferiority continued to haunt blacks even after the abolishment of slavery. Jim Crow laws, a system of legal segregation, resulted in the total exclusion of blacks from the mainstream culture of whites. This included ostracism in housing, employment, pubic transportation, etc. Flowers (1988) noted that ironically blacks had their status lowered during the Jim Crow years, after slavery had been abolished. As slaves they often received relatively equal treatment in restaurants and transportation. After the enactment of Jim Crow laws, blacks were denied virtually all civil rights, and suffered from open discrimination (Flowers 1988).

Jim Crow laws prevented blacks from association with whites in public places and from attending the best public universities and schools. It allowed them to be punished for social actions, such as talking with friends in public or making eye contact with a white person. Blacks were not allowed to reside in white neighborhoods and were often forced to live in inner-city neighborhoods with inferior schools. Employers refused to hire blacks, and unions excluded them from membership. Their Fifteenth Amendment right to vote was not upheld, and they were often prevented by whites from voting (Smith 2000).

Blacks were not just subjected to discrimination and ostracism during the post-slavery years. Whites commonly engaged in violence, harassment, and intimidation against blacks. Mobs were formed to prevent blacks from exercising civil rights such as voting, as well as to "put blacks in their place." It was not unusual during this time for blacks to be the victims of violence motivated by random hatred. The Southern Commission on the Study of Lynchings described the following as typical of the cruelties that white mobs were capable of inflicting:

> The sheriff along with the accused Negro was seized by the mob, and the two were carried to the scene of the crime. Here quickly assembled a thousand or more men, women, and children. The accused Negro was hung up in a sweet gum tree by his arms, just enough to keep his feet off the ground. Members of the mob tortured him for more than an hour. A pole was jabbed in his mouth. His toes were cut off joint by joint. His fingers were similarly removed, and members of the mob extracted his teeth with wire pliers. After further unmentionable mutilations, the Negro's still living body was saturated with gasoline and a lighted match

was applied. As the flames leaped up, hundreds of shots were fired into the dying victim. During the day, thousands of people from miles around rode out to see the sight. Not till nightfall did the officers remove the body and bury it (in Flowers 1988, 9).

Beginning shortly after the Revolutionary War, lynching was a popular method of terrorizing targeted groups. The definition of lynching is often mistakenly limited to hanging. In actuality, it encompasses any extra-legal killing by a mob consisting of three or more individuals. In many cases, lynchings were "legally sanctioned" through the presence of police and the lack of prosecution by courts of whites who participated in lynchings of blacks (Smith 2000).

The Ku Klux Klan embraced it as a trademark method of terrorism against blacks beginning in the post-Civil War era and continuing through the twentieth century. From 1882 to 1968, there were 4,743 recorded lynchings, with most of the victims being black. From 1889 to 1918, Georgia, Mississippi, Louisiana, Texas, and Alabama accounted for the majority of lynchings (Jacobs and Henry 1996). Lynchings were used to symbolically reinforce the economic and social position of inferiority for blacks. The practice often increased when blacks were threatening white economic dominance and stability. For example, studies have shown that lynchings were highest when cotton market prices were low (Smith 2000).

In addition to lynchings, whites often expressed their hatred toward blacks in the forms of riots. This was different from the individuality of lynchings, as riots were generally a response to the threat of blacks as a group, particularly the fear of a change in the status quo (Flowers 1988). In Mississippi, three blacks were tried in 1871 for making "incendiary speeches." During the trial, an argument resulted in a shooting spree that killed 25–30 blacks. Many blacks attempted to escape to the woods to hide but were caught and subsequently hanged by Klansmen. The three individuals on trial were also hanged. In addition to Mississippi, the early twentieth century saw Klan-led anti-black riots in Chicago, Tulsa, Memphis, and Washington, D.C. (Jacobs and Henry 1996).

Blacks were rarely protected by law enforcement or the courts. Codes in the criminal justice system allowed for race-based punishments that were harsh on blacks but often did not punish whites for crimes against blacks. The death penalty was applied in a discriminatory manner, and from 1800 through the mid-1900s, blacks who raped white women were often executed. It was rare for whites who committed rape to be sentenced to death (Smith 2000).

The most significant turn in the history of African Americans came during the Civil Rights Movement, at time when blacks began to openly and defiantly challenge Jim Crow laws and their inherent discrimination. While this movement is generally thought of in terms of black liberation, its scope is broad enough to be representative of the fight against oppression expressed by many minority groups in the United States. Given its significance in reducing intolerance in America, the remainder of the chapter will examine it in detail.

THE CIVIL RIGHTS MOVEMENT

Origins

It would be irresponsible of any theorist to pinpoint the catalyst or cause of a major social movement to any single element. However, many such movements can be anticipated or, in hindsight, at least partly explained by the presence of certain variables in a common formula. Most notably in the United States, upheaval or revolution has traditionally been preceded with rising expectations accompanied by slow social change (Eagles 1986). In the case of the Civil Rights Movement, the necessary components of such a formula were present by the 1950s when, according to Eagles, "the power to obtain results of Afro-Americans was running dangerously far ahead of the South's intellectual and institutional power to react constructively. Simultaneously, the racial attitudes in much of the rest of the nation were being transformed by that same potential power" (p. 7). Specifically, this imbalance was manifested in the cumulative impact of five social changes occurring by the 1950s for racial minorities: (1) a shift in the balance of power politics as the black vote began to influence marginal races; (2) rising incomes as higher education became accessible to blacks; (3) federal court decisions sympathetic to the plight of blacks; (4) a greater coalition with organized labor allowing for strength in the work force; and (5) a string of racial "firsts" that provided the race with proud and influential role models (e.g. Jackie Robinson joining the Brooklyn Dodgers in 1947, poet Gwendolyn Brooks winning a Pulitzer in 1949, and diplomat Ralph Bunche receiving the Nobel Peace Prize in 1950) (Eagles 1986).

Thus, as a product of collective psychology, the twentieth century witnessed a common people shedding fear and forthrightly establishing their willingness to force change on their own behalf, regardless of the interim consequences. Unfortunately, this often resulted in sad, tragic consequences, as the Movement can largely be classified as a violent one. Historical examination allows for the distinction of three modes of violent action with regard to race relations and the black revolt: violent forms of white resistance to black demands, black activism used as a tool to deliberately provoke white violence, and black violence against whites as an effort at self-defense (Geschwender 1973). The following section details the major events of the Movement, through which all three modes of violence are manifested.

A Chronology

Ruffins (1997) noted that a common myth about the Civil Rights Movement has been that the Movement began in 1955 and continued as "a magnificent example of a spontaneous uprising that freed an oppressed people" (p. 25). The author debunked this theory that the Movement was a direct result of the Montgomery Bus Boycott by noting that black people had been resisting oppression in various ways (e.g. circulating petitions, bringing court cases, and organizing against slavery) since before the American Revolution. However, Ruffins conceded that while the efforts against segregation had begun in the 1880s, they did not begin to have a marked impact until well into the twentieth century. An exhaustive examination of such racial events throughout American history is beyond the scope of this chapter. Thus, for the purposes of this discussion, the influence of the Civil Rights Movement from 1954 to 1968 will be considered.

In its 1954 decision in the case of *Brown v. the Board of Education of Topeka*, the United States Supreme Court ruled that the precedent of "separate but equal" established by *Plessy v. Ferguson* (1896) was inherently unconstitutional. The court however, failed to establish a directive on when desegregation should occur. Therefore in 1955 the National Association for the Advancement of Colored People (NAACP) requested that desegregation be immediate and complete. The Court rejected this proposal and instead declared that desegregation would occur with "all deliberate speed." In that same year, Emmett Till, a

14-year-old black boy who was visiting from Chicago was lynched in Mississippi for allegedly making suggestive remarks to a white woman. His assailants were tried and acquitted but later confessed to the crime. Toward the end of 1955, Rosa Parks refused to give up her bus seat to a white man that resulted in her arrest. Parks' action sparked the Montgomery Improvement Association, led by a young minister named Martin Luther King, Jr., to call for a bus boycott as a form of protest. This boycott was successful, for in the next year the Supreme Court ruled segregated busing unconstitutional (Black and Black 1987; Blumberg 1984; Cowan and Maguire 1994; Dudley 1996).

In 1956, the southern states took a collective stand against desegregation by delivering the Southern Manifesto, authored by Senator Harry Byrd of Virginia, to the United States Supreme Court. It was signed by all southern U.S. Representatives and all but three southern U.S. Senators, resulting in 101 congressional signatures. On June 1, Alabama statutorily prohibited the NAACP from operating within the state. The acrimony against the NAACP and its members was growing, and as a result King's home was bombed. Also during this year, blacks won a victory, as a federal court ordered the University of Alabama to admit Autherine Lucy. She never attended, however, because the school was able to "expel" her permanently, and it remained segregated for seven more years (Black and Black 1987; Blumberg 1984; Cowan and Maguire 1994; Dudley 1996).

The next year saw the first major civil rights legislation enacted with the passage of the *Civil Rights Act of 1957*. This act made some strides against discrimination, such as establishing a civil rights division at the Justice Department and providing penalties for tampering with voting rights. However, the Act was weakened by the elimination of several strong initial provisions for school desegregation. Also during this year, King and other black ministers, in an effort to link the many diverse nonviolent protest groups in support of civil rights, established the Southern Christian Leadership Conference (SCLC). King also organized a rally in support of voting rights of over 25,000 blacks at the Lincoln Memorial in Washington, D.C. The most notable events of 1957, however, occurred on September 4 and September 24 when the government of Arkansas refused to integrate its public schools. These events took place when Governor Orval Faubus ordered the National Guard to prevent nine black students from entering Central High School in Little Rock. President Eisenhower reacted by sending to Little Rock 1,000 paratroopers from the 101st Airborne Division with orders to enforce the federal court order (Black and Black 1987; Blumberg 1984; Cowan and Maguire 1994; Dudley 1996).

Students actively entered the integration movement when 10,000 participated in a Youth March for Integrated Schools in Washington, D.C., on October 25, 1958. Additionally, the NAACP Youth Council participated in sit-in demonstrations to integrate lunch counters in Oklahoma City. As if predicting the violence to come in the next few years, King was seriously, but not mortally, wounded this same year when an apparently deranged woman stabbed him in New York (Black and Black 1987; Blumberg 1984; Cowan and Maguire 1994; Dudley 1996).

Sit-ins continued in 1959, as college students forced desegregation at lunch counters in St. Louis, Chicago, and Bloomington, Indiana. The Tennessee Christian Leadership Conference also held sit-ins at major department stores in Nashville. Violence continued to escalate, as the first reported lynching since 1955 occurred when Mack Charles Parker was murdered for allegedly raping a white woman in Poplarville, Mississippi. California passed legislation prohibiting discrimination in public housing, and Memphis added

15,000 blacks to its registered voters list. Louisiana, however, removed 1,377 blacks from its voter rosters on a technicality (Black and Black 1987; Blumberg 1984; Cowan and Maguire 1994; Dudley 1996).

By 1960, sit-ins were a common form of protest spreading across the southern states. In Greensboro, North Carolina, four black students staged a sit-in at the lunch counter in Woolworth's, but sit-ins were also now occurring at hotels, movie theaters, libraries, and parks across the southern region. One such sit-in resulted in a riot when many black and white protestors were beaten in Jacksonville, Florida. The wide circulation of press photos brought national attention to the role played by police in protests. The student movement was solidified in April with the formation of the Student Nonviolent Coordinating Committee (SNCC) in Raleigh, North Carolina. SNCC would play a major role in the Civil Rights Movement in the coming years. Also in April came the first major demonstration of the Movement when 2,500 students and community members marched on city hall in Nashville, Tennessee. This march was prompted by the bombing of a black attorney. However, possibly the most important occurrence of 1960 may have been President Eisenhower's signing of the *Civil Rights Act of 1960*, which boosted the responsibility of the federal government in cases of civil rights violations.

January 1961 marked the beginning of both a tumultuous and progressive year for the Movement. It was in this month that the University of Georgia became the first state university to fully desegregate under court order (William J. Mathias, personal communication, 1998). On March 13, 1961, James Farmer, as national director of the Congress on Racial Equality (CORE), called for "Freedom Rides" across the South. Several of these rides resulted in arrests and assaults, after which CORE turned the Freedom Ride movement over to SNCC. President John F. Kennedy sent federal marshals to ensure the safety of participants in the rides. Later that spring, King and President Kennedy met secretly, at which time Kennedy disclosed his unwillingness to push for new civil rights legislation. Simultaneously, Robert Kennedy as U.S. attorney general urged civil rights leaders to disband the demonstrations and Freedom Rides and instead concentrate on winning suffrage. Ignoring Kennedy's plea, King led over seven hundred demonstrators at five separate marches on city hall in Albany, Georgia. Violence continued as police employed tear gas and canine units to disperse 1,500 peaceful demonstrators (Black and Black 1987; Blumberg 1984; Cowan and Maguire 1994; Dudley 1996).

King again returned to Albany in 1962, accompanied by leaders from SNCC, CORE, and the NAACP and held a mass sit-in and march against segregation. The year also saw the burning of nine black churches over a period of one month in Georgia by members of the Ku Klux Klan. Two Freedom Riders were wounded by shotgun blasts while participating in a voter registration drive in Mississippi, resulting in a demand by SNCC for a special White House Conference on safeguarding future drives. The University of Mississippi again came under fire when James Meredith sued on the grounds of racial discrimination after being denied admission to the Law School. Meredith won his suit, and Kennedy sent in the National Guard along with several hundred federal marshals to ensure Meredith's enrollment. A campus riot erupted, resulting in two deaths. In late 1962, Kennedy signed an executive order abolishing racial discrimination in federally financed housing (Black and Black 1987; Blumberg 1984; Cowan and Maguire 1994; Dudley 1996).

In 1963, against contrary urgings by Robert Kennedy, King, and other SCLC members led a civil rights campaign in Birmingham, Alabama, while CORE encouraged protesting against discrimination in the Northern states. The Birmingham march was met with hostility, and three thousand protesters, including King, were jailed after police chief Bull Connor used canine units and tear gas on the participants. The protest had been peaceful up until that point and, despite the confrontation with police, it was also successful. Within ninety days, lunch counters, rest rooms, and drinking fountains were desegregated in the city. This success was based partly on the public outcry over Connor's actions, which were televised nationally. Other marches were similarly successful; in Savannah, demonstrations forced business and civic leaders to desegregate hotels, bowling alleys, and theaters. Coinciding with a televised speech by Kennedy denouncing segregation as morally wrong, Black students Vivian Malone and James Hood integrated the University of Alabama despite resistance by Governor George Wallace. The very next day, on June 12, Medgar Evers, field secretary of the NAACP, was shot in his driveway in Jackson, Mississippi.

During this same year, the movement gained financial aid as many New York corporations pledged their support. However, New York was seeing its own problems as riots in the Harlem borough occurred after the shooting of a 15-year-old black youth by a police officer. In Washington, D.C., King delivered his "I have a dream" speech to 250,000 persons in attendance. He was met with opposition, however, from militant leader Malcolm X, who deemed the march a "Farce on Washington." Violence reached an all time high for the movement as four young girls were killed by a bomb in a Birmingham church and President Kennedy was assassinated in Dallas. Lyndon Johnson, Kennedy's successor, called for the passage of a civil rights act in his 1964 State of the Union address (Black and Black 1987; Blumberg 1984; Cowan and Maguire, 1994; Dudley 1996).

The U.S. Congress, under pressure from Johnson, did indeed pass the *Civil Rights Act of 1964* which prohibited discrimination in most public accommodations, education and employment, and created the Equal Employment Opportunity Commission. On June 21, 1964, Michael Schwerner, Andrew Goodman, and James Chaney were murdered in Mississippi. Schwerner and Goodman were white men from New York, and Goodman was a black Mississippian. All three were civil rights workers, and their murders formed the basis for the popular movie on the Movement, *Mississippi Burning*. One month later, civil rights leaders put mass marches and demonstrations in moratorium until after the upcoming presidential election on November 3. Johnson, with heavy black support, went on to win the election by a wide margin over opponent Barry Goldwater. In September, New York took an active step toward complete desegregation by busing students. At the end of the year, King was rewarded for his efforts with the Nobel Peace Prize. The year continued to bear witness to a wave of riots including ones in Harlem, Brooklyn, and Rochester, New York; Jersey City, and Elizabeth, New Jersey; Philadelphia, Pennsylvania; and Dixiemoor, Illinois. The Harlem riot was the most serious, resulting in one death, 140 injuries, and more than 500 arrests. This wave of riots marked the first recognition of a division in the Civil Rights Movement between nonviolent protestors and what Roy Wilkins of the NAACP called "the criminal elements" (Black and Black 1987; Blumberg 1984; Cowan and Maguire 1994; Dudley 1996).

The year 1965 opened with the assassination of Malcolm X, the most prominent militant of the Movement, in February. Ironically, three black men were ultimately convicted of the murder. On March 7, a day recorded in history as "Bloody Sunday," state troopers attacked six hundred marchers in Selma, Alabama, with tear gas, nightsticks, whips, and cattle prods. Two days later, King led a voting rights march in Selma but turned back upon reaching a state trooper barricade. Three more days passed before a Unitarian minister was beaten to death by local whites in Selma. Finally, on March 21, King, empowered with a federal court order and National Guard protection, led the successful voting rights march from Selma to Montgomery. In Watts, a black ghetto of Los Angeles, a riot occurred causing 35 deaths, 900 injuries, and more than 3,500 arrests. The six-day riot was the most severe in U.S. history, with property damage exceeding $46 million (Black and Black 1987; Blumberg 1984; Cowan and Maguire 1994; Dudley 1996).

James Meredith, participating in a one-man "march against fear," was shot by an unknown sniper in Mississippi on June 6, 1966. Meredith had been the first black to enroll at the University of Mississippi. His injuries were serious, but he survived. From June 7 to June 26, civil rights leaders including SNCC Chairman Stokely Carmichael and King completed what became known as "the Meredith March." During the march, Carmichael was the first to associate the phrase "Black Power" with the Movement. It was immediately controversial, as CORE adopted a resolution in support of Black Power at its national convention while the NAACP officially opposed it. As a result of Black Power, a militant group known as the Black Panther Party (BPP) was founded in Oakland, California. During this time, King was again injured while leading an integrated march in Chicago when whites threw bottles and bricks at the participants. Two days later, a riot broke out in Chicago's West Side, resulting in the deaths of two blacks. This, however, was not the only riot of the year. A riot in Cleveland killed four, injured fifty, and caused extensive damage. Other cities to see major race-related riots were Milwaukee, Atlanta, San Francisco, Lansing, Michigan, and Waukegan, Illinois. In December 1966, SNCC voted to exclude any whites from membership within the group (Black and Black 1987; Blumberg 1984; Cowan and Maguire 1994; Dudley 1996).

In 1967, President Johnson began to distance himself from the movement after King delivered his February 25 speech criticizing sharply the war in Vietnam. This speech also drew criticism from the NAACP. Rioting continued elsewhere as one at Jackson State College erupted following the shooting death of Benjamin Brown, a black deliveryman, on campus. This riot led to one death and two major injuries. Another in a black ghetto of Newark, New Jersey, killed 23 and injured 725, while a riot in Detroit saw 43 dead and 324 injured. In Boston, over 90 people were seriously injured in a riot that occurred after black welfare mothers barricaded themselves in a building to protest discrimination. A significant victory for the movement came with Thurgood Marshall's appointment as a U.S. Supreme Court justice. James Meredith came back on the scene and led a new "March Against Fear" in Mississippi. The Black Power movement had its first national conference in Newark with over fifty activist organizations represented (Black and Black 1987; Blumberg 1984; Cowan and Maguire 1994; Dudley 1996).

The term "black power" was initially coined in 1968 as Representative Adam Clayton Powell declared that nonviolence was no longer an effective civil rights strategy. He urged both blacks and whites to carry the banner and join the revolution. In February, another campus riot occurred when students attempting a march to integrate a bowling alley in Orangeburg, South Carolina, were met with attempts to force them to remain on the campus of South Carolina State College. Three students were shot and killed by police. On March 18, 1968, garbage workers in Memphis, Tennessee, went on strike, and Martin Luther King traveled there to help settle the strike. What may have been the most serious blow to the movement occurred on this trip when James Earl Ray assassinated King on the balcony of the Lorraine Hotel. The assassination tipped off riots in over one hundred cities across the nation. Shortly thereafter, Senator Robert Kennedy was assassinated in Los Angeles. In a testament to both President and Senator Kennedy's support of the Civil Rights Movement, King's widow Coretta Scott King joined Ethel Kennedy on the plane that returned Senator Kennedy's body to New York. The BPP was portrayed unfavorably in its first major news coverage as member Huey Newton was convicted of shooting a white police officer and later when three Black Panthers were arrested for attacking a police station in Jersey City with machine guns (Black and Black 1987; Blumberg 1984; Cowan and Maguire 1994; Dudley 1996).

The BPP received further attention in 1969, as party leader Bobby Seale was one of the "Chicago Eight" who were tried for conspiracy to incite a riot during the 1968 Democratic National Convention. Seale was gagged and chained during the trial after criticizing the judge, and his case was eventually separated from the others, who then became known as the infamous "Chicago Seven." Police later raided the Chicago headquarters of the BPP, killing two leaders in their beds and wounding four others. A grand jury condemned the raid as "excessive." Violence continued throughout the year, including rioting, firebombing, and sniping in Hartford, Connecticut, resulting in a dusk-till-dawn curfew. While civil rights events continued to occur through the next decade, the definitive end of the Movement came when, on October 30, 1969, in the case of *Swann v. Mecklenberg*, the Supreme Court replaced its 1954 statement calling for desegregation at "all deliberate speed" with a unanimous order demanding an end to segregated schools "at once" (Black and Black 1987; Blumberg 1984; Cowan and Maguire 1994; Dudley 1996).

Legal Issues

While the high visibility and mass publicity of protests during the Civil Rights Movement had great influence on attitudes, the true success of the Movement lay in the courts. Likewise, many of the most significant roadblocks to true desegregation and equality came in the form of official legal action. As Charles Hamilton (in Eagles 1986) stated:

> Changes in civil rights of Blacks resulted not just from protests and demonstrations carried out by individuals and organizations at the local level, but also from laws implemented by Congress and from the actions of federal judges (p. 97).

It should be noted that this discussion is oriented on the assumption that the movement *was* successful: overt discrimination was deemed unconstitutional, and black suffrage was ensured. It is from this perspective that the ramifications of legal action will be evaluated.

Prior to the twentieth century, the two most significant legal decisions pertaining to racial issues occurred in the form of the Emancipation Proclamation and the U.S. Supreme Court's decision in *Plessy v. Ferguson* (1896). While the Proclamation freed enslaved persons, the Court officially sanctioned segregation in *Plessy* with the notion that as long as schools and public places were equally provided, then separate facilities for blacks and whites were constitutional. The Court's decision of *Brown v. Board of Education of Topeka* (1954) reversed the *Plessy* decision and declared that desegregation should occur with "all deliberate speed."

In the wake of *Brown*, the federal courts were plagued with cases where local segregationists engaged in efforts to subvert the established laws and perpetuate *de facto* segregation. According to Killian (in Barkan 1984), "the slow pace of Southern school desegregation in the 1950s was created primarily by legalists who did not crudely defy the law but cleverly used it to limit change to a minimum" (p. 563). The contribution of the federal courts came in their willingness to overrule these efforts at subterfuge. The significance of these decisions was their origin in the federal, rather than state or local courts. According to Hamilton (in Eagles 1986):

> If Blacks relied solely on the established local institutions for redress of grievances, there was little likelihood of success. Thus, it was absolutely crucial that forces beyond the state and local governments intervene. And this meant turning to the federal government (p. 109).

The Supreme Court's rationale for *Brown* related primarily to the Fourteenth Amendment that provided equal protection under law. The Court reasoned that (1) states could not deny under law equal protection to any person within its jurisdiction; (2) racial segregation denied this equality; (3) the states were statutorily creating segregation; (4) Blacks qualified as "persons" falling within state jurisdiction; and (5) therefore states were unconstitutionally denying Blacks equal protection under law (Amaker 1988; Brisbane 1974).

The legal system was also used as an effort to derail the Movement. As Barkan (1984) stated, "At the state and local levels . . . the law served as an effective instrument of social control. . . . The entire legal machinery of the South became a tool for social control of civil rights protest" (p. 554). Such legal resistance manifested itself primarily in four forms.

First was the frequent use of arrest, prosecution, and other forms of legal harassment to suppress protest and dissent. Characteristic of this method was the Montgomery march, in which tear gas and dogs were used on the crowd and several hundred protestors were arrested. The second method was the use of police and civilian violence that undermined attempts by officials to use legal means to control dissent. Prime examples are the murders of three civil rights workers in Philadelphia, Alabama, and the bombing of a church in Birmingham resulting in the deaths of four young girls (Barkan 1984).

A third method was the passage of new statutes specifically outlawing behavior peculiar to protest activities such as sit-ins. Southern state and federal judges aided this effort by granting injunctions that limited these activities. Additionally, members of the courtroom workgroup such as judges, prosecutors, and jurors were often hostile to the goals of the Movement, making it extraordinarily difficult to win acquittals. There was also a shortage of defense attorneys who were willing to represent accused civil rights activists (Barkan 1984).

The two other branches of the criminal justice system, law enforcement and corrections, also presented barriers. Arrest was a constant threat as police were willing to make arrests at virtually any kind of protest regardless of how peaceful it was. They would also arrest known activists even when there was no protest activity in progress. Notably, most of these arrests were made for activities that were by and large legal outside of the South. Southern jails were hardly bastions of civil rights. Routinely, conditions were substandard for all inmates, including activists. Jail culture was similar to that of the surrounding society; thus, incarcerated activists were likely to meet hostility from both white prison guards and white inmates (Barkan 1984).

The fourth, perhaps most ambiguous form of maintaining the status quo was the failure of states to adequately prosecute offenders of racially motivated violent acts. The situation was further complicated by the fact that some of the state laws were unenforceable because they violated the rights to free speech and association that protected not only the activists but members of extremist groups as well. Even so, victims were not encouraged to take advantage of the well-established criminal and civil remedies that existed at the federal level since the passage of broad Reconstruction Era civil rights statutes. As Padgett (1984) indicated, the two-tiered approach of federal criminal and civil remedies combined with improvements in state legislation and enforcement was the most effective way to deter racial violence.

The weakness of state level acts against racially motivated violence was three-pronged: (1) the Constitutional problems with state legislation; (2) the inadequacy of state enforcement systems; and (3) the lack of appeal to enforcement from Reconstruction Era civil rights statutes. The result of these weaknesses was a complete failure on the part of the state to stymie violent activities of racist groups. "The failure of local prosecutors to bring suit against, and of local juries to convict, perpetrators of racial violence during the 1960s resulted in increased pressure on the United States Department of Justice to enforce the Reconstruction Era federal civil rights statutes" (Padgett 1984, 115).

The success of such federal prosecutions only served to highlight the failure of state court systems. This success relied primarily on the fact that when the Department of Justice acted as a private litigant or prosecuted in federal court, it had the opportunity to draw juries from much wider areas than that from which local juries were generally drawn, and therefore limiting the impact of the biases of local citizens on the initiation of the action. Padgett noted this as a pattern of history that "from the Reconstruction Era to the Civil Rights Movement, indicates that the federal government has of necessity become the primary guarantor of individual civil rights, especially the right to be free of injury or intimidation because of one's race or religion" (p. 130). These four manifestations of legal resistance to the civil rights movement resulted in what Barkan (1984) called a "characteristic protest dynamic" illustrated below in Figure 1-1:

One other legal aspect of the Movement merits attention in this discussion—the formal actions of the Executive branch. Ronald Brown (1993) in his work "Racial Stratification, Intellectual History, and Presidential Action in the Civil Rights Domain" noted three factors through which presidents shaped their administrations' policies on civil rights: interpretation of political history, black civil rights issues and social harmony, and the vote of the black community during election year. Brown argued that the U.S. Constitution was partly to blame for presidential constraints on the issue because it was a social contract written for and by whites. In fact, it was not until the 1830s that the term "civil rights" evolved, and even then it was used to describe the legal immunities commonly enjoyed by whites but routinely denied to blacks (Brown 1993).

---

black protest ⇒ white violence ⇒ federal intervention

FIGURE 1-1   Characteristic Protest Dynamic

As presidents interpret the political past from sources such as predecessors, scholars, and journalists, they usually desire to implement policies that demonstrate continuity with that racial history. Presidents have also been pressured to address black civil rights issues when political violence was used by whites to challenge reasonable racial harmony. Finally, the strategies of presidents may incorporate policies designed to secure the black vote, especially in the South, when black voters are in strategic locations during close elections (Brown 1993).

Harry Truman was the first president to bring black civil rights to the forefront as a national debate. It seems that the major catalyst for this was Gunner Myrdal's widely acclaimed book, *An American Dilemma* (1944), which urged the establishment of public policies to provide blacks with full social and political rights. Prior to Truman, presidents had been largely evasive on the civil rights issue, as was evident by the failure of civil rights groups to get a federal anti-lynching law passed, despite persistent attempts. This failure was not a result of passiveness on the part of the president; every president from Wilson to Truman flatly refused to use the office as a bully pulpit to support the passage of such a law. Even during the prime of the Civil Rights Movement, presidents rarely placed civil rights as a top priority. Kennedy and Johnson both were more likely to use the power of their administrations to support education and economic legislation than civil rights legislation. Johnson, however, was more likely than other presidents to support the Movement. He took a supporting position on civil rights legislation three times more frequently than the next most supportive president, Nixon, and twenty times more than the second most supportive, Kennedy. Nixon, however, did not neglect the white vote, as he was the first to challenge the legitimacy of the Supreme Court on the busing issue and had the U.S. Department of Justice and the U.S. Department of Health, Education, and Welfare drop their strict compliance with timetables for school integration. The Carter administration left its mark on the civil rights issue through the appointment of blacks to federal district courts (Amaker 1988; Brown 1993).

Race Relations

White Supremacy   While the foundation for race relations in the United States was most definitely laid through slavery, it was the official sanctioning from the U.S. Supreme Court that led to the establishment of white supremacy as a social system. In 1857, the Court issued its opinion in the case of *Dred Scott v. Sandford*. Regarding the Negro, the Court stated:

> It is difficult at this day to realize the state of public opinion in relation to that unfortunate race, which prevailed in the civilized and enlightened portions of the world at the time of the Declaration of Independence, and when the Constitution of the United States was framed and adopted. But the public history of every European nation displays it in a manner too plain to be mistaken . . . . [Negroes] had for more than a century before been regarded as beings of an inferior order, and altogether unfit to associate with the White race, either in social or political relations; and so far inferior that they had no rights which the White man was bound to respect; and that the Negro might justly and lawfully be reduced to slavery for his benefit . . . (Couch 1970, 432).

From this line of reasoning, the majority, consisting of the Chief and five concurring justices, formed the argument that the Negro was not a citizen at the time that the federal government in the United States was established. Therefore, the Congress lacked constitutional authority to bestow citizenship upon the Negro, and it was within the powers of the state to oppress the Negro if it was the state's choosing to do so (Couch 1970).

Even after the civil war and the Supreme Court's rulings in *Plessy* and *Brown*, White supremacy was the official position of the Southern states. Newby (1973) described the state of this policy in South Carolina:

> The tragedy of White supremacy was compounded by the fact that Whites never understood the horror of the policy they pursued. As it assumed institutional form in the segregation codes, they saw White supremacy as a device for regulating race relations and keeping interracial contact in acceptable channels. In their view institutionalized White supremacy minimized the danger of violence and other forms of trouble and guaranteed Blacks the opportunity to develop their own institutions. It was not, they felt, an exploitative system, nor even an unreasonable one, but rather a realistic accommodation to a difficult situation. Most White Carolinians never grasped the relationship between racial discrimination and White supremacy. Moderates and paternalists among them believed segregation, the institutional form of White supremacy, was discriminatory only if extremists made it so (p. 80).

While certainly the harshest and most visible varieties of supremacy came through racial violence and police discrimination, Newby (1973) noted three more subtle forms in which white supremacy was manifested: education, health care, and economics. It was essential to the survival of white supremacy that blacks be kept uneducated, unhealthy, poor, and dependent.

When it came to the education of blacks, the supremacists were divided into two philosophical camps. The majority was unsympathetic or indifferent to the idea of educating blacks at all, but others theorized that education was the best means through which to adapt blacks to segregation and white supremacy. The philosophy of the latter group incorporated three factors: (1) the need to preserve white supremacy; (2) the notion of industrial education as pioneered by Armstrong and Washington at the Hampton School and Tuskegee Institute; and (3) the innovative idea that education was a preparation for life's work (Newby). The result was a grossly undereducated class that only served to perpetuate the supremacist myth that blacks were intellectually inferior.

Discriminatory health care was also a product of the supremacist policy, and the result was a trend of poor health among the black population. They had higher mortality rates and shorter life expectancies primarily because they were more susceptible to diseases of all forms. Despite this demonstrated need for greater health care, they received much less of it than whites. This was obviously beneficial to the supremacist movement as a healthy, vigorous class of blacks might have been more resistant to oppressive social policies. The social significance of ill health, which drained the energies of the black person, was the perpetuation of a second myth: all blacks were lazy (Newby 1973).

Black Revolution
Belief Systems   By the late 1960s, the attitudes of many American blacks had shifted from nonviolent protest to militancy. When one applies a timeline to the beliefs of blacks concerning oppression, the evolution is clear. From 1948 to 1968, structured oppression,

from the black point of view, came in four areas. First, there were the efforts of the white community to increase opportunity for blacks, as mandated by the courts, without altering the basic institutional patterns. Second, whites made efforts to maintain domestic tranquility by controlling the welfare system. Third, there was community and economic resistance to integration. Finally, government support of wlack interests was sporadic and inconsistent (Pettigrew 1980).

Blacks developed their own beliefs to accompany these observations of the white culture. They believed that they had been discriminated against in the past and rejected legal segregation. Blacks did not subscribe to the view that they were inherently inferior to whites or were incapable of change. In fact, they believed that change was best accomplished by providing equal opportunities such as improving substandard schools and renovating black ghettos. Many blacks, especially those who participated in the Civil Rights Movement, adopted more progressive beliefs. For example, they argued that any manifestation of black "inferiority" was primarily a result of the cultural deprivation and undesirable environments they experienced under the control of whites. Progressive blacks also believed that the only path to racial harmony was through complete social integration, and if the opportunity for integration was not presented, than it should be forced (Pettigrew 1980).

As attitudes shifted from nonviolence to greater militancy, the manifestations of these attitudes shifted as well. With the abundance of ideological rhetoric during the Movement, it was relatively simple for the black American to move from the status of oppressed minority to that of revolutionary freedom fighter. A continuum of the changes in urban riot activity demonstrates this passage (see Table 1-1) (Eynon 1970).

The riots presented in Table 1-1 are not necessarily representative of the entire Civil Rights Movement. Many protests were nonviolent and peaceful; the activities represented in Table 1-1 that occurred during the Movement (i.e. urban riots from 1935 to 1968) can largely be attributed to black paramilitary groups: Black Muslims, Black Nationalists of New Libya, Black Panthers, Five Percenters, Harlem Mau Mau, Republic of New Africa, and the Revolutionary Action Movement.

Black Power   The issue of equality as the basis of the Civil Rights Movement had seen solidarity through the early 1960s. Groups such as the NAACP, CORE, SCLC, and SNCC had committed themselves to change through non-violent means. However, by the mid-1960s, the Movement had begun to split into two factions: those under the guidance of King, who maintained the ideal of nonviolent protest; and those under the guidance of a newcomer to the Movement, Stokely Carmichael, who no longer believed that nonviolent methods were effective.

TABLE 1-1   Urban Riot Activity in the 20th Century

Year	Number of Riots	Predominant Riot Activity
1900–1915	4	White mobs assaulting black people
1916–1934	12	Conflicts between black and white mobs
1935–1968	378	Black mobs looting and vandalizing property
1969	37	Conflicts between armed black militants and white authorities

King took the position that nonviolent resistance was the only way to achieve the goals of the Civil Rights Movement. As he stated, "The philosophy of nonviolent resistance . . . says that the means must be as pure as the end" (in Dudley 1996, 146). The nonviolent actions of the Movement came predominantly in three forms: (1) *nonviolent protest* in which activists went beyond verbal protest to actions, many of which were illegal, such as marches, picketing, and vigils; (2) *noncooperation* which consisted of activities where activists withheld or refused social, economic, or political cooperation such as walkouts, strikes, and boycotts; and (3) *nonviolent intervention*, the most militant version of nonviolent resistance, in which activists took action to intervene and initiated *de facto* social change by failing to observe laws or social customs. An example of this type was the frequent use of sit-ins (Wirmark 1974).

In order to perpetuate these activities, King started the aforementioned SCLC. The group had as its basic purpose to capitalize on the success of the mass action in the Montgomery bus boycotts. The SCLC sought to reproduce this pattern of mass resistance in other cities (Fairclough 1986). King was criticized, however, because his nonviolent tactics often were accompanied by violence—a phenomena that was characterized in 1965 as "the violence of nonviolence" (Colaiaco 1986). Many of King's actions opened the doorway for future violence; this included his support of the student group SNCC that was started by an $800 advance from the SCLC in 1960. The SCLC was interested in seeing the student sit-ins and peaceful protests continue and provided the money to help with the organization of the activities. By 1961, SNCC had 16 full-time staff, and by 1964 the number had grown to 150. The group participated along with the SCLC and CORE in many of the protest activities, including the Freedom Rides (Chambers 1968).

Stokely Carmichael started his career as civil rights leader when he unexpectedly, and through questionable means, secured the national chairmanship of SNCC. Almost immediately Carmichael, a militant, changed the focus of SNCC from that of a nonviolent organization working alongside King and the NAACP to one that was no longer willing to settle for such non-aggressive methods. From this new SNCC arose a dangerous and controversial concept of militancy known as "Black Power." It would not have been difficult to predict that organizations like SNCC would initiate such a radical departure from the traditional ideology of the Movement. After all, they were young and restless and impatient for change, unlike their older, more stable counterparts in the various other civil rights organizations (Brisbane 1974; Chambers 1968; Sellars 1990).

Carmichael initially coined the slogan "Black Power" during the Meredith march. As he defined it "Black power is not Black supremacy, does not mean the exclusion of White Americans from the Negro revolution, does not advocate violence and will not start riots" (Brisbane 1974, 145). It was instantly met with controversy and many organizations, including the NAACP, officially denounced it. Carmichael in defense of his stance stated:

> The racial and cultural personality of the Black community must be preserved and the community must win its freedom while preserving its cultural integrity. This is the essential difference between integration as it is currently practiced and the concept of Black Power (Dudley 1996, 219).

Carmichael's rhetoric, however, failed to convince members of the nonviolent sector. As Roy Wilkins, executive director of the NAACP, stated:

> Though it be clarified and clarified again, "black power" in the quick, uncritical and highly emotional adoption it has received from some segments of a beleaguered people can mean in the end only Black death (Dudley 1996, 229).

Wilkins had good reason to express such misgivings: Carmichael's followers were militant, black conscious, and violence oriented (Brisbane 1974). As the Black Power movement grew, a second group hailing it as their theme emerged in Oakland, California. They called themselves the Black Panther Party (BPP). The BPP along with SNCC continued to express its official position as being non-violent. However, police action often precipitated violence in encounter after encounter with the BPP. Likewise, the white media painted the group as militant and violent. By this time, Carmichael was no longer acting with moderation, and the BPP was growing ever more militant. The ideology had now reoriented itself around the philosophy that whatever the white culture would not give peaceably; the black activists would take forcefully (Chambers 1968).

A rather strange mutation of Black Power evolved simultaneously within a group calling themselves the Black Muslims. Their most significant role in the black revolution was serving as an emotional outlet for blacks whose expression of hatred of whites was more important than any constructive effort to improve their plight. Their spokesman was a self-proclaimed Muslim calling himself Malcolm X. One of his teachings was that every white man was a devil. Originating in the 1930s, the group boasted more than 100,000 members by the late 1960s. It did not support integration but advocated pure separation of the races and even demanded a separate share of the U.S. to be used only by blacks. Not surprisingly, this group had almost immediately alienated themselves from the mainstream members of the Movement. However, as the Movement evolved toward greater militancy, Malcolm X replaced King as the philosophical leader for many. Eventually, he was expelled from the Black Muslims after making public comments on the Kennedy assassination against the direct order of the Muslims' leader, Muhammad Elijah. He organized his own group, the Muslim Mosque, but he believed that he was being relentlessly pursued by Black Muslims and that his life was in danger. He was right; he was assassinated in 1965 by three black men. While two of the men professed to be Muslims, it was never clear who actually orchestrated the killing (Brisbane 1974; Muse 1964).

CONCLUSION

Intolerance has had many manifestations throughout American history, as is evidenced by the discussion presented in this chapter. Non-white racial groups, women, and non-mainstream religious practitioners have been targets and victims of white nativist rhetoric. It is unfortunate that the success of marginalized groups has only been achieved after years of oppression, strife, and resistance. However, it is important to note that success has occurred, despite the long odds, and these groups enjoy more freedom today than ever before. This is not to say that the American metamorphosis toward equality is complete. In this chapter, the long term development of intolerance against marginalized groups has been documented through historical fact. The remaining chapters will explore how this pattern of intolerance has impacted special populations and their participation as employees and clients of the American justice system.

REFERENCES

ALVAREZ, A. (2000). Unwelcome citizens: Latinos and the criminal justice system. In *Investigating difference: Human and cultural relations in criminal justice*, ed. Criminal Justice Collective of Northern Arizona University, 85–97. Boston: Allyn & Bacon.

AMAKER, N. C. (1988). *Civil rights and the Reagan Administration*. Washington, DC: Urban Institute Press.

BARKAN, S. E. (1984). Legal control of the Southern civil rights movement. *American Sociological Review, 49*, 552–65.

BARKAN, S. E., AND L. L. SNOWDEN. (2001). *Collective violence*. Boston: Allyn & Bacon.

BLACK, E., AND M. BLACK. (1987). *Politics and society in the South*. Cambridge, MA: Harvard University Press.

BLUMBERG, R. L. (1984). *Civil rights: The 1960s freedom struggle*. Boston: Twayne.

BRISBANE, R. H. (1974). *Black activism: Racial revolution in the United States 1954–1970*. Valley Forge, PA: Judson.

BROWN, R. E. (1993). Racial stratification, intellectual history, and presidential action in the civil rights domain. *Policy Studies Journal, 21*(3), 535–43.

CHAMBERS, B., ed. (1968). *Chronicles of black protest*. New York: Mentor.

COLAIACO, J. A. (1986, March). Martin Luther King, Jr., and the paradox of nonviolent direct action. *Phylon, 47*, 16–28.

COMSTOCK, G. D. (1991). *Violence against lesbians and gay men*. New York: Columbia University Press.

COUCH, W. T. (1970). *Culture in the South*. Chapel Hill: University of North Carolina Press.

COWAN, T., AND J. MAGUIRE. (1994). *Timelines of African-American history: 500 years of black achievement*. New York: Roundtable Press.

DUDLEY, W., ed. (1996). *The Civil Rights Movement: Opposing viewpoints*. San Diego: Greenhaven Press.

EAGLES, C., ed. (1986). *Is there a Southern political tradition?* Jackson, MS: University Press of Mississippi.

EYNON, T. G. (1970). Black equality: Revolution from the movement? *Sociological Focus, 3*(3), 23–31.

FAIRCLOUGH, A. (1986). Martin Luther King Jr., and the quest for nonviolent social change. *Phylon, 47*, 1–15.

FLOWERS, R. B. (1988). *Minorities and criminality*. Boston: Allyn & Bacon.

GESCHWENDER, J. A. (1973, Spring). The changing role of violence in the black revolt. *Sociological Symposium, 9*, 1–15.

HACKSTAFF, K. B. (2000). Women and criminal justice: Wielding the tool of difference. In *Investigating difference: Human and cultural relations in criminal justice*, ed. Criminal Justice Collective of Northern Arizona University, 129–46. Boston: Allyn & Bacon.

JACOBS, J. B., AND J. S. HENRY. (1996). The social construction of a hate crime epidemic. *Journal of Criminal Law and Criminology, 86*(2), 366.

MAGUIRE, K. (1995). Crime and the Ku Klux Klan: A study of political criminality in the USA. *The Criminologist, 19*(3), 131–37.

McCAGHY, C. H., T. A. CAPRON, AND J. D. JAMIESON. (2000). *Deviant behavior: Crime, conflict, and interest groups*. 5th ed. Boston: Allyn & Bacon.

MUSE, B. (1964). *Ten years of prelude: The story of integration since the Supreme Court's 1954 decision*. New York: Viking Press.

NIELSON, M. O. (2000). Stolen lands, stolen lives: Native Americans and criminal justice. In *Investigating difference: Human and cultural relations in criminal justice*, ed. Criminal Justice Collective of Northern Arizona University, 47–57. Boston: Allyn & Bacon.

NEWBY, I. A. (1973). *Black Carolinians: A history of blacks in South Carolina from 1895 to 1968.* Columbia, SC: University of South Carolina Press.

OGAWA, B. K. (1999). *Color of justice: Culturally sensitive treatment of minority crime Victims.* 2nd ed. Boston: Allyn & Bacon.

PADGETT, G. L. (1984, Spring). Racially motivated violence and intimidation: inadequate state enforcement and federal civil rights remedies. *The Journal of Criminal Law and Criminology, 75*, 103–38.

PERRY, B. (2000a). Exclusion, inclusion, and violence: Immigrants and criminal justice. In *Investigating difference: Human and cultural relations in criminal justice*, ed. Criminal Justice Collective of Northern Arizona University, 59–69. Boston: Allyn & Bacon.

PERRY, B (2000b). Perpetual outsiders: Criminal justice and the Asian American experience. In *Investigating difference: Human and cultural relations in criminal justice*, ed. Criminal Justice Collective of Northern Arizona University, 99–109. Boston: Allyn & Bacon.

PERRY, B. (2000c). Constructing sexual identities: Gay men and lesbians in the criminal justice system. In *Investigating difference: Human and cultural relations in criminal justice*, ed. Criminal Justice Collective of Northern Arizona University, 147–59. Boston: Allyn & Bacon.

PERRY, B. (2000d). In whose God we trust? Religious difference, persecution and criminal justice. In *Investigating difference: Human and cultural relations in criminal justice*, ed. Criminal Justice Collective of Northern Arizona University, 191–203. Boston: Allyn & Bacon.

PETTIGREW, T. F. (1980). *The sociology of race relations.* New York: Free Press.

PURPURA, P. P. (2001). *Police and community: Concepts and cases.* Boston: Allyn & Bacon.

RUFFINS, P. (1997). Ten myths, half-truths and misunderstandings about black history. *Black Issues in Higher Education, 13*(25), 23–26.

SELLARS, C. (1990). *The river of no return: The autobiography of a black militant and the life and death of SNCC.* Jackson: University Press of Mississippi.

SHELDON, R. G. (2001). *Controlling the dangerous classes: A critical introduction to the history of criminal justice.* Boston: Allyn & Bacon.

SMITH, B. (2000). Historical injustices, contemporary inequalities: African Americans and criminal justice. In *Investigating difference: Human and cultural relations in criminal justice*, ed. Criminal Justice Collective of Northern Arizona University. 71–84. Boston: Allyn & Bacon.

WIRMARK, B. (1974). Nonviolent methods and the American Civil Rights Movement 1955–1965. *Journal of Peace Research, 11*(2), 115–32.

2

African Americans in the Criminal Justice System

Catherine E. Burton and Marjie T. Britz

CHAPTER OUTLINE

INTRODUCTION

Many people feel the United States has two separate, unequal standards of justice—one for whites and one for minorities. There are a growing number of research articles, governmental reports, and anecdotal literature providing surveys of race-based inequality in the American Criminal Justice system. Instead of focusing on only one area of inequality (e.g. racial profiling, sentencing disparities, etc.), researchers are beginning to examine the broader problem of how the American criminal justice system interacts with minorities. The results of such examinations are often quite unnerving not only for African Americans, but for all minority groups.

Much of the research of the last two decades supports the theory that the offender's race is a strong predictor of sentence length and severity, likelihood of being stopped, type of plea bargain offered, and chances of being waived to adult court. Furthermore, there has been a steady expansion in the prison population over the past twenty-five years, and today the number of long-term incarcerated individuals in the United States totals over one million, with another million short-term prisoners moving in and out of jails (NIC 2005). This dramatic growth in prison population has had the greatest impact on the African American community. For many African Americans, particularly the poorest, the American experience has been marked by a historical pattern of crime, violence, and victimization on all sides (Cernkovich et al. 2000). This chapter examines the experience in the criminal justice system from the perspective of African Americans, describing it in three dimensions: employed professionals, victims, and offenders in the criminal justice community.

A BRIEF HISTORY OF AFRICANS IN AMERICA

The African experience of criminal justice and injustice in America dates back nearly four centuries. In 1619, a Dutch slave trader imported the first cargo of Africans in Jamestown, Virginia, beginning a long history of quasi-legal enslavement of Africans in North America. These first Africans were not slaves *per se*, but indentured servants in a similar legal position to poor Englishmen who bartered years of labor for passage to America. Africans' legal status began to be redefined by statute in the 1660s, however; although African Americans at this time were still referred to as "servants," they were now being owned, traded, and worked as slaves. By any reckoning, legal or otherwise, these unwilling immigrants to America were victims of a major crime.

The Jamestown colony had great success as an exporter of the popular new crop of tobacco, and concurrent with the success of tobacco planting, African slavery was recognized in Virginia and Maryland. A 1662 Virginia statute legalized indentured compulsory servitude for life. Slaves were already essential to the southern tobacco and cotton economy by the 1680s, but slaves lived and toiled in all the British colonies during the seventeenth and eighteenth centuries. Between 600,000 and 650,000 Africans had been forcibly taken to North America before Great Britain made slave trading by its subjects illegal in 1721. Among the new states, Pennsylvania abolished slavery first, in 1780, but the *Fugitive Slave Act of 1793* made helping a slave to escape or giving a runaway slave refuge crimes in themselves. Ironically, some northern African Americans themselves owned slaves, and African American freedmen lived unfettered throughout the south, if only at the whim of socially superior whites (Ellis 1990).

The 1857 *Dred* Scott decision by the U.S. Supreme Court involved a runaway fugitive slave residing in the Minnesota Territory. Scott brought suit in 1848 to claim freedom because he lived in a free territory. The Court ruled that Scott's place of residence did not make him free and, more tellingly, that slaves could not bring suit in federal court. This decision was consistent with various judicial doctrines that had been developed in order to undermine the increasingly powerful antislavery arguments and lawsuits (Pollak 2005).

While the Civil War was undoubtedly fought over slavery, abolition only came about through new acts of law. Slavery was abolished in the District of Columbia in 1862; in 1863, the Thirteenth Amendment abolished slavery, and in 1866 the Fourteenth Amendment finally granted citizenship to former slaves. The Fifteenth Amendment was approved in 1869, giving African Americans the right to vote. However, legal progress was not rapid. In *Plessy v. Ferguson* (1896), the Supreme Court found that "separate but equal facilities" (schools, restaurants, hotels) were still constitutional. This "separate but equal" doctrine remained in force until 1954, when the Court found it to be inherently unequal in *Brown v. Board of Education* (Pollak 2005).

After the Civil War, African Americans were nominally free to live and work wherever they chose, but *de facto* segregation and racism and *de jure* restrictions on voting, property ownership and other legal rights severely limited their social mobility and success, particularly in the South. Illegal lynching eventually became the established method whereby whites terrorized African Americans in order to maintain white supremacy. Between 1880 and 1940, lynchings remained a system of white social control using fear as the controlling mechanism and involving the open, public and often spontaneous murder of victims by white mobs, usually perpetrated against individuals suspected of crimes.

Lynching was generally performed by hanging or shooting, but sometimes included physical torture, dismemberment, maiming, and burning at the stake. The Tuskegee Institute reports that 4,730 people were lynched in the U.S. between 1882 and 1951, about 73% of whom were African American. Most lynching of African Americans took place in the South, but they were not unknown in the border states of Kentucky, Ohio, Indiana, and Maryland (Gibson 2005). Mob lynchings, indeed, were an ugly aspect of American justice from the time of the Revolution to the middle of the twentieth century. Lynching was used to exert social control and research has indicated that they vary by region and the economic well-being of lower-class whites (Beck and Tonlay 1990). Lynching also varied by region; the areas with the largest population of African Americans experienced the highest number of lynching (Corzine et al. 1983). It was basically domestic terrorism as a means of social control.

The Civil Rights Movement in the early 1960s forced the end of segregation, and the *Civil Rights Act of 1964* outlawed racial discrimination as such, but the long history of race crimes and oppression left many racist ideas and institutions engrained in American culture. In this context, African Americans for centuries were overwhelmingly the victims rather than perpetrators of crime. In 2005, the U.S. Senate finally issued a formal apology for the implicit tolerance of lynching that marked U.S. law for nearly a century, and the debate over reparations for slavery continues to revive memories of America's long history of injustice and its unresolved issues. This history explains the long-standing animosity between the African American community and police, and the assumption that African American victimization is as likely to come at the hands of authorities as from whites or other African Americans.

AFRICAN AMERICANS AS CRIMINAL JUSTICE PROFESSIONALS

Significant progress has been made in the integration of African Americans into America's criminal justice communities. Nevertheless, the lingering effects of centuries of exclusion and discrimination means that African Americans, Hispanics, and women will continue to be underrepresented at many levels for years to come. Municipal police departments and Federal agencies and prisons have probably made the most progress in integration, but considerable obstacles remain for African Americans seeking to rise to the higher ranks of police, prison and court systems (see Table 2-1).

Barely present as members of the law enforcement community until half a century ago, African Americans have recently become better represented as workers and professionals in the criminal justice system. This is due, in large part, to the aggressive implementation of Title VII provisions of the *Civil Rights Act of 1964,* and of Affirmative Action and Equal Opportunity laws in the various state, local, and federal agencies. African Americans are now employed as police officers, highway patrol officers, police chiefs, correctional officers, and judges. Nonetheless, the underlying racial tensions and African American-white animosities that have traditionally aggravated police relations with African Americans persist, and African American law enforcement personnel often express their own antipathy to tokenism, internal racism in police departments, and hostility toward them as "Uncle Toms" within the African American community.

A related problem is the use of political appointments to smooth over racial conflict, the lack of minority officers, and persistence of racial incidents and profiling. For example, in New Jersey in 2000, Governor Christie Whitman replaced a white chief with an African American chief as charges of police bias arose. Many officers still believe the only reason the white chief was replaced was to take racial conflict out of the limelight. Four months after firing Chief Williams, Whitman reaffirmed her belief that troopers should be able to use race as a factor in traffic stops. The former Chief Williams then sued the state for reverse discrimination. Such media-driven lawsuits cannot improve law enforcement conditions, but they do show that racial conflicts persist even as African Americans come to be better represented in law enforcement (Korobkin 2002).

In Law Enforcement

In the early 1900s, African Americans comprised only 2.7% of the police force, and by the middle of the century, African Americans continued to be substantially underrepresented. Affirmative action and diversity issues have affected the composition of police forces. American law enforcement has become more diverse over the last few decades. In 1988,

TABLE 2-1   Employees in Federal, State, and Private Adult Correctional Facilities by Race, 2000

Total	White	African American	Other
430,033	272,436	83,697	41,587

Source: Sourcebook of Criminal Justice Statistics, 2003.

African Americans held 12.3% of all police positions, up from 6.5% in 1975. Currently, there are at least five departments (Atlanta, Detroit, El Paso, Miami, and Washington, D.C.) in America's fifty largest cities in which white officers are a minority (Walker and Shelley 1999).

The lack of racial diversity in supervisory positions is problematic as well. In the mid-1990s in New York City, 28.7% of the population and 11.4% of the police were African American, but only 6.6% of police supervisors were African American. Jacksonville, Florida, reflected a similar situation, 25.2% of the population and 22.3% of the police force were African American, while only 4.8% of supervisors were African American (Walker and Shelley 1999). Again, the relatively recent integration of many departments makes the rise of African Americans in the ranks an issue, and will for years to come.

The Bureau of Justice Statistics examined a variety of trends in 62 of America's biggest cities concerning numbers of minorities and women who have joined police agencies. According to DOJ findings, the African American presence has almost doubled within some individual departments between the years of 1990 and 2000. In jurisdictions of more than 250,000 residents, numbers of full-time officers who belong to ethnic minorities rose from 30% to 38%. The percentage of African American police officers increased from 18% to 20% in that same period (Nislow 2002). On the federal level, more than 93,000 full-time personnel authorized to carry firearms and make arrests were employed by federal agencies as of June 2002. Of all these officers, 32.4% belonged to an ethnic or racial minority (BJS 2005).

African American sheriffs and police chiefs can also exert reforming influence, at least when their appointment is not a politically motivated as result of public opinion, as many believed was the case in Los Angeles after the Rodney King incident and verdict set off riots and assaults across the city. However, as the data demonstrate, African American detectives, police chiefs, and sheriffs have emerged most prominently in entirely African American or mostly African American locales, with relatively few exceptions outside of the nation's largest cities.

In the Courts

In a study of minority representation on the court bench, Graham (2003) sought to answer questions that have not been fully addressed in the past concerning the ethnic and racial composition of the judiciary in America. Previous studies focused on state appellate benches, with less attention paid to lower courts. The purpose of Graham's study was to supply a more complete overview of the ethnic/racial composition of American state and federal benches, and the results are revealing. The data reflect some progress by judges of color in gaining access to state and federal benches. However, they represent only about 6% of the total number of judicial officers and judges. The findings suggest that judges of color are still badly underrepresented

The National African American Prosecutors Association states that the 1,000 African American prosecutors of today represent only 3.3% of the U.S. total. Kenneth Montgomery, an assistant district attorney in Brooklyn, states that "A lot of African American and Hispanic males have an innate distrust of white prosecutors" (Kopp 2001, 2). He further reports that when he goes into African American communities, he senses disgust or resentment from the neighborhood residents, who often view him as an agent of a hostile, racist system (Kopp).

These problems persist and are to be expected in a period of change, but there are differences of opinion about how African American prosecutors should be perceived. Bryan Stevenson, an African American public defender in New York, says: "If you take a job in an office that has shown no concern for people of color, then you have to be prepared to deal with whatever people say, rather than faulting folks for raising questions" (Kopp 2001, 2). Resentment also comes from white prosecutors toward defendants, victims, and witnesses of color. African American prosecutors can be caught in the middle when their white colleagues show a lack of understanding about the attitudes of minority communities toward law enforcement personnel, or blame affirmative action programs for minority crime rates or failures to convict. On a more positive note, African American prosecutors can speak both to and for the community and help change the criminal justice system from the top down.

In the Correctional System

Ironically, in the criminal justice system, African Americans are best represented in numbers reflecting their population demographics as employees of the prison system. African Americans make up 21% of staff as well as 24% of correctional officers at the federal level. Similarly on the state level and in private corrections, similar percentages are reflected. In combing federal, state, and private correctional facility employees, African Americans represent more than 20% of the total employee population and more than half as many employees as any other minority race.

AFRICAN AMERICANS AS CRIME VICTIMS

Rates of Victimization

All of the reliable evidence shows that African Americans in the United States are disproportionately over-represented in the criminal justice system, both as victims and as offenders, by population as well as economic and social status. The Bureau of Justice Statistics reported the following figures for the year 2003:

- For each 1,000 persons in their group, 29 African Americans, 22 whites, and 16 persons of others races sustained a violent crime.
- African American and white persons experienced statistically similar rates of simple assault.
- Rates of rape/sexual assault were similar for African American, white, and other races.
- In comparisons of whites, African Americans, and other races, African Americans also had the highest rates of violent crime victimization (BJS 2005).

The FBI Uniform Crime Reports stated that in 2002, about 49% of murder victims were African American; clearly the frequency of violent victimization is much higher for African Americans than for others. Six of every ten thousand African Americans were victimized by a carjacker, as compared to 2 per 10,000 whites (BJS 2005). In short, the crime data confirms that African Americans have a much higher rate of crime victimization, that "African American on African American" crime is more prevalent than African American on white or white on African American crime, and that serious crimes of all kinds—robberies, assaults, rapes and murders—are still a very serious problem in most large African American urban communities today, despite the decline in violent crime rates over the last two decades.

Racial Profiling

In addition to ordinary crime, African Americans appear to be the targets of unusual police scrutiny as suspects. In the wake of growing complaints that police have long targeted African Americans for unwarranted interrogations and traffic stops, "racial profiling" has emerged in the media to describe an alleged police propensity to stop, search, and arrest minorities at rates far out of proportion to their numbers. In response, some states, counties, and municipalities have enacted programs to track police interaction with minorities, while others have resisted "race tracking" on the grounds that it is itself discriminatory. The profiling issue has attracted enormous attention in the mainstream media, and as a result racial profiling is being alleged, denied, denounced, and investigated from New Jersey to Illinois to California.

Although long viewed as a fact of life in America, the media debate over racial profiling ("driving while African American") only arose in the 1990s. During the mid-1990s, various minority groups complained of being singled out, typically by having their cars stopped and searched by police for minor traffic violations. Searches were conducted as a matter of course, with or without the permission of drivers or passengers. Police chiefs claimed that there were departmental policies against such racial discrimination, and at that time, in the absence of hard data, it was impossible to prove that profiling was being practiced.

Documenting the practice proved relatively easy once the data became available. Collecting data on traffic stops—why the driver was pulled over, identification by race or ethnicity, the basis of the search if one was conducted, and whether the driver received a warning, citation, or was arrested—provided the basis for a large-scale study. A *Traffic Stops Statistics Act,* introduced in the 105th Congress, and again in the 106th, legislated data collection about all traffic stops. Lawsuits filed concurrently with the debate on the bill shifted attention to the issue. In Maryland, for example, on a highway with a driving population 17% African American, African Americans made up over 70% of all the drivers stopped and searched by Maryland police (Harris 2003).

Hajjar (2002) described racial profiling as "the use of race as a proxy for criminality." To defend the practice, police have presented statistical evidence supporting the assertion that African Americans use and sell drugs at a proportionally higher rate than other races. The law enforcement perspective equates suspiciousness with race, and police act on this suspicion. This presumption, and the actions that it prompts, clearly singles out African American individuals on the basis of race. This practice is discriminatory and criminalizes targeted races in violation of two basic elements of the U.S. legal system: the individualization of criminalization and the presumption of innocence until proven guilty.

At the same time that racial profiling by law enforcement was expanding, the Supreme Court's sensitivity to Fourth Amendment rights was contracting. The constitutionality of pretexual traffic stops (i.e. using a minor traffic infraction, real or alleged, as an excuse to stop and search a vehicle and its passengers), reached the U.S. Supreme Court in 1996 in the case *Whren v. U.S.* The question before the Court was whether a search was constitutional even though it only occurred because the police were attempting to circumvent the requirements of the Fourth Amendment. In its friend-of-the-court brief, the ACLU argued that pretextual searches violated the core principles of the Fourth Amendment, and warned that to sanction such searches was to "invite discriminatory enforcement." The Court did not agree, however, and instead declared that any traffic offense committed by a driver was a legitimate legal basis for a stop, regardless of the officer's subjective state of mind (Schiller 2001).

In practice, some believe the *Whren* decision has given the police virtually unlimited authority to stop and search any vehicle they desire. Every driver probably violates some provision of the vehicle code at some time during even a short drive, because state traffic codes identify so many different infractions. For example, traffic codes define precisely how long a driver must signal before turning, and the particular conditions under which a driver must use lights. Vehicle equipment is also highly regulated. A small light bulb must illuminate the rear license plate. Taillights must be visible from a particular distance. Tire tread must be at a particular depth. All equipment must be in working order at all times. The police need only a superficial pretext to target a driver for a stop and search.

Since *Whren*, the Court has extended police power over cars and drivers even further. In *Ohio v. Robinette*, the Court rejected the argument that officers seeking consent to search a car must tell the driver he is free to refuse permission and leave. In *Maryland v. Wilson* (1997), the courts gave police the power to order passengers out of stopped cars, whether or not there is any basis to suspect they are dangerous. The dozens of stories in the press and on the airwaves, combined with the statistical reports, the lawsuits, and recent legislative action, make a powerful argument that racial profiling is not just an occasional problem.

The Racial Presumption of Guilt

The presumption of guilt leads to profiling individuals on the basis of a collective identity, i.e., their race. More importantly, profiling by race in lieu of evidence is shoddy police work and puts law enforcement in the position to cast a wide net and examine any people they profile. In other words, racial profiling leads to a self-fulfilling prophecy in which targeted investigation leads to more arrests, convictions and prison sentences. When race is seen as sufficient reason for suspicion, any characteristic that profiled individuals have distinguishing them from someone engaging in criminal activity can only be discerned after the fact. The blatantly discriminatory practice of profiling has damaged relations between minority communities and their law enforcement officers (Hajjar 2002).

Of course, nearly everyone who is stopped for a "routine traffic check" feels discriminated against, and persons who receive tickets or fines for minor infractions are often incensed; they wrongly conclude that they have been victimized. In many cases, moreover, we can not determine whether actual racial profiling comes from the individual officer or from the department itself; credible evidence of formal racist policies profiling minorities has not been presented. Nonetheless, new policies have been proposed and laws have been passed to either report alleged discriminatory acts, or to record the ethnicity, race, or gender

of persons being stopped. Without proper supervision, one cannot be certain that reform policies will be followed, or may in fact result in increased discrimination; it has been argued that
affirmative action to resolve past inequities may actually endanger the public (Lott 2000).
The calls for recording ethnicity, race and gender have also been opposed on the grounds that
this activity is itself "discriminatory" and hence illegal. On the other hand, many U.S. police
departments and highway patrols are now being carefully scrutinized to ensure that all traffic
stops, arrests and random interrogations/interviews are conducted with regard for the established legal principles of due cause, reasonable suspicion, and proper procedures.

AFRICAN AMERICANS AS OFFENDERS AND INMATES

Overrepresentation in the Criminal Justice System

There is a substantial body of research dealing with the over representation of African
Americans in the U.S. criminal justice system. The following is a brief list of some of those
findings (Walker et al. 1996; Mann and Zatz 1998; Schiller 2001):

- Nationwide, African Americans comprise 62% of drug offenders admitted to
  state prison. In some states, African Americans constitute between 80% and 90%
  of all people sent to prison on drug charges.
- Nationwide, African American men are sent to state prison on drug charges at
  13 times the rate of white men.
- Two out of five African Americans sent to prison are convicted of drug offenses,
  compared to one in four whites.
- African American men are incarcerated at 9.6 times the rate of white men. In
  11 states, they are incarcerated at rates that are 12 to 26 times greater than that of
  white men.
- Nationwide, one in every 20 African American men over the age of 18 is in prison.
  In five states, between one in 13 and one in 14 African American men is in prison.
- One in every 20 African American men over the age of 18 in the United States is
  in state or federal prison, compared to one in 180 white men.
- More people are sent to prison in the United States for nonviolent drug offenses
  than for crimes of violence.

The aforementioned statistics make it clear that African Americans are disproportionately represented in both jail and prison populations across the United States. Consider this:

On a given day in 1992, 372 whites and Hispanics were incarcerated for each 100,000 in the
overall population, while the rate for African Americans was 2,678 per 100,000. African
Americans, 13% of the U.S. population, represented 45% of those arrested for violent
felonies and roughly half of those held in state and federal prisons. On a typical day in 1994
nearly one-third of African American men aged 20–29 were either incarcerated, on parole or
on bail awaiting trial (Loury 1996, 23).

The overwhelming majority of federal inmates are African American. African
Americans are almost as heavily represented in the jail population as whites, although

TABLE 2-2   Prisoners in Federal, State, and Private Adult Facilities by Race, 2000

	White	African Americans	Other
Total	452,300	587,300	226,610
Federal	29,800	44,800	36,320
State	395,637	506,408	167,305
Private	27,905	36,066	22,024

Source: Sourcebook of Criminal Justice Statistics, 2003.

whites outnumber African Americans by five to one in the population. If one examines the total numbers of prison inmates in the U.S. by race or ethnicity, the gross disparity between African Americans and other ethic groups is evident across the board (see Table 2-2):

Today, the United States has the largest penal system in the world, and it is a growing industry. About 60% of all federal prison inmates and some 22% of inmates in local jails and state prisons are incarcerated for drug law violations, many for minor infractions (Delgado 2001). So great is the demand for new penal facilities that many states have resorted to contracting their prison management and operation out to private firms.

The numbers are nearly as stark in terms of arrests. For violent offenses such as murder, robbery, and aggravated assault, African Americans, despite their minority status are arrested for violent offenses nearly as much as whites who represent the majority (see Table 2-3).

Reasons for Overrepresentation

The racial disparity in prison populations has many explanations. Two of the leading arguments focus on the "War on Drugs" and economic inequality. The War on Drugs concentrated efforts of law enforcement on minority communities. Additionally, associated

TABLE 2-3   Adult Arrests by Race, 2004

Offense	# of Arrests[1]		% of Total Arrests[2]	
Violent Offenses	White	African American	White	African American
Murder	4,816	4,504	50.5	47.2
Robbery	35,439	41,774	45.2	53.3
Aggravated Assault	203,071	102,355	64.9	32.7
Property Offenses				
Burglary	149,525	56,894	71.0	27.0
Larceny-Theft	594,742	238,587	69.4	27.9
Motor-Vehicle Theft	66,948	35,952	63.5	34.1

Source: Uniform Crime Reports, 2004.

[1] Adults 18 and Over.

[2] Percentages reflect all races.

legislation with the movement resulted in disparate sentencing for minorities. Economic inequality explanations contend that concentration effect of social ills like poverty and segregation result in creating an urban underclass. One of the consequences of the creation of the urban underclass is that these neighborhoods are plagued, among other things, by high crime rates.

The War on Drugs   This policy stresses supply-side enforcement aimed at inner-city low-level dealers. In addition, in federal prison sentencing, there is a federal 100-to-1 disparity between "crack" or crystal and powder cocaine. Federal law enforcement is concentrated on crack offenses, and these factors contribute to the racial disparity as well (Coker 2003). It is argued that because police look for drugs primarily among African Americans and Latinos, they find a disproportionate number of them with contraband. Therefore, more minorities are arrested, prosecuted, convicted, and jailed, thus reinforcing the perception that drug trafficking is primarily a minority activity. Some feel that this perception creates the "profile" that results in more stops of minority drivers. At the same time, white drivers appear to receive far less police attention, many of the drug dealers and possessors among them go unapprehended, and the perception that whites commit fewer drug offenses than minorities is perpetuated (Massey and Denton 1993; Walker et al. 1996).

If this cycle does exist, it carries with it profound personal and societal costs. It is both symptomatic and symbolic of larger problems of race relations and the criminal justice system. It is offered by some that it may result in the persecution of innocent people based solely on their skin color. It could have a corrosive effect on the legitimacy of the entire justice system. Many argue that it deters people of color from cooperating with the police in criminal investigations. In the courtroom, it causes jurors of all races and ethnicities to doubt the testimony of police officers when they serve as witnesses, making criminal cases more difficult to win (Crews et al. 1996).

Although they are incarcerated at higher rates for drug offenses, data do not support a higher use of drugs by African Americans relative to whites. Rates of illicit drug use among African Americans were found to be 7.4%, 7.2% among whites, and 6.4% among Hispanics (Substance Abuse and Mental Health Service Administration 2001). Nevertheless, of the U.S. state prison population incarcerated for drug offenses, African Americans comprise 57% of the inmates.

Disproportionate incarceration affects African American women as well. The numbers of incarcerated women have risen sharply, at a much faster rate than those of men. The biggest increase is in the number of incarcerated African American women. The combination of federal mandatory sentencing laws and drug enforcement policies is particularly destructive to African American women charged with drug crimes. The women involved in drug transactions often had minor roles, while their intimate partners played large parts.

Mandatory sentencing leaves no room for leniency for these women. Although prosecutors are willing to recommend shorter sentences in exchange for useful information, these women often play such a peripheral role that they have no useful information to impart, and so receive longer sentences than their culpable male partners in crime (Coker 2003). Brownell (1998) analyzes the profile of women in prison:

> Most women prisoners and detainees are from uneducated, urban, poor sections of the population. They are disproportionately women of color: African American women comprise

> 46 percent of women prisoners and 43 percent of women in jail . . . This is compared with white women, who comprise 40 percent of women in prison and 38 percent of women in jail. Hispanic women comprise 12 percent of women in prison and 16 percent of women in jail. Because African Americans comprise 13 percent of the overall population in the United States, their overrepresentation in prisons and jails is startling (p. 328).

The disparate use of search warrants for drug offenses also contributes to racial disparities in arrest and incarceration rates. Other factors, such as use of search warrants to locate and deport illegal alien felons or habitual criminals, also play a role. Significant racial disparities in the issuance of search warrants in drug cases were found in a San Diego study, although not as one might first expect. African Americans make up 6% of the population and search warrants were issued in 26% of their cases. Hispanics make up about 24% of the population of San Diego County, and were subjected to search warrants in 43% of their cases; whites, who make up fully 61% of the population, were subjects of search warrants in 35% of cases.

Death penalty sentences show profound racial disparities as well. In the years 1995–2000, 682 defendants were charged with crimes with the death penalty as a potential punishment. African Americans were defendants in 48% of these cases, Hispanics in 29%, and whites in just 20%. The disproportionate number of African Americans for whom the death penalty is sought, and to whom it is applied, has been the basis for lawsuits and appeals by opponents for more than four decades (Dieter 2005).

Plea agreements that spared the defendants a death penalty prosecution were entered by 48% of white defendants, 38% of Hispanics, and just 25% of African Americans (U.S. Department of Justice 2001). Another relevant statistic is that prosecutors seeking the death penalty were 99% white, and the ranks of prosecutors at all levels are still heavily segregated; there has never been an African American attorney general of the United States, and Attorney General Alberto Gonzales was the first non-white to hold that post in the more than 200 years of American history (Dieter 2005).

Poverty and Economic Inequality   Wilson (1987) emphasizes the concentration of poverty in our inner cities and its resulting effects as influential in the investigation of the determinants of crime. His analysis stresses the transformation of the inner city during the past several decades as a result of changes in the urban economy and movement of the middle class away from the central city. This has resulted in the most disadvantaged segments of the central city population being concentrated in an environment with minimal vertical class integration and little sustained contact with individuals and organizations that represent mainstream society (Shihadeh and Ousey 1996). According to Wilson (1987), the concentration of poor families in urban communities constitutes an underclass characterized by features such as high unemployment rates, fewer two-parent families, and higher crime rates (Cuciti and James 1990). Related to the development of this underclass are concentration effects such as reduced access to jobs and reduced opportunities for exposure to conventional role models (Wilson 1987).

While Massey and Denton (1993) agree with much of Wilson's (1987) argument about the change in the character of the central city, they maintain that his argument does not adequately take into account the effect of segregation on the transformation of the inner city into a locus of poverty. Their arguments strongly suggest that in an urban area, degree of segregation of a racial or ethnic group from the Anglo population, which represents mainstream society, may itself be positively associated with group homicide rates. Further, residential segregation has an impact on the social control that inhibits crime, both at the formal level of law enforcement and at the informal level of neighborhood organization (Peterson and Krivo 1993), and this also suggests that segregation may affect crime rates (Shihadeh and Flynn 1996). Much of the research in this area suggests that a main feature of poor urban communities is that poor families are racially segregated into neighborhoods that are overwhelmingly poor (Wilson 1987; Massey and Denton 1989, 1993). This trend suggests that not just poverty but concentrated poverty may play a part in determining homicide rates.

Other explanations include the urban culture of gang violence. However, in the final analysis, the larger numbers of African Americans in the prison population reflect a criminal justice system that is predominantly administered and adjudicated by whites, with charge and sentence outcomes that heavily favor wealthier white defendants over virtually every other ethnic group. The effect of this imbalance is to arrest, convict and incarcerate African Americans in disproportionate numbers. While the overwhelming majority of all prisoners are indeed guilty of the crimes for which they have been convicted, the highly selective focus of the criminal justice system on African American street crime means that many other lawbreakers—drug importers and buyers, white collar criminals, and others—go largely untouched by law enforcement.

CONCLUSION

In striking contrast to the numbers of African Americans employed in the criminal justice system, they continue to be disproportionately represented as victims of crime and as offenders and prisoners, with the result that African Americans now comprise nearly half of all prison and jail inmates. Whether this is a lingering effect of centuries of economic and social inequality and injustice, or a simple reflection of higher crime rates among African Americans, it is a situation that poses serious problems for the long-term stability and racial harmony of the United States. Unfortunately, there is evidence that there may in fact be two separate criminal justice systems in the United States: one for whites and a separate one for minorities. However, the progress that has been made, although not enough, gives hope that the promise of the criminal justice system, equal justice for all, can be achieved.

REFERENCES

BECK, E. M, AND S. E. TONLAY. (1990). The killing fields of the deep south: The market for cotton and the lynching of blacks, 1882–1930. *American Sociological Review, 55*, 526–39.

BROWNELL, P. (1998). Female offenders in the criminal justice system: Policy and program development. In A. R. Roberts (ed.), *Social work in juvenile and criminal justice settings* (2nd. ed., pp. 325–49). Springfield, IL: Charles C. Thomas.

Bureau of Justice Statistics. (2005). *Victim characteristics.* Washington, DC: Department of Justice.

CERNKOVICH, S. A., P. C. GIORDANO, AND J. L. RUDOLPH. (2000). Race, crime and the American dream. *Journal of Research in Crime and Delinquency, 37*(2), 131–70.

COKER, D. (2003). Supreme Court Review: Forward: Addressing the real world of racial injustice in the criminal justice system. *Journal of Criminal Law and Criminology, 93*, 827–79.

CORZINE, J., J. CREECH, AND L. CORZINE. (1983). Black concentration and lynchings in the South: Testing Blalock's power-threat hypothesis. *Social Forces, 61*, 774–96.

CREWS, G. A., R. H. MONTGOMERY, AND W. R. GARRIS. (1996). *Faces of violence in America.* Needham Heights, MA: Simon & Schuster.

CUCITI, P. AND J. FRANKLIN. (1990). A comparison of Black and Hispanic poverty in large cities of the southwest. *Hispanic Journal of Behavioral Sciences, 12,* 50–75.

DIETER, R.C. (2005). *The death penalty in African American and white: Who lives, who dies, who decides.* Washington, DC: Death Penalty Information Center.

DELGADO, M. (2001). *Where are all the young men and women of color? Capacity enhancement practice in the criminal justice system.* New York: Columbia University Press.

ELLIS, D. (1990). The volume, age/sex ratios, and African impact of the slave trade: Some refinements of Paul Lovejoy's review of the literature. *Journal of African History, 31,* 485–92.

GIBSON, R. A. (2005). *The Negro holocaust: Lynching and race riots in the United States, 1880–1950.* Retrieved from http://www.yale.edu/ynhti/curriculum/guides/1979/2/79.02.04.x.html.

GRAHAM, B. L. (2003). *Descriptive representation on the American bench.* An assessment. Paper prepared for presentation at the 61st Annual National Conference of the Midwest Political Science Association, Palmer House Hilton, Chicago, IL, April 3–6, 2003.

HAJJAR, L. (2002). In times of trouble: The problem of racial profiling. *Race Matters Lecture Series*, University of California-Santa Barbara.

HARRIS, D. A. (2003). The reality of racial disparity in criminal justice: The significance of data collection. *Law and Contemporary Problems, 66*(3), 71–98.

KOPP, E. (2001). Black prosecutors: Dealing with race in the criminal justice system. Kenneth Montgomery Law Firm, http://kjmontgomerylaw.com/BlackProsecutors.pdf.

KOROBKIN, D. S. (2002). *Racial profiling: A new challenge.* Swarthmore School of Public Policy.

LOTT, J. R., Jr. (2000). Does a helping hand put others at risk? Affirmative action, police departments and crime. *Economic Inquiry, 38*(2), 239–57.

LOURY, G. (1996). The impossible dilemma between African American crime and judicial racism. *New Republic*, 21–25.

MANN, C. R., AND M. S. ZATZ. (1998). *Images of color.* Los Angeles, CA: Roxbury.

MASSEY, D. S., AND N. A. DENTON. (1989). Residential segregation of Mexicans, Puerto Ricans, and Cubans in selected U.S. metropolitan areas. *Social Science Research, 73,* 73–83.

MASSEY, D. S., AND N. A. DENTON. (1993). *American apartheid: Segregation and the making of the underclass.* Cambridge, MA: Harvard University Press.

National Institute of Corrections. (2005). *What is the difference between jail and prison?* Washington, DC: Department of Justice.

NISLOW, J. (2002). Female, minority ranks are up, but it's more than just numbers. *Law Enforcement News, 28,* 579.

PETERSON, R. D., AND L. J. KRIVO. (1993). Racial segregation and Black urban homicide. *Social Forces, 71,* 1001–26.

POLLAK, L. H. (2005) Race, law & history: The Supreme Court from Dred Scott to Grutter *v.* Bollinger. *Daedalus, 134*(1), 29–41.

SCHILLER, B. R. (2001). *The economics of poverty and discrimination* (8th ed.). Upper Saddle River, NJ: Prentice Hall.

SHIHADEH, E. S., AND N. FLYNN. (1996). Segregation and crime: The effect of Black social isolation on the rates of black urban violence. *Social Forces, 74,* 1325–52.

SHIHADEH, E. S., AND G. C. OUSEY. (1996). Metropolitan expansion and Black social dislocation: The link between suburbanization and center-city crime. *Social Forces, 75,* 649–66.

Substance Abuse and Mental Health Service Administration. (2001). *National household survey on drug abuse highlights.* Washington, DC: Office of Applied Studies, U.S. Department of Health and Human Services.

U.S. Department of Justice. (2000). *The Federal death penalty system: A statistical survey (1988–2000)*. Washington, DC: Department of Justice.

WALKER, S., C. SPOHN, AND M. DELONE. (1996). *The color of justice: Race, ethnicity, and crime in America*. Belmont, CA: Wadsworth.

WALKER, S. AND T. O. SHELLEY. (1999). Affirmative action, diversity, and law enforcement. 187–99. In D. J. Kenney and R. P. McNamara (eds.), *Police and policing: Contemporary issues* (pp. 187–99). Westport, CT: Praeger.

WILSON, W. J. (1987). *The truly disadvantaged*. Chicago: University of Chicago Press.

CASES

Brown v. Board of Education (1954), 347 U.S. 483
Dred Scott v. Sanford (1896), 60 U.S. 393
Maryland v. Wilson (1997), 517 U.S. 806
Ohio v. Robinette (1996), 519 U.S. 33
Plessy v. Ferguson (1896), 163 U.S. 537
Whren v. U.S. (1996), 517 U.S. 806

3

Hispanics and Latinos in the Criminal Justice System

Lynne L. Snowden

❖

INTRODUCTION

The Latino population is the United States' largest minority group. In July 2004, one out of every seven people was Latino, and this ratio is expected to increase because of continued family reunification via immigration (Jelinek 2005). The Latino birthrate now outpaces both African Americans and whites in the United States. For example, the Latino growth rate for the 12 month period starting in July 2003 was 3.6% compared to the overall United States population growth rate of 1% (Jelinek 2005). If this growth continues, the Latino population will eventually rival that of the majority, in spite of the fact that there is already substantial intermarriage with both the African American community and the white majority. For this reason, many authors have labeled the massive immigration from Mexico, Central America, and South America "the browning of America." Future amnesty and guest worker programs may accelerate this phenomenon. The following discussion examines the profound impact of Latinos on the United States criminal justice system.

Before beginning our discussion about Latinos and criminal justice, some definition of terms is in order. The term *Hispanic*, most frequently used by the U.S. government, categorizes U.S. citizens, permanent residents, and temporary immigrants who come from the Spanish-speaking countries of Latin America or a Spanish-speaking culture (Jelinek 2005). According to the U.S. Census Bureau, Hispanics form an ethnic group, not a race.

The term *Latino* has become more popular in common usage because it has a geographical connotation and does not carry the cultural meaning implied in the term Hispanic. It also does not carry the historical stereotype that *Hispanic* bears. *Latino* refers to people who come from Mexico, Central America, and South America. *Latino* is considered to be the more precise definition of this very diverse group, and it will be the term of choice for the rest of this chapter.

Since Latinos are such a diverse group, counting them or speaking about them in a combined way is a difficult endeavor. Many people who answered the 2000 U.S. census used two or more categories to describe their ethnicity, so it is important to remember that any statistic describing particular ethnic groups can easily be skewed by those who self-report their status. For example, many second-generation Latinos do not consider themselves to be anything besides American, nor do they speak a language other than English. These people may or may not self-report an ethnicity. Other Latinos are temporary workers with great mobility, so they miss regularly any attempts to count them, such as in a census, and do not consider themselves to be anything other than Mexican, Guatemalan, Colombian, etc. Some Puerto Rican immigrants do not report being Hispanic or Latino since they are born American citizens, etc. The term Latino will be used to describe this group, except in cases where surveys used the specific term Hispanic in collecting their data.

LATINOS AS CRIMINAL JUSTICE EMPLOYEES

The nomination and confirmation of Alberto Gonzales to the nation's top law enforcement position of U.S. Attorney General embodies America's changing demographics. Latinos continue to take a growing place in the criminal justice system "as both prisoners and prison guards, defendants and prosecutors" in what some have termed "the latest step in the Browning of Justice" (Lovato 2005, 1). "The implications of the browning of justice are huge for the country and Latinos as a whole. Traditional notions of a united Latino community and a united political family crumble as some families lose money as their children are arrested and others make money to build their family's future as they begin careers as police officers, correctional officers, and lawyers" (p. 2). In some states, such as California and Texas, Latino employees are the fastest growing population of any U.S. group.

Professionalism

While Latino employees remain under-represented in many areas of the U.S. criminal justice system, they have made great strides in policing over the last few years. Perhaps the most difficult area to attract qualified Latinos has been the police departments in larger cities. Table 3-1 shows the minority and female composition in police departments in major urban areas of the United States. The far right section of the table compares the percentage of sworn personnel who were Latino in 1990 and 2000 in the largest cities of the United States. Only four cities in the sample failed to increase the number of sworn Latino personnel. While it appears to be slow going in many Midwest areas, many other cities more than doubled their percentage of Latino officers during the last ten years. One border city, El Paso, Texas, has a majority (72%) of Latino officers (Reaves and Bauer 2003).

Table 3-1 also compares the percent female and the percent of any minority in sworn personnel. Including all minorities, many of the largest U.S. cities are near or over the 50% mark in minority sworn officers. The last column in the table shows the officer to resident ratio in the year 2000. Latinos eliminated the total disparity in the officer to resident ratio only in the city of Tampa, Florida, with most city ratios at about 60% parity. This percentage is quite respectable given the rapidity with which Latinos have increased in the population of U.S. major urban areas. Clearly Latinos have made some gains in local policing, but what about federal law enforcement and corrections?

TABLE 3-1   Minority Employees in Policing 1990 to 2000

	Female		Any Minority		African American		Hispanic/Latino	
	% of sworn personnel		% of sworn personnel		% of sworn personnel		% of sworn personnel	
City	1990	2000	1990	2000	1990	2000	1990	2000
NY	12.3	15.5	25.5	34.7	12.6	13.3	12.1	17.8
LA	12.5	18.4	37.5	53.9	13.4	13.6	21.0	33.1
Chi	13.0	21.3	30.4	40.3	23.6	25.9	6.3	12.7
Hou	9.6	12.4	26.3	39.7	14.4	19.4	11.4	17.9
Phi	14.7	24.2	26.5	41.1	23.2	34.5	2.8	5.6
Pho	8.1	15.0	15.5	17.9	3.6	3.9	11.0	12.0
SD	12.7	14.5	24.0	30.7	7.7	8.7	11.4	15.9
Dal	13.3	15.8	22.7	36.8	15.5	21.4	6.2	13.5
SA	5.7	6.0	43.9	48.0	5.8	5.8	37.9	41.7
LV	10.2	10.9	13.4	19.3	7.5	9.3	3.7	7.3

Source: U.S. Department of Justice, Bureau of Justice Statistics, 2002, 11.

Like their local counterparts, federal law enforcement agencies and the federal correctional system also made significant gains in hiring male Latinos. During the period from 1996 to 2002, the minority representation in federal officer ranks rose from 28% to 32.4% (BJS 2005). Since African American representation rose only 0.4%, from 11.3% to 11.7%, most of this rise can be attributed to increases in the number of Latino officers, 13.1% to 16.8%, from 1996 to 2002 (Reaves and Bauer 2003). The rise in the number of minority officers occurred in all agencies as well, with each of 12 federal agencies reporting gains in the number of their minority officers, including the Immigration and Naturalization Service, the Federal Bureau of Prisons, U.S. Customs Service, Federal Bureau of Investigation, Drug Enforcement Agency, and several other agencies with arrest and firearm authority. This list did not include the Transportation Security Administration because it conducted a major expansion in the Air Marshals program during this period. The thousands of officers hired are "not included in the BJS survey because of classified information restrictions" (p. 10). Targeted hiring of women also does not explain the increase in minority employment since the percentage of female officers increased only 1.1% from 1996 to 2002, with most of these officers being hired in the Internal Revenue Service and the U.S. Postal Inspection Service (Reaves and Bauer 2003).

To summarize the employment findings, trends toward the "browning" of the criminal justice system were strong during the last decade. However, the trends occurred in the local and federal governments rather than uniformly throughout all levels of the system and all areas of the country. State law enforcement organizations show that a much different dynamic occurred at that level. Unlike their federal and local counterparts, the state police organizations throughout the country have failed to increase Latino representation among their full-time sworn personnel. As a result, the percentage of Latino officers is very low in all but a few states. The percentage of females and other minority groups (with the possible exception of African Americans in a handful of states) is also extremely low. Some statistics explain the magnitude and distribution of this problem: only two U.S states have a sizeable percentage of Latino state police officers: Texas, with 22% of its force being Latino, and New Mexico, with the largest percentage of Latino officers at 40%. Three other states, Arizona (14%), California (15%), and Florida (10%) are the only ones out of the remaining states to have double digit percentages which, when averaged represent parity with the U.S. Latino population. The majority (45) of states range from 0 to 8%, with the average being only 1.95% Latino officers (BJS 2005).

Lifestyle and Culture

Why is the percentage of Latino state law enforcement officers substantially lower than their local and federal counterparts? A federal workforce study by the Congressional Hispanic Caucus Institute provides some answers. "Latinos are the only minority group to remain under-represented in the federal workforce [general, not criminal justice]," comprising 11.8% of the national civilian labor force (Cortez and Zazueta 2003, 1). "However, only 6.6% of permanent federal employees are Latino. Moreover, the career paths of Latinos already in the federal government (all sectors) show less progress than other groups" (p. 1). This report found that the reasons for the inequity were several institutional barriers, which included: (a) poor lines of communication between the federal government and the Latino community; (b) the hiring/job seeking practices of the government revolve around kinship and friendship networks, as do those in the criminal justice system. "These practices do not facilitate boosting the number of Latino employees in the federal government, given the fact that there are so few to begin with [and] . . . the government tends to advertise its job opportunities internally, rather than [in] the community at large" (p. 2); (c) Latinos have the highest high school drop-out rates in the nation. In 2000, the U.S. Census Bureau found a 21.1% dropout rate for all Latino 16 to 19 year olds, more than three times the "white alone" rate (Fry 2003). As a measure of future schooling, social, and job prospects among teen populations, the aggregate status dropout rates clearly underline the Latino disadvantage for entry into adulthood (Fry); and (d) a demographic problem exists because the Latino community is the youngest in the United States, with more than a third of all Latinos under the age of 18 (Cortez and Zazueta).

These institutional barriers to success are extremely difficult to overcome. They help to explain the low percentage of Latinos in state criminal justice agencies and the court sector as well. Most if not all of the state organizations require four-year college degrees for entry into their recruiting pool, with military or local policing experience an added plus. Few naturalized Latinos have the time or the educational background to meet these standards unless they are second- or third-generation U.S. citizens who were educated in this country. The success of the federal law enforcement agencies' Latino recruitment effort versus that of the states is most likely due to the higher salaries that the federal government offers. The small pool of qualified Latino candidates are probably choosing federal over state jobs because the application requirements are fairly similar and the pay and benefits are generally better.

VICTIMIZATION AND VICTIM CHARACTERISTICS

Latinos, like other groups who are disproportionately young and poor, continue to suffer from criminal victimization in the United States. Some criminologists argue that scholars have neglected research on Latino criminal investigations, especially homicides. For example, Martinez (1997) claims that researchers have an incomplete understanding of Latino homicides because the crimes take place in a unique environment created by the interaction of immigration and economic deprivation. This environment creates Latino-specific links to homicide that could aid in reducing the extent of homicide in the Latino community. However, in a 2002 study of five major American cities, Martinez found that the presence of Latino homicide is not as high as expected relative to the rate of other impoverished minorities. Dr. Martinez, who is one of the few scholars who have studied Latino homicide, used both individual and neighborhood level data from the 1980s to the 1990s. Although the arrival of a large number of immigrants substantially altered the demographics of the United States Latino population during this period, making it younger and poorer, Martinez contends that this did not engender a substantial rise in homicide rates or other violent crime (Martinez 2002). He finds that the most plausible explanation for Latino homicide patterns being lower than expected is the strength of the Latino family networks and the immigrant communities (Martinez).

Regarding other types of violent crime, Latino persons aged 12 and over were victims of 733,000 simple and aggravated assaults, rapes, and sexual assaults in 2003

(Reaves and Bauer 2003). This violence most often took the form of simple assault, which made up 67% of all Latino victimizations. While such substantial numbers of crimes may be difficult to comprehend, it is important to note that Latino persons were no more likely to be victims of violence than were non-Latinos. Latinos aged 12 and older experienced 14% of all violent crimes and made up 13% of the population in 2003 (NCVS 2005). Although there were no differences for simple assault and robbery, Latinos were significantly more likely to be victims of aggravated assault than other people in America. Reasons for these differences in victimization are not revealed in the National Crime Victimization Survey data, but a look at a trend study conducted by the Office of Justice Programs in the U.S. Department of Justice helps to shed some light on the overall victimization of Latinos in the United States.

"Among Hispanics over the period 1993–2000, those most vulnerable to violent crimes were males . . .; juveniles aged 12 to 17 . . ., those with household incomes under $7,500 . . ., and those who had never married. Violence against Hispanics, as with most other victims, most often took the form of simple assault" (Rennison 2002, 1). But this trend data also showed that the rate of violent crime fell at a higher rate for Hispanics than for all other groups. This rate declined 56% for Hispanics, 50% for whites, and 51% for blacks from 1993 to 2000 (Rennison). For every demographic characteristic considered in the BJS study, the rate of violence against Hispanics declined from 1993 to 2000. Some of the largest groups who benefited are: females (a 63% decline), middle-aged persons from 35 to 49 years old (66% decline), divorced or separated persons (64% decline) those in households with incomes from $15,000 to $24,999 (71% decline) and those living in rural areas (71% decline) (Rennison). The percentage of violent crimes reported to authorities was similar for Hispanics, whites, Asians, blacks, and Native Americans. Characteristics of their typical offenders were a stranger armed with a weapon, usually a firearm. Twenty-eight percent of Hispanic victims perceived the offender to be under the influence of alcohol or drug use which was slightly lower than whites (32%) (Rennison).

Because of the tolerance of physical violence among married partners in many Latin American cultures, Latino victims are often stereotyped as victims of violence by an intimate partner or some other relative. The BJS survey showed this was not true of Latino violence in the U.S. since the percentage of Latinos who were victimized by an intimate partner was only 9% and 4% who were assaulted by some other relative. These rates were similar to the non-Latino groups examined 1993–2000 (Rennison 2002). However, some studies have found a strong tendency towards Latino under-reporting of sexual assault and abuse. For example, in a sample of 1,121 Mexican American and white non-Latino adolescent females, white adolescents were twice as likely to report sexual assault compared to the Mexican American population (Arellano et al. 1997). Both white and Latino abuse victims were more likely to come from homes with parental substance use and family conflict.

During 2003, property crime rates, motor vehicle theft rates, and fraud rates were higher for Latino households. In general, property crime bore no relationship to household income except for those who earned less than $7,500. These low-income households were robbed at a significantly higher rate and also suffered greater rates of assault than persons of higher incomes (Rennison 2002). Since Latinos are disproportionately poor, they are more likely to live in high crime areas and so be at higher risk of victimization, especially for robbery and assault. Latino households were almost twice as likely to have a motor vehicle stolen than non-Latino households (NCVS 2005).

Latino Offenders

Unfortunately police departments and the U.S. Federal Bureau of Investigation (FBI) do not generally collect or publish data on ethnicity in conjunction with their arrest statistics. The FBI publishes the Uniform Crime Report on an annual basis, but it only contains data on race in the following categories: *White, Black, American Indian*, and *Alaskan Indian/other*. Sometimes they use only *White, Black*, and *Others*. It is anyone's guess where a Latino enters into this schematic. They could be classified as white, black, or other and more probably are classified as all three. So, rather than examine UCR statistics on Latino crime, this section looks at several types of crime with which Latinos are often associated. Three specific areas of crime with which Latinos are stereotypically and sometimes rightfully connected are youth gang activity, criminal and drug gangs (trafficking), and human trafficking (immigration law violations).

Latino Gang Activity

Social science researchers have actively investigated gangs for decades. In spite of this fact, the U.S. center responsible for collecting uniform gang data, the National Youth Gang Center in Tallahassee, Florida, stated that "definitions continue to pose problems in evaluating youth gang activity on a national level" (Wilson 2000, 30). The reason that no two gangs exhibit identical behavior, sociologists have found, is that youth gangs are not traditional groups, but rather groups which are in a constant state of flux (Barkan and Snowden 2000). These transitional groups may evolve toward adult organized crime or they may be moving in a more positive direction such as becoming community advocates. At different times, a particular group may even move from one direction to the other. Differing community perceptions also cause problems in definition. For example, local police, neighbors, friends, or community agencies may regard them as simply "unsupervised and troublesome youth groups" instead as of "criminal gangs." Certainly no community wants to portray itself as a "gangland." If a group has specific racial or class connotations, such as being Latino, neighborhood residents and schoolmates may or may not regard them as a gang. Nevertheless, most gangs do share some common behavioral patterns that can help law enforcement officers understand them better.

Snowden (2001) suggests that Latino youth form gangs because they are actively and jointly engaged in challenging or blaming someone or something in their environment as being the cause of their personal problems. The group joins together to fight whomever or whatever they label as being the "cause" of their problem. Their gang association reinforces and reaffirms each member's individual position. For example, they may join together for protection from feared neighborhood members, another gang who has claimed a certain territory, the high crime area where they live, boring schools, neglectful parents, the scrutiny of law enforcement officers, or all of the above. While some youth gangs may not engage in violent or criminal behavior, it is highly likely that any group which forms to "fight" something will engage in violence sooner or later.

Data from the *National Youth Gang Survey* shows that Latinos were the predominant ethnic group among youth gang members in all areas of the country except rural counties. Large city gangs were 47% Latino, small cities 46%, suburban counties 47%, and rural counties 32%. African American youth made up 36% of rural gangs. In 1998, Latinos were the predominant racial/ethnic group among all gang members nationwide. Latinos accounted for 46% of all gang members nationwide, followed by African Americans at 34%, Caucasians at 12%, Asians at 6%, and all other groups at 2% (Wilson 2000). That percentage has stayed firm, varying from 46% to 47% Latino in all the recent youth gang surveys up until 2002 (Egley 2002). However, youth gangs are not necessarily homogenous. Respondents from the gang survey estimated that about one third of all gangs (36%) were significantly mixed with two or more types of racial/ethnic group members, which usually predominated in smaller cities in Midwest America (Wilson 2000, 46). In addition, although crimes were not linked to specific gangs, crime related homicides were a serious problem that occurred in over half the reporting cities as well as motor vehicle theft, larceny/theft, aggravated assault, and robbery. Surprisingly, drug sales and property crime were greatest in suburban counties and rural areas, where the lowest concentration of Latino gangs exist.

In 1998, the U.S. Bureau of Justice Statistics surveyed 40 of the nation's largest urban counties and found that 62% of the juvenile felony defendants were black, 20% were white, 16% were Latino, and almost 2% were another race. In 2003, there were about 20 million males who identified themselves as Latino in the U.S., and about 10 million of those males were under the age of 25, so it is probably not surprising that there are so many Latino gangs in the United States. Two hundred eighty-four cities (population +25,000) with persistent gang activity from 1999 to 2000 reported gang homicide statistics, with 91% reporting at least one or more homicides related to gang activity. In the following year, 47% reported an increase in homicide activity, and 42% reported a decrease (Egley 2002, 1–2). Although Latinos are not a distinct category in the following FBI data, it shows that juveniles were responsible for a lot of violent activity. There were 2,261,000 juvenile arrests in 2002. The arrest figure has decreased each year since 1995. In 2002, juveniles were involved in 10% of arrests for murder, 12.5% of drug abuse violations, 20% of weapons violations, and 25% of arrests for robbery (Snyder 2002).

International Criminal Latino Gangs

Since the 9/11 terrorist attacks in the United States, criminal justice scholars and law enforcement officials have argued that some Latino criminal gangs with well developed and extensive networks could be the future face of terrorism. Some believe that Colombian drug gangs and other Latin American gangs may become the foot soldiers for al-Qaeda and other terrorist groups.

The *Mara Salvatrucha* is an international criminal gang that developed from Los Angeles Latino youth gangs. Latino gangs in California separated into two rival factions, the *Nortenos* (Northerners), primarily found in Northern California, and the *Surenos* (Southerners), found to the south. Latino gangs aligned under the *Nortenos* generally add the number 14 after their gang name, while those aligned under the *Surenos* add the number 13 (Swecker 2005). This is why the *Mara Salvatrucha* gang also became known as MS-13.

The U.S. *Immigration Law of 1998* (IIRIRA) allowed the "expedited removal" of immigrants who had committed crimes, even relatively minor ones. Passage of this act led to the deportation of thousands of Central American gang members, including Salvadorans and confederates of MS-13 like the 18th Street gang. Many Salvadorans who immigrated to the U.S. during El Salvador's civil war had found themselves needing protection in the most violent sections of Los Angeles, so they formed Los Mara Salvatrucha. The gang became well known for its organizational skills and its violence (Vaquera and Bailey 2004). Since MS-13 had recruited immigrant members from all over Central America, the deportations sent Los Mara members home to many weak countries where criminal gangs flourished. These members quickly formed Los Mara branches, who taught local youth the gang's tactics and culture (Vaquera and Bailey).

Estimates suggest more than 200 gangs affiliated with the Mara Salvatrucha (MS-13) and the 18th Street gang formed in Latin America and now congregate around the border between Guatemala and Mexico. They have created an "enormous violent crime wave" in that region which includes murder, drug trafficking, contraband weapons, and the illegal migrant trade from those two countries (Vaquera and Bailey 2004). Los Mara is also expanding their membership in Honduras and El Salvador, as well as throughout Mexico, bringing violence and death along with them, particularly among vulnerable illegal migrants whom the gangs rob and assault as they travel through Mexico on their way to the United States.

Other MS-13 members left Los Angeles before the deportation and began gangs in their new neighborhoods. Los Mara spread quickly across the United States. For example, in 1993, three MS-13 gang members from Los Angeles moved to the Washington, D.C. metropolitan area to recruit additional MS-13 members. Today there are as many as 1,500 members of MS-13 in the Northern Virginia/D.C. area (Swecker 2005). MS-13 now has a presence in more than 31 states, with 8,000 to 10,000 hardcore members (Swecker).

Los Mara gangs are certainly closer to organized crime groups than they are to political terrorists, but the current world paranoia about terrorism leads security experts to worry about the two types of groups developing an alliance. MS-13 in the United States is still a loosely structured street gang; however, its threat is based on its violence and its potential to grow, not only geographically, but also in its organization and sophistication. "Gang members affiliate themselves into groups known as cliques. Each clique will have a local leader called the 'shot caller,'" but there is no evidence of a single organizational leader (Swecker 2005, 6). "There are multi-clique meetings in which gang members pay a fee to attend, coordinate their activities, exchange information regarding law enforcement actions and efforts, and issue punishment and/or sanctions for infractions of the gang's code" (p. 7). The FBI reports that some MS-13 members have taken over existing Latino gangs. MS-13 members instill discipline through violence and some are engaged in retail drug trafficking, primarily powdered and crack cocaine and marijuana, and, to a lesser extent, methamphetamines and heroin. The drug proceeds are laundered through seemingly legitimate businesses. MS-13 members are also involved in a variety of other types of criminal activity, including rape, murder, extortion, auto theft, immigrant smuggling, and robbery (Swecker).

The FBI considers the Mara Salvatrucha gangs such a threat that they established a MS-13 National Gang Task Force to combat the gang and to spread intelligence at both the national and international level. An example of the MS-13 National Gang Task Force coordination efforts took place in early 2005 when the Federal Bureau of Investigation, the U.S. Customs, the U.S. Border Patrol, the Texas Department of Public Safety, and the East Hidalgo Detention Center worked together to arrest a key MS-13 figure alleged to have been involved in a bus massacre that took place in Honduras on December 23, 2004 (Swecker 2005). Twenty-eight people were assassinated in the massacre, including six children, and fourteen other individuals were seriously wounded. A note left at the scene indicated the massacre was in retaliation against laws targeting gang members in Honduras, with MS-13 members identified as being responsible for the attack (Swecker).

There have also been some isolated and unsubstantiated reports of MS-13 members meeting with al-Qaeda operatives, but there is no information regarding outside financing of the MS-13 organization (Swecker 2005). Rather than liaison with terrorist groups, who are always in need of resources, the MS-13 organization is more likely to develop fund-raising projects with them rather than ideological mergers.

Latino Drug Gangs, Narcoterrorism, and the War on Drugs

One reason why Latinos are stereotyped as "drug abusers" is because of the thriving drug industries that exist in Colombia, Mexico, and Central America. Just as the 1996 immigration law stimulated the deportation of MS-13 members and the rebirth of a gang movement, so too did a need for new resources provoke the Fuerzas Armadas Revolucionarias (FARC) to revitalize its organization. The group successfully mobilized new funding from the Columbian drug trade. Although FARC continues to call itself a Marxist insurgency group, it has failed to gain support for its ideas from the broader Columbian population since the 1960s. By 1980, FARC had completely failed to garner the public sentiment and appeared to dying out (Franco 2000).

In the late 1980s, FARC moved into the illegal drug industry to gain the resources which it could not raise in the public sector. Today FARC makes several billion dollars a year from drug trafficking. FARC's activities and association with drug cartels prompted a United States Ambassador to Columbia, Anne Patterson, to label FARC a cynical and hypocritical drug-trafficking organization who claims to be seeking social justice, but is really only seeking drug money (Stoller, personal communication, 2001). Most of FARC's successful activities are connected to the drug trade. Throughout the last decade, FARC has developed a symbiotic relationship with the *cocaleros* (coca growing farmers) whom they protect. FARC taxes all coca crops, paste production, and the transportation of narcotics in and out of the rural regions which they control (Franco). FARC is involved in arms trafficking—they use the drug money to buy weapons on the international black market. FARC also "exchanges drugs for weapons and cash with organized crime groups in Chechnya, Russia," and other Eastern European countries (p. 5).

Though FARC has succeeded by facilitating a favorable environment for drug activities in Colombia, it has also destabilized the government enough to draw the attention of the United States and Columbia's neighbors. The worse the crisis becomes in Colombia, the more likely it is that the United States will intervene in the conflict. Since FARC cannot draw its power from the people, it must move closer to the drug trade. As it does, it greatly increases the probability that the United States will be forced to step up their law enforcement activity in the region.

Immigration: Latino Victims or Criminals?

Each year the United States admits 25 to 30 million non-immigrants into the country. About a third of these people come from Europe, and the rest come from areas all over the world. Many of the U.S. unauthorized immigrants come from the non-immigrants who overstay their visas by not leaving the country when their legal visas expire. When they are no longer allowed to legally live in the U.S., they usually disappear into the general population, obtain some type of false documentation and then go on as if they were a normal immigrant. The other large segment of the unauthorized population enters the country through clandestine means, such as sneaking over the border with the aid of friends, family, or Mexican smugglers known as *coyotes*. In January 2000, the U.S. Immigration and Naturalization Service estimated that the unauthorized population residing in the United States was 7 million (INS 2002). "California is estimated to have the most unauthorized residents, about 2.2 million or 32% of the total, and . . . Mexico is the largest source country for unauthorized immigration into the U.S. with 69% of the total population. . . . In addition to Mexico, six countries had more than 100,000 authorized residents . . . El Salvador, Guatemala, Columbia, Honduras, China, and Ecuador" (p. 1). Only one of these countries, China, is not in Latin America, so it is clear that most of our unauthorized immigrants are Latinos. Two important disclaimers about this population should be noted: (a) Immigration scholars often disagree with the INS regarding the number of unauthorized people in the country—estimates range as high as 14 million, and usually average about 10 million; (b) This population is not consistent—in other words, while there may only be 7 million unauthorized people in the country at any one point in time, in a month or two there may be a million different people here because most of the border crossers return home on a cyclical basis and others come to take their place. However, all 7 million of these people are in violation of criminal law so they know that they can be arrested and deported at any time. As a result, they usually remain hidden. Their illegal status makes this group of people very vulnerable to more serious criminal elements who often use the undocumented to hide illegal operations, such as drug smuggling. The criminals know that the immigrants are unlikely to report them because they fear the police. The unauthorized population also can shield the criminal element. Employers who hire illegal immigrants do not bother to investigate or report that their farm or business is also the front for a drug-smuggling operation.

The unauthorized Latinos are often victimized directly via robbery, illegal drug and alcohol sales, theft, petty larceny, prostitution, and just about every other crime one can imagine. Many of the Latinos who make up the unauthorized population come from remote villages in Mexico and Latin America. They are unsophisticated and do not consider themselves criminals. They hear many untrue things about working in America and usually cross the border via *coyotes*. These human traffickers must be paid large sums of money. Since the immigrants usually do not have such sums (often they come from such poverty that their families literally do not have enough food to eat without the sums of money that the workers send home), they are frequently brought into the criminal network by drug smugglers. These criminals offer to pay part of the passage if the immigrant will carry some drugs into the United States. Upon arrival, they turn in the drugs for money to help pay the *coyotes*. The *coyotes* must be paid, or they will kill the immigrant's family. Thus, in spite of the farm workers being seen by themselves, their families, and by the local farmers (whose farms need the Mexicans for labor) as heroes, the entire illegal immigration process is actually steeped in criminality.

The Border Patrol, using IBIS card readers and the IDENT system, looks especially for criminal immigrants, those with prior arrests or convictions. These immigrants are detained in INS detention centers or, if these are full, they are housed in local jails and prisons. Frequently, unauthorized entrants detained in the interior of the country are also housed in regular prisons. Immigrants who are convicted of crimes, whether here legally or illegally, must serve out their sentences in U.S. prisons and then await deportation in the INS detention centers (prisons). The Border Patrol and Immigration and Customs Enforcement (ICE) report their principal activities and accomplishments on an annual basis. In 2003, the Border Patrol apprehended 946,684 deportable persons, 95% of whom were Mexican immigrants working in agriculture or seeking employment (INS 2005). The number of deportable immigrants captured by the Border Patrol is down sharply from a few years ago.

In 2003, the total of apprehended, deportable immigrants was 59% smaller than in the year 2000 (INS 2005). The Department of Homeland Security (DHS) also has an immigration investigations program. They perform criminal, employer, fraud, and smuggling investigations. Types of immigration violations/convictions encountered in 2003 are listed above in Table 3-2 along with the number of violations handled by the immigration agents. Most convictions are for entry violations, but a number of other federal convictions, such as drug trafficking, etc. also occur. While about a million immigrants are apprehended each year, only approximately 20,000 immigrants choose to go through the legal process. The rest take voluntary departure and many immigrants re-attempt the border

TABLE 3-2   Convictions for Selected Immigration and Naturalizaion Violations in Fiscal Year 2003

Type of Violations	Number of Convictions
All Violations	**22,478**
Immigration Violations	**21,820**
Entry of aliens illegally	14,199
Reentry of deported aliens	4,938
Bringing in/Harboring illegal aliens	1,612
Fraud and False Statements for Benefits	270
Fraud and misuse of Visas/Alien Registration	253
Fraud and misuse of Identification Documents	390
Conspiring to defraud the U.S.	6
Employing unauthorized aliens	72
Naturalization Violations	**137**
False Representation as Citizens of U.S.	101
Fraud, Misuse of Passports or Citizenship Papers	36
Other Violations	**521**
Racketeering	173
Money Laundering/Financial Fraud	17–20 (Avg.)
Weapons Trafficking	67
Drug Trafficking	158
Obstructing Justice	35
Other Violations	63

Source: 2003 Yearbook of the Immigration and Naturalization Service, DHS.

crossing as soon as possible. Finally, government figures show that a great deal of drug seizures take place at the border every year. For example, in 2003, there were 8,528 marijuana seizures, worth $1,434,000,000, weighing 1,562,368 pounds; there were 742 cocaine seizures, worth $598,000,000, weighing 21,030.8 pounds; and 119 seizures of heroin, worth $42,000,000, weighing about 389 pounds (INS 2004).

LATINO INMATES

Many Latino agencies have argued that the over-representation of Latinos "at every stage of the criminal justice system from police stops to penitentiary and parole" (Woodbury 2004, 1) is the result of stereotyping and discrimination. On the opposite side, law enforcement proponents insist that Latino criminality is the reason for "the browning of the criminal justice system" at the offender level. Several states with the most alarming statistics, such as Connecticut and Illinois, have done studies to assess why Latinos appear to be arrested and incarcerated at higher than normal rates. Their findings will be summarized in the conclusion to this section. According to the National Council of La Raza, a Latino civil rights organization, juvenile and adult Latinos are involved in the "browning of justice" as they are being arrested, charged, and convicted of felonies in numbers that far surpass their 13% share of the U.S. population (Woodbury 2004). La Raza released a study with the following findings:

- Latinos are overrepresented at every stage of the criminal justice system, from police stops to penitentiary and parole.
- Latinos account for nearly one-third of the federal prison population and stand a one in six chance of being imprisoned during their lifetime.
- In the courts, Latino males are sentenced to prison three times as often as whites, despite being the least likely ethnic group to have a criminal history.
- Nonviolent offenders, particularly substance abusers, receive the most serious injustice, as Latino youths charged with drug offenses are incarcerated at rates of 13 to 1 relative to whites.
- In 2000, La Raza said that Latinos account for over 43% of all convicted drug offenders and DEA continues to arrest them at rates nearly triple their proportion in the general population and many are incarcerated for low-level nonviolent drug offenses.
- At the arrest and prosecution level, a combination of racial profiling and disproportionate reliance on public defenders have caused Latino prison rates for low-level offenses and immigration violations to skyrocket.

Colorado statistics from several sources support the above findings and suggest that the disparities are worsening. From 1998 to 2003, Latino prison commitments rose nearly 23% and in a 12-month period, the incarceration rate for Latino drug offenders was four times that for Anglos (Woodbury 2004). The *Los Angeles Sentinel* reported that when prosecutors make the decision on trying juveniles as adults, race matters. For example, in an Illinois study of 393 youths automatically transferred to adult court during 1999–2000, 99% were either African American or Latino. In addition, 99% of the youth imprisoned for drug crimes in Cook County were nonwhites. More than half of the juvenile drug-transfer cases had never received court services before, and 34% had no previous juvenile-court convictions. A speaker from the Justice Policy Institute said that the state has automatic transfer laws that mandate those aged 15 and up must be sent to adult court if arrested for dealing drugs within 1,000 feet of a school or a public housing project (McKissack 2001). Nationwide, juvenile African American drug offenders are sentenced to 90 days more in state correctional facilities than whites, and Latinos are sentenced to 160 days longer than whites.

Statistics like the ones stated in the La Raza report led to the 98th American Assembly finding that "there is significant racial disparity in most aspects of law enforcement, including disparate treatment by the police, selective prosecution, and discriminatory sentencing" (American Assembly 2001, 10). This report states that racial disparity represents a crisis situation that destroys families and creates a sense of hopelessness in minority communities. "While in prison, non-violent offenders face a penal system that often results in further criminalization as opposed to rehabilitation" with two million people currently incarcerated in America and over two-thirds of them people of color (American Assembly, 2001, 10–11). While most white Americans are more or less aware of this situation, many of them have no idea about the extent of the problem as it relates to Latinos.

Latinos often run afoul of the law because they come from countries where there is extensive police corruption. As a result, they have little or no idea how to deal with a police system that does not revolve around bribes. In addition, the Latino immigrant population isolates itself from the mainstream of American communities where they work. They receive most of their community information by word of mouth or from Spanish-speaking radio stations. This oral system is especially sensitive to inaccurate information. It also magnifies any type of disparate treatment as word spreads through the Latino community.

There are two problems connected with Latino youth. The first is that law enforcement officials often assume that a group of young Latinos is "out for trouble" or is engaging in gang violence without observing a consistent pattern of such behavior. Latinos usually travel in groups because of their poverty and their large families, not necessarily because they want traveling companions. Many Latino youth gangs do not engage in criminal activity and should not be prejudged simply because of their ethnicity. The second problem is the temptation to allow institutional discrimination to creep into legislation and to make first-time offender punishments too harsh. The long-term effects of moving youthful offenders to adult court must be considered. A minor felony record will act as a road block to job and educational opportunities, making the immigrant a user of public services rather than a tax-paying citizen who funds social benefits.

A *Human Rights Watch Briefing* conducted on February 22, 2002, documented racial disparities on a state-by-state basis in the incarceration of Africans Americans and Latinos. The figures reveal a continuing and extraordinary magnitude of minority incarceration, including a stark disparity in their rates of incarceration compared to those of whites. Out of a total population of 1,976,019 incarcerated in adult facilities, 63% are black and Latino, though these two groups constitute only 25% of the national population (Human Rights Watch 2002, 1). Extreme state violators include New York, with a 15% Latino population and a 26.7% incarceration rate; Massachusetts, with 6.8% Latinos and 26.1% incarceration; and West Virginia, with 0.7% Latinos and 3.3% incarceration, giving it a whopping ratio of 4.9 times as many Latinos incarcerated than reside in the state (Commission on Racial Disparity 2004).

Another major problem area is the federal jurisdiction, where in 1998, 30% of all federal prisoners were Latinos, a figure which has probably worsened today. Two areas with disparity problems, the city of Chicago and the state of Connecticut, ran studies to determine why the disparity had occurred. Connecticut has one of the severest disparity problems in the nation so the state set up a commission to study several points in the criminal justice system that might be likely to cause disparity, including police discretion, the awarding of bail, and minority representation on juries. Although they did have significant findings in a few areas such as, "Caucasians were granted no-financial release at nearly twice the rate of" (Commission on Racial Disparity 2004, 20) the minority group for both felonies and misdemeanors, the value of the study lies more in model that it presents for future studies rather than in its results. All sections of the arrest and conviction areas were surveyed, as well as other data, such as the U.S. Census, and were incorporated into the study. Hopefully more states will follow the example of Connecticut in opening the door to understanding the mechanisms for disparity which exists in the United States legal system.

Another landmark study is still in progress in the city of Chicago. In 1993 Chicago instituted on an experimental basis the Chicago Alternative Policing Strategy, known as CAPS, to improve police effectiveness "by identifying and solving problems through community interactions (community policing)" (Skogan et al. 2002, 1). Several National Institute of Justice reports have summarized key findings from the CAPS program evaluations, and one discusses how CAPS has benefited Latinos in Chicago. Findings included how Chicago's Latinos viewed and participated in CAPS, the characteristics of the city's Latino residents, and local population trends. They are (Skogan):

- In 1999, more than 45% of surveyed Latinos did not graduate from high school and less than 10% had a college degree. Regarding income levels, 44% of the Latinos earned less than $20,000 a year compared to 38% of blacks and 16% of whites.
- Almost 79% of Latino households included children while 44% of the black households had children, and only 22% of white households had children.
- Chicago's Latino neighborhoods have more criminality and physical decay. In addition, the Latino residents did not share the perception of other Chicagoans that there has been general improvement in their neighborhoods over the last decade (p. 7), in spite of the fact that actual crime statistics indicated a decline in these neighborhoods. Non-English speaking Latinos also rated each neighborhood measure as a more serious problem than did English-speaking Latinos and African Americans.
- Language preferences again divided Latinos in their views of the CAPS program and police performance. English speakers rated police higher on helpfulness, concern, and fairness. Levels of income and education were also positively linked with Latinos ability to speak English.

To summarize the important point of this study—some aspects of disparity may be linked to people's ability to positively interact and communicate with criminal justice personnel, rather than factors embedded within the criminal justice system itself. Just as we suspect that disparity is positively linked with poverty and low levels of education, so might low levels of communicative ability ruin everything positive we try to do to enlist minority community support.

CONCLUSION

This chapter on Latinos and United States criminal justice has taken a broad view of the problems which Hispanics and Latinos have with the system and the problems which the system has with Latinos. One thing is evident—there are many difficulties on both sides. There are also far too few studies that illuminate the Latino situation. Perhaps this is because the numbers of Latinos have risen so dramatically in the last few years, but more likely it is because Latinos have been marginalized in American society and the American criminal justice system. Latino numbers have now propelled them to be the largest minority in the United States, and by 2050 it is predicted they will share the majority with whites. This means that the country must increase Latino education, communication, and income levels quickly or the criminal justice system will continue to be a warehouse for illegal and impoverished immigrants.

REFERENCES

American Assembly. (2001). Racial equality: Public policies for the twenty-first century. *Report of the Proceedings of the Ninety-Eighth American Assembly*. New York: Columbia University.

ARELLANO, C. M., J. A. KUHN, AND E. L. CHAVEZ. (1997). Psychosocial correlates of sexual assault among Mexican American and White Non-Hispanic Adolescent Females. *Hispanic Journal of Behavioral Sciences, 19*(4), 446–60.

BARKAN, S. E., AND L. L. SNOWDEN. (2000). *Collective violence*. Englewood, NJ: Allyn & Bacon.

Bureau of Justice Statistics [BJS]. (2005). *Sourcebook of criminal justice statistics*. Retrieved from http://www.albany.edu/sourcebook/.

Civil Rights Division. (2003). *Guidance regarding the use of race by federal law enforcement agencies*. Washington, DC: U.S. Department of Justice.

Commission on Racial and Ethnic Disparity in the Criminal Justice System. (2004). *Annual report and recommendations, 2003–2004*. Hartford, CT: State of Connecticut.

CORTEZ, J., AND E. ZAZUETA. (2003). Latinos in the federal workforce. *CHCI Policy Brief.* Washington, DC: Congressional Hispanic Caucus Institute.

EGLEY, A., Jr. (2005). *Highlights of the 2002–2003 National Youth Gang Survey*. Washington, DC: U.S. Department of Justice.

EGLEY, A., Jr. (2002). *National Youth Gang Survey trends from 1996 to 2000*. Washington, DC: U.S. Department of Justice.

FRANCO, G. H. (2000). Their darkest hour: Colombia's government and the narco-insurgency. In *Parameters, US Army War College Summary, 30*(2), 83–93.

FRY, R. (2003). High school dropout rates for Latino youth. In *ERIC Digest*. Publishing Source: ERIC Clearinghouse on urban Education, # ED482920. Retrieved from http://www.ericdigests. org/2004–3/latino.html.

HOWELL, J. C., AND A. EGLEY, Jr. (2005). *Gangs in small towns and rural counties*. Washington, DC: National Youth Gang Center.

HOWELL, J. C., A. EGLEY, Jr., AND D. K. GLEASON. (2000). *Youth gangs: Definitions an age-old issue*. A paper presented at the American Society of Criminology 2000 Annual Meeting in San Francisco, California, November 2000.

Human Rights Watch. (2002). *Race and incarceration in the United States*. Retrieved from http://www.hrw.org/reports.

Immigration and Naturalization Service [INS]. (2005). Table 22: Nonimmigrants admitted by selected class of admission and region and selected country of last residence. In the *Yearbook of the Immigration and Naturalization Service, 2004*. Washington, DC: Department of Homeland Security.

Immigration and Naturalization Service [INS]. (2004). *Yearbook of the Immigration and Naturalization Service, 2003*. Washington, DC: Department of Homeland Security.

Immigration and Naturalization Service [INS], Office of Policy and Planning. (2000). *Estimates of the unauthorized immigrant population residing in the United States: 1990 to 2000*. Washington, DC: U.S. Immigration and Naturalization Service.

JELINEK, P. (2005). 1 in 7 people in the U.S. Hispanic. *Star-News*. June 9., Wilmington, NC.

LOVATO, R. (2005). *Gonzales appointment latest step in browning of justice*. Los Angeles: Pacific News Service and North California Media.

MARTINEZ, R., Jr. (1997). *Facing violent crime among Latinos*. Working Paper No. 35 in Julian Samora Research Institute Research and Publications Working Paper Series. East Lansing, MI: Michigan State University.

MARTINEZ, R., Jr. (2002). *Latino homicide: Immigration, violence, and community*. New York: Routledge.

McKISSACK, F. (2001). Huge racial disparities in juvenile sentencing. *Los Angeles Sentinel*. June 20. Retrieved from www.highbeam.com/library.

National Center for Victims of Crime [NCVS]. (2005). *Crime and victimization in America 2005: Statistical overview*. Washington, DC: National Center for Victims of Crime.

Rand Corporation. (2001). Drugs and insurgents in Colombia. In *Rand Research Brief*. Retrieved from http://www.rand.org/publications.

REAVES, B., AND L. BAUER. (2003). *Federal law enforcement officers, 2002—Bureau of Justice Statistics Bulletin* [NCJ 199995]. Washington, DC: U.S. Department. of Justice.

RENNISON, C. M. (2002) *Hispanic victims of violent crime, 1993–2000* [NCJ 191208]. Washington, DC: U.S. Department of Justice.

SKOGAN, W., J. STEINER, J. DuBOIS, J. GRUDILL, and A. FAGIN. (2002). *Community policing and the new immigrants*. Boston: Northwest University.

SNOWDEN, L. (2001). *Preventing Terrorism*. North Chelmsford, MA: Erudition Books.

SNYDER, H. N. (2002). *Juvenile arrests 2000*. Washington, DC: Office of Juvenile Justice and Delinquency Prevention.

SWECKER, C. (2005). Statement of Chris Swecker, Criminal Investigative Division Federal Bureau of Investigation Before the Subcommittee on the Western Hemisphere House International Relations Committee, April 20, 2005. In *Congressional Testimony*. Retrieved from http://www.fbi.gov.

VAQUERA, T., AND D. BAILEY. (2004). Latin gang in the Americas: Los Mara Salvatrucha. *Crime and Justice International, 20*(83).

WILSON, J.J. (2000). *1998 National Youth Gang Survey*. Washington, DC: Office of Juvenile Justice and Delinquency Program.

WOODBURY, R. (2004). La Raza reports overrepresentation of Latinos in U.S. jails. In *La Voz de Colorado*. Retrieved from http://www.highbeam.com.

4

Native Americans in the Criminal Justice System

Skip Grubb

❖

INTRODUCTION

Native Americans have historically been portrayed in a negative light. Recently, however, the image of Native Americans has begun to change in popular culture. Films such as *Thunderheart*, *Dances with Wolves*, and *Windtalkers* highlighted the ingenuity and nobility of the Native American peoples. In addition, Native Americans began to improve their economic future with the construction and operation of Indian-owned gambling casinos. Other cultural aspects innate to Native Americans and their involvement in the legal system as victims, offenders, and criminal justice personnel are explored in this chapter. Issues of identity and cultural heritage for Native Americans will provide a backdrop to further enhance the understanding of their position in the United States; thus the discussion begins there.

NATIVE AMERICAN IDENTITY AND CULTURE

The terms *Native American*, *American Indian*, and *Indian* are synonymous with the tribal peoples of the United States. Most tribal members prefer to be identified with their specific tribes and by their given native names but have tolerated these broader terms in an effort to pacify local community members and ease tension between themselves and the dominant culture. In fact, most Native Americans have not identified themselves as one group with these terms but prefer to maintain a separate identity and refer to this vast group of tribes as "The People" or "The Friends." This distinction demonstrates the pride individual tribes feel and their respect for members of other tribes (Shusta et al. 2002).

Much like Anglo-Americans, Indian tribes have names which are not precisely correct but which serve as descriptors, much like "nicknames." For instance, in the Anglo culture, men who are named Robert may be called "Bob," and women who are named Margaret are referred to as "Peggy." Many tribes were named in an effort to identify attributes of members of that specific group (e.g. "fierce fighters," "horseback riders," etc.). Members of the Sioux tribe were called "Snakes" by rival tribes, and this moniker was adopted by European settlers. According to researchers (Shusta et al. 2002), even the term *Indian* is not a proper term, but one erroneously applied by Christopher Columbus, who thought he had landed in the East Indies rather than the "New World."

While Native Americans have a rich cultural history, much of this culture has been destroyed or manipulated to favor the European-descended majority. A review of student textbooks will reveal an interpretation of historical events that favors the dominant population. American Indians were portrayed as vicious, bloodthirsty savages who stubbornly resisted religion, education, and acculturation. Some examples would be the frequent references to the practice of scalping enemies, burning enemy camps, and enslaving enemy women and children. In addition, references to Native Americans' pagan-like religions and native languages contributed to the demonization by European settlers. This portrayal has led to several centuries of historical and cultural baggage and often reveals itself in the form of poor self-esteem and a repudiation of cultural identity. In some cases, a self-fulfilling prophecy is evident in the individual as well as the beliefs of community members in surrounding towns and villages.

Unlike other minorities, the population of the Indian people has not rapidly expanded. Native Americans currently represent only 1.5% of the total population, and this figure includes the Inuits and Aleuts of Alaska. While some individuals deny their heritage in an attempt to avoid stigmatization, others falsely proclaim a heritage to which they are not entitled. Why? These fraudulent claims are made in an effort to obtain educational preferences, scholarships, or other entitlements which would otherwise be unavailable. Certain tribal members are eligible to receive annual stipends as a result of profits netted from gambling casinos and other capital ventures, in addition to certain tax benefits accorded Indian reservations. Membership in tribal communities varies, as many tribes have different criteria for inclusion. Since membership is a matter of tribal sovereignty, the federal government is very reluctant to interfere. Even some tribes fail to be recognized by the federal government due to historical and political considerations. At this point, over 500 tribes are recognized by the government. Every tribe has an administrative body that may be contacted to authenticate membership status, and the federal government utilizes the Bureau of Indian Affairs (BIA) for guidance in these matters.

While the federal government has recently made strides in attempting to reconcile a rather suspect relationship with the Indian people, Native Americans remain skeptical. Trust is easy to lose and extremely difficult to re-establish. In an effort to regain the trust of the tribes and make amends for past transgressions, President Clinton signed an Executive Order in 2000 to renew the government's commitment to tribal sovereignty.

This feat was to be accomplished through an effort to establish meaningful consultation and collaboration with tribal officials in the development of federal policies having tribal implications, to strengthen the administration's government-to-government relationship to tribes, and to reduce the imposition of unfounded mandates by ensuring that all executive departments and agencies consult with tribes and respect tribal sovereignty as they develop policies on issues that impact Indian communities (Shusta et al. 2005, 255).

President George W. Bush reaffirmed this sentiment in 2002 in a White House news release by proclaiming:

> My administration is working to increase employment and expand economic opportunity for all Native Americans. Several federal agencies recently participated in the National Summit on Emerging Tribal Economies to accomplish this goal. In order to build upon this effort, my administration will work to promote cooperation and coordination among federal agencies or the purpose of fostering greater economic development of tribal communities. By working together on important economic initiatives, we will strengthen America . . . with hope and promise for all Native Americans (Shusta et al. 2005, 255).

While these statements are broad in scope and promise a great deal concerning the treatment of Native Americans, the United States government has not historically demonstrated good faith in maintaining its promises. An unbiased review of the past will reveal the gathering of Plains Indians from the Dakotas and their internment on reservations. Tribes were relocated from their native lands and reservations across the country to areas deemed more suitable for their habitation. This was also known as the "Trail of Tears," but the government viewed this move as a benevolent gesture—an opportunity for a less fortunate people to be provided for by a paternal authority. The government would provide food, clothing, and housing as well as an education. Yet starvation, isolation, and lack of education have plagued the American Indian. Today most reservations still suffer from poor educational opportunities, high unemployment, and a proliferation of substance abuse. According to Shusta et al. (2005),

> Mortality rates attributed to alcohol consumption are nearly seven times as many for American Indians and Alaska Natives as for other races. Alcoholism is the leading health and social problem of American Indians; 75% of the deaths for people under 45 years of age most often follow alcohol use (p. 261).

This combination of factors may also account for the fact that suicide rates for Native Americans are significantly greater than that for other races and almost double that among young males aged 15–35. Indians who leave the reservation to pursue education or employment opportunities express a high degree of discomfort and anxiety as a result of "feeling caught between two worlds." By leaving the reservation, they are abandoning their traditions—however temporarily—and suffering a sense of personal loss and insecurity. In entering a new world, this sense of loss and insecurity is heightened and becomes exacerbated, particularly if they do not experience success or acceptance in the new environment.

These individuals, who are neither successful nor accepted in either world, experience feelings of abandonment and subsequent depression. If success and acceptance in the new world occurs, these individuals still suffer the pangs of abandonment since they can never fully return to the reservation. They may endeavor to make life better for the ones who dare to follow them, but seldom are they able to fully embrace their native culture. While they do not abandon their culture, it becomes more diluted in that individual. In some cases, forced assimilation has extinguished the culture from many Indians as their grandparents and parents were forced to abandon the old ways in order to become more American.

In an attempt to increase local employment opportunities, many tribes have turned to gambling casinos and the collateral businesses which support these ventures. Since tribal lands are under the sovereignty of the tribes, gambling casinos provide a much needed stream of revenue and limited regulation from governmental agencies. This revenue is not taxed in the same manner as other casinos. The revenue comes from guests who frequent the casinos that are located in areas not generally zoned for development by local or state governments, thereby reducing or eliminating many sources of competition. Preferential hiring practices will increase the opportunity for local tribal members to become gainfully employed and thus raise their standard of living.

The Choctaw-owned Golden Moon and Silver Star casinos are located in Philadelphia, Mississippi. Only 100 miles from the state capitol of Jackson and located in Neshoba County, this sleepy community has been revitalized due to the influx of guests seeking entertainment in a charming southern environment. Visitors who previously came to Neshoba County for the Fair each July only to hear political candidates build their platforms for state office now frequent the area year round. However, casinos alone cannot solve all the woes of the local tribe, let alone other tribes in the Indian nation. Many communities experience problems associated with the promotion and enhancement of gaming establishments. These problems include but are not limited to addictive behaviors, crimes of moral turpitude, and the possibility of associated increases in motor vehicle accidents.

NATIVE AMERICANS AS LAW ENFORCEMENT PROFESSIONALS

What role is law enforcement playing in attempting to resolve these community issues? Law enforcement in the Indian community is a complicated matter. Law enforcement services may be comprised of tribal, municipal, county, state, and federal officers. Jurisdictional issues are confusing with regard to arrest powers, prosecution, and detention facilities. Training for each of the previously mentioned officers varies widely, as well as the condition of detention facilities and their ability to confine juveniles and adults. Uniformed tribal officers report to the BIA superintendent (Bureau of Indian Affairs) who generally has no law enforcement background. Investigations are usually handled by officers from local, county, state, or federal agencies who have received extensive training and are certified by the state or federal government. While tribal officers have the authority to arrest reservation inhabitants, they detain non-Indians until local, county, or state officers arrive. Their jurisdiction has historically been limited to the land under the sovereignty of the tribe. Even in traveling from one part of the reservation to another, tribal officers' power on public roadways is restricted.

Local, county, and state officials have jurisdiction on native lands but in conjunction with the tribal police and tribal leaders. Even federal officers must respect the sovereignty of the reservation. Most local, county, and state officers are reluctant to respond, much less become embroiled in tribal offenses as a result of the confusion surrounding the above-mentioned issues of jurisdiction and authority to act. In an effort to eliminate or at least reduce some of this confusion, the *Final Report of the Executive Committee for Indian Country Law Enforcement Improvements* (1994) to the United States Attorney General and the Secretary of the Interior offered the following options:

Option A
Consolidate the three major law enforcement programs under the line and budgetary authority of BIA's Office Of Law Enforcement Services (OLES). DOJ (Department of Justice) will assist OLES by expanding the availability of technical assistance and training.

Option B
Transfer all three major law enforcement programs in BIA (criminal investigations, uniform police, and detention services) to DOJ, maintaining Indian hiring preference and contracting/compacting authority. DOJ will create liaison positions to assure that community accessibility and tribal input on local law enforcement issues and priorities are maintained (p. 4).

Most uniformed officers attend the BIA Indian Police Academy (IPA) at Artesia, New Mexico, a satellite facility of the Federal Law Enforcement Training Facility (FLETC) at Glynco, Georgia. The academy's course is 16 weeks in length and covers a wide array of basic law enforcement topics. These topics range from basic report writing and laws of arrest through the use of force continuum and emergency driving techniques. Each academy class is composed of 50 cadets or recruits. These recruits may wait up to a year to attend the academy. Once the training begins, only about 50% of the class actually graduates. These 25 officers return to their reservations for patrol duty but seldom remain. Within two years, another 50% of this number leave tribal policing. Only about 12 officers thus remain to police communities with ever-increasing problems. This attrition rate is not completely out of line with municipal policing. Most municipalities send cadets or recruits to the academy within a year of being hired. To have a class of 50 cadets, 500 applicants must be screened. Only 10% will be accepted for the training academy, which may last from 12 to 24 weeks, depending upon state certification requirements. Very few recruits fail to graduate and are assigned to patrol duty. The attrition begins at year three and continues until the tenth year. Of the original 50 academy classmates, about 40% will leave municipal policing prior to completing the 20 or 25 years of service needed for retirement. Law enforcement academies nationwide are facing a recruiting and hiring crisis. This crisis is due in part to poor salaries, difficult working conditions, and the inherent danger associated with policing. The lack of available law enforcement officers puts a tremendous strain on the present level of staffing for municipalities and especially Indian officers. Officers routinely patrol very large areas with little or no assistance. The best staffed tribally operated law enforcement agency, the Navajo Nation Department of Law enforcement in Arizona had one officer for every 100 square miles of territory.

According to the Bureau of Justice Statistics:

> The total number of American Indian arrests for violent crime increased 1.7% from 2000–2001. . . . Compared to all races, American Indians were less likely (16–27 arrests per 100,000) to be arrested for robbery but more likely to be arrested for aggravated assault. . . . In 2001 the arrest rate among American Indians for alcohol violations—driving under the influence (DUI), liquor law violations, and drunkenness was double the national rate (Perry 2004, 16–17).

When surveyed, 83% of Village Public Safety Officers (VPSO) reported that a lack of adequate pay was problematic, 60% reported a need to supplement their salaries, 20% reported using food stamps, and 72% stated they feared for their own lives or safety while dealing with dangerous situations. In fact, more than a third (37%) were injured while making an arrest (Wood 2000). Since 1995, 19 officers have lost their lives in the line of duty; all have their names inscribed on the walls of the National Law Enforcement Officers Memorial.

NATIVE AMERICAN VICTIMIZATION

According to a Bureau of Justice Statistics Profile, *American Indians and Crime*, "American Indians experience violence at a rate (101 violent crimes per 1,000 American Indians) more than twice the rate for the Nation (41 per 1,000 persons), 1992–2001" (Perry 2004, I). Is this just an isolated occurrence or the result of neglect? Perhaps this increase in crime is the result of outsiders attempting to create new markets for drugs or utilizing native lands as factories or distribution centers for shipping illicit products to larger markets. In any event, a rise in violent crime has occurred that is contrary to the national trend for the years stated. In the boom decade of the 1990s, crime in general suffered a significant decline as a result of economic prosperity and the availability of new jobs. A review of certain crime facts may prove useful in attempting to explain this anomaly.

- On average, American Indians experienced an estimated 1 violent crime for every 10 residents age 12 or older.
- From 1976 to 1999, 7 in 10 American Indian juvenile murder victims were killed by another American Indian.

- The violent crime rate in every age group below age 35 was significantly higher for American Indians than for all persons.
- Rates of victimization for both males and females were higher for American Indians than for all races.
- The rate of violent victimization among American Indian women was more than double that among all women.
- Offenders who were strangers to the victims committed most of the robberies (71%) against American Indians.
- American Indians were more likely to be victims of assault and rape/sexual assault committed by a stranger or acquaintance rather than an intimate partner or family member.
- Overall about 62% of American Indian victims experienced violence by an offender using alcohol compared to 42% for the national average.
- American Indians faced an offender with a weapon in nearly a third of the violent crime incidents. (Perry 2004, iv–vi)

Statistically, for the young to be victims of violent crime is not unusual. Reviews of NCVS (National Crime Victimization Survey) data and other self-reported studies reveal that young people take more risks, frequent places which may place them in peril, as well as stay out later in the evening. Alcohol use and substance abuse have also played a historical role in risky and aberrant behavior.

The use of weapons has risen nationwide with the ready availability of purchase from reputable arms dealers and/or the ease of purchase from illegitimate sources. While the federal government has instituted background checks and waiting periods, most customers can legitimately acquire a firearm in less than a week. Purchases from gun shows and other sources require less than an hour. Weapons are used most frequently to commit robberies, and most of the robberies committed are intraracial in nature. Native Americans appear to be victimized by their own people, and this finding contradicts conventional thinking concerning attacks by perpetrators from outside the Native American community. In addition, Native American women appear to be the victims of violence at twice the rate of all women. These two factors are disturbing when considered alone, but in combination may provide an interesting topic for further exploration and discussion. In rapes/sexual assaults, however, nearly 80% of the offenders were identified as white or Caucasian. Empirically this would be a logical assumption, since most reservations are near areas currently populated by a majority of Caucasians.

TABLE 4-1   Median Age of Single-Race U.S. Residents By Race (Census 2000)

Race	Median Age
Total Population	35.3
American Indian	28.0
White	37.7
Black	30.2
Asian	32.7

Source: A BJS Statistical Profile, American Indians and Crime, 1999–2002, 3.

TABLE 4-2   States with the Largest American Indian Population
(Census 2000)

Area	American Indian	Percent of State Population
California	333,346	1.0
Oklahoma	273,230	7.9
Arizona	255,879	5.0
New Mexico	173,483	9.5
Texas	118,362	0.6
North Carolina	99,551	1.2
Alaska	98,043	15.6
Washington	93,301	1.6
New York	82,461	0.4
Michigan	58,479	0.6

Source: A BJS Statistical Profile, American Indians and Crime, 1999–2002, 3.

NATIVE AMERICANS AS OFFENDERS AND INMATES

One possible explanation for the rise in violence may be the frustration felt by young Indians who face a future they believe is filled with a lack of opportunity and hopelessness. Robert Merton theorized that normlessness or *anomie* was an explanation for delinquent behavior. Individuals who experience failure or find their legitimate path to success blocked seek to adapt their behavior in an effort to discover some measure of success. This success will be defined by measures created by each individual. One measure of success, according to Merton, is *innovation*, whereby the individual accepts the goals of society (wealth, power, status) but rejects the means. In other words, in order to achieve wealth and status, illegal means may be utilized. One manner by which to achieve status is to become a member of a gang. According to Major et al. (2004) the following characteristics can be used to define a youth gang in Indian country:

- Claims a turf or territory
- Commits crime together
- Has a leader or several leaders
- Has a name
- Displays or wears common colors or other insignia
- Hangs out together (p. 10)

These characteristics parallel gang membership outside the reservation, but the order of characteristics may differ by rank and importance depending upon the size of the gang and the location of the gang (urban, suburban, or rural).

To the downtrodden, gang membership brings many benefits. Chief among these is acceptance, being a part of something which the member believes enhances his/her personal identity. Since some Native Americans experience a negative self-image or a sense of ambiguity concerning their heritage, gang membership aids in filling this perceived void. Membership also provides protection for individuals in the group that may be very appealing for members of a minority. Particularly for individuals who believe they are surrounded by the majority (usually Caucasians or Latinos in border towns) and who believe they are denied opportunity due to their minority status. Parental apathy and erosion of the family structure also contribute to gang membership. In some cases, natives who return to the reservation from prison or metropolitan public housing areas bring a gang mentality to younger tribal members.

According to a 2004 report by the Office of Juvenile Justice and Delinquency Program (OJJDP), *Youth Gangs In Indian Country*, ". . . approximately one-half of responding communities indicated that almost all gang members (more than 90 percent) were of this race" (Major et al., 6). The demographics of the Native American gangs mirror those of most other gangs (race, gender, age, etc.).

Gang membership is neither easy nor automatic, since most have an initiation process and require adherence to a strict set of rules or a code. The initiation process may require being beaten by gang members—referred to by some groups as being "thumped in"—or by stealing some item for the group. In some extreme cases, even murder is used as an initiation rite in order to gain full unrestricted membership. These rites are meant to evaluate the bravery, determination, and fidelity of prospective members. However, most tribal communities surveyed by the OJJDP ". . . reported no gang related homicides during 2000, and few Indian country and comparison sample respondents indicated more than one gang-related homicide" (Major et al. 2004, 8).

Most violence in tribal communities appears to be the result of individual action rather than gang action. Gang action appears to be centered primarily on property crimes, such as graffiti, vandalism, group solidarity, and substance abuse. These crimes have historically been linked with boredom and a lack of constructive alternatives for young people, factors which plague the Native American population. In fact, most tribal communities report gang activity near the bottom of the list in terms of social problems plaguing their members. The most frequently cited social problems are centered upon alcohol abuse and domestic violence. Immaturity and substance abuse have created many situations which have necessitated police action. Law enforcement officers loathe dealing with underage intoxicated offenders since they are usually released to the custody of the parents instead of being incarcerated. In some cases, these offenders run away from their parents or guardians only to be arrested again later the same day.

One infamous crime committed by a Native American individual occurred on March 21, 2005, in Red Lake, Minnesota. Jeff Weise, a 16-year-old tenth grader, killed his grandfather, Red Lake Tribal Police Sergeant Daryl "Dash" Lussier, took his grandfather's bullet-resistant vest, service weapon, and police cruiser, drove to Red Lake High School, and killed seven of his classmates. This episode was marked as the second-worst school shooting in United States history at the time it took place (O'Driscoll and Kenworthy 2005).

NATIVE AMERICANS AS DEFENDANTS AND INMATES

In fiscal year 2000, "just under seventy-five percent of suspects investigated in Indian country involved a violent crime compared to the national total of five percent. . . . The number of charges filed against American Indians for violent crimes increased 27% from 1997 to 2000. While the [total] number of suspects declined [by] 21%" (Perry 2004, 18–19). These statistics tend to indicate that while a smaller number of individuals are being arrested, the crimes for which they are arrested are more serious in nature. The

TABLE 4-3   Criminal Cases Filed in U.S. District Courts (2000) (by type of offense)

	Percent of Offenses Charged	
	Indian Country	
Type of Offense	All Cases	Cases Only
Violent	4.7	73.3
Property	19.5	9.4
Drugs	39.3	2.1
Other	36.4	15.3
Total	100	100
Total Number	77,990	924

Source: U.S. Bureau of Justice Statistics, 2004.

majority of these suspects were from South Dakota, Arizona, and New Mexico. A quarter of these suspects were investigated for property, drug, or other offenses.

These investigations led to 751 American Indians being incarcerated in federal prisons. "American Indians were more likely to be serving a sentence for a violent offense than Federal prisoners of other races. In fiscal year 2001, 55% of American Indians entering Federal prison were serving a sentence for a violent crime compared to 4% of white offenders, 13% of black offenders, and 5% of Asian offenders" (Perry 2004, 22). While Indian reservations come under federal jurisdiction, not all criminal offenses are prosecuted in federal courts. Many are referred to the state courts or local tribal authorities. These confinement facilities are operated under the authority of the Bureau of Indian Affairs. State courts or tribal councils usually handle those matters deemed to be less serious and not meeting the criteria for federal prosecution. The distinction for determining jurisdiction is as follows:

- **Federal Jurisdiction.** Fourteen (14) crimes under the Major Crimes Act of 1885. 18 U.S.C. §1153
- **State Jurisdiction.** All crimes on tribal lands specified under Public Law 280. 18 U.S.C. §1162
- **Tribal Jurisdiction.** Crimes committed by Indians in Indian country. Sentences are limited to one (1) year and a $5,000 fine per offense or both. 25 U.S.C. §1302 (7)

In an effort to maintain tribal sovereignty and authority over members of the Indian community, many tribal councils seek to maintain jurisdiction and punish local offenders. In Indian jails, "At midyear 2002 more than a third of the offenders were held for violent offense, 15% specifically for domestic violence. Eleven percent of all offenders (226) were being held for DWI/DUI" (Minton 2003, 1). Confinement of inmates locally allows for visitation by relatives and restitution to the tribe through work details. More than 80% of inmates were held for misdemeanors. Crowding is an omnipresent problem with eight of the ten largest jails operating at more than 100% capacity. The five largest Indian jails are located in Arizona. The Tohono

O'odham Detention Center (the second largest facility in Arizona) was operating at three times its rated capacity, or 297%.

The November 2003 Bureau of Justice Statistics bulletin reported that "seven jails were under multiple court orders or consent decrees to limit the number of inmates they can house and for conditions of inmate confinement. Six facilities were ordered to detain inmates in a humane condition" (Minton, 4). Of the 70 Indian jails, some had been constructed as early as 1929 with new facilities being completed in 2001. The average age of these 70 institutions is 22 years. Physical structure is not the only problem facing these institutions. Staffing is a major issue as well. In the 2001 fiscal year, almost 450 new employees were added to the staff. In 2002, Indian country jails still reported 233 vacancies, and nearly two-thirds of the jails were still understaffed.

Sir Robert Peel noted that the best evidence that the police were doing their job was the absence of crime. Perhaps prevention is the key to reducing or eliminating criminal behavior since incarceration does not appear to be effective. A study conducted by the Bureau of Justice Statistics in 1994 reported that, "Within the first six months of their release, 26% of the 1712 American Indian offenders were arrested for a new crime—a felony or serious misdemeanor. By the end of 36 months from their release, an estimated 60% were arrested . . ." (cited in Perry 2004, 23).

CONCLUSION

A good deal of behavior is modeled after observed behavior. As previously mentioned, many Native American children are raised in single-family homes or homes hindered by domestic violence. Frequently the adults responsible for these children are formally uneducated or undereducated. As a result, their communication skills are not as developed as others, and they may not possess the problem-solving skills of their more educated neighbors. For these children to overcome these inadequacies, the school system must provide them with more than "the three Rs" (reading, writing, and arithmetic).

Programs must be developed and implemented that teach problem solving skills, communication skills, and anger management. While many schools begin this training in the sixth grade targeting twelve year olds, some proponents of these training programs recommend implementing some of the basic principles within the first year of school. The Law Related Education (LRE) program is designed for students K-12 and teaches them about the role of law in key social systems such as the family, the community, and the courts. Responding in Peaceful and Positive Ways (RIPPW) is directed toward sixth graders and teaches them the causes of violence and the consequences of violent acts. The Safe School Unit of San Diego County (California) Department of Education has developed a Violence Prevention/Intervention (VPI) team. This team was created in an effort to provide a safe school environment, aside from the use of metal detectors, security officers, and locker checks. VPI was meant to be a comprehensive approach to safety by involving teachers, aides, and administrators in the prevention and resolution of crisis situations. Schools should be a safe haven for learning not a daily battle for survival. Modeling these programs in the Indian schools and other schools attended by Native Americans could prove very beneficial in reducing the amount of violence on the reservation, as well as improving the negative self-image held by many Indian youth.

Interaction between Native Americans and criminal justice officials may be improved by observing a few simple guidelines:

- Understand the initial resistance to your efforts to establish rapport and goodwill and do not take it personal.
- Make an effort to get to know the community in your particular effort. Make positive contact with American Indian organizations and individuals.
- Convey a respect for Native American values.
- Have empathy for the conditions which may have led some Native Americans to make poor decisions.
- Do not interrupt Indians when they are speaking. That behavior is considered rude.
- Do not take advantage of Native Americans if they are silent or do not speak correctly.
- Respect elder members of the tribe.
- Ask elders for their advice whenever possible.
- Consider members of the tribal community who may be responsible for children other than the mother and/or father.
- Whenever possible, do not separate children from their parents.

Adherence to these few guidelines may improve communication and trust between a group that considers themselves disenfranchised and the government that has historically betrayed them.

REFERENCES

Final Report of the Executive Committee for Indian Country Law Enforcement Improvements to the Attorney General and the Secretary of the Interior. (1997). Washington, DC: United States Department of Justice.

Major, A. K., A. Egley, Jr., J. C. Howell, B. Mendenhall, and T. Armstrong. (2004). *Youth gangs in Indian country.* Washington, DC: Office of Juvenile Justice and Delinquency Prevention.

Minton, T. D. (2003). *Jails in Indian country, 2002* [NCJ 198997]. Washington, DC: Bureau of Justice Statistics.

O'Driscoll, P., and T. Kenworthy. (2005). Nazi web link eyed in killings: Echoes of Columbine emerge; gunman, 15, admired Hitler. *USA Today.* March 23.

Perry, S. W. (2004). *American Indians and crime* [NCJ 203097]. Washington, DC: Bureau of Justice Statistics.

Shusta, R. M., D. R. Levine, P. R. Harris, and H. Z. Wong. (2002). *Multicultural law enforcement: Strategies for peacekeeping in a diverse society.* 2nd ed. Upper Saddle River, NJ: Prentice Hall.

Shusta, R. M., D. R. Levine, P. R. Harris, and H. Z. Wong. (2005). *Multicultural law enforcement: Strategies for peacekeeping in a diverse society.* 3rd ed. Upper Saddle River, NJ: Prentice Hall.

Wood, D. S. (2000). Officer turnover in the Village Public Safety Officer Program. *Alaska Justice Forum, 17*(2), 1, 4.

5

Asian Americans in the Criminal Justice System

Skip Grubb and Gordon A. Crews

CHAPTER OUTLINE

INTRODUCTION

Asian American is a collective term that refers to a variety of ethnic minority groups. In this chapter the term "Asian" is being used to encompass the racial groups of Filipinos, Chinese, Japanese, and Koreans, as well as Indo-Chinese groups (Vietnamese, Laotians, Cambodians, and Thais). Due to the perceived economic success of Asians in America, they are often referred to as the "Super Minority" or "Model Minority." This stereotype has possibly contributed to the animosity between Asian Americans and other racial groups in the country. The term "model minority" was first used in print in the 1960s. At that time, the view held by many was that the Japanese cultural traits of strong family values and ethic kept the Japanese from becoming a "problem minority."

ASIAN AMERICAN CULTURE AND LIFESTYLE

Asian Americans, like most other minority groups, suffer from applications of stereotypes by the dominant culture. These stereotypes result in a variety of discriminatory practices to which Asian Americans are subjected. One of these is economic discrimination. For example, there are still licensing and credentialing barriers to some occupations as well as housing and finance discrimination. Asian Americans in business report a *bamboo ceiling* where they are not able achieve higher positions of management. They have been accused of being too aggressive, communicating poorly, and suffering from megalomania. They are pigeonholed into technology jobs and are considered to be lacking in non-technical abilities (Nisbett 1993). Because Asian Americans are more likely than other minorities to take on extra jobs and to place a high priority on saving their income for investment and/or retirement, they are sometimes viewed as ruthless and cutthroat. They frequently experience a backlash against their perceived economic success (Nisbett 1993).

The American educational system is another source of discrimination for Asian Americans. American teachers perceive Asian children to be well behaved, obedient, self-reliant, and respectful of education. While this is a positive stereotype, it is nonetheless one that omits a portion of the target population. Truants, dropouts, teen mothers, gang members, and underachievers are also present among Asian American youth. However, these problem juveniles may go undetected by an inattentive system that assumes all Asian American youths are successful conformers. The needs of these youths will then go unmet. Asian American students also suffer enormous pressures from the "model student stereotype" and their parents to do well in school. These pressures sometimes lead to mental disturbance, suicide, homicide, and the use of drugs (Kitano and Daniels 1995). Due to some aspects of their indigenous Asian culture, Asian American children can have a particularly strong fear of being ridiculed, especially by teachers or other authority figures. Problems are acute for Asian American teenagers who cannot achieve well in school. There are no proper counseling programs, and the shame may push the youngster into a life of crime.

Social discrimination is a fact for many minority groups, and Asian Americans are no exception. Many Americans do not understand or accept the some of the familial aspects of the Asian-American culture. For instance, most other racial and ethnic groups within the United States do not practice ancestor worship. For Asian Americans, familial roles are well-defined and based on ancient tradition. Mothers are to provide sons for fathers, and there are still attempts to arrange suitable marriages. The purpose of this system is to prevent unattractive women from becoming "old maids" and to keep elderly people out of nursing homes. There is also a rather unfortunate tendency for the wife to commit suicide rather than seek divorce in an unbearable marriage (Aquirre and Turner 1998). These non-mainstream familial characteristics can further marginalize the Asian American in society.

Social discrimination has resulted in almost no opportunities for interaction in private or professional organizations. There are few national organizations representing the interests of Asian Americans. Political parties tend to ignore Asian American candidates, and neither of the major political parties has agenda items helpful or relevant to Asian American concerns. In fact, candidates from both parties have exploited anti-Asian senti-ment at times to get votes (Kitano 1997). Asian Americans are acutely aware that they come from past enemy nations of the U.S. This is particularly true for immigrants from China, Japan, Korea, and Vietnam.

Asian Americans suffer from Hollywood-style stereotypes regarding how romantic, exotic, and sensual they are. This is a further source of discrimination. Movies and popular imagery have portrayed the Asian theatre as a heavy-drinking, sex-laden paradise. American soldiers and sailors tell stories about Asian prostitutes. Child prostitution rings have been uncovered in places like the Philippines. Rock music celebrates the "looseness" of places like Bangkok, and rap music celebrates the looseness of Asian females. The American fascination with Asian American interracial sex has been a titillating feature of American society since the West Coast brothels of the Gold Rush days (Shusta et al. 1995).

ASIAN AMERICANS AND THE PROFESSION OF CRIMINAL JUSTICE

Asians have made tremendous strides in obtaining college educations and pursuing grad-uate or professional studies in the United States. The number of Asian lawyers has increased in the last several decades, but Asian involvement in law enforcement has not been as successful. Even in metropolitan areas with a significant Asian population, these individuals are under-represented in local and state law enforcement agencies. Even corrections officers are overlooked by administrators. A review of the *Sourcebook of Criminal Justice Online* (2003) under the heading of "Characteristics of Federal Bureau of Prisons Correctional Officers" fails to identify Asian officers as a specific category but collectively lumps them into one category identified as *Other*. This category includes Asians, Native Americans, and non-Hispanic employees in Puerto Rico. Perhaps they have not been specifically targeted for recruitment, or perhaps they fail to see the value in the role of local policing. In any event, they are conspicuously absent from these govern-mental agencies. Just as curious is the lack of governmental tracking concerning their involvement in correctional institutions. Again, utilizing the *Sourcebook of Criminal Justice Online* (2003), Asian inmates are not specifically assigned a category but listed under *White non-Hispanic* or *Black non-Hispanic*. While Caucasian, African American, and Hispanic involvement is recorded, Asians are listed in a category making their partici-pation extremely difficult to determine.

An examination of recently published peer reviewed journals reflect the lack of attention to Asian victims, perpetrators, and criminal justice personnel. In the December 2003 issue of *Police Quarterly* in an article entitled "The Impact of Citizen Perceptions of

Community Policing on Fear of Crime: Findings from Twelve Cities," Scheider et al. (2003) ". . . examined the relationship between citizen perceptions of community policing and fear of crime . . ." (p. 363). In twelve major cities studied, Asians were once again overlooked as a major variable. In the June 2005 issue of *Police Quarterly*, Frank, Smith, and Novak's study, "Exploring The Basis of Citizen Attitudes Toward the Police," surveyed 613 citizens of a Midwestern city to determine their general and specific attitudes toward the police. Since the city was not identified, a significant Asian population may not have been present to include in the study. Yet again, the variable list included Caucasian, African American, income, and education level, but no mention of Asians. In "Citizen Satisfaction with Police Encounters," Skogan (2005) singled out groups by race and age including whites, blacks, and Latinos, but excluded Asians.

Societal changes have traditionally come from the point of service of those individuals most affected by the status quo. In this case, law enforcement officials are the first visible level of the criminal justice system. How can they assist Asians in becoming more comfortable with local government agencies and utilizing these agencies in such a manner as to improve their quality of life by prosecuting and imprisoning predators? A police department in Monterey Park, California, is already taking the first steps. With a population of 60,000 residents and a large percentage of Asians (61.5%), the Police Chief Jones Moy developed a collaborative program with the local library to introduce non-native speakers to local police officers and to have these non-native speakers ask the officers questions through an interpreter. The police and the interpreter create scenarios where the citizen would interact with police officers, such as traffic stops, how to report a crime, and how to respond should the police want to question him/her about a crime. Then together the officers and the citizens practice basic English skills and the native tongue or dialect of the resident population (Moy and Archibald 2005). Through this type of non-threatening interaction, local residents have an opportunity to dispel urban myths or rumors and relieve themselves of historical baggage from contact with the police in their native countries. While this program is an excellent first step, local officials need to become familiar with the local Asian communities. They need to determine who the community leaders are and establish a relationship of trust with these individuals. A concerted effort to recruit young people from these communities into criminal justice positions, such as law enforcement and corrections, should be made. The community also needs to develop a stake in the quality of communities outside their own, a vested interest in the quality of life city- and state-wide.

ASIAN AMERICAN VICTIMIZATION

In the previous discussion, there is a substantial lack of data on Asian Americans and the various roles they encounter in the criminal justice system. While some of this missing data can be attributed to the aforementioned methodological issues, other explanations can be considered for missing data on Asian American victims. Cultural status, immigrant status, generational status, and fear all contribute to a collective lack of crime reporting. For instance, older Asian Americans are faithful to their cultural traditions. They may be reluctant to trust governmental authority and prefer to handle "problems" within the context of the family or community. Justice for the Chinese, for example, was designed to protect the emperor and his lineage of privilege, not enhance the lives of the populace. Therefore, a regard for law and order in the formal governmental sense has not been embraced by Chinese Americans. They believe its application will not uniform but subject to the whim of the present ruler. An informal system of social control is relied upon instead. Inherent in this system is the Chinese collective mentality of equity and decency. Society should be filled with virtuous citizens who govern themselves. Individuals who fail to follow this group collective philosophy bring shame and disrepute upon themselves as well as upon their family members. For many individuals, this type of psychological pressure to conform is highly effective. However, individuals who view this type of conformity as stagnating, oppressive, or unnecessary seek an opportunity to rebel or break away from this type of individual responsibility.

Much like the Chinese, the Japanese value harmony and conformity. In some cases, these individuals embraced the same philosophical principles of Confucius and Tao. Individualism and individual rights are subordinate to the collective good. To bring attention to oneself is shameful since it detracts from the cohesion of the group. This sense of shame is borne by all members of one's family and imposes a terrible burden upon the family unit. Loyalty, fidelity, and respect are highly prized virtues and deeply ingrained in the fabric of Japanese society. Conflict is to be avoided whenever possible, as it may be viewed as a sign of disrespect or personal weakness. In the last sixty years, even with the influence of American culture as well as other Western nations, Japanese citizens have remained stoically loyal to traditional customs. The likelihood of first generation immigrants seeking assistance from outside sources such as law enforcement officers, social assistance agencies, or the courts is remote. The language barrier may also prove to be insurmountable since Japanese is one of the most difficult languages in the world to speak and write fluently. According to Tarver et al. (2002), 57.7% of Japanese households "do not speak English very well" and 33% are "linguistically isolated" (p. 97). The language barrier is a problem in Asian American communities, inhibiting crime reporting and cooperation with police. "Yes" sometimes means "no" or "yes, I hear what you're saying, but I may not agree with you" in conversations with Asian Americans (Kitano 1997).

TABLE 5-1   Language Barriers

	Speak Asian or Pacific Islander Language at Home	Do Not Speak English "Very Well"	Linguistically Isolated
Total Asian	65.2	56.0	34.9
Chinese	82.9	60.4	40.3
Filipino	66.0	35.6	13.0
Japanese	42.8	57.7	33.0
Asian Indian	14.5	31.0	17.2
Korean	80.8	63.5	41.4
Vietnamese	92.5	65.0	43.9

Source: (Tarver, Walker, and Wallace 2002, 97).

Asian families are much more likely to have more children than their non-Hispanic White counterparts. ". . . 18 percent of Asian and Pacific Islander families had five or more members, compared with 11 percent of non-Hispanic White families" (Reeves and Bennett 2003, 2). Additionally Asian and Pacific Islanders are much less likely to divorce than their non-Hispanic white neighbors. With these basic facts as a backdrop, one can understand why members of these minority groups are hesitant to report crime committed against them or against others in their communities to the appropriate government agency.

One of the few areas where there is data on Asian American crime victims is in domestic violence. Glicken and Sechrist (2003) discuss the difficulty in properly documenting family violence. They refer to methodological differences as well as ones concerning the definition of family violence. Should incidents of pushing and shoving be included, and do same-sex couples qualify as a family? How are Asian victims identified? Are they individually counted or lumped together under a category such as "Other?" At this point in time, no clearly delineated category for abused Asian women exists.

Glicken and Sechrist cite in their 1988 text that twelve million married women have been or were currently being assaulted by their husbands. As late as 1995, four women a day were killed by men who batter. Since most Asian families are patriarchal in nature, and Asian families experience a low divorce rate with a higher than average birth rate, Asian women are at significant risk to be in an abusive situation. As Asian families are likely to be isolated by a limited linguistic ability or fear associated with previous contacts with local law enforcement officers or cultural taboos forbidding relationships outside the nuclear family, an environment may exist which would benefit abusers or potential abusers.

Abusers have many characteristics in common, among these is a family history of battering. Often this pattern of behavior is passed from one generation to the next and becomes an accepted part of the marital union as the batterer models the behavior of the father and the grandfather. Not viewed as abuse, this pattern of behavior is noted as establishing dominance in the household and maintaining a sense of discipline. Substance abuse, while uncommon among the older generations, often leads to spouse abuse and child abuse. While remorse may follow the act of violence, the batterer relies upon the need to establish and maintain discipline as integral to the maintenance of the nuclear family. Isolated family members in a country with foreign customs, who have experienced the corruption or inefficiency of their own law enforcement officials, are very reluctant to contact local authorities, especially if a language barrier exists and the likelihood of being ostracized by their community is a distinct possibility. The loneliness associated with being a victim of abuse and being ostracized from family and friends is compounded when the people who should be your saviors espouse hatred and loathing toward one's own culture.

Michele Yoshida describes an incident which occurred in San Francisco in late July 1999. In this particular instance, Ms. Yoshida, a Special Assistant to a Commissioner of the U.S. Commission on Civil Rights, received a vitriolic telephone call from an individual who threatened her life and that of her boss. A week prior to this call, Chinatown had been inundated with fliers stating, "We are being ripped off by these sneaky little yellow [expletive deleted] and we can't do a damn thing about it . . . This has got to stop . . . Stop the yellow scum do something today for us White people" (Hall and Wang 2001, 30). Victor Hwang believes that ". . . Asian Pacific America lives not in the Chinatowns or Little Tokyos but in the hearts of those who recognize that incidents of anti-Asian violence are not random or isolated attacks, but rather a part and practice of the historical treatment of Asian Pacifics in America for the past two hundred years" (Hall and Wang 2001, 44). When public officials are confronted by this type of blatant racism and academics postulate that prejudice and discrimination have been a historical part of this county's landscape for two centuries, what possible hope is there for a blending of cultural identities?

ASIAN AMERICAN CRIMINAL BEHAVIOR

Asian crime is difficult to investigate, even harder to prosecute because of the aforementioned reluctance of the victims to approach the police. Because of long standing mistrust and suspicion directed against the police and the government—attitudes that took shape overseas in the face of brutal political oppression—it is difficult to gauge the extent of the crime problem (Lyman 1986). Gangs are often regarded as the worst crime problem in Asian American communities. Besides traditional concerns over organized groups like the *Tong* and *Triad*, there's concern about the emergence of violent, defiant youth gangs. Moore and Terret (1998) estimated that 5% of the estimated 846,000 gang members in the late 1990s were Asian. These gang members were primarily urban residents but moving to suburban and rural areas. Relocation may be the result of nuclear family expansion or gang members seeking new markets and increased profits.

Historically, the Triads were secret criminal societies that were organized in the seventeenth century to oppose the rule of the Ming Dynasty in China. They continued to flourish in Hong Kong, Malaysia, Singapore, Thailand, Burma, and Taiwan through the modern era. Hong Kong triads turned up in Great Britain and Australia long before the British relinquished control of their colony to China (Ebbe 1989). The first American-based "Tong"— the literal translation means "meeting hall"—is an extension of the merchant associations that were first organized in 1847 in San Francisco as a means of preserving cultural identity and providing a social outlet. Not every member of a Tong is criminally inclined. The crime-affiliated gangs of the Tong are well organized and entrenched in their respective communities.

Asian gangs with close links to sophisticated criminal organizations are involved in money laundering, illegal gambling, counterfeiting, the theft of computer software, and the smuggling of illegal aliens into the United States (Ebbe 1989). The traffickers who deal in human cargo are known as "snakeheads." For a $15,000 commission, the snakehead, who is based in China, will smuggle an illegal alien into the U.S. with the vague promise of employment and a stable life awaiting them at the end of a journey fraught with all kinds of hardship and peril (Ebbe 1989).

The Japanese also have a history of organized crime and gangs. Peter B.E. Hill (2003) a British Academy Postdoctoral Fellow in Sociology at the University of Oxford, states that "the groups commonly referred to as *yakuza* lay claim to a long lineage" (p. 36). Initially these groups were utilized by merchants as a form of protection from unscrupulous traders, both foreign and domestic. Having been reasonably successful in this endeavor, these groups expanded into the area of gambling and were tacitly supported by the Tokugawa shoguns. As governmental control weakened in the early 1800s, these "yakuza" supplied an illegitimate source of protection and security for local communities.

After gaining popularity and support from local community leaders, yakuza members began to exert influence among local politicians and people of influence. They served as strike breakers and personal protection for business leaders. As the century progressed, the business opportunities for the yakuza did as well as they began to supply "comfort women" to certain influential citizens as well as the Japanese military (Hill 2003). Still not satisfied with their profits, they began to exert an influence over the distribution and protection of opium dens for Chinese customers.

At the end of World War II, Japan's economy was devastated. In the absence of a viable free market enterprise, the yakuza developed and maintained a vibrant black market economy. The black market helped to maintain and stabilize supply, demand, and price structures. Hill (2003) notes that within "only two months after the surrender, it was estimated that there were 17,000 such markets throughout the country" (p. 43). One notorious documentation of Asian gang influence may have been in 1997 when President Bill Clinton accepted a $250,000 campaign contribution from Stanley Ho. Mr. Ho was a noted Macao gambling tycoon with established ties to a Chinese Triad. After the revelation of Mr. Ho's connections, a congressional investigation was initiated. Prior to being summoned to testify before a congressional committee, Mr. Ho fled the United States.

There is a growing affiliation between Asian organized crime and Asian American gangs. Asian organized crime often uses traditional gangs in supporting organized crime efforts. Asian gangs are used as "muscle" or to do "dirty work." They are used in trafficking drugs and in controlling a neighborhood or community (Purvis 2001).

The West Coast remains the stronghold of Asian organized crime activity. The importation of drugs from the "Golden Triangle" region of Thailand, Burma, and Laos is a prime source of revenue as the gangs take root in their respective communities. "Ice," the crystalline, smokeable form of methamphetamine, has turned up on the West Coast in recent years. Ice originated in Japan reportedly around 1919, but is now being produced in Hong Kong, South Korea, Japan, Thailand, and the Philippines for distribution in the U.S. Thus far, the drug is mostly confined to West Coast communities, but the situation is likely to change as the Asian street gangs and tong groups shift their base of operation to the hinterland. Tong gangs have fanned out across the U.S. and are particularly active in Maryland, Los Angeles, and New York City. Houston's Asian community was hit particularly hard in 1996 with numerous drive-by shootings and continuous gang warfare (Purvis 2001).

During the 1970s and 1980s, the Wah Ching, a Chinese street gang organized in 1966, came to control most of the criminal vices in the Chinatowns of Los Angeles, New York, and San Francisco. Their extortion and protection rackets are reminiscent of decades-old Mafia activity. The power of the Wah Ching on the West Coast was never seriously threatened until 1989 when a new criminal organization, the Wo Hop To triad of Hong Kong began moving into the San Francisco Bay Area. In recent years, there has been a consolidation of power between these two groups and the evolution of an Asian "super gang" (Purvis 2001).

Having realized the benefits of applying structure and organization to their criminal endeavors, some West Coast Vietnamese and Chinese "gangsters" are being recruited into the *Crips* and *Bloods* gangs. Their presence has been detected in the greater Midwest, notably in Minneapolis-St. Paul and central Wisconsin where Hmong youth have formed a dozen Crip gangs, and at least five Blood-affiliated gangs (Purvis 2001).

Asian American street gangs range in size from 5 to 200 gang members; and their crimes include residential and business robberies, auto thefts, and burglaries. Rarely are they involved in drive-by shootings. The gang members vary in age from 15- to 25-years-old, and the older gang members are usually the leaders. Early formation of Asian gangs was loose-knit, and the gang members did not associate with each other on a continuous basis. They had little, if any, loyalty to a particular gang. Unlike Hispanic and African American gangs, Asian American gangs began with no unique characteristics such as tattoos, hand signs, or graffiti. They had no names for their gangs, nor were they organized or turf oriented. There were no female Asian gangs and few female Asian gang members (Purvis 2001).

A few of the Asian gangs have now recruited female gang members who carry weapons for male gang members and assist male gang members in committing crimes such as home invasion robberies. Some of the female gang members have formed their own gangs and operate independently of their male counterparts. In Orange County, female gangs—such as the Wally Girls, Pomona Girls, and Dirty Punks—average 20 to 50 members between 13- to 20-years-old. Each female gang is allied with one or more male gang such as the Santa Ana Boys or Cheap Boys. Several of the female gang members have been arrested for auto burglary, shoplifting, and petty theft.

By 1985, Vietnamese gangs were committing organized auto thefts, extortions, firearms violations, home-invasion robberies, witness intimidations, assaults, and murders. They frequently used some type of weapon during the commission of their crimes. Vietnamese gang members began targeting their own communities with ruthless and vicious crimes and would often travel to various Vietnamese communities throughout the country to commit these crimes (Purvis 2001). Extortion of Asian business owners is a principal Vietnamese gang crime since many of the extortion victims fear to report the crime. Gang members engage in burglarizing, ransacking, or vandalizing businesses and then demand payment as insurance against further trouble; and others have extorted protection money from business owners by threatening to kill them and their families. Auto thefts by these gang members are on the increase, and it is not uncommon for a gang member to be arrested for auto theft and have in his possession an altered ignition key used to start the stolen vehicle. Often, the vehicles are stolen and used during the commission of a crime, then later abandoned (Purvis 2001).

The Laotian and Cambodian gangs remained predatory. They became turf oriented, and their crimes were random property crimes—usually involving some form of robbery or burglary. They are still principally representative of Vietnamese, Laotian, and Cambodian gangs; and their gang members vary in age from 13- to 35-years-old. They continue to terrorize and prey upon their communities with violent crimes, occasionally resulting in murders. They have increased their traveling patterns from coast to coast committing these crimes. Their growing level of mobility and violence has made them a national crime problem. Many of the Asian gangs have begun to emulate other ethnic gangs; and they are adopting certain gang characteristics such as gang names, hand signs, tattoos, and graffiti.

One of the most frightening aspects of Asian gangs is their brutal home-invasion robberies. In a typical home invasion, gang members enter a home, tie up the inhabitants, then terrorize, torture, beat, rob, and—at times—kill them. More than 300 such robberies were reported in California one year, and the attacks are becoming more widespread and violent. Many Asian gang-related crimes go unreported because of the victims' fear of revenge from the gang members. For each reported robbery, experts believe there may be as many as three to five robberies going unreported. Other crimes—which include robberies, burglaries, auto thefts, and extortions—are often marked with extreme violence. Many of them are conducted with precision, suggesting some form of structure, organization, and planning.

Violence by Asian gangs continues to increase. They have threatened to kill and have shot at police officers. Turf-related gang wars between some Asian gangs and other ethnic gangs are occurring. Their weapons of choice are handguns, rifles, and automatic or semi-automatic firearms, and they show little or no remorse for the victims of their violence (Purvis 2001).

CONCLUSION

In 2001, the National Council on Crime and Delinquency held a symposium on issues affecting Asian Americans. Several critical themes emerged at the symposium including: (a) the need to combat the "model minority" stereotype, (b) the need to develop culturally relevant intervention models, (c) the need for more documentation and research on Asian American communities and issues, and (d) the need to apply best practices to Asian American youth-at-risk. As the introduction to this chapter explained, the stereotype of Asians as a model minority may put the group in a position of benign neglect when it comes to government resources. These resources may apply to the issue of funding for pertinent research on the Asian American population, as well as support for effective programs for at-risk-youth. Law enforcement must strive to achieve a cultural model of interaction that enhances communication with the Asian American community. Cultural norms in both the dominant and minority societies must be recognized in order for the criminal justice system to effectively respond to Asian American victimization and the issues of gang related crime.

REFERENCES

AQUIRRE, A., AND J. TURNER. (1998). *American ethnicity: The dynamics and consequences of Discrimination.* Boston, MA: McGraw-Hill.

EBBE, O. (1989) Crime AND Delinquency in Metropolitan Lagos. *Social Forces, 67,* 751–65.

FRANK. J., B. W. SMITH, AND K. J. NOVAK. (2005). Exploring the basis of citizens' attitudes toward the police. *Police Quarterly, 8*(2), 206–28.

GLICKEN, M. D., AND D. K. SECHRIST. (2003). *The role of the helping professions: In treating the victims and perpetrators of violence.* Boston: Allyn & Bacon.

HALL, P. W., AND V. M. WANG, eds. (2001). *Anti-Asian violence in North America.* Walnut Creek, CA: AltaMira Press.

HILL, P. B. E. (2003). *The Japanese Mafia: Yakuza, law, and the state.* Oxford, UK: Oxford University Press.

KITANO, H. (1997). *Race relations.* Englewood Cliffs, NJ: Prentice Hall.

KITANO, H. AND R. DANIELS. (1995). *Asian Americans: Evolving minorities.* Englewood Cliffs, NJ: Prentice Hall.

LYMAN, S. (1986). *Chinatown and Little Tokyo: Power, conflict, and community among Chinese and Japanese immigrants in America.* Milwood, NY: Associated Faculty Press.

MOORE, J., AND C. TERRETT. (1998). *Highlights of the 1996 National Youth Gang Survey.* Washington, DC: OJJDP.

MOY, J., AND B. ARCHIBALD. (2005, June). Reaching English-as-a-Second-Language Communities: Talking with the police. *The Police Chief,* 54–57.

NISBETT, R. (1993). Violence and the U.S. regional culture. *American Psychologist, 48*(4), 441–49.

REEVES, T., AND C. BENNETT. (2003). *The Asian and Pacific Islander population in the United States: March 2002*. Washington, DC: U.S. Department of Commerce.

SCHEIDER, M. C., T. ROWELL, AND V. BEZDIKIAN. (2003). The impact of citizen perceptions of community policing on fear of crime: Findings from twelve cities. *Police Quarterly, 6*(4), 363–86.

SHUSTA, R. M., D. R. LEVINE, P. R. HARRIS, AND H. Z. WONG. (2002). *Multicultural law enforcement: Strategies for peacekeeping in a diverse society*. 2nd ed. Upper Saddle River, NJ: Prentice Hall.

SHUSTA, R. M., D. R. LEVINE, P. R. HARRIS, AND H. Z. WONG. (2005). *Multicultural law enforcement: Strategies for peacekeeping in a diverse society*. 3rd ed. Upper Saddle River, NJ: Prentice Hall.

SKOGAN, W. G. (2005). Citizen satisfaction with police encounters. *Police Quarterly, 8*(3), 298–321.

Sourcebook of Criminal Justice Statistics Online. (2003). Available at http://www.albany.edu/sourcebook/pdf/t627.pdf.

Sourcebook of Criminal Justice Statistics Online. (2004). Available at http://www.albany.edu/sourcebook/pdf/t1106.pdf.

TARVER, M., S. WALKER, AND H. WALLACE. (2002). *Multicultural issues in the criminal justice system*. Boston: Allyn & Bacon.

6

Arab Americans in the Criminal Justice System

Angela W. Crews

INTRODUCTION

Violent death and political, religious, and social upheaval in the Middle East grab newspaper headlines daily. Most of us cannot remember a time when there was not conflict in that region of the world. Historically, conflict "over there" was of little concern to the average American. However, since the mid-1990s, "over there" has crept closer to American soil, landing solidly "over here" with the first World Trade Center attack in 1993 and the horrific follow-up acts of terrorism on September 11, 2001, in New York, Washington, D.C., and in the peaceful Pennsylvania countryside.

Although terrorism and the Middle East are inexorably linked in the minds of many, this tendency unfortunately subjects Middle Eastern individuals to undeserved prejudice, stereotyping, and discrimination. We frequently teeter precariously on the fine line between threat recognition and discrimination based on religion and on racial, ethnic, and national origin. It usually is quite easy to determine that natives of this region living in the United States are of "other" national origin, race, and ethnicity simply from skin tone, speech, and manner of dress. When one also considers that these "others" often are perceived to be Islamic, the potential for bias is dramatically and unfortunately increased.

It is important to examine the role of Middle Eastern individuals, aside from their perceived link to terrorism, both as participants and as victims in the American criminal justice system. According to most historians, humankind and all of its social, political, and cultural progeny originated in this region of the world. Law, for example, was first codified by Hammurabi (c. 1750 B.C.), ruler of ancient Mesopotamia, who ordered that laws be written and publicized so that all citizens would be able to see them. This code was carved on a diorite column and consisted of 3,600 lines of cuneiform that addressed business and family relations, private party and personal injuries, and labor relations (*Columbia Encyclopedia* 2006). In general, his code was humanitarian, but featured literal retributive punishment (i.e. "an eye for an eye"), a philosophy and practice still followed in many Middle-Eastern countries today.

The term "Middle East" generally refers to a collection of two dozen or more countries spanning three continents (Europe, Asia, and Africa). Different sources consider different countries to be part of this area, but most sources have several members of their lists in common. The countries most frequently held to be part of the "Middle East" include Iran, Iraq, Syria, Turkey, Saudi Arabia, United Arab Emirates, Lebanon, Israel, Palestine, Jordan, Yemen, Oman, Kuwait, Bahrain, Qatar, Afghanistan, Pakistan, and the North African countries of Egypt, Libya, Sudan, Tunisia, Algeria, Morocco, Western Sahara, and Mauritania (see Figure 6-1). Sources disagree as to whether Pakistan and the westernmost North African countries (Morocco, Western Sahara, Mauritania) should be included, but the broadest classification will be used for this chapter. Additionally, the term Arab-American will be used to describe individuals with a Middle-Eastern heritage, as defined above, who currently live in the United States.

According to the 2000 U.S. Census, the American Arab community has grown approximately 40% since the 1990 census. The figures, however, undoubtedly underestimate the actual number of individuals of Middle-Eastern origin in the United States. The growth of this community is reflected in the American Arab representation in political

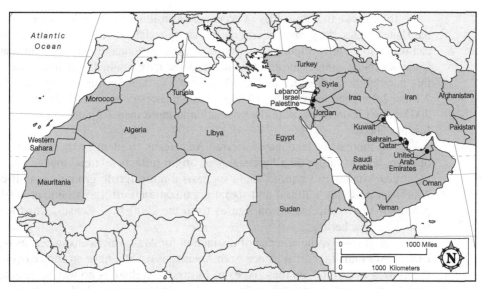

FIGURE 6-1   Map of the Middle East. Available online: http://www.mideastweb.org/ maps.htm

venues. In the 2006 United States political campaigns, for example, there are 41 Arab Americans running for elected office, ranging from mayor to United States Senate (Arab American Institute 2006).

We constantly attempt to count and measure societal demographics, but currently have few mechanisms in place to do so within our Middle-Eastern community. The phenomenon of "racial profiling" within some law enforcement communities led to one attempt, although separate categories for individuals of Middle Eastern descent were not differentiated. In 1999, President Clinton issued a *Memorandum on Fairness in Law Enforcement* that outlined the procedures for the law enforcement collection of data regarding race and ethnicity, providing five racial categories (American Indian/Alaskan Native, Asian, Black/African American, Native Hawaiian/Other Pacific Islander, and White) and one category for ethnicity (Hispanic or non-Hispanic). All federal programs collecting data were required to comply with this categorization no later than January 1, 2003.

In its response to the Executive Memorandum, the Department of Justice proposed that "additional ethnic groups should be recognized, as the agencies deem appropriate, so as to permit the monitoring of encounters involving other ethnic groups. Additional categories may include Arabic/Middle Eastern or Southeast Asian" (Department of Justice 1999, 3). Unfortunately, however, no standards for identifying ethnicity beyond Hispanic have been promulgated by the government (Department of Justice 1999, 3). Opponents of refining the classification system fear that the "monitoring of encounters" involving Arab Americans and Southeast Asians may actually exacerbate tendencies toward profiling.

To illustrate the difficulties of accurately measuring the Middle Eastern presence in the United States, the Census questionnaire has no racial/ethnic category for "Arabic" and can only capture this origin in the section of the questionnaire that determines ancestry. Under-sampling, non-response, and under-response have resulted in an inaccurate count of this population. Although the 2002 American Community Survey estimates between 2.1 and 2.3 million individuals of Middle-Eastern ancestry as defined above (U.S. Census 2002), other sources estimate the population at more than 3.5 million (Arab American Institute 2005).

The increasing tendency for Arab Americans to identify themselves as being of Arab descent rather than by country of origin reflects a "trend towards pan-ethnic identities, similar to Latinos," and "suggests a more fertile ground for unified Arab American political, cultural and social organizational efforts" (Samhan 2004, 1). A profile of this group, based on figures from the 2000 U.S. Census, illustrates their reported ethnic heritage.

Unfortunately, the absence of distinction for Arab Americans in census reporting carries over into other areas. Since Arab Americans usually have no choice but to report themselves as "white" on these types of forms, often there is no way to determine the prevalence of Arab Americans in the workplace, in the criminal justice system (either as offenders or as victims) or in other political and social service areas. Therefore, research into the role of Arab Americans in American society is extremely difficult and usually only is measured by organizations specializing in representing and protecting the rights of this population, such as the American-Arab Anti Discrimination Committee, the Arab Defense League, the Arab American Institute, the Muslim Public Affairs Council, the American Muslim Alliance, the Council on American Islamic Relations, the Islamic Society of North America, the Islamic Institute, the Islamic Supreme Council, the American Muslim Council, and the American Lebanese Heritage Club.

ARAB AMERICANS AS EMPLOYEES

Again, given the lack of specificity regarding Middle Eastern heritage, it is impossible to determine the representation of Arab Americans as employees in the criminal justice system. According to information from the U.S. Census (2000), about 64% of American Arab adults are in the work force with an unemployment rate of about 5%. Nearly three-quarters of the working Arab Americans are employed in managerial, professional, technical, sales or administrative fields. Fewer American Arab workers are employed in service occupations as compared to Americans overall (12% versus 27%, respectively), and approximately 12% are government employees.

LIFESTYLE OF ARAB AMERICANS

Despite an American culture and political environment that often questions American Arab loyalty, more than 80% of Arabs living in the United States are citizens and have a higher naturalization rate (54%) than others in the foreign born population (40%). Furthermore,

60%–75% of individuals indicating an Arab ancestry in U.S. Census polls are native-born Americans (Arab American Institute Foundation 2005).

Arabic immigrants "work in all sectors of society and are leaders in many professions and organizations," and have a strong commitment to family, economic, and educational achievement, and making contributions to all aspects of American life" (Arab American Institute Foundation 2005, 1).

Arab Americans tend to be more affluent and more highly educated than other Americans (Armas 2005). The median income of $47,000 in 1999 was slightly higher than for other households in the United States ($42,000), and nearly one-third of Arabic households reported annual incomes of more than $75,000. While only 24% of non-Arab Americans hold a bachelor's degree or higher, more than 40% of Arab Americans have reached that level of educational attainment. Moreover, Arab Americans hold post-graduate degrees at nearly twice the rate of other Americans (17% versus 9% respectively) (Arab American Institute Foundation 2005).

As with most groups who have immigrated to the United States, individuals of Middle Eastern origin tend to settle in specific areas of the country. Lebanese individuals comprise the largest group of Middle Easterners in most states, except New Jersey, where persons of Egyptian heritage dominate, and Rhode Island, where individuals of Syrian ancestry are most prevalent. Illinois is home to the largest number of people with Palestinian heritage. Illinois, along with the states of Michigan and California, is home to a significant number of persons with Iraqi and Assyrian/Chaldean background. Persons from Morocco, approximately 3% of the Arabic-speaking population, comprise a new immigrant community settling primarily along the coast between Massachusetts and Virginia (Samhan 2004).

RELIGION

The religion most closely associated with the Middle East is Islam, the fastest growing religion in the United States (Kozaryn 1999). Islam, along with Christianity and Judaism, is a monotheistic religion, with followers of each religion believing in one divine creator, or "god." While Christians and Jews call this creator "God," followers of Islam, or Muslims, call this creator "Allah." Although Islam is a religion in the strictest terms, followers view it much more broadly. It is a way of life, practiced in such a way as to "bring God into the center of one's consciousness, and thus one's life" (Council on Islamic Education 1995, 1).

The majority of Arab Americans are Christians, however, with only 24% identifying themselves as Muslim (Arab American Demographics 2000, 2). Contrary to common belief, anyone can become a Muslim, regardless of gender, race, nationality, color, or social or economic status. All that is required is recitation of the Shahadah (the declaration of faith containing the basic creed of Islam), witnessing that "there is no deity but Allah, and Muhammad is His Messenger" (Council on Islamic Education 1995, 1). In fact, despite the common conception that Islam is exclusively a Middle Eastern religion, Arabs comprise only about 15%–18% of all Muslims. Indonesia, a Southeast Asian country, has the largest number of Muslims (over 160 million), and

South Asian peoples (from India, Pakistan, Bangladesh, and Sri Lanka) constitute 1 in 4 Muslims. African Muslims constitute another 20% of the total (Council on Islamic Education 1995, 3).

Although approximately 3.5 million people claim Arabic descent (U.S. Census 2000), there are approximately 6 million Muslims living in the United States. Of these, over half are Americans who have joined the religion rather than having been born into it, and only slightly more than 12% of the American Muslims is of Arabic origin; the majority is of African American (42%) and South Asian (24%) origins (Council on Islamic Education 1995).

ARAB AMERICANS AS OFFENDERS, VICTIMS, AND INMATES

It is unfortunate to follow a section on religion with a section on acts of violence, but given the origin and history of terrorism, it is appropriate. First, however, you are asked to consider an exercise in logic:

Some Arabs are Muslim.
Some Muslims are terrorists.
Therefore, some Arabs are terrorists.

This syllogism is true. Some Arabs are terrorists. One also can infer from this statement that some terrorists are Arabs and some are Muslims. However, human beings have developed the tendency to substitute the word "some" in the above series with the word "all." We over generalize and stereotype, which leads to prejudiced attitudes and discriminatory behavior. We tend to judge a particular race, ethnicity, culture, national origin, or religion by the actions of a few of its members. We do this because we cannot observe everything ourselves and because we have a need to neatly, quickly, and efficiently categorize everything, including people, into groups wherein all the individual members share certain traits and characteristics.

Sadly, we often are incorrect in our assumptions and our classifications because we create syllogistic fallacies or invalid arguments. For example, Gordon, a young police officer, repeatedly is called to homes on his beat where women have been the victims of domestic violence perpetrated by young Hispanic males. Gordon could eventually conclude that "All Hispanic males commit domestic abuse," that "All domestic abuse is perpetuated by Hispanic males," or that "All women in relationships with Hispanic men are in danger of domestic abuse." Inevitably, Hispanic ethnicity will become linked to domestic violence in Gordon's mind. He fails to consider that his beat is over 90% Hispanic, that rates of domestic abuse in other (non-Hispanic) neighborhoods may be even higher than in the Hispanic neighborhoods, or that women in relationships with Hispanic men may be more likely to report incidents of domestic violence. As a result, Gordon is in danger of developing selective observation, noting only behaviors that affirm his beliefs and ignoring those that do not.

It is likely that society has developed this type of perception and reasoning with Arab Americans and with individuals that follow Islam. Religious beliefs impact the daily lives of many Arab Americans, as they do the lives of many other Americans. Unfortunately, extreme religious beliefs contribute to terrorism, along with other extreme political, social, or cultural beliefs.

A history of terrorism and a complete description of the consequences of the events of September 11, 2001, are beyond the scope of this chapter. However, a short definition of terrorism and a brief description of its effects is required to completely understand the social, economic, and political positions in which the United States currently finds itself and to describe the impact on the Arab American community in the United States.

The Federal Bureau of Investigation (FBI) defines "terrorism" as "the unlawful use of force and violence against persons or property to intimidate or coerce a government, the civilian population, or any segment thereof, in furtherance of political or social objectives" (28 C.F.R. Section 0.85) (FBI 1999). These acts can be domestic or international. Domestic terrorism involves acts "committed against persons or property to intimidate or coerce a government, the civilian population, or any segment thereof, in furtherance of political or social objectives" conducted "by a group or individual based and operating entirely within the United States or its territories without foreign direction" (FBI 1999, 3). International terrorism involves acts that "occur outside the United States or transcend national boundaries in terms of the means by which they are accomplished, the persons they appear intended to coerce or intimidate, or the locale in which the perpetrators operate or seek asylum," and either violate "the criminal laws of the United States or any state," or would violate those laws "if committed within the jurisdiction of the United States or any state" (FBI 1999, 3).

We have daily "terror alerts" that remind us to be vigilant for potential acts of terror. In the minds of most Americans, this translates to awareness of acts such as airplane hijackings and suicide bombings committed by "extremists" like those involved with 9/11. In reality, however, prior to 9/11/2001, there had been "no successful acts of international terrorism perpetrated in the United States" for six years (FBI 1999, 1).

The "growing internationalism" of crimes against the United States, such as the bombings of the World Trade Center in 1993, of Khobar Towers in Saudi Arabia in 1996, of two U.S. embassies in East Africa in 1998, and of the USS Cole in the Yemeni port of Aden in 2000, led the FBI to expand its international presence, establishing legal attaché offices in 44 countries by 2001 and changing the name of the annual terrorism report from "Terror in the United States" to "Terrorism" (FBI 2001). The limited scope of publications prior to 2000 did not adequately convey the "breadth and width of the terrorist threat" facing the U.S.

Surprisingly, prior to 9/11, the United States primarily was under attack by domestic terrorist groups. The FBI reported 1999 to be characterized by a "sharp increase in domestic terrorism . . . carried out by animal rights and environmental extremists" (FBI 1999, 1). In fact, "these special interest or single issue terrorists committed eight of the ten terrorist incidents recorded in the United States" during the year, and that the remaining two incidents were committed by "rogue right-wing extremists" (FBI 1999, 1). The Animal Liberation Front (ALF) was credited with six incidents and the Earth Liberation Front (ELF) with two. Their acts resulted in losses and damages estimated to be more than four million dollars and in the deaths of lab animals. No human injuries or casualties were reported (FBI 1999).

Middle Eastern participation in acts of terrorism perpetrated against the United States can be tied to a handful of groups and individuals. The 26 individuals on the FBI's "Most Wanted Terrorists" list in 2006 are from Saudi Arabia (5), Egypt (5), Lebanon (4), the Philippines (3), Kenya (3), Palestine (2), Yemen (2), Libya (1), and the United States (1).

The lone American citizen was born in the United States of Iraqi parents who moved back to Iraq shortly after his birth. The three Philippine terrorists are tied to a Muslim extremist group, Abu Sayyaf Group (ASG), whose members fought in Afghanistan with future Al Qaeda members. The remaining terrorists are tied to Saudi and Lebanese Hizballah groups, and to Palestinian and Egyptian Islamic Jihad groups (PIJ, EIJ), although the EIJ group, also known as Al Jihad, merged with Al Qaeda in 2001. In general, these groups are Islamic extremists, dedicated to the promotion of Islam, to the overthrow of non-Islamic governments, and to the liberation of Jerusalem and elimination of Israel (Country Reports on Terrorism 2006b).

During 2005, 56 citizens of the United States lost their lives as a result of terrorist incidents around the world, and 47 of those deaths were in Iraq. Iraq also was the place where Americans were most at risk of kidnapping. Ten of the eleven U.S. Citizens kidnapped around the world were kidnapped in Iraq. However, American citizens were most likely to be injured in terrorist incidents in Indonesia and in the United Kingdom (Country Reports on Terrorism 2006a).

Current focus is on Al Qaeda ("Base" or "Foundation"), created in 1988 by Osama bin Laden after fighting alongside American forces to repel the Soviet invasion of Afghanistan. Bin Laden's philosophies evolved from his tutelage under various followers of Islamist movements, specifically those of the Muslim Brotherhood. This Brotherhood also is the source of the Palestinian Islamist group, Hamas (Katzman 2005; Country Reports on Terrorism 2006b).

As an Islamic fundamentalist group, Al Qaeda believes that the correct interpretation of Islam evolves solely from the Qur'an, which Muslims view as the word of God, revealed to Muhammad through the Archangel Gabriel. These individuals believe that secular influences have caused the problems of the world, and that peace and justice can only be attained by returning to the original message of Islam, emphasizing traditionalism and rejecting innovation.

Al Qaeda is an extremely well-organized and well-developed organization, with an extensive infrastructure of businesses and non-governmental organizations that provide documentation, financing, and legitimate cover for its operations. These operations include resource acquisition, tactical planning, logistics, surveillance, procurement, and strategies for the precise execution of an operation (Katzman 2005).

When Iraq invaded Kuwait in 1990, bin Laden argued against U.S. involvement and advocated "the raising of a 'mujahedin' army" to repel the Iraqis (Katzman 2005, 3). Subsequently, he moved to Sudan, and then to Afghanistan in 1996 after the Sudanese government, under pressure from the U.S. and Egypt, expelled him. There, he joined with the Taliban and assisted them in gaining and maintaining control of the Afghan government (Katzman 2005). The Taliban is a Sunni Islamist Nationalist movement. The Sunnis are the largest denomination of Muslims, following a strict Islamic tradition.

The growing presence and influence of the United States within the Middle East, specifically within Saudi Arabia, was probably the catalyst for Al Qaeda's wrath against the United States. Saudi Arabia is home to the most holy sites in Islam, the sacred cities of Mecca and Medina. The development of permanent U.S. military installations there represented a lack of Saudi control over the territory. Further, Miniter (2003) reported that bin Laden despised Americans as "infidels" who supported "corrupt" and "insufficiently Islamic Saudi elite."

By September 11, 2001, Al Qaeda had developed into a "coalition of factions of radical Islamic groups operating throughout the Muslim world," with locations in more than 70 countries (Katzman 2005, 3). The following groups represent only a sampling in the Al Qaeda coalition: the Islamic Group and Al Jihad (Egypt), the Armed Islamic Group and the Salafist Group for Call and Combat (Algeria), the Islamic Movement of Uzbekistan (IMU), the Jemaah Islamiyah (Indonesia), the Libyan Islamic Fighting Group (Libyan opposition), and Harakat ul-Mujahedin (Pakistan, Kashmiri) (Katzman 2005).

After the attacks of September 11, 2001, the U.S. strongly suspected that the Taliban had supported bin Laden and, as a result, the U.S. government began military operations to force the Afghans to turn over bin Laden. Although this was not fruitful, intense financial and political pressure, along with military force, deposed the Taliban leadership in December 2001, although insurgent resistance still operates to this day (Katzman 2005). Osama bin Laden is thought to be eluding authorities in Pakistan, with the suspected assistance of the Pakistani government. Despite reports of his death from either kidney failure (Ledeen 2006), or an earthquake that struck Kashmir in 2005 (White 2005), authorities determined on May 24, 2006, that the voice on a recent videotape was that of bin Laden (CNN 2006).

VICTIMIZATION OF ARAB AMERICANS

Even before the atrocities of the middle 1990s and early 2000s, Arab Americans were feeling the heat of discrimination. During and after American military operations in the Middle East related to the Iraqi invasion of Kuwait in 1990, Rutledge (1991) reported that Arab Americans in the United States were targeted by the FBI for questioning only because of their perceived or actual national origins. He describes airline policies at this time that refused to allow Iraqi nationals to fly, despite American citizenship, and Immigration and Naturalization Service (INS) policies that required the keeping of a "close record" of anyone entering the United States with Iraqi or Kuwaiti passports (1991). Australian scholars also have noted troubling patterns of anti-Arabic behaviors and perceptions among Australians and New Zealanders (Sydney Institute of Criminology 2004; Weber et al. 2002; Poynting et al. 2001).

Not surprisingly, these discriminatory tendencies only have worsened since 2001, with the targets becoming younger and younger. A study of peer relations among 748 fifth grade students during the year following 9/11 found that Middle Eastern children experienced significant drops in positive peer relations and popularity. These drops were accompanied by significant increases in the reported bullying of Hispanic and Middle Eastern students (DeRosier 2004).

Other crimes targeted toward Arab Americans have increased since 2001. The Federal Bureau of Investigation's annual collection of hate crime statistics suffers from the same shortcoming as other attempts to measure many things within Middle Eastern communities. Any ethnicity/national origin-based hate or bias-motivated offense directed at persons of Arabic origin are potentially captured in the "Ethnicity/National Origin" category of "Anti-Other Ethnicity/National Origin" and in the category of "Religion" which measures "Anti-Islamic" crime.

This type of inference, however, suffers from serious shortcomings. Ethnicities and origins other than Arabic are captured in the "Anti-Other Ethnicity/National Origin" designation and all the "Anti-Islamic" crime is not likely to have been directed at Arab Americans given that most Muslims in the United States are not of Arabic origin and that most Arab Americans are Christian, rather than Muslim. However, much of hate crime is generated by perception, and perpetrators of hate crime may perceive any Arabic or Arabic-looking person to be a follower of Islam.

In 2000, Anti-Islamic (AI) crime and Anti-Other Ethnicity/National Origin (AOENO) crime comprised less than 5% of all bias motivated crime incidents, offenses and victims. In 2001, approximately 20% of all bias motivated crime incidents, offenses, and victims were AI and AOENO. Since 2001, these figures have declined, but still remain at nearly twice the rate (about 9%) measured in 2000 (FBI, 2000, 2001, 2002, 2003, 2004).

In addition to "street" crimes perpetrated against Arab Americans, these individuals also face increased likelihood of discrimination in the workplace. The Equal Employment Opportunity Commission (EEOC) routinely monitors charges received under Title VII of the 1964 Civil Rights Act alleging discrimination based on race, religion, and national origin. On December 11, 2001, Ziad Asali, President of the American-Arab Anti-Discrimination Committee, described 115 incidents of employment discrimination documented by the EEOC that had occurred since September 11, 2001. These cases included incidents of "job termination, complaint abuse, discriminatory policy, hostile work environment and ethnic slurs, national origin discrimination, and termination after questioning by the FBI," originated in several different geographical locations, and involved public and private employers (Retrieved from: http://www.eeoc.gov/abouteeoc/meetings/12-11-01-adc.html).

Prior to September 11, 2001, EEOC already was tracking the number of charges filed nationwide alleging discrimination on the basis of several specific religions, including the Muslim faith. Between September 11, 2001, and May 7, 2002, the Commission received 497 charges on the basis of Muslim religion. During the same comparable time frame in the previous year, only 193 charges were processed (EEOC 2002b).

To further monitor charges filed by individuals who believed they had experienced "backlash" discrimination as a result of 9/11, the Commission implemented code "Process Type Z" retroactive to September 11, 2001 (EEOC 2002a). This code, derived from Title VII of the Civil Rights Act of 1964, as amended, 42 U.S.C. § 2000e, was created to track charges filed by persons who were, or were perceived to be Muslim, Arab, Middle Eastern, or South Asian, or filed by persons alleging retaliation relating to the events of September 11.

Between September 11, 2001, and September 10, 2002, 654 such charges were filed alleging a combination of national origin, race, and religious discrimination. Discharge and harassment were the most frequently cited issues (EEOC 2002a). Through March 11, 2003, 765 charges were filed. More than 450 charges of alleged discriminatory discharge and more than 300 charges of alleged harassment were filed as the adverse actions taken by employers. As of March 11, 2003, 80 individuals aggrieved by September 11-related employment discrimination received close to $1.2 million in monetary benefits through EEOC efforts (EEOC 2003).

While the number of filed charges actually has declined since 1999, the proportion of charges alleging discrimination based on national origin and on religion has increased in both number and in proportion of total charges. In 1999, charges filed because of alleged national origin discrimination were about 9% of all charges filed, with charges based on alleged religious discrimination about 2%. The proportions have been steadily increasing ever since. In 2005, filed charges based on national origin discrimination were nearly 11% of all filed charges, with religious-based charges representing over 3% of all charges (see Table 6-1).

Although the number of total charges has been decreasing since peaking in 2002, reaching its lowest point since before 1999, the proportion of filed charges alleging discrimination based on national origin and religion remains unchanged. In fact, the figures in Table 6.1 represent a *3% decrease* in the number of charges filed between 1999 and 2005, but a *13% increase* in the charges filed due to national origin discrimination and a *30% increase* in those filed due to religion discrimination. This indicates that EEOC efforts to educate corporations and business owners may not be having that strong of an impact on the corporate culture or on corporate behavior as it pertains to perceptions and bias directed toward individuals due to their national origin or religion. On the contrary, things seem to be getting worse.

TABLE 6-1 Annual distribution of charges filed with the EEOC alleging discrimination based on National Origin or Religion: 1999–2005*

Year	Total	National Origin (% of Total)	Religion (% of Total)
1999	77,444	7108 (9.2)	1811 (2.3)
2000	79,896	7792 (9.8)	1939 (2.4)
2001	80,840	8025 (9.9)	2127 (2.6)
2002	84,442	9046 (10.7)	2572 (3.0)
2003	81,293	8450 (10.4)	2532 (3.1)
2004	79,432	8361 (10.5)	2466 (3.1)
2005	75,428	8035 (10.7)	2340 (3.1)

*Based on EEOC (2005b). Charge statistics FY 1992 through FY 2005. Available online: http://www.eeoc.gov/stats/charges.html

ARAB AMERICANS AS INMATES

Inadequate classification once again prohibits a detailed examination of Arab Americans as inmates within the American criminal justice system. There simply is no readily available breakdown of American prisoners by national origin. Information about religious practices, however, is more readily available. Caution should be used in extrapolating information about incarcerated individuals of Middle Eastern origin from information about incarcerated Muslims. Unfortunately, this risky inference may be the closest proxy.

The Islamic religion is popular in American prisons, and the courts have made significant accommodations for Muslims within U.S. correctional facilities. In general, facilities must make accommodations for individuals to practice their faith and to follow religious (e.g. prayer, religious services) and cultural requirements (e.g. hair styles, clothing, diet), as long as doing so does not present a security threat, compromise hygiene, or incur prohibitive costs (Hudson 2006).

It is possible that tens of thousands of state and local inmates around the United States are practicing Muslims; nearly one quarter of the jail inmates at New York's Rikers Island are of the Islamic faith (Associated Press 2005). California alone is home to an estimated 10,000 to 11,000 Muslim inmates who won the right to wear their six-inch beards and to practice Jumu'ah, a weekly religious ritual that previously had been denied the inmates (Egelko 2002). According to the Bureau of Prison's Chaplaincy Services Branch, approximately 9,000 inmates in the federal prison system, or about 6% of the total federal inmate population, seek Islamic religious services. This population is served by fewer than a dozen Muslim chaplains (Office of the Inspector General 2004).

ARAB AMERICANS AS DETAINEES

In addition to incarceration within American prisons, Arab Americans may be kept within "detention centers," developed after 9/11 to house potential, suspected, or actual terrorists for questioning. In the year following the attacks of 9/11/2001, the FBI used immigration laws to round up and detain 762 aliens for questioning (Office of the Inspector General 2003). Other sources, however, indicate that at least 1,200 immigrants were detained and questioned (Zogby 2003).

Extensive debate has swirled around the legal status of detainees. Some argue that their status depends in part on whether the military actions of all involved parties can be called "war." Participants in wars generally are protected under the 1949 Geneva Conventions and the 1977 Protocols that require humane treatment and respect for prisoners of war (POWs) (Guide to the Geneva Conventions 2003). Participants in wars generally also are known as combatants, rather than as civilians. Strangely, however, the United States has given these individuals the status of "illegal combatants," a term not found in any of the Conventions or Protocols. The use of this term was to deny that the detainees had the protections given POW captives (Moran 2002).

The Office of the Inspector General (OIG) examined the treatment of these individuals, including how they were processed, their bond decisions, their removal from the United States or custody release, the conditions of their confinement, and their ability to access counsel. The OIG issued a 198-page report that focused on individuals held at the Passaic County Jail in Paterson, New Jersey, a county facility contracted by the INS to house federal immigration detainees, and those held at the Federal Bureau of Prisons' Metropolitan Detention Center (MDC) in Brooklyn, New York. Immediately after 9/11/2001, these two facilities held the majority of detainees and were the source of numerous complaints of detainee mistreatment.

After the investigation, Inspector General Fine concluded that, "while our review recognized the enormous challenges and difficult circumstances confronting the Department in responding to the terrorist attacks, we found significant problems in the way the detainees were handled" (Office of the Inspector General 2003, 1–2). As a result, the OIG issued 21 recommendations indicating problems related to "arrest and detainee classification policies," "procedures for confining aliens arrested on immigration charges who are suspected of having ties to terrorism," and the "oversight of detainees housed in contract facilities" (Office of the Inspector General 2003, 4). Moreover, Inspector General Fine concluded that "while the chaotic situation and the uncertainties surrounding the detainees' connections to terrorism explain some of the problems we found in our review, they do not explain them all" (Office of the Inspector General 2003, 4).

In addition to domestic facilities, the American government also used existing international military facilities in various countries to house detainees. When the Iraqi government fell in 2003, American military forces assumed control of the Abu Ghraib prison, renamed it the Baghdad Central Confinement Facility, and used it as a detention center that they named "Camp Redemption." Allegations of detainee abuse surfaced in 2003 and were confirmed in 2004 when Sergeant Joseph Darby provided photographic evidence of detainee torture by U.S. military personnel (Hersh 2004). Since that time, the facility has been attacked several times by local insurgents, resulting in numerous military and detainee deaths and injuries. Several U.S. military personnel were tried and convicted for their roles in the torture. A recent announcement by the U.S. government will result in the permanent abandonment of Abu Ghraib by the U.S. and the transfer of inmates to Camp Cropper, a lockup near the Baghdad airport (*Sydney Morning Herald* 2006).

Detainees and others also were housed at Guantanamo Bay, a U.S. Navy facility leased from the Cuban government. Although the facility is in Cuba, U.S. District Court Judge Ricardo Urbina recently ruled that the *1993 Religious Freedom Restoration Act* applies to American installations at Guantanamo because the U.S. exercises control over the area. His ruling meant that four British citizens held at the site for nearly three years, who were forced to shave their beards and harassed as they worshipped, had the right to file suit against the U.S. government for violations of their religious freedoms. Shfiq Rasul, Asif Iqbal, Rhuhel Ahmed, and Jamal Al-Harith are seeking $10 million in damages from U.S. Defense Secretary Donald Rumsfeld and ten U.S. military commanders (Times Online 2006).

"Camp X-Ray" at Guantanamo Bay, Cuba, held 759 detainees since the detention center began taking prisoners related to terrorism in January 2002. About 275 detainees have been released or transferred, and the United States has filed charges against only 10 detainees. The camp has since been shut down after concerns surfaced related to prisoner abuses. Despite repeated calls from foreign governments and others concerned about detainee treatment, the United States is refusing to cease operations at the Guantanamo location "as long as the detainees held there represented a threat to the U.S. and its allies" (Times Online 2006, 2).

FUTURE DETENTIONS OF ARAB AMERICANS

In January 2006, KBR, a subsidiary of Halliburton Industries, was awarded an Indefinite Delivery/Indefinite Quantity (IDIQ) contingency contract for $385 million by the U.S. Department of Homeland Security to construct Immigration and Customs Enforcement (ICE) facilities in the event of "an emergency influx of immigrants, or to support the rapid development of new programs" in the event of other emergencies like natural disasters.

ICE, created in 2003, is the Department of Homeland Security's largest investigative branch. As indicated in Halliburton's press release, this contract also may provide immigrant detention support to other U.S. Government organizations in the event of an *immigration emergency* (emphasis added) (Halliburton Press Release, January 24, 2006).

The potential for immigrant detention centers brings to mind the Japanese interment camps during WWII and Oliver North's Rex-84 "readiness exercise" in 1984 that called for the Federal Emergency Management Agency (FEMA) to collect and detain 400,000 imaginary "refugees" to control population movements over the Mexican border into the United States. Daniel Ellsberg, the former military analyst who in 1971 released the Pentagon Papers detailing American activities in Vietnam, says that the proposed detention centers are "almost certainly" in "preparation for a roundup after the next 9/11 for Mid-Easterners, Muslims and possibly dissenters" (Scott 2006, 1). Ellsberg also reminds us that the government already has done this "on a smaller scale, with the 'special registration' detentions of immigrant men from Muslim countries, and with Guantanamo" (Scott 2006, 1).

As of year end 2004, there were more than 19,000 detainees being held under ICE jurisdiction, the majority within local jails through intergovernmental agreements (Sourcebook of Criminal Justice Statistics 2004). At mid year 2003, American state and federal prisons held more than 90,000 "non-citizen" prisoners. The definition of "non-citizen" is unclear, with several states reporting "foreign born" inmates as "non-citizens" (Harrison and Karberg 2004).

Muller (2003) argues that this type of profiling, while possibly warranted, is uncontrollable in the hands of law enforcement. He states that the most egregious error made in the past was not that our government used profiling (i.e., inferring suspicion from national origin) as the rationale for large scale internment, but rather the "enormity of its deprivations" (p. 130). He urges us to understand the "twin realities that profiling might sometimes be rational and that profiling will very likely get out of hand" (pp. 130–31).

CONCLUSION

Perhaps is it a good thing that our system currently does not have the ability to describe the involvement of individuals with the American criminal justice system based on national origin. Unfortunately, this limits our ability to analyze participation of those with Middle Eastern origins as employees, as offenders, and as victims.

We only can infer from FBI statistics on hate crimes related to religion and national origin about those of Middle Eastern origin as victims. We only can infer from Federal Bureau of Prisons statistics related to participation in the Islamic religion about those of Middle Eastern origin as participants in the correctional system. Finally, we only can infer from statistics related to terrorism about those of Middle Eastern origin as criminal offenders. Given that law enforcement agencies, courts, jails, and departments of correction count those of Middle Eastern origin among the "white" or "black" populations, those inferences are the best that we can do at the present time. A serious flaw in this method is the inability to distinguish that someone indicated on papers as being "Islamic" or "Muslim" may not in fact be Middle Eastern. For example, Islam flourishes in American prisons, but many of the practitioners are African Americans who converted to the religion.

Our system recognizes the inadequacies of this approach. However, many leading authorities are reluctant to become more specific with respect to national origin because they fear that it would result in increased tendencies for profiling and targeting individuals because of their national origins, rather than their behaviors.

We know that there are cultural and religious differences *between* individuals of Middle Eastern origin and others, and *among* those of Middle Eastern origin. The Turks, for example, recently have attempted to embrace democracy and Islam in order to join the European Union. This cultural blend differentiates the Turks from all other Middle Eastern individuals. Therefore, categorizing the Turks with the Syrians and the Pakistanis and the Iraqis would be an egregious error, but one that would be unavoidable if our system attempted to distinguish those of Middle Eastern heritage from all others.

Increased levels of hate crimes and discrimination against individuals of Middle Eastern origin can be ameliorated with social and political effort. Current and future treatment of those that we question, detain, and arrest must be based on actual offenses, not suspicion or perception based on skin color, national origin, religion, or affiliation. James Zogby, American Arab and President of the Arab American Institute reminded us that "Arab Americans died in the attacks. Arab Americans were also part of the rescue effort. Dozens of New York City Police and rescue workers who bravely toiled at Ground Zero were Arab Americans" (2003, 2).

A rich and valued part of United States history is in our tradition as a melting pot, where individuals with varied cultures, beliefs, and backgrounds can become a part of American society. Integral to that tradition is the priority placed on human rights. Although we must remain vigilant in the protection of our citizens, domestically and abroad, part of that vigilance must be directed at protecting our citizens from unwarranted and unfair stereotyping, bias, and discrimination based on race, national origin, and religion.

REFERENCES

Arab American Institute (2006). *Arab American Candidates in 2006*. Retrieved from: http://www.aaiusa.
   org/AAcandidates/arab_american_candidates.htm.

Arab American Institute Foundation (2005). *Arab American Demographics*. Arab American
   Institute. Retrieved from: http://www.aaiusa.org/AAIF?Census/demographics.htm.

ARMAS, G. (2005). Census: Arabs in U.S. tend to be affluent. *San Francisco Chronicle*. March 8.
   Retrieved from: http://sfgate.com/cgi-bin/article.cgi?file=/n/a/2005/03/08/national/
   a121902S61.DTL.

Associated Press (2006). Pentagon to release Guantanamo detainee list to Public. May 15.
   Retrieved from: http://www.foxnews.com/story/0,2933,195559,00.html.

Associated Press (2005). Fertile ground? Muslim inmates seen as potential terrorists. *Winston-
   Salem Journal*. June 5. Retrieved from: http://www.journalnow.com/servlet/Satellite?pagename=
   WSJ%2FMGArticle%2FWSJ_BasicArticle&c=MGArticle&cid=1031783109872&path=!nation
   world&s=1037645509161.

BBC News (July 20, 2004). Al-Qaeda's origins and links. Retrieved from: http://news.bbc.co.uk/1/
   hi/world/middle_east/1670089.stm.

CNN News (May 24, 2006). Voice on tape is that of Osama bin Laden.

CLINTON, W. J. (1999). Executive Memorandum on Fairness in Law Enforcement.
   1999 Presidential Documents, 35(23), 1049–83. Government Printing Office: Washington, DC.
   June 9. Retrieved from: http://www.aele.org/fedprof.html.

Columbia Encyclopedia. (2006). Hammurabi. Retrieved from: http://www.encyclopedia.com/html/
   H/Hammurab.asp.

Council on Islamic Education (1995). Teaching about Islam and Muslims in the public school
   classroom. Retrieved from: http://www.aaiusa.org/PDF/CIE.pdf.

Country Reports on Terrorism (2006a). *Terrorism deaths, injuries, kidnappings of private U.S. Citizens,
   2005*. Office of the Coordinator for Counterterrorism, Bureau of Consular Affairs. U.S. Department
   of State, Washington, D.C. Retrieved from: http://www.state.gov/s/ct/rls/crt/2005/65970.htm.

Country Reports on Terrorism (2006b). *Chapter 8—Foreign Terrorist Organizations. Office of the
   Coordinator for Counterterrorism, Bureau of Consular Affairs*. U.S. Department of State,
   Washington, D.C. Retrieved from: http://www.state.gov/s/ct/rls/crt/2005/65275.htm.

DeROSIER, M. (2004). The social climate of school in the aftermath of 9/11: Ethnic differences in
   children's peer relations. *Journal of School Violence, 3*(1), 5–16.

Equal Employment Opportunity Commission (2003). Plan of the Equal Opportunity Commission
   for improving access to services for persons with limited English proficiency. Available online:
   http://www.eeoc.gov/abouteeoc/plan/lep/lep.html.

EGELKO, B. (2002). Muslim inmates win appeals court ruling: Friday rites, beards allowed in
   Solano prison. *San Francisco Chronicle*. December 28. Available online: http://sfgate.com/
   cgi-bin/article.cgi?f=/c/a/2002/12/28/BA241560.DTL.

Federal Bureau of Investigation (2000). *Hate Crime Statistics*. Crime in the United States-2000, 11.
   Uniform Crime Reporting Program, Washington, D.C. Retrieved from: http://www.fbi.gov/ucr/
   cius_00/hate00.pdf.

Federal Bureau of Investigation (1999). *Terrorism in the United States-1999*. Available online:
   http://www.fbi.gov/publications/terror/terror99.pdf.

Federal Bureau of Investigation (2001). *Hate Crime Statistics*. Crime in the United States-2001, 13.
   Uniform Crime Reporting Program, Washington, D.C. Retrieved from: http://www.fbi.gov/ucr/
   01hate.pdf.

Federal Bureau of Investigation (2002). *Hate Crime Statistics*. Crime in the United States-2002, 13.
   Uniform Crime Reporting Program, Washington, D.C. Retrieved from: http://www.fbi.gov/ucr/
   hatecrime2002.pdf.

Federal Bureau of Investigation (2003). *Hate Crime Statistics*. Crime in the United States-2003, 9. Uniform Crime Reporting Program, Washington, D.C. Retrieved from: http://www.fbi.gov/ucr/03hc.pdf.

Federal Bureau of Investigation (2004). *Hate Crime Statistics*. Crime in the United States-2004. Section 1, Table 1. Uniform Crime Reporting Program, Washington, D.C. Retrieved from: http://www.fbi.gov/ucr/hc2004/hctable1.htm.

Federal Bureau of Investigation (2004). *Terror 2000/2001*. Retrieved from: http://www.fbi.gov/publications/terror/terror2000_2001.pdf.

Guide to the Geneva Conventions (2003). *Convention III: Relative to the treatment of prisoners of war, Geneva, 12 August 1949*. Society of Professional Journalists. Retrieved from: http://www.genevaconventions.org/.

Halliburton Press Release. January 24, 2006. Retrieved from: http://www.halliburton.com/default/main/halliburton/eng/news/source_files/news.jsp?newsurl=/default/.

HARRISON, P., AND J. KARBERG. (2004). *Prison and jail inmates at midyear 2003* (NCJ 203947). Bureau of Justice Statistics Bulletin, U.S. Department of Justice, Washington, D.C. Retrieved from: http://www.ojp.usdoj.gov/bjs/pub/pdf/pjim03.pdf.

HERSH, S. M. (2004). Torture at Abu Ghraib. *New Yorker*. April 30. Available online: http://www.newyorker.com/fact/content/?040510fa_fact.

HUDSON, D. (2006). Prisoners rights: Overview. First Amendment Center. Retrieved from: http://www.firstamendmentcenter.org/rel_liberty/free_exercise/topic.aspx?topic=prisoner_rights.

KATZMAN, K. (2005). *Al Qaeda: Profile and threat assessment. CRS Report for Congress* (Order Code RS22049). Washington, D.C. Retrieved from: http://www.usembassy.it/pdf/other/RS22049.pdf.

KOZARYN, L. D. (1999). *Muslim troops highlight nation's diversity*. American Forces Information Services. U.S. Department of Defense: Washington, D.C. Retrieved from: http://www.defenselink.mil/news/Jan1999/n01261999_9901261.html.

LEDEEN, M. (2006). One moment in time. *National Review Online*. January 9. Available online: http://www.nationalreview.com/ledeen/ledeen200601090808.asp.

MINITER, R. (2003). *Losing bin Laden: How Bill Clinton's failures unleashed global Terror*. New York: Regnery.

MORAN, D. (2002). "Illegal combatants" and the law of armed conflict. *Strategic Insights*. August. Monterey, CA: Center for Contemporary Conflict. Retrieved from: http://www.ccc.nps.navy.mil/si/aug02/law.pdf.

MULLER, E. (2003). Inference or impact? Racial profiling and the internment's true legacy. *Ohio State Journal of Criminal Law, 1*, 103–31.

Office of the Inspector General (2003). *Press release: The September 11 detainees: A review of the treatment of aliens held on immigration charges in connection with the investigation of the September 11 attacks*. June. U.S. Department of Justice, Washington, D.C.

Office of the Inspector General (April, 2004). *A review of the Federal Bureau of Prisons' selection of Muslim religious service providers*. U.S. Department of Justice, Washington, D.C. Retrieved from: http://www.usdoj.gov/oig/special/0404/final.pdf.

POYNTING, S., G. NOBLE, AND P. TABAR. (2001). Middle Eastern appearances: "Ethnic gangs," moral panic and media framing. *Australian and New Zealand Journal of Criminology, 34*(1), 67–90.

RUTLEDGE, B. (1991). Hate crimes: Arab-Americans feel the heat of bigotry. *Human Rights: Journal of the Section of Individual Rights and Responsibilities, 18*(1), 30.

SAMHAN, H. H. (2004). By the numbers. *Arab American Business Magazine*. http://www.allied-media.com/Arab-American/Arab_demographics.htm.

SCOTT, P. D. (2006). *Homeland Security Contracts for Vast New Detention Camps*. Pacific News Service. Feb 8. Retrieved from: http://news.pacificnews.org/news/view_article.html?article_id=eed74d9d44c30493706fe03f4c9b3a77.

Sourcebook of Criminal Justice Statistics (2004). *Table 6.61.2004: Detainees under Bureau of Immigration and Customs Enforcement (ICE) jurisdiction.* Available online: http://www.albany. edu/sourcebook/pdf/t6612004.pdf.

Sydney Institute of Criminology (2004). *Bin Laden in the suburbs: Criminalising the Arab other.* Sydney Institute of Criminology: Sydney.

Sydney Morning Herald. (2006). U.S. to transfer Abu Ghraib prisoners. March 10. Retrieved from: http://www.smh.com.au/news/world/us-to-transfer-abu-ghraib-prisoners/2006/03/10/ 1141701667799.html.

Times Online. (2006). British Guantanamo detainees sue U.S. for $10m. May 11. Retrieved from: http://www.timesonline.co.uk/printFriendly/0,,1-2-2175790-2,00.html.

U.S. Census Bureau (2002). *American Fact Finder.* PCT026: Ancestry for people with one or more ancestry categories reported. Data Set: 2002 American Community Survey Summary Tables, 1–2. U.S. Census Bureau: Washington, D.C.

U.S. Department of Justice (1999). Department of Justice proposal: *Responding to the Executive Memorandum on Fairness in Law Enforcement,* 1–3. October 8. Government Printing Office: Washington, D.C.

U.S. Employment Opportunity Commission (2005a). *FY 2005 annual report on the operations and accomplishments of the Office of the General Counsel.* Available online: http://www.eeoc.gov/ litigation/05annrpt/index.html#IA.

U.S. Equal Employment Opportunity Commission (2005b). *Charge statistics from the U.S. Equal Employment Opportunity Commission FY 1992 through FY 2005.* Retrieved from: http://www. eeoc.gov/stats/charges.html.

U.S. Equal Employment Opportunity Commission (2003). *Plan of the Equal Employment Opportunity Commission for improving access to services for persons with limited English proficiency.* Footnote 3. Retrieved from: http://www.eeoc.gov/abouteeoc/plan/lep/lep.html.

U.S. Equal Employment Opportunity Commission (2002a). *Commission's response to September 11th. Annual Report-2002,* 7. Retrieved from: http://www.eeoc.gov/abouteeoc/annual_reports/ annrep02.html.

U.S. Equal Employment Opportunity Commission (2002b). *Fact Sheet: EEOC provides answers about workplace rights of Muslims, Arabs, South Asians, and Sikhs.* Retrieved from: http://www.eeoc.gov/press/5-15-02.html.

WEBER, L., B. P. Bo, AND S. POYNTING. (2002). Special issue: Refugee issues and criminology. *Current Issues in Criminal Justice, 14*(1), 9–101.

WHITE, D. (2005). Senator Harry Reid told Osama bin Laden killed in Pakistan earthquake. Retrieved from: http://usliberals.about.com/b/a/222193.htm.

ZOGBY, J. (2003). *Statement before the United States Committee on the Judiciary.* Hearing on "America after 9/11: Freedom preserved or freedom lost?" Nov. 18.

7

Women in the Criminal Justice System

Catherine E. Burton

❖

CHAPTER OUTLINE

INTRODUCTION

Victim, offender, professional—these are the primary roles women play in the U.S. criminal justice system. However, women did not always occupy all of these roles. Women's roles in the criminal justice system have changed over time, paralleling their struggle for social, political, and economic equality. Society influences a woman's position and status. In a patriarchal or male-dominated society, women were men's subjects. Therefore, it is no surprise that women's earliest roles in the justice system were as victims. The feminist movement and women's struggle for equality have coincided and, some feel, enable women to take their places as offender and professionals. This chapter will examine the various roles of women in the criminal justice system as professional service providers, victims, and offenders.

WOMEN IN THE CRIMINAL JUSTICE FIELD

There has been a striking increase in the number of women working in the criminal justice system since 1975. The field of criminal justice has traditionally been dominated by men. Before the 1970s and the gender equality movement, women held very few positions in the criminal justice system. The few positions they did occupy were considered "specialist" slots that drew on the "qualities and skills associated with their gender" (Martin and Jurik 1996, 1). During the 1960s and 1970s, the legislative process extended equal employment opportunities to previously excluded groups, including women (Ex., Title VII of the *Civil Rights Act of 1964* and the *Equal Employment Opportunity Act of 1972*). Although the numbers of women in the field are increasing, there are still serious issues and inequities that remain. Some of these issues include obstacles to recruitment, retention, and advancement; training opportunities; and sexual harassment (Martin and Jurik 1996; Gowdy et al. 2003).

Women in Law Enforcement

The duties of women in law enforcement began to expand in the 1960s in response to judicial involvement and legislation began to support demands for equality. Gowdy et al. (2003) examine the status of women in law enforcement from 1971 to 1995:

- In 1971, 1.4% of the 225,474 police officers in municipal police departments were women.
- In 1975, out of a force of 8,500 FBI special agents, 30 were women. Of the 1,200 special agents of the Secret Service, 7 were women.
- In 1995, women represented 24% of all police employees, 9.8% of all sworn officers, and 62% of all civilian employees in some 13,000 agencies.

In 2001, women still held only 12.7% of all sworn law enforcement positions in large agencies, 8.1% in rural and small agencies, and 14.4% in federal agencies (Reaves and Hart 2001). In law enforcement training academies, only 17% of recruits who completed their training in 2002 were female (Bureau of Justice Statistics 2005b). Furthermore, women's representation in large police agencies declined from 1999 to 2001, slipping from 14.3% in 1999, to 13.0% in 2000, and even further to 12.7% in 2001. It will take women several generations to achieve equality in large police agencies at the present rate, particularly in the absence of specific strategies on the part of major agencies for bringing more women into their ranks (Lonsway et al. 2003).

Societal expectations and attitudes dictate the gender inequity that is firmly established in the workplace. Martin (1991), in analyzing workplace gender inequity, finds that there are barriers in law enforcement and corrections, both male-dominated areas. Women find it difficult to rise to management levels due to denial of training and limits imposed by traditional organizational behavior.

It is even more difficult for African American women to join the "all boys club." Because they face discrimination on the basis of both race and gender, researchers have labeled this "double jeopardy" (Van Wormer and Bartollas 2000). McCoy (1993) further notes that while affirmative action has improved hiring practices where female officers are concerned, advancement into the higher ranks of law enforcement agencies has not occurred. A major obstacle women have yet to overcome is the negative attitudes that male peers and supervisors hold about women's roles in policing (Hale 1992). Executives within policing organizations have not created organizational cultures that place value on the diversity that women bring to law enforcement (Gowdy et al. 2003). Supervisors may have perceptions of female employees based on perceptions they understand, i.e., females as daughters and wives (BJS 1995). Women in the field have reported that they are not taken seriously by male colleagues, that managers do not perceive women as pursuing a career track, and that they must constantly prove themselves (BJS 1994).

Women in the Corrections System

The corrections component of the criminal justice system remains male-dominated and sex-segregated to a greater extent than others. Women's rights to equal opportunity have been given less weight than inmate privacy, security, and the women's physical qualifications. Throughout the 1980s and 1990s, the number of female correctional officers in jails increased dramatically. In terms of executive positions, women have been wardens of female institutions since the late nineteenth century. Today, more women are seeking the top positions at male institutions (Van Wormer and Bartollas 2000).

Female correctional employees have been the least examined by academicians with the exception of female correctional officers in male prisons. Rowan (1996) studied the safety of female officers in maximum-security prisons and found that male correctional officers were assaulted 3.6 times more often than female officers. Further research on assault rates found that female officers listened more effectively than men, had a calming effect, were not confrontational, and did not use force to exercise control (Martin and Levine 1991).

Gowdy et al. (2003) reported on the representation of women in the correctional field:

- Seventeen percent of the wardens or superintendents in state correctional systems and 20% in juvenile systems are female.
- Thirty percent of all jail payroll staff and 24% of all jail correctional officers are female.
- Women hold 12% of the supervisory and 12% of the nonsupervisory correctional officer positions in the federal adult system.
- Women make up nearly 30% of all correctional personnel in state adult correctional facilities.
- Seventeen percent of women in state adult correctional systems are wardens or superintendents.
- Nearly 7% of all federal wardens are female.

Similarly to law enforcement, women have made gains in terms of representation. However, a clear path to the top echelons of correctional management does not yet exist. Research focusing more attention on the issues women in the corrections field face and a change in organizational culture may begin to address the problem.

Women in the Legal Profession

In terms of employment, women have made the most significant advances in the legal profession. Again, equal rights legislation and the political struggles of women have been major contributors to this progress. Approximately 80% of female attorneys have entered the profession since the 1970s. As of 2003, women comprise more than 29% of all practicing lawyers in the United States. In U.S. law schools, 49% of law students and 32.8% of the faculty are women. Women have even ascended to the judiciary. In 2003, the ABA (2003) collected the statistics on the presence of women on the bench:

- One woman out of nine justices of the U.S. Supreme Court
- More than 17% of the U.S. Federal Court of Appeals judges
- More than 16% of the U.S. District Courts judges
- Twenty-eight percent of justices on State Courts of Last Resort

Despite the fact that the percentage of female professionals in the court system has grown since the mid-1970s, gender bias remains. There are still fewer women making partner than their male counterparts and fewer still who ever achieve the executive position of managing partner. Since the 2003 report, Sandra Day O'Connor, the first woman on the Supreme Court, resigned her position, leaving only one woman serving on the highest court in the land.

The Glass Ceiling

However, barriers still remain for women. Opportunities have been opened in the lower rank and non-managerial positions, but by and large women and minorities still face barriers to the upper-level management and executive positions as criminal justice practitioners

(Gowdy et al. 2003). In 1991, government research conducted by the Bureau of Labor Statistics (1991) verified that the "glass ceiling effect" does still exist in the United States. They hold that there are still points beyond which women are not permitted to advance.

The field of corrections has taken some positive steps. Gender-neutral hiring policies have been adopted by state and federal corrections systems. Rison (1994) finds that correctional administrators had taken steps to address gender bias in their managerial practices. Court mandates, union pressure, and recognition of equal opportunity are all factors that have contributed to gender-neutral policies. Not only is fundamental fairness a reason to employ women in corrections, but purely pragmatic reasons have also influenced some of the managerial changes. The pool of correctional personnel must be expanded. The recruitment, retention, and promotion of women are means to achieve that goal.

Sexual Harassment

The courts recognize two types of sexual harassment: quid pro quo, involving sexual favors, and "hostile work environment," i.e., suggestive comments or pictures, jokes, unwanted physical contact, or other situations that adversely impact work performance. The development of programs to deal with sexual harassment is insufficient unless support for the programs comes from the top. The attitude of management toward harassment can advance or inhibit effectiveness. Overlooking, trivializing the issue, or refusing to acknowledge the issue are all factors that contribute to harassment (Gowdy et al. 2003).

As a result of the fact that criminal justice agencies are largely populated with men, sexual harassment has been tolerated at the highest levels and permeates all levels of the criminal justice system. Women employed in large agencies as well as those employed by small town police departments complain of sexual harassment. Although the media and prominent legal cases (*Arnold v. Seminole*, 1985) have brought this issue to the forefront, there is much evidence that the problem still exists. For example, even as late as the 1990s, research demonstrated that 53% of the female respondents employed in small town agencies have experienced sexual harassment during their career, primarily by supervisors. An even higher percentage (83%) of the respondents reported that male coworkers expressed negative attitudes about and toward women (Van Wormer and Bartollas 2000).

VICTIMIZATION OF WOMEN

Women as victims is one aspect of the greater issue of exploitation of women in society at large. Many writers relate this victimization to the concept of patriarchy upon which society is structured. This male power structure is then replicated in the paternalistic response of the criminal justice system to female victims of crime. The system in itself becomes a mechanism of control. The state becomes the victim in any cases brought forward for prosecution, with prosecutors relegating the real victims to roles of complainant and witness, both represented by the prosecution. Women victims have little input into this process; their voices are muted, leaving them with little control over situations. The frustration caused by this lack of control results in "secondary victimization" (Elias 2000; Van Wormer and Bartollas 2000), the sense that not only have these women been victims of crime but also of the criminal justice system.

Crime Victims Movement

Women pushed to gain some control during the political struggles of the late 1960s and early 1970s. Women no longer accepted the concept that they were somehow to blame for their own victimization. Female victims of crime started referring to themselves as *survivors*, not *victims* (Van Wormer and Bartollas 2000).

In the late 1970s and early 1980s, the crime victims' movement made critical progress. In 1975, the *Report of the LEAA Task Force on Women* suggested that research was necessary to determine whether crime victimization was different for men and women, marking a surge of interest in providing assistance to the victims of crime. The National Organization for Victim Assistance (NOVA) became the first of many service organizations dealing with a wide range of women's issues, including domestic violence, sexual assault, and child-abuse prevention.

In 1984, the *Victims of Crime Act* led the way for the establishment of the Office for Victims of Crime under the U.S. Department of Justice. With the passage of the *Victims of Crime Act* (VOCA) and the subsequent *Violence Against Women Act of 1994* (VACA), crime victims started to receive basic rights within the criminal justice system. These rights include (1) access to information about the offender's case and disposition, sentence, and release, (2) the right to introduce a victim's impact statement to the court and the parole board, (3) the right to participate in all proceedings in which an offender may participate, and (4) the right to receive services such as treatment and restitution (Gowdy et al. 2003; Doerner and Lab 2005).

Measuring Victimization

When crime against women is examined, victimization is frequently regarded as more significant because women are victims of many unreported crimes, ranging from domestic abuse to rape. Bachman and Saltzman (1995) note the difficulty in measuring the extent of violence against women, particularly sexual assault and other forms of violence committed by intimates or acquaintances. Women may consider these incidents to be private events or feel stigmatized by the nature of the events and, as a result, do not report these crimes. One of the most striking findings is that the victimizations of women predominantly arise from intimate relationships or personal acquaintances rather than from random violence or organized criminal activities.

Two major sources of data, official police reports and victimization surveys, measure the extent of crimes against women. The most widely used dataset based on official police reports or arrest records is the Uniform Crime Reports (UCR), collected by local law enforcement and maintained by the Federal Bureau of Investigation. The most commonly used victimization survey is the National Crime Victimization Survey (NCVS).

Uniform Crime Report   Produced by the FBI, the UCR began in 1931, providing data on eight index crimes: murder, forcible rape, robbery, aggravated assault, burglary, larceny-theft, and arson. This data source has several limitations; three are of particular concern to the study of female victimization. The first is the concept that Doerner and Lab (2005) refer to as the *dark figure of crime*, crime that is not known to police. The second limitation is that only the most serious offense is reported in the dataset. For example, if during a single incident, multiple crimes—for example, rape and murder—were committed, only murder would be recorded. The third limitation is that there is little information about the victim.

The National Incident-Based Reporting System (NIBRS) combats some of these limitations. The NIBRS is an expanded data-collection system that includes detailed information on the victim, victim–offender relationship, injuries, and property loss and reports multiple crimes in a single incident. The NIBRS provides an opportunity to learn more about victims. However, due to the increased data-entry requirement on the part of local law enforcement, the program is not available nationwide. As a result, the UCR provides a valuable but limited picture of victimization (Doerner and Lab 2005).

National Crime Victims Survey. The NCVS is the fourth generation of victimization surveys that began in 1979 in their present incarnation. One of the most serious limitations of the NCVS, and all victimization surveys, is the issue of *recall.* Two primary problems exist with recall: *telescoping* and *memory decay.* In telescoping, the incident occurs outside the timeframe of the survey. In memory decay, the incident occurs within the timeframe of the survey, but the respondent does not remember it and/or does not report it accurately. Protecting the respondents' identities creates another limitation to this data; researchers are unable to link the incidents of victimization to geographical locations. Therefore, the statistics are only available in a national aggregate (Doerner and Lab 2005).

The NCVS is used to construct reasonably accurate reports of rape, sexual assault, and other crimes committed by family members or intimates. The NCVS uses the following definitions for relationships:

- *Intimates:* spouses, ex-spouses, girlfriends, boyfriends, and ex-boyfriends and girlfriends
- *Acquaintances/friends:* former friends, friends, stepchildren, children, brothers, sisters, or other relatives
- *Strangers:* anyone not known previously by the victim

All the NCVS data over the last quarter century support the assertion that females are more likely to be victimized by acquaintances, friends, or intimates than are males. This is particularly true with the violent crimes of rape, assault, battery, manslaughter, and homicide.

Trends in Violence Against Women   Violence against women is a matter for serious concern. Lawsky (2000) reports that violence is the leading cause of injuries to American women between the ages of 15 and 44, more common than the combination of deaths from muggings, car accidents, and cancer. Four million American women are the victims of domestic violence yearly. Based on the best projections from arrest records, reported crimes, and surveys of victimization, 75% of American women will be victimized by violent crimes at some point in their lives. However, these figures may well be understating the reality of violence against women in America today. Despite increasing publicity and new policing standards for mandatory arrests in domestic disputes involving violence or the threat or attempt of violence, many women remain reluctant to report crimes against themselves by intimate relations. Underreporting may also stem from the repetitive nature of many domestic assaults, some of which go on for years before the recorded police call, assault, or homicide arrest occurs.

While NCVS data demonstrate that violent victimization of women has followed the national downward trend of the 1990s, levels of violent attacks against women remain unacceptably high. Craven (1996) reports that, between 1992 and 1994, violent crimes against women reached nearly 14 million. In 1994, statistics from the NCVS and the FBI's Uniform Crime Reporting (UCR) Program reflected 1 rape per every 270 women, 1 robbery per every 270 women, 1 assault per every 29 women, and 1 female homicide victim per every 23,000 women age 12 or older.

Generally, women have a lower risk of homicide than men; however, the predominant pattern is one of men attacking and murdering women (Craven 1996). The overwhelming number of homicides in the U.S. are perpetrated by men regardless of the gender of the victim. However, in incidents of both non-fatal and fatal violence, women are at a higher risk than men to be victimized by an intimate; females who are victims of homicide are more than twice as likely to have been murdered by boyfriends or husbands as male victims are to have been killed by girlfriends or wives. In sum, female homicide victims are predominantly the victims of intimate associates rather than of casual acquaintances or strangers. In 1992–93, for example, women sustained over one million violent victimizations perpetrated by an intimate and were more likely than men to suffer violent victimization by a relative. In this same period, 78% of women victims reported that they knew the offender.

Craven (1996) identified the following trends:

• Men are victimized at higher rates in all categories of violent crime except rape and sexual assault.
• Women who live in families with less than $10,000 annual income are more likely to experience violent victimization.
• Ethnicity or race of the female is not associated with risk level for victimization by intimates.
• Women are more likely to be injured when victimized by intimates.
• Women who are injured in violent crimes are more likely to report the incidents to law enforcement than women who are not injured.
• Women aged 16–24 experienced the highest per-capita rates of intimate violence, 19.6 victimizations per 1,000 women.

The most current data for criminal victimizations of women paint a clear picture of the striking difference between women who were the victims of intimate crimes of violence and those who were victims of more conventional violence, such as robbery. On average, from 1976 to 1998 the number of murders by intimates decreased by 1% per year for female victims. Intimate violence is primarily a crime against women. In 1998, females were the victims in 72% of intimate murders and the victims of nearly 85% of non-lethal intimate violence. In 2002, women experienced an estimated 494,570 rape, sexual assault, robbery, aggravated assault, and simple assault victimizations at the hands of intimates, down from 1.1 million in 1993. A recent government report, BJS (2005b), indicated that during 2003:

• 70% of the sexual assault/rape victims who were female stated that an intimate, relative, acquaintance, or friend was the offender
• 45% of females who were robbed stated that the offender was a stranger

The data examining sexual assault perpetrated against women yield some frightening statistics. Bachman and Saltzman (1995) find that women (aged 12 or over) annually report about 500,000 sexual assaults and rapes. More than half of the aforementioned crimes were committed by friends or acquaintances. Strangers perpetrated about one in five. Research indicates that nearly half of the female victims of violence by intimates stated that the perpetrator was either using illegal drugs or drinking at the time the crime was committed. This pattern is similar to the substance-use levels reported in surveys of prison and jail inmates. Female offenders who admitted to having committed violent acts against an intimate partner when they had been drinking reported consumption of an average of about 5 ounces of alcohol, the equivalent to 10 mixed drinks or beers, just prior to the incident. Comparable data for drug use are more difficult to develop because of the wide variety of substances and tests, but most researchers agree that drug use plays a significant role in many violent assaults, whether among users or from users attacking women in the course of property crimes or intimate disputes.

Weapons also seem to be frequently present during attacks on women. Among women reporting violence by armed intimates, firearms, knives, and other objects pressed into service as weapons were used with roughly the same frequency (Bachman and Saltzman 1995). There are many anecdotal accounts that suggest that women are more likely to use knives than guns, but, as victims, women experiencing assaults by armed intimates are about as likely to find themselves attacked by guns, knives, or blunt objects. Marriage, separation, and divorce are critical factors in determining the likelihood of a violent assault by a boyfriend, husband, or ex-husband. Among women victimized by violence committed by an intimate, the rate for women separated from their husbands was three times higher than for women who were divorced and about 25 times higher than that of married women. These rates show that the separation process is an acutely dangerous and unstable one for many women.

Law Enforcement Response to Domestic Violence and Sexual Assault

The above data suggest two main categories of violence against women: domestic violence and sexual assault. The criminal justice system has not traditionally considered these crimes high priority and/or has constructed barriers for victims. However, progress has been made in the processing and disposition of both domestic violence and sexual assault.

Domestic Violence   The criminal justice system has not always pursued domestic violence enthusiastically for a myriad of reasons, including an unwillingness to treat violence perpetrated by someone other than a stranger as equal to other crimes and the lack of the victims' cooperation. Historically, women have not been willing to participate in court proceedings because of the economic and psychological entanglements of their relationships with the offenders. Many states did not even allow law enforcement to make arrests for domestic disturbances unless the police officers witnessed the attack. Additionally, most domestic charges were classified as misdemeanors. Because of this classification and the problems with the victim's participation, prosecutors often assigned these cases a low priority (Gowdy et al. 2003).

As a result of the women's movement of the 1960s, a change began in the way law enforcement began to respond to domestic violence. Between 1976 and 1981, the LEAA funded various projects including shelters for battered women, treatment for abusers, and special prosecution units. Further change was brought about in the 1980s with the inception of the Minneapolis Domestic Violence Experiment (Sherman and Berk 1984; Gowdy et al. 2003). This initiative is partially responsible for the shift of attention by the criminal justice system from mediation and counseling to making arrests in domestic disturbances. Research indicates that subsequent episodes of domestic violence decreased by 50% when the suspect was arrested. These positive results led to replications of the study in other cities (including Atlanta, Charlotte, Colorado Springs, Miami, and Milwaukee) but results were often inconsistent with the findings of the pilot study in Minneapolis. The replication studies report three outcomes of an arrest: (1) no deterrent effect, (2) only certain types of offenders were deterred from subsequent violence, and (3) violence escalated. The last outcome suggests a need for more intervention by the courts in conjunction with increased arrests by law enforcement. In addition to coordination between the police and the courts, victim advocates and other community service organizations should be included in order to provide the three-pronged approach needed to combat domestic violence (Gowdy et al. 2003; Doerner and Lab 2005).

Sexual Assault   The response of the criminal justice system toward sexual assault victims has also been influenced by feminism and the women's movement. Similar to domestic violence, some stringent legal requirements provided a framework to determine whether or not rape complaints were pursued. For instance, the complaint had to be filed promptly; a delayed report would not be acted upon. Also, the incident had to have corroborating witnesses (which we now know are rare in rape cases). Finally, the victim had to physically resist the attacker (Gowdy et al. 2003; Doerner and Lab 2005).

By the mid-1980s all states had changed their statutes to focus on the offender and not the victim's behavior. With the encouragement of victims' rights organizations, 14 states passed laws making it illegal for a man to rape his wife. Additionally, rape shield laws were enacted which limited using the victim's prior sexual conduct in court (Gowdy et al. 2003; Doerner and Lab 2005). Beyond legislative changes, the criminal justice system has made a great deal of progress in the way they handle sexual assault cases. Many departments and agencies have in-house victim advocates that are trained to deal with sexual assault victims and can help them get the community services they will need to facilitate recovery. The criminal justice system needs to continue to work with community programs and facilities in order to develop a systemic approach regarding how the system responds to crimes of sexual assault. One such joint endeavor is the Sexual Assault Nurse Examiner Program (SANE). This program trains registered nurses to guide the victim through the physical examination process. The victims are provided with compassion, sensitivity, and immediate attention to their physical and emotional distress. Furthermore, SANE also administers a rape kit that enables law enforcement to obtain and preserve evidence in order to successfully prosecute cases. There is a need for more research and collaborative efforts. Although a great deal of progress has been made, there is more to accomplish (Doerner and Lab 2005).

Theories of Spousal Abuse and Sexual Assault

Two broad categories of theories explaining spousal abuse and sexual assault emerge from the literature: (1) psychological/physiological and (2) sociocultural. Psychological theories involve the psychopathology of the individual as an explanation for the abuse. For example, violent behavior in a domestic relationship may stem from issues that include substance abuse, depression, mental illness, and intergenerational abuse. Alcohol and drugs could affect the abuse in two ways: the perpetrator could engage in the abusive behavior as a result of being under the influence of the substances, or the drugs and/or alcohol could allow the perpetrator to feel free of inhibitions that would normally encourage the individual from refraining from the act. Depression and mental illness and low self-esteem may cause an individual to relieve frustrations by perpetrating violence on family members (Doerner and Lab 2005).

Early psychological theories that attempt to explain sexual violence as a result of repressed sexual desires or past female domination as the cause of sexual aggression. Some physiological theories argue that rape is caused by an uncontrollable sex drive derived from the evolutionary need of males to procreate with more than one woman due to the lengthy gestation period (Ellis 1989; Scully 1990; Doerner and Lab 2005). Sociocultural theories such as these stem from the concept of patriarchy or a male-dominated society. Throughout much of history women have been viewed as chattel, or the property of men. These theories largely explain crime, with males using violence to solve problems and maintain the status quo (their power). The criminal justice system, being male-dominated, has often turned a blind eye to domestic abuse. Sociocultural explanations of rape also stem from a patriarchal society and are linked to the learning theory approach in which behavior is learned through formal and informal mechanisms—that "rape is the result of males exerting their learned position in society" (Doerner and Lab 2005, 156). Abuse often follows intergenerational patterns. Abusers have observed role models or figures of authority deal with life's problems through violence. These types of theories gained momentum and support from the women's movement as emphasized the ills of traditional sex roles.

The social learning theories can also be applied to the victimization aspect of domestic violence to explain why some women do not leave abusive relationships. Women who are abused often lack resources to leave relationships—such as money, skills to gain employment, or even a place to go. A *learned helplessness* syndrome can develop when women believe they have no control over their environment and are helpless to alter their circumstances (Walker 1979; Doerner and Lab 2005).

The cause of spousal abuse and sexual assault is still debated. The aforementioned theories only provide a broad overview of some of explanations the field has offered. The most accurate explanation probably includes a myriad of factors and is not easily explained. While sociocultural explanations are by far the most accepted to date, it does not mean that some psychological theories do not have merit and validity.

WOMEN AS OFFENDERS

We have seen a steady increase in female offense rates over the past 40 years. However, although their contribution to serious crime has increased, they are still responsible for relatively little serious crime (murder, forcible rape, robbery, and aggravated assault). Women have typically been arrested for crimes such as larceny-theft, drunk driving, substance-abuse violations, and prostitution (often filed as a charge of disorderly conduct) (Chesney-Lind 1997). In contrast to the widely unreported or underreported cases of victimization of women, there is a reliable and uniform body of data on female offenders, from such records as police complaints, arrest reports, and data on incarcerated females in local, state, and federal prison systems. According to the FBI, women accounted for 23.2% of the total arrests for that 2004. This figure is slightly higher but fairly consistent with previous findings that report that women accounted for approximately 22% of the arrests for 1998. The five-year trend from 1999 and 2003 showed a slight increase in the number of female arrests (2.8%). The majority of the arrests for 2003 were for larceny-theft (Table 7-1), followed by drug-abuse violations and arrests for driving while intoxicated. These three categories accounted for more than 70% of female arrests for that year. Prior research supports this finding, indicating that many of the women in state prisons in 1997 had arrest records showing such offenses as property theft and driving while intoxicated (Greenfield and Snell 1999).

The broad conclusions to be drawn regarding women offenders are fairly clear. Women's arrest and conviction rates have been rising steadily over the last 40 years; and the age of female offenders in arrest, conviction, and incarceration is critical: female juveniles are about twice as likely to be arrested as female adults, more than three times as likely to be arrested for larceny (e.g. shoplifting and petty theft without violence), and more than four times as likely to be arrested for car theft (FBI 2004; Greenfield and Snell 1999; Snell 1994).

Part of the decades-long increase in the number of arrests and convictions of women can be ascribed to the "war on drugs" with its attendant mandatory sentencing laws for those convicted as drug offenders. Criminal activities (typically larceny, prostitution, or drug sales) typically supply the money to support women's drug habits. Nearly three decades ago, a study of women incarcerated in New York City jails conducted by Feinman (1976) found that about 85% of the women being held there were narcotics addicts. When this study was conducted, fewer women than men were steadily employed, possibly accounting for the greater number of women who relied on illegal means of obtaining drug money. Although women have entered the labor force in much

TABLE 7-1   Adult Female Arrests, 2003[a]

Offense	#of Arrests[b]	% of Total
Violent Offenses		
Murder	868	10.3
Robbery	6,264	10.4
Aggravated Assault	55,307	20.7
Property Offenses		
Burglary	20,985	13.7
Larceny-Theft	211,501	37.1
Motor-Vehicle Theft	12,458	16.6
Drug Abuse Violations	192,312	18.3
Driving Under the Influence	179,867	18.2

Source: Uniform Crime Reports, 2003;

[a]Adult=18 and over;

[b]Includes all males and females.

greater numbers over the last few decades, the economic circumstances of women offenders had not changed appreciably by the end of the 1990s. To a greater extent than men, women offenders appear to be driven by economic necessity and constraints upon their employment options.

Violent Offenders

The approximately 2.1 million violent female offenders account for about 14% of all violent offenses, as opposed to approximately 23% of all types of criminal offenses. Seventy-five percent of these violent female offenders perpetrated simple assault. "Simple assault," as defined by the Bureau of Justice, is an attack without a weapon that results either in a minor injury or an injury that requires less than two days of hospitalization. Simple assault also includes verbal threats of assault and attempted assault without a weapon (BJS 2005a; BJS 2005b; FBI 2004).

Females accounted for approximately 10.3% of the murder and non-negligent manslaughter arrests in 2003. As with victimization of women by intimates, the majority of homicides committed by females are against persons well known to them (FBI 2004; BJS 2005a). The Bureau of Justice Statistics (2005a) examined data from 1973 to 2003 and indicated that over 60% of the murders committed by women between 1976 and 2003 were committed against a family member or intimate. Over half of women who committed murder used a firearm. Additional findings from the BJS report include the following:

- About 28% of violent female offenders are juveniles.
- Seventy-five percent of the victims of violent female offenders were also women.
- Almost two-thirds of victims had a prior relationship with the female perpetrator.
- An estimated 40% of women perpetrating violence were thought by the victim to be under the influence of alcohol or other drugs when the crime took place.

Some of the economic variables that have impacted women's offense rates were (1) whether or not they were in primary or secondary breadwinner positions, (2) their length of time in or out of the labor market, (3) their level of income, and (4) unemployment. Unemployment is very high among female offenders, but basic unemployment rates tend to misrepresent the nature and extent of unemployment. Minority status is also a significant predictor of both property and violent crime by women, but minorities are also more likely to have been involved in violence than in property crime. Educational status as a student or graduate is negatively related to crime, indicating that female students or women with more education show less criminal behavior (BJS 2005a; BJS 2005b; FBI 2004).

Employment and higher wages significantly decrease both property and violent crime rates, and this relationship holds true for young females as well as young males. As a group, younger females significantly increased the rates of property crime offenses, but not drug and violent crimes. The conclusion there may be that drug addiction and domestic violence persist over time into adulthood, whereas larceny, car theft, and delinquency are crimes of younger females (BJS 2005a; BJS 2005b).

Theories of Female Criminality

Theories of criminal behavior have ranged from biological to societal (social, political, economic). These theories have largely been developed to explain male criminal behavior. Women make up only a small part of the criminal population and many researchers have not investigated why women commit crime or, perhaps more importantly, why they do not. The earliest biological theories by Cesare Lombroso linked criminal behavior to atavistic features. In women, he defined atavistic features as those features that were the opposite of feminine (e.g. excessive body hair). Much of the research that examined female criminality involved society's view of women and their sexuality. Thomas (1923) and (1907) asserted that women engaged in criminal activity, particularly prostitution, in order to satisfy their desire for excitement. Finally, in the 1960s, research began to examine the connection between the economic and social status of women in relation to criminal behavior (Grana 2002).

It was not until 1975 and the development of the women's liberation theory that the research focus shifted to explaining the behavior of female offenders. Adler (1975) and Simon (1975) suggest that the women's equality movement increased crime rates. However, Adler (1975) contended that violent crime would increase, whereas Simon (1975) held that property crime would increase. Simon further held that violent crime would decrease as new career and educational opportunities decreased women's frustrations (Adler 1975; Simon 1975; Belknap 2001).

The women's liberation theory was not supported by later research. Steffensmeier (1980) finds that female violent crime rates have remained stable since the inception of feminism in the 1970s. However, research has indicated that female property crime rates have increased since the 1970s (Steffensmeier and Streifel 1992). Further examination of the issue indicates that female property crime rates may be related to a dearth of employment opportunities rather than an abundance of them. The higher the number of women and their dependents living in poverty, the higher the rates of female property crime. This concept is known as the "feminization of poverty." In fact, the crimes women were most often associated with after the feminist movement of the 1970s were crimes such as prostitution that did not support the notion of the emancipated female (Smart 1982; Steffensmeier and Allan 1988; Belknap 2001; Grana 2002).

A reworking of feminist theory takes into account race, gender, and class and the way those three issues intersect and influence both male and female crime. Messerschmidt (1993) focuses on the concept of "masculinity" as an explanation of criminality. In other words, it is masculinity that accounts for criminal behavior. Lower-class males and males of color do not have as many opportunities for legitimate structures that allow them to establish masculinity (good education, good job, etc.) and, therefore, have increased rates of criminal activity. In an effort to explain lower female crime rates when they too have decreased opportunities to legitimate power structures, Messerschmidt (1993) contends that females do not have a need to establish masculinity or to demonstrate power, i.e. resulting in lower female crime rates (Naffine 1996; Belknap 2001).

Belknap (2001) argues that life-course theory supports a pro-feminist perspective. This theory contends that life events (especially those that took place during childhood and adolescence) can impact criminal behavior. From birth to death, the formal and informal controls such as family, peers, school, and work can all influence whether or not a person engages in offending behavior. Much of the research regarding life-course theory supports the validity of the theory. In order to trace life events over a long period, researchers have employed longitudinal datasets. A significant limitation of these datasets is the fact that the data collection began when interest in studying female offending was not as significant as it is today. Therefore, a great deal of the research to date has only been conducted with males (Sampson and Laub 1990; Sampson and Laub 1993; Maguin and Loeber 1996).

Belknap (2001) links feminist pathways research, as it is currently referred to, with life-course theory in that it examines events that influence a woman's risk of offending. However, instead of using longitudinal data, this research explores data at one point in time. These studies usually include incarcerated women and sometimes self-identified prostitutes. Furthermore, not all of the research uses women's first person accounts or "voices." Some has used official records such as pre-sentence investigation reports. The common thread among this type of research is the use of women's histories and past traumas or abuses to examine subsequent criminal behavior. Although relatively new, these pathways studies lend support to the argument that childhood and adult traumas may predict criminal behavior for girls and women.

WOMEN IN PRISON

Just as the number of female offenders has increased, so has the number of women behind bars. In 2003, more than 100,000 women were under the jurisdiction of the federal and state corrections authorities. Since 1995, the number of female inmates has averaged a 5.1% increase a year (Table 7-2). This number reflects a rate of about 1 woman for every 100,000 U.S. residents (BJS 2003). The majority of incarcerated offenders in local jails are male. However, an exploration of demographic data on offenders housed in local jails from 1995 to 2004 demonstrates that female rates are increasing faster than males (BJS 2005c). Even with the increasing numbers, women's prisons are smaller and fewer in number than those facilities used to house male offenders. The small number of female prisoners compared to the male population has allowed an "institutional sexism" to exist. For instance, in addition to women's facilities being smaller, they are farther away from friends and family, which results in physical and

TABLE 7-2   Female Prisoners Under State or Federal Jurisdiction, 1995 and 2003[a]

	2003	1995[a]
All Female Inmates	68,468	100,102
Sentenced to more than 1 year	63,963	90,946
Incarceration rate[a]	61	47

Source: Bureau of Justice Statistics, Prison and Jail Inmates at Midyear 2003;
[a]Total number of prisoners with a sentence of more than 1 year per 100,000 U.S. residents.

emotional isolation. They are characterized by few educational and vocational programs as well as specialized treatment. This lack of resources at female institutions is often justified by the "small" numbers they represent when examining the correctional system as a whole (Belknap 2001).

The War on Drugs

The sharp increase in women's rates of incarceration has been attributed to the criminal justice policy referred to as "The War on Drugs." Many argue that the increased attention by law enforcement to drug-related crimes has been directly responsible for the increase in women's arrest and imprisonment rates. In fact, some have labeled the "War on Drugs" actually a "War on Women." Research supports that argument to an extent, but there are some significant interstate differences (Morash and Schram 2002). In New York, from 1986 to 1995 drug convictions were responsible for more than 80% of the increase in women's convictions. Minnesota did not see a dramatic increase in female convictions for drug-related crimes. Furthermore, studies held that the large majority of African American and Latino (59% and 77%, respectively) women incarcerated were convicted of drug-related offenses as opposed to only 34% of white women. The focus of law enforcement on street-level drugs places African Americans, and Latinos to a lesser extent, at greater risk of arrest. The women studied were certainly not drug lords, but low-level dealers and users who played no significant role in drug trafficking, and frequently introduced to offending behavior by an intimate (Morash and Schram 2002; Pollock 2002).

The federal system has seen the most dramatic increase of female convictions for drug offenses due to the impact of U.S. Sentencing Guidelines. These guidelines do not allow jurists to take into account gender or whether or not a defendant is a single parent when handing down sentences (Pollock 2002). However, sentencing has not always been gender neutral. Prior to the 1970s, women were often given lighter or indeterminate sentencing due to the belief among many practitioners that women were more responsive to rehabilitation. In legal challenges to this practice the Court held that men and women could be sentenced differently on the basis of sex (*Kansas v. Heitman*, 1919). Subsequent cases rejected this rationale. The civil rights and feminists movement as well as new legislation attempted to eradicate sex-based discrimination. Several hypotheses have been developed to explain disparate sentencing of women and men. The *chivalry hypothesis* (an extension of paternalism) contends that male practitioners view women as less dangerous than men and as a result issue less severe sentences. The *evil woman hypothesis* takes the opposite approach and holds that male officials view women as more dangerous than men and consequently sentence them more harshly (Crew 1991; Morash and Schram 2002).

Demographics of Women Serving a Sentence

Racial disparities are apparent when examining the demographics of women in the correctional system. Nearly two-thirds of women on probation are white, while almost two-thirds of women confined to jails and prisons are minority. This statistics is staggering in light of the fact that minority women only make-up 26% of the U.S. population. We are seeing more Latino women facing incarceration, but there are some significant differences in their representation in state and federal facilities. In state prisons only one in seven women are Latino. However, under the jurisdiction of the federal correctional system, one in three female offenders are Latino (Greenfield and Snell 1999; Morash and Schram 2002).

In terms of family structure, only 17% of incarcerated women were married before being sentenced to prison, but 65% had children under the age of 18. Of those 65%, more than half were the primary care-givers for those children before incarceration. In situations where males are convicted of residential sentences, the mother usually already has custody, and the father's incarceration does not lead to the state guardianship. However, this situation is not often the case when women with children go to jail. About two-thirds of women incarcerated in the state system and half of those in the federal system lived with their young children before entering prison. Many of the children do not have another parent or family member to assume guardianship when their mothers go to prison. As a result, the rising rates of incarcerated women have had a severe impact on the American family (Greenfield and Snell 1999; Morash and Schram 2002; Pollock 2002).

Educational and employment demographics are bleak for female offenders. The large majority of women involved in the criminal justice system (incarcerated or on probation or parole) have at least graduated from high school or earned a GED. However, 7% have only completed up to an eighth-grade education. Data indicate that men had a much easier time securing employment at a livable wage. Economic circumstances are generally more difficult for women before entering prison than for men. Only 40% of women in the state prisons report that they were employed full-time before their arrests. Approximately 37% of women earned incomes of less than $600.00 a month before their arrest, and almost 30% of women had been receiving welfare assistance prior to incarceration (Greenfield and Snell 1999; Morash and Schram 2002; Pollock 2002).

Two background issues are prevalent among women in prison: the residual emotional effects of psychological and physical abuse, and addictions to alcohol and drugs. Nearly 60% of the women in state prisons were past victims of physical or sexual abuse, about one-third of women in prison had suffered abuse by intimates, and just below 25% reported prior abuse by a family member. Overall, physical or sexual abuse was reported by 44% of women under correctional authority and 69% of women who reported an assault stated that it occurred before age 18 (Greenfield and Snell 1999; Pollock 2002). Explorations of these childhood scars may provide some link to their offending behavior.

Many of the women in correctional facilities have serious substance-abuse problems. Approximately 50% of female offenders in state prisons reported that they were using drugs, alcohol, or both at the time they committed the offense for which they were incarcerated. Twenty-nine percent of the female offenders were under the influence of alcohol and 40% under the influence of drugs at the time the offense was committed. Nearly one-third of the women incarcerated in state prison said they committed the crime to get money to support a drug habit (Greenfeld and Snell 1999; Morash and Schram 2002).

CONCLUSION

Women have been playing an increasing role in the criminal justice system for more than a quarter of a century. Academics and practitioners alike should work toward reducing the number of women coming into contact with the criminal justice system as victims and offenders, while continuing to increase female representation as employees in the criminal justice system. Regardless of the progress women have made in terms of employment opportunities since the 1970s, they still continue to be underrepresented as criminal justice practitioners. This lack of representation can be partially explained by an organizational culture that views women less favorably than men. The criminal justice system, in particular correctional agencies, can be difficult, dreary work environments. In order to attract more women into careers as criminal justice practitioners, recruitment needs to be accelerated and retention issues addressed. Perhaps it is time to provide additional incentives through bonuses; part-time employment opportunities; and specialized, flexible training programs for women interested in this challenging and rewarding line of work. One example that agencies might look to as a model is the Part-time Special Agent Employment Program (PTAP) at the Federal Bureau of Investigation. This program allows men and women who cannot devote themselves full-time to a career the opportunity to pursue employment in federal law enforcement. This type of program may be especially attractive to women and may be a part of the solution necessary to increase female representation in the criminal justice system (for more information go to http://www.fbi.gov).

REFERENCES

ADLER, F. (1975). *Sisters in crime: The rise of the new female criminal.* New York: Free Press.

American Bar Association. (2003). A current glance at women in the law, 2003. Commission on Women in the Profession.

BACHMAN, R., AND L. E. SALTZMAN. (1995). *Violence against women: Estimates from the redesigned survey.* Bureau of Justice Statistics, U.S. Department of Justice.

BELKNAP, J. (2001). *The invisible woman: Gender, Crime, and Justice.* Belmont, CA: Wadsworth Thomson Learning.

Bureau of Justice Statistics. (1994). *Sourcebook of criminal justice statistics, 1994.*

Bureau of Justice Statistics. (1995). *Sourcebook of criminal justice statistics, 1995.*

Bureau of Justice Statistics. (2005a). *Crime characteristics.* U.S. Department of Justice, Office of Justice Programs.

Bureau of Justice Statistics (2005b). *State and local law enforcement statistics.* U.S. Department of Justice.

Bureau of Justice Statistics. (2005c). *Jail statistics.* U.S. Department of Justice, Office of Justice Programs.

Bureau of Labor Statistics. (1991). A report on the glass ceiling initiative. U.S. Department of Labor.

CHESNEY-LIND, M. (1997). *The female offender: Girls, women and crime.* Thousand Oaks, CA: Sage Publications.

CRAVEN, D. (1996). Female victims of violent crime. Bureau of Justice Statistics, U.S. Department of Justice.

CREW, K. B. (1991). Sex differences in criminal sentencing: Chivalry or patriarchy? *Justice Quarterly, 8*(62).

CURRIE, E. (1985). *Confronting crime: An American challenge*. New York: Pantheon.

DOERNER, W. G., AND S. P LAB. (2005). *Victimology*. Cinncinati: Anderson Publishing.

ELIAS, R. (2000). Historical treatment of victims. In *Encyclopedia of Women and Crime*, ed. N. H. Rafter. Phoenix: Oryx Press.

ELLIS, L. (1989). *Theories of rape*. New York: Hemisphere.

Federal Bureau of Investigation. (2004). Crime in the United States. U.S Department of Justice. Washington, DC.

FEINMAN, C. (1976). *Women's development unit project annual report, January 1, 1975 to April 9, 1976*. New York: NYC Correctional Institution for Women.

FEINMAN, C. (1994). *Women in the criminal justice system*. Westport, CT: Praeger.

GOWDY, V. B., T. CAIN, AND R. SUTTON (2003). *Women in criminal justice*. Hauppauge, NY: Novinka.

GRANA, S. J. (2002). *Women and (in) justice*. Boston: Allyn & Bacon.

GREENFIELD, L. A., AND T. L. SNELL. (1999). *Women offenders*. Bureau of Justice Statistics, U.S. Department of Justice.

HALE, D. C. (1992). Women in policing. In *What works in policing: Operations and administration examined*, ed. G.W. Cordner and D.C. Hale. Cincinnati: Anderson Publishing.

LAWSKY, S. B. (2000). A nineteenth amendment defense of the Violence Against Women Act. *Yale Law Journal, 109*, 783.

LONSWAY, K., M. MOORE, P. HARRINGTON, E. SMEAL, AND K. SPILLAR. (2003). *Retaining more women: The advantages to law enforcement agencies*. National Center for Women and Policing, A Division of the Feminist Majority Foundation.

MAGUIN, E., AND R. LOEBER. (1996). Academic performance and delinquency. Crime and Justice, 20, 145–264.

MARTIN, S. E. (1991). Effectiveness of affirmative action: The case of women in policing. *Justice Quarterly, 8*, 489–504.

MARTIN, S. E., AND N. C. JURIK. (1996). *Doing justice, doing gender: Women in law and criminal justice occupations*. Thousand Oaks, CA: Sage Publications.

MARTIN, D., AND M. LEVINE. (1991). Status of women in law enforcement. *Law Enforcement Technology, 18*, 26.

MCCOY, D. G. (1993). Women in law enforcement: A positive work environment. *Law Enforcement Tomorrow, 2*, 5–9.

MESSERSCHMIDT, J. W. (1993). *Masculinities and crime*. Lanham, MD: Rowman & Littlefield.

MORASH, M., AND P. J. SCHRAM. (2002). *The prison experience: Special issues of women in prison*. Prospect Heights, IL: Waveland Press, Inc.

NAFFINE, N. (1996). *Feminism and criminology*. Philadelphia: Temple University Press.

NYE, I. F. (1958). *Family relationships and delinquent behavior*. New York: Wiley.

POLLOCK, J. M. (2002). *Women, prison, and crime*. Belmont, CA: Wadsworth Thomson Learning.

REAVES, B. A., AND T. C. HART. (2001). *Federal law enforcement officers, 2000*. Bureau of Justice Statistics, U.S. Department of Justice.

REISS, A. J. (1951). Delinquency as the failure of personal and social controls. *American Sociological Review, 16*, 196–207.

RISON, R. (1994). Women as High-Security Officers. *Federal Prison Journal*. Bureau of Prisons: Washington, DC.

ROWAN, J. R. (1996). Female correctional officers said to reduce prison violence. *Criminal Justice Newsletter, 27*, 2–3.

SAMPSON, R., AND J. LAUB. (1990). Crime and deviance over the life course: The salience of adult social bonds. *American Sociological review, 55*, 609–627.

SAMPSON, R. J., AND J. H. LAUB. (1993). Turning points in the life course: Why change matters to the study of crime. *Criminology, 31*, 301–25.

SCULLY, D. (1990). *Understanding sexual violence*. Boston: Unwin Hyman.

SHERMAN, L. W., AND R. A. BERK. (1984). The specific deterrent effects of arrest for domestic assault. *American Sociological Review, 49*, 261–72.

SIMON, R. (1975). *Women and crime*. Lexington, MA: D. C. Heath.

SMART, C. (1982). The new female offender: Myth or reality? In *The Criminal Justice System and Women*, ed. B. R. Price AND N. J. Sokoloff. New York: Clark Boardman.

SNELL, T. L. (1994). *Women in prison*. Bureau of Justice Statistics, U.S. Department of Justice.

STEFFENSMEIER, D. (1980). Sex difference in patterns of adult crime, 1965–1977: A review and assessment. *Social Forces, 58*, 1080–1108.

STEFFENSMEIER, D., AND E. ALLAN. (1988). Sex disparities in arrests by residence, race, and age: An assessment of the gender convergence/crime hypothesis. *Justice Quarterly, 5*, 53–80.

STEFFENSMEIER, D., AND STREIFEL, C. (1992). Time-series analysis of the female percentage of arrests for property crimes, 1960–1985: A test of alternative explanations. *Justice Quarterly, 9*, 77–104.

Thomas, W. (1907) *Sex and Society: Studies in the social psychology of sex*. Chicago: University of Chicago Press.

Thomas, W. (1923). *The Unadjusted girl: With cases and standpoint for behavior analysis*. Boston: Little, Brown, and Co.

VAN WORMER, K. S., AND C. BARTOLLAS. (2000). *Women and the criminal justice system*. Boston: Allyn & Bacon.

WALKER, L. E. (1979). *The battered woman*. New York: Harper & Row.

8

Gays and Lesbians in the Criminal Justice System

Reid C. Toth

❖

CHAPTER OUTLINE

INTRODUCTION

In this chapter, issues and problems facing homosexuals as employees, victims, offenders, and inmates are examined. Like many of the racial and ethnic minorities, gays and lesbians are confronted with unique struggles at every stage of the criminal justice system. In particular they must confront rampant discrimination and hatred in many cases without the benefit of protective legislation. Sexual orientation is not included as a covered condition by the *Civil Rights Act,* the *Americans With Disabilities Act,* or the *Equal Rights Amendment.* Such conditions have allowed the environment of the criminal justice system to be unusually harsh for the gay employee, victim, or inmate.

EMPLOYEES

While the exact percentage of gays and lesbians employed as police officers is unknown, Arnott (1994) suggests that as a demographic reflection of society, the proportion can be expected to be approximately 10%. Following this logic, it may also be assumed that the employment rates of gays and lesbians in other areas of criminal justice are equally high. A review of the literature revealed few studies of gays in criminal justice areas other than policing. For that reason, the discussion on employment in this chapter will center on gays and lesbians who have entered into the profession as police officers. However, efforts are also made to peripherally address issues facing homosexuals employed in other forms of criminal justice work.

Lifestyle

The problem of ensuring quality policing in the gay community is a difficult one. It makes sense to have gay officers in such locations; yet hiring gay officers is difficult due to the unwillingness of the officers to be open about their sexuality (Barlow and Barlow 2000). Such openness is restricted as a reaction to the fear present in the gay community. The problem thus becomes self-perpetuating. In the United States, police agencies have historically been reluctant to hire gays despite the obvious benefits and have in some cases openly campaigned against the presence of homosexuals. For example, the Los Angeles Police Department (LAPD) issued a statement in a 1975 departmental memorandum that homosexuality was an automatic bar to be hired by the agency. The LAPD did not repeal such a discriminatory policy until 1991. In 1988, it was discovered that the LAPD required recent members of its academy class to list at least one member of the opposite sex with whom they had been romantically involved. Until 1991, the psychological exam administered to LAPD applicants contained questions inquiring into the applicant's attraction to members of the same sex. Other agencies also allowed discrimination against gays well into the 1980s and 1990s: the Atlanta Police Department was still openly rejecting candidates if background checks revealed homosexual tendencies in 1981; police officers in New Jersey could be fired for homosexuality until 1989; by 1991, the Chicago police department still did not have a single officer who was openly gay; until 1993 the Dallas Police Department refused to hire homosexuals, citing state law criminalizing such behavior; and as recently as 1992 the Federal Bureau of Investigation fired investigators who were discovered to be homosexual (Barlow and Barlow 2000).

The first major crack in the wall of discrimination came when Sergeant Charles Cochrane became the first serving police officer to publicly announce that he was gay. He did so while testifying before a New York City Council in favor of a gay rights bill (Barlow and Barlow 2000). Since his declaration, limited efforts have been made to actively recruit gay and lesbian police officers. As of 1992, only ten American cities had enacted policies aimed at recruiting homosexual individuals into police work (Arnott 1994). Some police departments have begun actively recruiting gay and lesbian officers as a result of better organization in the gay community and the resulting intense demands to end anti-gay discrimination. Other police departments are not so proactive, and have simply refrained from excluding applicants who are homosexual (Barlow and Barlow 2000).

Such efforts are limited because of the law enforcement communities' subscription to heterosexist society's blanket rejection and condemnation of the homosexual lifestyle (Barlow and Barlow). Given the environment, one may wonder why a homosexual would actively seek employment in criminal justice. Marcy L. Kahn, a New York State Supreme Court Justice, stated that she was drawn to the legal profession as a gay person because she felt that it would give her the best opportunity for protecting her own civil rights and the civil rights of others (Buhrke 1996). This same justification can be found in other arenas of criminal justice, where gays are drawn by their desire to make a difference in the gay community.

The majority of openly gay and lesbian officers are employed in the large urban police departments where they are more likely to be accepted and tolerated than in the smaller, more rural police agencies. However, even in the larger agencies, gay and lesbian police officers are often forced to live a double life, hiding their true sexual orientation from their fellow officers. The result is often great personal strain and pressure (Arnott 1994). Homosexual police officers that remain "in the closet" and lead a double life have high rates of suicide, alcoholism, and stress-related health problems (Arnott 1994).

As law officers, gays and lesbians have reported many shared life experiences, including:

- Living a double life
- Being expected to protect the identity of other gay and lesbian officers
- Being expected to perpetuate the myth of police as "straight" and loyal to each other
- Experiencing sophisticated and subtle forms of discrimination within the police department
- Becoming victims of slur campaigns such as accusations of being child molesters
- Enduring the stereotype that gays and lesbians are bound by a covenant of sex; it is the only thing held in common with other gays and lesbians (Arnott 1994).

Gay officers often report fear of being exposed and the potential for becoming victims of harassment and discrimination by fellow officers and supervisors. These officers have to be careful when socializing in the gay community while off-duty for fear of being stopped and identified by the police. Gay officers report avoiding taking any kind of police action, even when directly witnessing victimization, while in off-duty social circumstances that may reveal their sexual orientation. Much like the discrimination and harassment associated with having other police officers know their lifestyle, gay officers also fear ostracism from the gay community for being a police officer (Barlow and Barlow 2000).

Such ostracism is a direct result of the chronic victimization that the gay communities suffer directly at the hands of law enforcement.

Stress for gays in criminal justice lies not only in the negative reaction of the gay community, but also in the converse such as unwanted advances from other gays who are simply attracted to the uniform or power they perceive on behalf of the criminal justice employee (Buhrke 1996). Like many heterosexuals who experience being pursued because they are considered to be attractive or have exceptional bodies, homosexuals who attract potential mates because of the uniform often feel objectified. Leinen (1993, 1) quoted a gay police officer as stating "It's a big turn-on to people. They love it. They eat it up. The uniform, the authority, the image. You are on a very high pedestal as a rule. Guys like to say they went home and went to bed with a cop. That's hot. It's the fantasy thing to have a relationship, to have sex with a policeman."

Professionalism

Agency characteristics such as organization, power, and status appear to have an impact on the quality of life for a gay employee. Buhrke (1996) found that in terms of general organization, issues such as size, locale, number of openly lesbian and gay officers, and anti-discrimination policies all contributed to environments conducive to gay employees. The larger agencies seem to allow for more positive experiences. Likewise, agencies that were located in or near large gay communities such as San Francisco allowed for better quality of life for the gay officer. The presence of a large number of gay officers who are able to be open about their orientation is an indicator that hostilities toward gays within the agency are low. Finally, anti-discrimination policies are valuable as long as they are supported and enforced by the administration.

Status issues such as gender or race impact quality of life for gays in criminal justice agencies. On average, lesbians are subjected to less hostility than gay men. This may be due, in part, to the belief that lesbians are hyper-masculine and therefore conform to the image of a criminal justice employee as "macho," and that gay men are effeminate and weak. Lesbian relationships are frequently stereotyped by males as erotic, and gay men are considered to be HIV carriers. Like heterosexuals, minority individuals who least resemble the white, Anglo-Saxon, macho male image are more frequently targeted for anti-gay harassment (Buhrke 1996).

There is often an unwritten perception among police that homosexuals should conform themselves to heterosexual standards (Arnott 1994). Gays and lesbians who do not conform to this ideal may be subjected to harassment and torment unless they have been able to rebuke such actions in another manner. Buhrke (1996) determined that gay employees who exuded some form of power were less likely to be harassed. Power could come from many sources. Those employed at higher ranks or in positions of authority experienced less abuse. Personality could also serve as a source of power. Those employees who were open and confident about their orientation were more readily accepted by fellow officers. Such confidence may be related not only to internal belief systems, but also to feeling secure in an ability to find other suitable employment if necessary. These individuals are often less intimidated and therefore targeted less frequently for abuse and harassment (Buhrke). The ability of gay and lesbian officers to exert influence over police department policy is directly linked to their ability and willingness to become visible as members of the gay community (Barlow and Barlow 2000).

Much of the resentment toward gay and lesbian officers is fed not only by the fear that such officers may be carriers of HIV, but also the contemporary belief that such behavior is immoral and reprehensible. Such resentment can often be life-threatening as was the case of a gay Miami police officer whose calls for emergency backup were ignored by fellow officers on five separate occasions. Because the police occupation is populated overwhelmingly by men, which leads to issues concerning their perceptions of their own masculinity, the presence of a gay officer may be interpreted as a threat to the straight officer's masculine identity (Barlow and Barlow 2000). Given this threat, it is not surprising that lesbian officers are marginally more acceptable to the law enforcement community. It is not uncommon for the stereotype of a lesbian as being exceptionally masculine to contribute to the belief that lesbians in fact would make better officers than heterosexual women. The converse, however, is that gay male officers are less masculine and therefore less qualified for the job (Barlow and Barlow 2000).

Regardless of the size of the agency, the presence of policies concerning homosexuals, or the clandestine nature of a gay officer's lifestyle, many gays and lesbians are subjected to abuse when they become employed by the criminal justice system. Such harassment rarely has to do with how competent an employee is at their assigned tasks, or how discreet they are in their private lives. The following are examples of incidences of harassment experienced by gay or lesbian criminal justice employees:

- A jailer for a California Sheriff's Department, who was a known lesbian, was accused by an inmate of making sexual advances. As the jailer describes, she was assigned to the jail system after graduating the Academy. Her duties included housing, feeding, counseling, and disciplining female inmates. One inmate who was frequently disciplined by the deputy made the allegation that she had been sexually assaulted by the officer. Although eventually cleared, the deputy stated, "if I had been heterosexual, I don't even think there would have been an investigation" (Buhrke 1996, 138).

- A correctional officer for the Massachusetts Department of Corrections reported various incidents of harassment that he was subjected to by both inmates and other officers. ". . . this officer was telling the inmates to whip their dicks out at me; they took their penises out underneath their aprons. It was a big joke in the kitchen. I was humiliated. I'd be walking around the kitchen and the officer would say to an inmate, 'Show him.' He'd lift his apron, and there it was sticking out" (Buhrke 1996, 157). This particular officer was assigned to kitchen guard duty and felt that he was constrained in being able to carry out his duties. He avoided doing pat searches of inmates who left the kitchen to ensure that knives or other items weren't being stolen. This resulted from an accusation of the food service director that he had grabbed inmates inappropriately. He noted that some inmates were genuinely afraid to have him touch them. He also noted a serious decline in respect from the inmates after they witnessed the behavior of other correctional officers. "Inmates figured, 'If an officer is doing this to him, we can do it.' So inmates wouldn't respond to me; they would never listen to me" (Buhrke, 158).

- A lesbian dorm supervisor for the San Francisco Sheriff's Department described abuse she received from inmates while conducting strip searches during the intake process. Inmates made statements such as, "You god damn bull dyke; all you want to do is see me naked." The officer remembered thinking in response to such comments, "I hope I can hold my breath long enough so I don't have to smell this woman who's been living on the street for three weeks" (Buhrke 1996, 148). Ironically, this same officer believed that she received her job not in spite of her sexual orientation but because of it. The sheriff was actively recruiting in the gay community and she applied as a lesbian, and continued to declare herself a lesbian at every stage of the process. She believed that it was the sheriff's intention to have all aspects of San Francisco's communities represented including racial minorities and homosexuals (Buhrke 1996). The dorm supervisor also reported that inmates frequently attempted to use her sexuality as a power ploy. They might try flirtation to see if she would respond. Those inmates who considered themselves to be lesbians (not just "jailhouse lesbians") expected special treatment from her because they believed she should understand and empathize with them for any discrimination they had received (Buhrke).

- A gay shift lieutenant for the Massachusetts Department of Corrections indicated that his sexuality influenced his decision to become a correctional officer. "Subconsciously, I almost think it was buying insurance that I wasn't gay, because it was this macho job—'No fags are in there. I can play the role of the straight macho guy. Nobody'll ever suspect me.' Looking back on it I was big time into proving to myself that I wasn't gay" (Buhrke 1996, 165). This particular officer received very little harassment on the job. In fact, he was treated with respect for the most part after revealing his sexual orientation. He stated that even the inmates gave him a lot of respect for it. In fact, he believes that coming out contributed significantly to getting promoted (Buhrke 1996).

- A gay deputy director in the New York City Department of Correction described reactions of inmates to his sexuality. "Sometimes it would get violent. I've had inmates come into my office, stand in front of me, and flex their muscles. I pushed them out of my office, 'What the hell's the matter with you? Give that sex stuff to somebody else. That's not what I'm here for'" (Buhrke 1996, 173).

- A compound sergeant for the New Jersey Department of Corrections was openly lesbian. She recounts that when she was initially employed she was told, "If you want to get anywhere, you can't tell anybody you're a lesbian." Her response was, "I can't not tell anybody I'm a lesbian" (Buhrke 1996, 163).

It is the goal of various gay advocacy groups to see that homosexuals are eventually readily received in the criminal justice employment community. A 1995 study conducted by Commander Dan Watson of the Los Angeles Police Department in response to inquiries made by the Commission on Peace Officer Standards and Training identified ten theoretical events that would have the greatest impact on assimilation of openly gay and lesbian police officers into the law enforcement culture. In descending order these events were (Watson 1995, 16):

- Passage of domestic partnership law
- High ranking law enforcement officer identifies self as gay
- Cure for AIDS discovered

- Sexual orientation becomes protected under EEOC
- Military ends ban on homosexuality
- A church takes a stand supporting gays/lesbians
- Mandatory hiring goals for gay/lesbian officers
- Police union takes stand supporting gay officers
- Chief of Police participates in major gay event

Assimilation is important to the productivity of an agency. In environments where intolerance is the norm, efficiency is lost. In an effort to the loss of morale and productivity that can accompany an environment where homosexuality is not tolerated, police departments should: (a) realize the positive contributions made by gays and lesbians to the criminal justice system, (b) understand the unique professional experiences faced by gay and lesbian police officers, and (c) be aware of personal prejudices and stereotypes concerning gays and lesbians. Internally, police administrators should make certain changes to ensure a better environment for gay and lesbian officers (Arnott 1994, 227–28). These changes include

- developing a welcoming environment in which policies and procedures prohibit discrimination based on sexual orientation,
- holding supervisors accountable by demanding enforcement the nondiscriminatory policies and procedures,
- demonstrating administrative commitment to ensuring equal treatment for all officers,
- recruiting and training gay and lesbian officers,
- supporting gay and lesbian police officer organizations,
- forming task forces to open channels of communication between the gay and lesbian communities and the police departments,
- paying attention to public relations by ensuring that media representation reflects the welcoming environment,
- improving crime solving among the gay and lesbian community.

Some states are indeed making strides to ease the assimilation of gay officers. In response to a 1990 California state directive, the Commission on Peace Officer Standards and Training developed a cultural awareness curriculum for law enforcement. As part of this curriculum a *Sexual Orientation Training Course for Law Enforcement* was developed. The course had seven learning objectives: cultural awareness training guidelines, background of sexual orientation issues, legal issues, stereotypes, demographics and diversity, police points of contact, and community resources (Commission on Peace 1992). In many areas, gay advocacy groups are developing to help with the assimilation. For example, the Society of Law Officers (SOLO), based in San Diego, California, is a support group for gay and lesbian police officers in that area (Arnott 1994). Agencies are also beginning to see the benefit to having a contingent of gay officers. In areas where there is a large gay community, police leaders are finding it politically savvy to assign openly gay officers to cases of anti-gay victimization (Barlow and Barlow 2000).

VICTIMIZATION

Becoming a crime victim is one of the most significant issues facing the gay and lesbian community today. Studies show that the prevalence of victimization is already at an alarming proportion and that it is steadily increasing. In 1984, the National Gay and Lesbian Task Force (NGLTF) conducted the first study on anti-gay violence. They sampled 2,074 subjects, consisting of gay men and lesbians from eight cities including New York, Boston, St. Louis, Atlanta, Seattle, Los Angeles, and Dallas. The results indicated a 19% rate of physical assault, a 44% rate of threats of physical violence, and a 94% rate of victimization in general (including interpersonal as well as property victimization). Moreover, 92% of the subjects reported knowing another homosexual individual who had been victimized, and many subjects reported multiple victimizations. Other early studies have shown similar findings (Berrill 1992).

Jenness and Broad (1997) report four trends concerning anti-gay violence. First, it is the most common, visible, violent, and socially acceptable form of hate crime. Second, it is the fastest growing form of hate crime. Third, such violence involves a wide spectrum of offenders ranging from intimate partners to strangers, and in some cases includes whole institutions (e.g. state, religious, and medical organizations). The fourth trend suggests that anti-gay violence crosses ethnic and cultural boundaries that other crimes do not. For example, the majority of violent crime is intra-racial (i.e. victim and offender are the same race), but anti-gay crime is not necessarily limited to being committed by the same race offenders.

Anti-gay violence can often be explained (although not necessarily accepted) when homophobia considered as a motivating factor. Berrill (1991, 114) defines *homophobia* as "the long-standing persistent, and baseless notion that gay and lesbian people are sick, evil, predatory people who hate and fear the opposite sex and who molest children." Berrill further points out that homophobes equate gay people with their homosexuality, as if gays have no other dimensions. Sexuality is seen as only one aspect of a heterosexual's life, yet there is a perception that sexuality consumes a homosexual's life. Homophobes often hold gays responsible for three perceived threats to the American public: AIDS, pedophilia, and religious blasphemy (Perry 2000). AIDS, however, is less likely a cause of homophobia and anti-gay prejudice than it is a justification for these as pre-existing conditions. To support this, one must note the lack of hate-motivated violence against other groups considered to be at high risk for AIDS such as intravenous drug users. Berrill (1991, 113) suggests that the AIDS epidemic is closely tied to a second epidemic, "an epidemic of fear, hatred, discrimination and violence which is effecting [*sic*] both lesbians and gay men." Anti-gay prejudice certainly predated the AIDS epidemic, but it is Berrill's contention that AIDS inflamed such prejudice and provided fodder for those individuals who already hated gays and lesbians.

There is also a correlation between anti-gay violence and the presence of biblically supported anti-homosexual rhetoric. Perpetrators of anti-gay victimization often consider the victims to be an "abomination" as defined by the Biblical chapter of Leviticus, or as being unnatural and violators of God's law (Perry 2000).

Primary and Secondary Victimization

Berrill and Herek (1992) suggest that homosexuals may experience victimization in two ways. *Primary victimization* is the event of becoming the victim of a crime. *Secondary victimization* is the negative response from others, including family, friends, and colleagues, as a result of the victim's sexual orientation. This may come in the form of indifference, rejection, stigmatization, and outright discrimination. Secondary victimization is widespread and legally condoned. It has a significant impact on the ability of the victim to process and deal with the consequences of primary victimization.

In terms of primary victimization, homicides against gay males have been noted to be particularly brutal in nature. According to Berrill (1992), it is rare for a hate-motivated murder against a homosexual to be a simple gunshot wound. More often the victim has been repeatedly beaten, tortured, or disfigured in some way, seeming to suggest that the perpetrator was attempting to "rub out" all evidence of humanity in the victim due to their sexual orientation. "Approximately 70% of the gay homicides are characterized as overkill" (Bufkin 1999, 164).

Sexual assault is another prevalent form of primary victimization faced by homosexuals. In 1994, Hickson (in Hodge and Canter 1998) studied 930 adult homosexual males on the subject of nonconsensual sex. He found that 28% had been forced to have sex against their will at some point in their lives and 11% of the assaults involved more than one offender. The study also showed that a significant proportion of the attacks involved homosexually active perpetrators as well as victims. Unfortunately, sexual assault of gay men is often underreported and goes unrecognized by the public. This may be due to the public's resistance to accepting the notion that a crime has been committed when a male is sexually accosted.

There are several myths concerning sexual assaults of males. Many believe that males cannot be, or are rarely, the victims of sexual assault. Further, it is believed that males who have been assaulted were victimized while residing in same-sex correctional institutions. A third myth is that sexual assault of males is only committed by homosexual rapists who are targeting heterosexual men and boys. Another frequently held belief is that women are rarely the perpetrators of sexual assaults against men. Studies have shown that male victimization may account for anywhere between 5% and 10% of all sexual assaults. Stermac and Sheridan (1996, 63) examined 29 men who were victims of sexual assault or attempted sexual assault. They found that 86% had been assaulted by male perpetrators and that half of the male-on-male assaults were committed by someone known to the victim. In cases where females were the perpetrators, all of the victims knew their assailants. When strangers were involved, only a few of the assaults were characterized as anti-gay in nature. Most disturbingly, the majority of these victims were young gay men who had a physical or mental impairment. The varieties and prevalence of assault described by the victims in this study included:

- Touching and fondling (7%)
- Fellatio performed on the assailant (43%)
- Receptive anal intercourse (54%)
- Attempted intercourse (11%)
- Force vaginal intercourse with female perpetrators (7%)
- Unsure of method due to intoxication or incoherence (17%)

Stermac and Sheridan (1996) were unable to conclude, based on this study, that gay men were more likely than non-gay men to be sexually assaulted despite an indication of high prevalence of victimization in the former. As the researchers suggested, there are other factors that could explain the difference between the two groups. For instance, gay men may be more willing to report sexual assault than heterosexual men either because they wish to take advantage of victim's services or because they simply feel less stigmatized.

The NGLTF reported the following examples of other prevalent forms of primary victimization taken from its 1993 report of *Anti-Gay Violence and Victimization* (3):

- On January 7, a Latino woman leaving a Washington, D.C., gay bar was accosted by a man who crudely described how he would make her have sex with him. The man shot her point blank in the face, killing her.
- A teenager dragged a 55-year-old Vietnamese man to the rocks on Laguna Beach, California, kicked him with steel-toed boots and beat him unconscious on January 9. The teen admitted driving to Laguna Beach looking for gay people to harass.
- The Tampa, Florida home of a HIV-positive lesbian AIDS activist was burned to the ground on April 24, while she attended a national march for gay rights. The activist received numerous threatening phone calls prior to the arson.
- Oregon Citizens Alliance supporters distributed a flyer in the Salem, Oregon public library in early 1993 calling for the execution, castration, and imprisonment of lesbians and gay men. The flyer called on its readers to demonstrate their "love" for gay men by slashing their throats and bleeding them to death.
- Two men who admitted to stalking "faggots" shot a gay man and robbed him of his wallet when he stopped to help them dislodge their car in Wichita, Kansas, on January 12. The shooting left the man a quadriplegic.
- A man hiding in the back seat of a car forced a lesbian to drive to a field near Woodhaven, Michigan, and raped her on October 14. During the attack, the man said, "This should teach you not [sic] be a queer . . . It's wrong . . . This is what you need."
- Seventy skinheads and neo-Nazis held a rally called "Gay Bash '93" in a state park near New Hope, Pennsylvania, on November 6.
- Three men forced a gay man into a car at gun point in Tyler Texas, drove him ten miles away, and shot him at least 15 times, killing him on December 2. The three men boasted that they had assaulted and robbed several other gay men.
- A woman who dressed, acted, and talked like a man, and who dated women was murdered on December 31 in Humboldt, Nebraska. One of the men charged with her murder stripped her in public on December 24 to prove she was a woman, then kidnapped and raped her.

In addition to the types of brutal, stranger related attacks described above, gays and lesbians face the frequently undisclosed problem of domestic violence. Island and Letellier (1991) estimated that of America's 9.5 million adult gay men, as many as 500,000 are victims of domestic violence and an equal number are perpetrators. Gay men and lesbians in violent relationships are susceptible to the same deceptive cycle of violence as men and women in heterosexual relationships. Like battered heterosexuals, battered gays experience learned helplessness, fear retaliation for trying to leave, and are often hunted, followed, and attacked by their partners. Gays however have the added complications of homophobia, heterosexism, and ignorance in the general public to contend with. Such complications result in public attitudes such as "men are not victims," or "fights between men are normal and therefore not domestic violence" (Island and Lettelier 1991).

While the brutal nature of primary violence against homosexuals is appalling, it is even more appalling to realize that gays and lesbians are often victimized subsequently through secondary victimization. This victimization occurs after the initial crime and is a result of prejudice and bias often found among the homosexual's friends and family, as well as the criminal justice system. For example, in the courtroom, gays and lesbians are fearful of not receiving a fair or sympathetic hearing. Supporting this fear is the recent use of the "gay-panic" defense in which the perpetrators claim fear of being advanced upon by a homosexual as a mitigating factor in the commission of the crime (Perry 2000), there are also circumstances where victims find themselves blamed for the crime and experience indifference and prejudice from the prosecutors, judges, and juries. Berrill (1991) describes two instances in which judges exposed their own biases:

> In December 1988 a Dallas judge sentenced a defendant convicted of murdering two gay men to less than the maximum sentence of life in prison. In justifying the sentence, Judge Hampton stated, 'I put prostitutes and queers at the same level, and I would be hard put to give somebody life for killing a prostitute.' In another 1988 case involving the beating death of an Asian-American gay man, a Broward County Circuit Judge in Florida jokingly asked the prosecuting attorney, 'That's a crime now to beat up a homosexual?' When the prosecutor answered, 'Yes, sir. It's also a crime to kill them,' the judge replied, 'Times have really changed' (122).

The gay-panic defense has been employed by a number of assailants to absolve them of criminal responsibility when the crime involved a gay victim. This defense is a legal strategy akin to temporary insanity or diminished capacity in which the defendant claims to be the target of a homosexual advance by the victim. The defendant supposedly is so threatened that he strikes out violently against the victim either in self-defense or because he finds the overture so reprehensible that he loses all self-control. Some have suggested that the psychological basis for this behavior on the part of the defendant is a latent homosexual tendency or a homophobic reaction due to childhood homosexual abuse. In some cases, the jury has found a homosexual advance to be sufficient provocation for a violent reaction or loss of control, thereby mitigating murder to manslaughter. In other cases, juries have determined that the advance was sufficient to induce a psychotic episode, preventing the defendant from distinguishing right from wrong (Wall 2000).

The gay-panic defense is grounded in the myth that gay men are by nature sexual predators. This defense has been particularly successful when the victims are deceased and unable to refute accusations of aggression (Berrill 1991). Originally, gay panic was conceptualized by Dr. Edward J. Kempf, a psychiatrist, in 1920. "Kempf's Disease," as it became known, was described as "the sudden onset of 'feverish panic or agitated furor, amounting sometimes to temporary manic insanity, which breaks out when a repressed homosexual finds himself in a situation in which he can no longer pretend to be unaware of the threat of homosexual temptations'" (Wall 2000, 455). Despite its legal usefulness, gay panic has not been recognized by the psychological community since 1952 when it was eliminated from the DSM.

The following are significant legal cases utilizing the gay-panic defense (Wall 2000):

- **People v. Rodriquez** (1967): This was the first reported use of homosexual panic as a defense. The defendant employed an insanity defense in the murder of a victim whom the defendant claimed had come up behind him in an alley as the defendant was urinating and grabbed him. The defendant argued that he assaulted the victim out of "acute homosexual panic brought on him by the fear that the victim was molesting him sexually" (Wall 2000, 456). The jury convicted the defendant of second-degree murder.

- **Shick v. State** (1991): The judge instructed the jury to consider voluntary manslaughter in convicting the defendant who reacted violently after an alleged homosexual overture by the victim. Shick reportedly was hitchhiking after being stranded by his automobile when the victim offered him a ride. Shick, who was intoxicated, accepted. The two rode around looking for women with whom to engage in sex. When none were to be found, the victim supposedly offered to perform oral sex on the defendant. When the victim pulled down his pants and embraced Shick, the defendant reacted by violently beating the victim to death. Shick claimed that the advance caused him to lose all self-control. The jury heeded the judge's instructions and convicted Shick of voluntary manslaughter.

- **State v. Wallace** (2000): The defendant was convicted of manslaughter instead of first-degree murder based on his defense that the victim had groped him. The defendant claimed that he was urinating when the groping occurred and that he instantly reacted by turning and firing a gun. The jury accepted this despite the fact that the victim was shot in the back of the head and not at close range.

In some cases, the gay-panic defense has been unsuccessful. For example in the case of gay victim Matthew Shepard, the judge ruled that the gay-panic defense could not be used at trial because it was not supported by State law. In *Commonwealth v. Halbert* (1991) it was found by the court that the overture by a gay victim of placing his hand on the defendant's knee was not considered reasonable provocation. In 1987, a Pennsylvania jury rejected the gay-panic defense and sentenced Richard Laird and Frank Chester to death for the murder of Anthony Milano. This case was significant because it marked the first time that a maximum sentence had been given for a crime that was clearly antigay in motivation (Rosaga 2000). There have not yet been any cases where a female defendant employed a gay-panic defense, nor has there been a case where a homosexual defendant used a "straight-panic" defense in response to a heterosexual overture. Despite the fact that the gay-panic defense does not always result in acquittal, legal experts contend that openly discussing the homosexuality of the victim in court may prejudice juries in unforeseen ways (Wall 2000).

Defense attorneys use several arguments to justify the use of the gay-panic defense. They argue that in many cases it is the only defense available to the defendant and that the defendant should not be denied using a provocation argument to mitigate criminal responsibility. They also argue that since an intimidating sexual advance could conjure memories of previous sexual abuse, the defendant may legitimately believe his life was in danger because of his past experiences. A third argument for the gay-panic defense is that the defendant's ability to understand and perceive reality under certain circumstances could place in doubt his ability to form criminal intent. Additionally, defense attorneys argue that juries are more likely to be sympathetic to defendants who have killed because of confusion and rage during a homosexual attack than those who claim to simply be unable to control their violent tendencies. A final argument is that since men are more likely to be violent than women, the gay-panic defense should be allowed because it highlights the male-oriented nature of the crime (Wall 2000).

Arguments against the use of the gay-panic defense begin with the theory that it exploits homophobia that may be present among jury members or judges. In such cases the jury may blame the victim for his sexual orientation, or a judge may allow the gay-panic defense hoping that it will negatively bias the jury toward the victim. Second, this defense essentially places the victim on trial, and may encourage the jury to ignore the rules of self-defense. Finally, this defense reinforces crimes against gays and lesbians rather than encouraging, through the judicial system, tolerance, and self-restraint (Wall 2000).

Victim Characteristics

The NGLTF (1994) noted that as of 1993, anti-gay violence was widespread against racial minorities, women, Jews, and the disabled. Studies of anti-gay violence that have included race or ethnicity as a variable have shown that minority individuals among both gay men and lesbians are more likely to experience violent victimization. In particular, African Americans and Hispanics who are homosexual are most likely to be victimized. This may be explained by the compounding effects of a higher risk for victimization because of sexual orientation and a higher risk for victimization due to their minority status in general (Berrill 1992).

Waldner-Haugrud et al. (1997) studied gender differences in victimization among 283 gays and lesbians. They found that 47.5% had been victimized by a same-sex partner compared to 29.7% of gays. Lesbians also had a higher overall perpetration rate, 38%, compared to 21.8% for gay men. Lesbians were more likely to be classified as victims and perpetrators of violence, to report pushing or being pushed, and to have experienced a greater variety of victimization tactics. Berrill (1992) suggests four reasons for the variation in victimization rates between gay males and lesbians: (1) on average, American men are more likely to be victims of violent crime than American women; (2) gay men tend to have a higher visibility than do lesbians because of the greater number of establishments such as gay bars and bath houses which cater to gay men, increasing their vulnerability of gay men; (3) gay men often discover their sexual orientation earlier than lesbians, implying that the longer period of time a person has been "outed," the greater the likelihood of victimization; and (4) lesbians are more likely to modify their behavior out of fear for their personal safety, thereby reducing the opportunities for victimization.

Perpetrators of Anti-Gay Crime

Studies suggest that the "typical" perpetrators against gay individuals are young males who are strangers to the victim and who are often acting in accordance with other young males (Berrill 1992). For example, the NGLTF found that homosexuals were victimized 48% of the time by multiple attackers. They report that there is an average of 1.47 attackers for every victim (Bufkin 1999). One such group reportedly organized for the specific purpose of attacking homosexuals is the "Blue Boys." Collins (Bufkin 1996, 161) quotes a group leader's description of the group:

> The Blue Boys are real men. . . . Blue Boys are male. We're heroes. We have wives and girlfriends. We're out fucking chicks every night. . . . We chose blue baseball bats because it's the color of the boy. The man is one gender. He is not female. It is male. There is no confusion. Blue is the color of men, and that's the color the men use to defeat the anti-male, which is queer.

In general, organized hate groups do not seem to be a major source of crime committed against homosexuals. However, rhetoric espoused by these groups may influence and encourage individuals to commit such crimes. While not prominent, hate group actions against gays and lesbians is on the increase. The Skinhead movement seems to be responsible for the majority of these incidents (Berrill 1992).

Police response has been a problem in preventing anti-gay crime, and in some cases the police are perpetrators. The gay community is paradoxically both under-policed and over-policed. It is under-policed in the sense that victimization of gays is often not responded to immediately or seriously; yet it is over-policed in the sense that the police often target homosexuals for arrest on minor infractions. There have been many documented cases of police becoming perpetrators of crime and harassment against homosexuals. Such cases include incidents of physical abuse, blackmail, entrapment, unequal enforcement of the law, and failure to respond fully to cases of anti-gay violence (Berrill 1992).

Police abuse was the cause for the most notorious act of the gay movement. Known as the "Stonewall Rebellion," it ensured that the gay cause of protected civil liberties would continue to escalate as a public issue. Stonewall Inn was a popular gay and lesbian hangout throughout the 1960s. Due to frequent police raids and harassment, the Stonewall Inn had implemented a flashing light system at the door to warn patrons of individuals entering the premises that might be police officers. When the light flashed, the patrons would cease dancing. On June 27, 1969, the police arrived at the Stonewall Inn with a warrant for liquor violations. Some patrons were allowed to leave, while others were taken to the police station for interrogation. As police loaded patrons into vans, a gathering crowd began to pelt officers with beer cans and bottles. The police fled for cover to the bar and waited for reinforcements. The environment outside escalated to full scale rioting that continued for several nights. It was estimated that more than 2,000 people participated on the behalf of the gay patrons (Buhrke 1996).

Settings of Anti-Gay Crime

According to Harry (1992), a homosexual is most likely to experience victimization when the following elements are present: (a) an obvious departure from heterosexually defined gender roles, (b) groups of immature males who have deviated from strict adhesion to typical moral standards, and (c) opportunities for gay bashing, particularly districts defined as gay neighborhoods or hangouts.

Aside from crimes committed on the street, homosexuals frequently experience victimization in schools, homes, and prisons. In 1990, an NGLTF study of 40 colleges reported 1329 reported cases of anti-gay incidents. Ranges of 16% to 41% of study respondents have reported being victimized in their homes by relatives. In 1987, a 4-year-old Chicago boy was burned, stuck with pins, beaten, scalded, starved, gagged, and hung upside down for hours by his mother and her boyfriend because they judged him to be effeminate. The boy was eventually beaten to death. The boy's brother also experienced similar torture but survived (Berrill 1992).

Individuals who live in an area defined as a "gay neighborhood" are more likely to be victimized than those who reside in other areas. Presumably this is because there are greater opportunities for perpetrators to find targets for their crimes in areas where the ratio of gay residents is higher. However, simply living in a gay-defined district does not alone mean that one will be victimized. Even within these quarters, victims generally attract the attention of perpetrators by conforming to that individual's perception of a gay man or lesbian. Those persons who are effeminate or hyper-masculine in appearance are more than twice as likely as other homosexuals to experience victimization (Harry 1992).

Responses to Anti-Gay Crime

In response to anti-gay crime, Berrill and Herek (1992) suggest that criminal justice agencies (1) enact policies that stringently assert to officers that such victimization is a crime and should be treated as such, (2) respond vigorously to incidents of anti-gay crime; (3) develop procedures to train officers in the recognition of and response to hate crimes; (4) coordinate with community organizations in effort to prevent anti-gay crime; (5) closely monitor incidents that have possible hate undertones in an effort to thwart further violence; (6) deploy additional officers in areas where hate-crimes are concentrated; and (7) establish special task units to cope with areas where hate epidemics seem to be present. Hamner (1992) suggested that removing lesbians and gay men as an out-group from heterosexual society would be an effective strategy for preventing victimization. This would require changing the negative stereotypes against homosexuals by the general heterosexual public.

Anti-gay violence has resulted in the establishment of hundreds of gay and lesbian advocacy groups, community centers, and antiviolence projects. The presence of such groups, and the high visibility that they have brought to violence against gays and lesbians, has been largely responsible for the categorization of such acts as hate crimes (Jenness and Broad 1997). Regardless of size and funding, there are two primary reasons for the appearance of gay and lesbian advocacy groups: (1) they are founded in response to a specific hate crime incident in the community which implied that such anti-gay sentiment was likely to erupt in other violent acts; or (2) they were founded because of a generalized awareness of the epidemic nature of violence against gays and lesbians (Jenness and Broad 1997).

Gay and lesbian advocacy groups were founded as early as the 1950s, with the Mattachine Society in 1950 and the Daughters of Bilitis in 1955. However, it was a full decade before gay and lesbian groups mobilized into a political movement to fight anti-gay acts and discrimination. From its beginnings, this movement sought to challenge the stereotype that homosexuality was an aberrant condition. Gradually the movement broadened this concept to include homosexuality as an acceptable alternative to heterosexually defined norms; an alternative that deserved equal acceptance and legal protection. As was to be expected, gay and lesbian groups were met with resistance on many fronts including institutional and legal ones. Twice, in 1976 and again in 1986, the United States Supreme Court ruled that state laws against homosexuality were Constitutional. Undaunted by such setbacks, the gay and lesbian movement has continued to push for civil liberties and legal protection for homosexuals resulting in the elimination of penalties against private sexual relationships in many states (Jenness and Broad 1997).

San Francisco has one of the largest and most well funded of the advocacy groups. Community United Against Violence (CUAV) responds to anti-gay violence by offering services to victims of such crimes. It was founded in 1979 as a response to the increase of violent crime against gays and lesbians. New York City also founded an advocacy group in 1980. Similar to the motivation of CUAV, the New York City Gay and Lesbian Anti-Violence Project was established in response to an increase in anti-gay crime and the perceived failure of the criminal justice community to act. It provides various services to victims including information and referrals, counseling, and advocacy. Victims range from survivors of homosexual domestic violence to sexual assault and other bias-motivated crimes. The New York City project also documents these acts and uses this information to educate the public. It is their hope that education of the public will reduce intolerance of the gay lifestyle and indifference to anti-gay crimes. CUAV and the New York City Gay and Lesbian Anti-Violence Project are atypical, however, of most advocacy groups. The great majority of these organizations are small, community-based, staffed solely by volunteers, and supported by private donations (Jenness and Broad 1997).

Noticeably absent from the gay and lesbian advocacy movement are the issues of race and religion. Jenness and Broad (1997) believe this is manifested in three ways. First, very few, if any, gay advocacy groups identify themselves as being advocates for minority gays and lesbians. Second, although these groups are addressing a type of hate crime, they rarely take stances on other types of hate crimes such as racism or anti-Semitism. Third, very few of these organizations aim their message specifically at minority gays and lesbians. The result is that, throughout the history of the gay and lesbian movement, the participants have been primarily white. This can be a problem because studies have shown that gays and lesbians of color are at increased risk for violent victimization.

The most prevalent activity by advocacy groups aimed at combating anti-gay crime is the collection and documentation of anti-gay episodes of violence. These efforts are generally made with the intention of challenging official law enforcement reports and legislative findings. Advocacy groups often distribute their own findings to police, government officials, the gay community, and the general public. They release such information either by publicizing statistics through independently produced press kits, annual reports, flyers, pamphlets, and books; or they report their findings to the NGLTF which compiles statistics from different communities and produces a national report similar to the Federal Bureau of Investigation's (FBI) Uniform Crime reports (UCR) (Jenness and Broad 1997).

The following describes the mission of the National Gay and Lesbian Task Force:

> Founded in 1973, the NGLTF is a civil rights organization dedicated to building a movement to promote freedom and full equality for all lesbians and gay men. The Task Force exists to eradicate anti-gay prejudice, discrimination, and violence; advocate on behalf of lesbian and gay people regarding major health issues, including AIDS; and serve its 32,000 members in a manner that affirms and reflects the diversity of gay and lesbian communities. The NGLTF Policy Institute houses the Task Force's educational and organizing programs, including the Anti-Violence Project. The Anti-Violence Project was initiated in 1982 to promote an appropriate official response to anti0gay violence, improve the treatment of lesbians and gay men by the criminal justice system, and assist local communities in organizing against prejudice and violence (NGLTF 1994, i).

OFFENDERS

Statutorily Prohibited Behavior

Much of the "crime" committed by homosexuals is less likely to be typical of street crime than it is to be behavior unique to gays and lesbians that has been outlawed by statute. Many states have statutes restricting the freedom of gays and lesbians. The punishments range from life imprisonment to fines. In the South, the practice of "buggery" (anal intercourse) may result in life imprisonment. In Massachusetts, homosexual activity is punishable by 20 years incarceration. Until the early 1960s, all states prohibited same sex relations. Presently 20 states still outlaw homosexuality. Prosecution under these statutes is rare, but their presence nevertheless serves to marginalize and stigmatize the gay community (Perry 2000). During 1971, 110 men were sentenced for "sodomy and oral copulation" in the United States. The sentences ranged from 15 years to life (Buhrke 1996).

The first state to repeal a sodomy law was Illinois when it adopted the Model Penal Code in 1961, decriminalizing private consensual acts such as adultery, fornication, and sodomy. This sparked a trend as other states throughout the 1960s and 1970s altered laws by dropping or lightening penalties for consensual private sex acts. However, from the mid-1970s through the 1980s a backlash occurred during which some states, while decriminalizing sodomy for opposite sex partners, enacted new statutes criminalizing homosexual sodomy. This backlash may be in part explained by the new growth and visibility of the gay community (Eskridge and Hunter 1997).

The federal courts addressed the issue of homosexuality in the case of *Bowers v. Hardwick* (1986). The U.S. Supreme Court failed to overturn state statutes that made sodomy a criminal offense. They further upheld that even in the privacy of consenting adults, intercourse between two men is illegal (Arnott 1994). In this case, an Atlanta police officer followed Hardwick to his home in an attempt to issue a warrant on an unrelated charge. A third party allowed the officer to enter Hardwick's home. When the officer entered a bedroom he observed Hardwick engaging in sodomy with another male (Wallace and Roberson 2001).

While gays are rarely subjected to legal prosecution under sodomy statutes, they are still harassed by law enforcement that zealously pursues enforcement of sexual solicitation laws. Since soliciting sex is illegal, police may frequent gay bars and cruising areas looking for individuals seeking homosexual activity. It is not necessary that this activity be commercial (i.e. prostitution) in order to be criminal (Perry 2000). Vice squads have been reported to use entrapment methods because they are confident that their authority will not be challenged. They are frequently correct in this belief. Many gay men and lesbians plead guilty to such charges, even when there is a clear lack of sufficient evidence, just to avoid additional public exposure (Buhrke 1996). Reportedly, Miami policemen were at one time entrapping gay men who violated statutes against lascivious behavior by pretending to engage in oral sex with each other, inviting gay men to join them, and then arresting them for lewd behavior (Buhrke).

In some states, the tide of legal intolerance against homosexuals seems to be turning. In July 2000, Vermont became the first state to legalize marriage-like civil unions (known as "CUs") of gay and lesbian couples. Carolyn Conrad and Kathleen Peterson of Brattleboro, Vermont, waited at the town clerk's office at midnight to fill out the paperwork. They became the first lesbians in the country to be civilly united when they exchanged vows before a justice of the peace and a crowd full of supporters. Only a handful of protesters were present (Goldberg 2000).

Criminal Conduct

Like the criminality of other minorities, crimes committed by homosexuals are not exclusively confined to statutorily prohibited consensual behavior. Homosexual crime is particularly high profile when it involves sex offenses. Walsh (1994) asserts that sex offenders are the most detested form of criminal, especially when they have committed crimes against children. The public's revulsion is further compounded when the offender is homosexual or has committed the crime against a child of the same sex. Outrage is particularly heightened when the child is male. In the eyes of the public, the homosexual child molester is deviant on three levels. First, the offender has broken the public taboo against homosexuality. Second, by inference, the offender has committed the offense against the wishes of the victim. Finally, the offender has chosen a victim who is of an inappropriate age. According to Horowitz and Willging (in Walsh), judges tend to hold attitudes and values that mirror those of mainstream society. Therefore it can be assumed that American courts reflect the same social rejection and revulsion of homosexual child molesters as does the general public. Given this atmosphere, it is not surprising that homosexual child molesters are 6.79 times more likely to be imprisoned than their heterosexual counterparts.

Walsh (1994) conducted a study of 255 convicted male sex offenders who had chosen children as their victims. He concluded that homosexual child molesters received harsher legal sanctions, and that these sanctions could be directly related to the homosexual status of the offender. This conclusion was based on the lack of influence from mitigating factors that typically resulted in lesser punishments for heterosexuals. The homosexuals in the study scored significantly higher on virtually all variables believed to be mitigating in nature when present in other cases. They were of a higher SES; they had higher IQs, they were less likely to have forced their victims or used coercion; they were less likely to have engaged in extended sexual activity with the victim; they were more likely to have cooperating victims; and they were more likely to have fully accepted responsibility for their actions. This last factor is particularly significant because Traver (in Walsh) noted that sex offenders were more likely to receive probation recommendations from probation officers if they accepted fully responsibility for their actions. The admittance of culpability is also frequently viewed by the court as evidence of remorse for the crime. According to Walsh, 40% of his homosexual offenders accepted complete blame compared to 25% of heterosexual offenders. Yet the expected mitigating effect of these admissions is not present for the homosexual offenders. McCaghy (in Walsh 1994) reasoned that the willingness of homosexual offenders to take responsibility for the actions was connected to the notion that by being homosexual, that had already come to accept themselves as a deviant in the eyes of the general society. This prior acceptance may have an impact on their willingness to accept the second label of deviance as a child molester. To the contrary, heterosexual child molesters are frequently in denial that they are anything but an upstanding citizen with an unsullied self-image (Walsh 1994).

In a 1998 study conducted by Blanchard and Dickey on homosexual and heterosexual child molesters, it was found that the homosexual offenders reached puberty on average at an earlier age than the heterosexual offenders. This included, in addition to physical advancement, experiencing their first orgasm, ejaculation, or sexual experience. Mayer (1992) cites three studies documenting the prevalence and characteristics of women sex offenders in which it was found that homosexual abuse was not uncommon. In one of the studies, 60% of the female subjects had molested their daughters. In two others, it was found that the majority of offenses included homosexual assault. Mayer suggests that a reasonable conclusion based on previous studies as well as her own is that some females who molest children are latent homosexuals who have not accepted their true sexual orientation. These types of offenders may use overly nurturing and affectionate parenting, or what Mayer refers to as "pseudo-incest" to satisfy their homosexual impulses.

As previously discussed in this chapter, domestic violence is a problem in many homosexual relationships, especially those involving lesbians. Data on lesbian batterers is difficult to obtain because (a) the victims are more likely to reach out for help or services than the batterer themselves and (b) the lesbian community has focused its attention on the victims, rather than spotlighting the aggressors (Margolies and Leeder 1995). While the public has welcomed the establishment of treatment for abusive male spouses or partners, there are few studies or services for lesbian batterers. A lesbian who is physically abusive in one relationship is likely to be abusive in successive relationships unless treatment is sought. Margolies and Leeder suggest that lesbian batterers are usually female survivors of childhood family violence but have broken the norm of the compliant victim. All of the batterers in Margolies' and Leeder's study had a family history of violence. Seventy percent had been child victims of sexual abuse, 65% experienced physical or verbal abuse, and virtually all of them witnessed abuse from their father or stepfather directed at their mother.

While lesbian batterers share some similarities with male heterosexual batterers and women who have survived abuse, they are also different in significant ways. For instance, gender is not an issue between same sex partners which brings to light the issue of power. Because the batterer is both a woman and a lesbian, she has significantly less power in society than the heterosexual male batterer. The partners in an abusive lesbian relationship are already social outcasts who may have experienced discrimination and homophobia. The internalization of these experiences can cause and maintain the violence present in the relationship (Margolies and Leeder 1995). Lesbian batterers are driven by an intense emotional need for constant attention and emotional involvement from their partners. This dependence may become a source of anger in and of itself. They may feel controlled by the partner's influence on their emotional state which at times results in a dependent rage. In some occasions when the batterer is feeling deprived of attention, they engage in violence to reestablish an intense connection with their partner. Ironically, they used violence to induce closeness and intimacy (Margolies and Leeder 1995).

INMATES

Males

It is an American stereotype that homosexual rape is rampant in male correctional institutions. Like most stereotypes, there is a bit of truth and a lot of fiction to this standard. In prison, inmates who are homosexual or perceived to be homosexual by other inmates are significantly more likely to be sexually assaulted. The assailant is most likely to consider himself to be heterosexual. Other commonly reported incidents include "wide-spread beatings, rapes, verbal harassment, and other abuse of those who are gay or HIV-positive, or perceived to be so. The consequence for many gay inmates is unrelenting fear, isolation, humiliation, and violence. Moreover, such attacks are often ignored and even encouraged by prison officials" (Berrill 1992, 35). The following are a few examples of the difficulties faced by homosexual inmates:

- A gay deputy director in the New York City Department of Correction states his position on gay inmates. "I always felt an affinity toward the gay inmates. Gay male inmates are looked at as clowns, comic relief, and objects of humor. They're not looked at as though they have special counseling needs" (Buhrke 1996, 171).
- In Washington, D.C., a lesbian inmate was placed in administrative segregation for 62 days. The Department of Corrections stated that the isolation was necessary to ensure that the inmates understood that homosexual behavior would not be tolerated (NGLTF 1994).
- In 1993, a Vacaville, California, corrections officer allegedly raped a gay inmate, The inmate received no response from prison officials after reporting the incident (NGLTF 1994).

There are strong inconsistencies in the research literature concerning prevalence of consensual homosexual activity in male prisons. For example, Nacci and Kane conducted a study in 1983 on 330 federal inmates' sexual behavior and found that 30% reported engaging in some form of consensual homosexual relations (in Hensley 2001). Tewksbury found that 19.4% of 150 male inmates in Ohio engaged in consensual homosexual activity during the previous year (in Hensley). In studying 101 inmates in Delaware, Saum found that only 2% engaged in consensual homosexual activity (in Hensley). One explanation for the disparity between the studies is that many inmates may choose not to report homosexual activity for fear of being seen as weak by other inmates. One conclusion, however, that is consistently supported in the literature is that inmates who consider themselves to be homosexual in orientation prior to incarceration also engage in homosexual activity during incarceration (Hensley 2001).

The research literature on homosexuality provides discussion on two theories of origin. The importation model is based on the theory that homosexuality in prison is condoned and accepted by the inmates because they are more likely to come from subcultures in society that are more likely to accept homosexuality than other subcultures. Therefore, the inmates "import" attitudes of acceptance when they enter the institution. A second model theorized that sexual behavior in prison is a result of the unnatural circumstances of a unisexual environment and the inevitable sexual deprivation. The deprivation model asserts that inmates develop social structures to alleviate the "pains" associated with such isolation. In other words, inmates have a choice of celibacy or homosexuality. Many inmates find celibacy to be the least desirable of the two (Eigenberg 1992).

Eigenberg (1992) distinguished between two broad categories of homosexual inmates: those inmates who are true homosexuals (i.e. they were homosexual prior to being incarcerated) and those inmates who are situational homosexuals (i.e. men who engage in homosexual act due to heterosexual deprivation). The literature indicates that true homosexuals, or "fags" in prison jargon, are more likely to play the "passive" or "female" role as inmates, and will choose to do so even if women are available. Situational homosexuals, also referred to in prison lingo as "punks," are held in more contempt than true homosexual by the other inmates. This is because the punks are believed to have caved into pressure and sacrificed their masculinity. Therefore they are seen as cowardly and weak. Other inmates consider punks to be men who have been turned into women by a forced act of submission. Fags on the other hand are less despised because they have chosen the lifestyle rather than being forced to assume it (Eigenberg 1992).

Situational homosexuals assume various roles within prison. Some are known as "canteen punks" and are latent homosexuals who provide sexual relief for other inmates who have been unsuccessful at attracting a "queen" or in coercing a weaker inmate into participating without payment. New inmates are often approached sexually after having been "seduced" with offers of protection, loans, or gifts. These new inmates will find themselves threatened with physical violence if the loans are gifts are not repaid. Such violence will likely be of a sexual nature. Feeling they have no choice and that a sexual encounter is inevitable, the new inmate becomes a canteen punk (i.e. one that can be purchased) by accepting the gifts in return for the sexual favors. Inmates who commit forcible rape are also considered situational homosexuals and are known as "wolves," "jockers," or "voluntary aggressors." Unlike other situational homosexuals however, wolves are not considered to have lessened their masculinity because they are performing the "male" role during the sex act, and they have initiated and controlled the encounter. To summarize, there are three roles for situational homosexuals: rape victims, prostitutes, and rapists (Eigenberg 1992).

Females

Fishbein (2000) makes a distinction between sexual relationships in men's and women's prisons. Women are more likely to have familial type relationships, while men use homosexuality to establish dominance, manifest aggressive tendencies, gain economically, and provide a sexual outlet. It has been determined that only a small proportion of women actually commit to homosexuality as a lifestyle.

Empirical evidence suggests that lesbianism and unusual masculinity are present at a higher rate among incarcerated women than those in the general population. Fishbein (2000) found that lesbian detainees were more masculine, were more hostile, and had experienced more physical child abuse than heterosexual detainees. Although it was not found that lesbians committed more violent crimes, it was determined that they are often incarcerated for longer periods of time and in general treated more harshly by the criminal justice system. One explanation for this may be that hyper-masculine lesbians tend to be treated more like males in the criminal justice system. Since male offenders typically receive longer sentences than females for the same offense, the hyper-masculine lesbian may experience the same bias. Fishbein also makes the suggestion that since many of the lesbian subjects in her study reported a higher rate of hostility and anger than the non-lesbian subjects, the longer sentences may be a result of a negative reaction by judges, police, and other criminal justice personnel to the hostile demeanor.

Kathryn Ann Farr (2000, 57) examined 35 case studies of women on death row. She found that hyper-masculine or those who met the "butch" stereotype of lesbians, were over-represented in a typical death row case. She argued that such offenders were portrayed during their trials as being man-haters with an irrational rage and desire for revenge through murder, and that the homosexual perception became an "aggravating circumstance" for the jury or judge when considering the death sentence. She gives the example of a case in which a lesbian was sentenced to death for killing her 3-year-old son, despite the fact that similar cases involving heterosexual mother or fathers rarely resulted in a sentence of death. She provided the following summary of the case (reported verbatim; all emphasis, punctuation, and insertions are part of the original text):

> Case #2. Sentenced to death in April of 1992 for the murder of her three-year-old son, the defendant in Case #2 was the only woman on death row in 1993 for having murdered her child by abuse. The identification of the child's mother, a Cuban immigrant, as his killer, and the news that she was a lesbian whose lover was also implicated in the crime, fueled the public fire. The defendant's lover testified against her in exchange for a plea agreement (a guilty plea to the charge of second-degree murder and child abuse) in regard to her own involvement in the murder. The prosecutor made routine references to the defendant's lesbianism, arguing at one point that it should be considered as an "aggravating circumstance" (Brownworth, 1992b), and, at another time, that the lovers hated the victim because he was male (Anderson, 1996). Additionally, the press provided the public with courtroom representations of the defendant's deviance, such as a prosecutor's description of her as "a cocaine-addicted mother who neglected and repeatedly abused [the victim] before killing him with a baseball bat" (*Sun Sentinel*, 1992, p. 3b). Her volatile courtroom behavior upon hearing her sentence was also widely reported. For example, the *Sacramento Bee* (1992) stated that "[the defendant] shouted hysterically in Spanish at [the judge] after he announced the sentence" (p. A10). And, reporter Yanez (1992) wrote that "[the defendant] shook visibly in her seat as [the judge] pronounced the death sentence. She then jumped to her feet in a fit of fury. 'They call this justice?' she yelled" (p. 1B).

Propper (1997) examined homosexuality rates of juvenile females (ages 13–17) in seven correctional institutions. She found that 14% of those participating in the study considered themselves in a committed relationship with another female (referred to as "going with" or "being married"), 10% had engaged in passionate kissing, 10% had written love letters, and 7% had engaged in sexual contact beyond simple hugging or kissing. Given that several of the institutions were coed, Propper concluded that this study did not support the typical assessment of sexual deprivation as an explanation for the presence of homosexuality in confined settings.

The terms "lesbian" or "homosexual" are rarely used by incarcerated females to describe romantic or sexual encounters. Instead, jailhouse slang includes terms such as "girl-stuff," "playing," "the doll racket," "bull-dogging," "having people," "being together," "tying in," and "making it." The avoidance of formal labeling may serve the function of distinguishing erotic encounters in an incarcerated setting from a long-term, committed, homosexual relationship on the outside. Such encounters may include "having a close asexual friendship or make-believe family, an erotic emotional crush, limited physical contact such as light kissing, hand holding, or embracing, or overt sexual relations such as tongue kissing, fondling of breasts or genitals, tribadism, cunnilingus, or anilingus" (Propper 1997, 98). What is clear, however, is that by using informal or slang labeling, the female inmate is attempting to avoid a description that coincides with the more traditional lesbian relationships found in society.

CONCLUSION

The gay or lesbian faces unusual challenges when traversing through the criminal justice system. This is true whether they entered it voluntarily, as an employee, or involuntarily as a victim, offender, or inmate. Discrimination against homosexuals is presently at a level once experienced in the pre-civil rights era by racial minorities. The gay and lesbian movement is at an early stage, and its members are frequently confronted with the truth about the American justice system: it is a slow, rusty beast when change is afoot. The establishment of gay advocacy groups, and the resulting greater awareness of the public, will continue to impact the response of the criminal justice system. In the next chapter, the authors examine problems faced by the disabled as they navigate through the American system of justice; this group confronts many barriers similar to those encountered by gays and lesbians.

REFERENCES

ARNOTT, J. S. (1994). Gays and lesbians in the criminal justice system. In *Multicultural perspectives in criminal justice and criminology*, ed. J. E. Hendricks and B. Byers, Springfield, IL: Charles C. Thomas. Pp. 211–31.

ATLAS, R., AND R. DUNHAM. (1990). Are prisons any better? Twenty years of correctional philosophy, changes in Prison Facilities as a Function of Correctional Philosophy, Sage Criminal Justice System Annuals Publications, Sage, Beverly Hills, CA.

BARLOW, D. E., AND M. H. BARLOW. (2000). *Police in a multicultural society: An American story.* Prospect Heights, IL: Waveland.

BERRILL, K. T. (1991). Anti-gay violence: Causes, consequences, and responses. In *Bias crime: The law enforcement response*, ed. N. Taylor. Chicago: University of Illinois at Chicago.

BERRILL, K. T. (1992). Anti-gay violence and victimization in the United States: An overview. In *Hate crimes: Confronting violence against lesbians and gay men*, ed. G. M. Herek and K. T. Berrill. Newbury Park, CA: Sage. Pp. 19–45.

BERRILL, K. T., AND G. M. HEREK. (1992). Primary and secondary victimization in anti-gay hate crimes: Official response and public policy. In *Hate crimes: Confronting violence against lesbians and gay men*, ed. G. M. Herek and K. T. Berrill. Newbury Park, CA: Sage. Pp. 289–305.

BUFKIN, J. (1999). Bias crime as gendered behavior. *Social Justice, 26* (1), 155–176.

BUFKIN, J. L. (1999). Bias crime as gendered behavior. *Social Justice, 26* (1), 155–77.

BUHRKE, R. A. (1996). *A matter of justice: Lesbians and gay men in law enforcement.* London: Routledge.

Commission on Peace Officer Standards and Training. (1992). *Sexual orientation training course for law enforcement.* Sacramento: Author.

EIGENBERG, H. M. (1992). Homosexuality in male prisons: Demonstrating the need for a social constructionist approach. *Criminal Justice Review, 17*(2), 219–34.

ESKRIDGE, W. N., AND N. D. HUNTER. (1997). *Sexuality, gender, and the law.* Westbury, NY: Foundation Press.

FARR, K. A. (2000). Defeminizing and dehumanizing female murderers: Depictions of lesbians on death row. *Women and Criminal Justice, 11*(1), 49–66.

FISHBEIN, D. (2000). Sexual preference, crime, and punishment. *Women and Criminal Justice, 11* (2), 6–84.

GOLDBERG, C. (2000). Vermont law in effect; gay couples wed. *Sunday Star-News.* July 2. Wilmington, NC.

HAMNER (1992). Gay-Bashing: A social identity analysis of violence against lesbians and gay men. In *Hate crimes: Confronting violence against lesbians and gay men*, ed. Gregory M Herek and Kevin T Berrill. Pp. 179–190.

HARRY, J. (1992). Conceptualizing anti-gay violence. In *Hate crimes: Confronting violence against lesbians and gay men*, ed. G. M. Herek and K. T. Berrill. Newbury Park, CA: Sage. Pp. 113–22.

HENSLEY, C. (2001). Consensual homosexual activity in male prisons. *Corrections Compendium, 26*(1), 1–4.

HODGE, S., AND D. CANTER. (1998). Victims and perpetrators of male sexual assault. *Journal of Interpersonal Violence, 13*(2), 222–40.

ISLAND, D., AND P. LETELLIER. (1991). *Men who beat the men who love them: Battered gay men and domestic violence*. New York: Haworth Press.

JENNESS, V., AND K. BROAD. (1997). *Hate crimes: New social movements and the politics of violence*. New York: Aldine De Gruyter.

LEINEN, S. (1993). Gay cops. New Brunsick, NJ: Rutgers.

MARGOLIES, L., AND E. LEEDER. (1995). Violence at the door: Treatment of lesbian batterers. *Violence against women, 1*(2), 139–58.

MAYER, (1992). *Women sex offenders*. Holmes Beach, FL: Learning Publications.

National Gay and Lesbian Task Force. (1994). *Anti-gay/lesbian violence, victimization, and defamation in 1993*. Washington, DC: Author.

PERRY, B (2000). Perpetual outsiders: Criminal justice and the Asian American experience. In *Investigating difference: Human and cultural relations in criminal justice*, ed. Criminal Justice Collective of Northern Arizona University, Boston: Allyn & Bacon. Pp. 99–109.

PROPPER, A. M. (1997). Lesbians in female and coed correctional institutions. *Journal of Lesbian Studies, 1*(1), 97–107.

ROSAGA, A. (2000). Ritual killings: Antigay violence and reasonable justice. In *States of confinement: Policing, detention, and prisons*, ed. J. James, New York: St. Martin's. Pp. 172–88.

STERMAC, L., AND P. M. SHERIDAN. (1996). Sexual assault of adult males. *Journal of Interpersonal Violence, 11*(1), 52–65.

WALDNER–HAUGRUD, L. M., L. V. GRATCH, AND B. MAGRUDER. (1997). Victimization and perpetration rates of violence in gay and lesbian relationships: Gender issues. *Violence and Victims, 12* (2), 173–184.

WALL, B. W. (2000). Criminal responsibility, diminished capacity, and the gay panic defense. *Journal of the American Academy of Psychiatry and the Law, 28*(4), 454–59.

WALLACE, H., AND C. ROBERSON. (2001). *Principles of criminal law*. 2nd ed. Boston: Allyn & Bacon.

WALSH, A. (1994). Homosexual and heterosexual child molestation: Case characteristics and sentencing differentials. *International Journal of Offender Therapy and Comparative Criminology, 38* (4) 339–353.

WATSON, D. (1995). *Assimilation of openly gay and lesbian police officers into the law enforcement culture*. Sacramento: Commission on Peace Officer Standards and Training.

9

The Disabled and Physically Challenged in the Criminal Justice System

Reid C. Toth

❖

INTRODUCTION

Disabled individuals often have great difficulty when dealing with the criminal justice system. Unlike other types of discrimination, the barriers faced by the disabled are not usually tied to a "hate" ideology, but rather are the product of fear, ignorance, and apathy on the part of criminal justice agencies and the public. For instance, it may be considered reasonable by some to assume that a person who is legally blind cannot perform the duties of a law enforcement officer. It may also be believed that a wheelchair-bound person cannot commit a crime. It may be assumed that a deaf person would have no more trouble than the average convicted criminal when it comes to adjusting to prison life. It may be the public's perception that a victim who is disabled would receive the same services and attention as any other victim from the criminal justice system. All of these attitudes are in fact based on inaccurate perceptions of the disabled person. As will be discussed in this chapter, disabled people *are* capable of being employed as law enforcement or corrections officers; they *are* able to commit crimes just as serious as any other criminal; they *do* have a much more difficult time in prison; they *are* often ignored and mistreated as victims. Fortunately for the disabled person, federal legislation has been enacted with the intent of changing many of these misperceptions and preventing further discrimination. While not specifically written for the criminal justice system, such legislation has nonetheless been applied to cases of criminal justice employees, offenders, defendants, inmates, and victims. This chapter will examine in detail the problems and issues associated with being a disabled person involved with the criminal justice system. It is not reasonable to attempt a discussion of every single disability, so the authors have selected impairments that would, in combination, provide examples of the most common scenarios for the disabled individual. Specifically discussed are mental, visual, mobility, and hearing impairments, as well as the problem of HIV and AIDS. This chapter will begin with a general discussion of the centerpiece of the legal framework which impacts the criminal justice system as it relates to disabilities: *The Americans With Disabilities Act of 1990.*

The ADA and Its Impact on Criminal Justice

Accessibility   According to Schneid and Gaines, the ADA could be the most important legislation since the passage of the Civil Rights Act of 1964 in terms of affecting law enforcement. Although the ADA has "significant implications for the criminal justice system, law enforcement is mentioned only once in the legislative history of the ADA, and even that is only in reference to persons with a history of illegal drug use. Yet experts believe the impact on criminal justice has been major" (Rubin 1).

As Randall Atlas (1992, 1) stated, "the need for reasonable access is evidenced by the fact that one in five people in the United States will become disabled." Atlas (15) further stated that the ADA would profoundly affect correctional architecture and suggested that it would spark a "tremendous amount of legal action against building owners and public entities." The intent of the law was to create a non-discrimination policy in the built environment for people with disabilities (Atlas). However, despite the possible legal encounters, "application of the ADA to Criminal Justice facilities is particularly difficult and cumbersome because of the prime directive of security in the day-to-day operations" (Atlas 15). Smith and Alpert (1993, 554) reported that "In addition to the changes necessary to those portions of police facilities generally open to the public, law enforcement agencies have the additional concern of making lockup and other secure areas safe and accessible to disabled prisoners. Modifications also may be required for vehicles used to transport disabled persons."

Schneid and Gaines pointed out that under the ADA, police agencies, as well as all covered employers, will have to modify facilities so that disabled individuals can perform and participate in services. Although many criminal justice facilities may need little modification to come into compliance, others may need a considerable overhaul. Courthouses are a good example. Courthouses serve a wide variety of individuals who may be disabled and must be assured accessibility, including litigants, jurors, victims, witnesses, beneficiaries in probate proceedings, volunteers, social service workers, attorneys, judges, and court personnel (Wood 1990). However, courthouses throughout history have been designed with the image of strength and dignity in mind in an effort to pay reverence to the law. This has been reflected in features such as numerous steps, large columns, and heavy doors, all of which may impede accessibility (Wood 1990).

Aside from courthouses, accessibility in other aspects of the criminal justice system is equally questionable. As Long and Sapp (1992) pointed out, the state of programs and facilities in a state prison when accessibility for disabled inmates is an issue, is poor at best. Even in states where institutions are trying to accommodate and provide for disabled inmates, the results are often only marginally adequate. In no case has a state reported full accessibility for the disabled to programs and facilities (Long and Sapp 1991). Long and Sapp suggested, based on the results of their study, that the needs of physically disabled inmates are not being met by State level correctional facilities.

Atlas and Dunham (1990) suggested that a reason for the lack of attention given to disabled inmates is that humanitarian and rehabilitative concerns fall second to the primary need for security. This results in prison designs and architecture that do not consider the needs of physically disabled inmates (in Long and Sapp). Such arrangement of priorities can, however, result in an inexcusable denial of inmates and disabled individuals' rights. For example, one study (Wertlieb 1991) found a Texas prison where paralyzed inmates had been denied wheelchairs for mobility, and were literally left to crawl onto toilets. They had been completely denied any access to dining halls or other communal areas. In another situation, People, Inc., found that even when agencies for the disabled did exist, they often were reluctant or demonstrated outright refusal to serve offenders, particularly in residential programs (Wertlieb 1991).

The future for disabled persons in the criminal justice system is not entirely bleak. "States are beginning to develop new institutional and community programs for mentally retarded individuals who find themselves involved in the criminal justice system

(Wertlieb 1991, 343). Two examples of improved programs include the states of New York and South Carolina. New York has developed a "sensorially disabled unit" for housing hearing or visually impaired inmates. The general inmate population is not admitted to this unit, but the disabled inmates are permitted entry to the general population if they so choose (Wertlieb 1991). In South Carolina, the South Carolina Criminal Justice Academy now focuses two-hours of its training curriculum on disabilities, for new police officers (Montgomery 1982, in Wertlieb 1991).

Exemptions for Criminal Justice Agencies, Litigation and Client Remedies   After the enactment of the ADA, the International Association of Chiefs of Police (IACP) sought exemptions from the employment standards for state and local police as well as sheriffs' departments, by working with congressional delegations on behalf of its membership. The IACP's exemption request was denied. The ADA guidelines gave no exemptions except in the case of the Federal Government. Therefore the Federal Bureau of Investigation (FBI) and the Drug Enforcement Administration (DEA) are not required to comply, but all state and local agencies are (Bosarge 1991).

However, despite the litigation costs that may occur, "the preservation of these rights is crucial in all realms of life from educational settings to prison settings" (Wertlieb 1991, 332). Because the ADA is a law, certain remedies are available to individuals who have been discriminated against by law enforcement agencies in light of their disability. These remedies are the same as those found in Title II of the *Civil Rights Act of 1964* and can include injunctive relief, reinstatement, back pay, and attorney fees and costs (Smith and Alpert 1993). "With the passage of the *Civil Rights Act of 1991*, ADA plaintiffs who were intentionally discriminated against may also recover compensatory damages of varying amounts, depending on the size of the employer as well as punitive damages in an appropriate case" (Smith and Alpert 1993, 554). Smith and Alpert (1993, 549) stated that "because the substantive provisions of the ADA are virtually the same as those of the *Rehabilitation Act of 1973*, courts are likely to regard the *Rehabilitation Act* cases as highly persuasive when construing the ADA." The foremost issue confronted by the courts was whether the person alleging discrimination was disabled under the meaning of the statutes.

"While some of the ramifications of the ADA for law enforcement agencies can be predicted, the full impact of the ADA on the law enforcement community will take many years to sort out" (Smith and Alpert 1993, 543).

The Disabilities

Each type of disability will pose unique problems for criminal justice agencies. Compounding these problems is the issue of whether the disabled person is a criminal justice employee, victim, offender, defendant, or inmate, as each of these would demand a specific type of response. Such responses have not always been humane or compassionate. At one time in the United States, a person could be institutionalized and sterilized solely because of their disability (Wertlieb 1991).

Persons with disabilities, whether it is a suspect, witness, or victim, interact at least as frequently with police as do non-disabled individuals (McAfee and Musso 1995). As a result, new attention is being given to their presence in the criminal justice system. Such attention, while a good start, is not without its flaws. For example, much of the program modification focus in terms of training has been oriented toward the needs of the mentally retarded. Individuals with physical disabilities such a blindness and deafness are largely ignored (Wertlieb 1991). Furthermore, those who supervise offenders with disabilities rarely have specialized training (Wertlieb 1991).

The ADA has had a significant impact on the way criminal justice agencies are required to adapt to disabled persons, but it also has its limits. The ADA does not cover illegal drug use, whether an addiction is present or not, unless the individual is undergoing drug rehabilitation and is no longer using illegal drugs. The ADA also specifically excludes from protection individuals in the following categories: 1) homosexuality, bisexuality, transvestism, transsexualism, pedophilia, exhibitionism, voyeurism, gender identity disorders not resulting from physical impairments, or other sexual behaviors; 2) compulsive gambling kleptomania, or pyromania; or 3) psychoactive substance use disorders resulting from current illegal use of drugs (Martin 1998). The disabilities focused on in this chapter, however, all fall under the protection of the ADA.

Mental illness is probably the most common of all disabilities facing the criminal justice system. In terms of police training, mental illness is the only disability category that has received significant attention in the police training literature (McAfee and Musso 1995). According to the ADA a mental disability is defined as "mental or psychological disorder, such as retardation, organic brain syndrome, emotional or mental illness, or specific learning disability." The ADA also makes a distinction between mental illness and mental retardation. Mental illness is defined as " . . . a group of disorders causing severe disturbances in thinking, feeling, and relating. They result in substantially diminished capacity for coping with ordinary demands of life . . . A mental illness can have varying levels of seriousness. Identical illnesses can cause different reactions in different people or different reactions at different times in the same persons" (in Rubin and Campbell 1995, 3). Personality traits such as a bad temper or poor judgment do not qualify as a disabling condition under the ADA.

Deafness is another significant problem for the criminal justice system. It is a disability that is much more difficult to accommodate than many of the others. Communication alone is quite complicated. There are three different versions of sign language used in America: American Sign Language (ASL), Signed English (SE), and Pidgined Signed English (PSE). The majority (75%) of prelingually deaf Americans use ASL (McAlister, 1994). American Sign Language is a separate and distinct language that does not translate literally into English. For example, a hearing person may ask, "Are you a good student?" which would be translated by an ASL interpreter to "You good learn person you" (Vernon 1995). There are very few signs in ASL that cover correctional and legal terminology. There are significant differences between the terms "correctional officer," "parole officer," and "police officer," yet there are no signs to distinguish between them (Vernon 1995).

Individuals with minimal language skills may have to be accommodated through "relayed interpretation" during which a hearing ASL interpreter passes information to a deaf ASL-Minimal Language Skills Interpreter who then conveys the message to the defendant by using rudimentary ASL, pantomime, drama, and gestures. The defendant then responds and the process is reversed (McAlister 1994).

While most professionals in the criminal justice system recognize that deaf defendants need special accommodations, problems still arise. Many personnel in law enforcement and the court systems do not understand that each deaf defendant presents a unique communication problem. For example, individuals who speech-read or use hearing aids need to be no further than six feet from the speaker in order to understand what is being said. A person who relies on ASL requires an interpreter fluent in that system, and then others may use oral interpreters exclusively (McAlister 1994).

In 1991, only 15 states used a sign language interpreter upon a person's arrest, and of those, only three required a police officer to obtain an interpreter to deliver the Miranda warnings. Due to the deficit many deaf individuals have in formal sign language, interpreters may have great difficulty communicating the complete intent of the Miranda warnings. In addition, the Code of Ethics for official sign language interpreters does not allow the interpreter to interject any personal opinions. Given these difficulties, many interpreters simply inform suspects that they should wait for an attorney before relaying any information (Wertlieb 1991).

Not only do individuals with minimal language skills require a specialized interpretation expert, they also require significantly more time for the interpreting process. This is not simply a case of translating the legal concepts into "another language." It is estimated that an interpreter dealing with such a defendant will require 5 to 6 hours just to communicate the Miranda warnings (McAlister 1994).

The ADA requires agencies to accommodate deaf individuals in arrest and detainment situations. Likewise, agencies that are responsible for administering a community's emergency response system must be able to accommodate deaf citizens. The law mandates that 911 services must provide direct access to people who use TDDs (Rubin and Dunne 1994). In one case, a deaf man's wife died after complications with the 911 communications system. The man used a special communicator to call a 911 operator and report that his wife was having difficulty breathing. The operator, unfamiliar with the TDD technology, hung up. The woman died before paramedics were able to arrive (Rubin and Dunne 1994). Some criminal justice officials have expressed objections to TDD calls because they cannot be monitored (Gardner 1994).

Obesity is commonly overlooked as a debilitating condition. A person is generally considered to be obese when they are more than 20% above their ideal weight (Frisk and Hernicz 1996). However, obese individuals do face many of the same challenges and acts of discrimination that are experienced by other types of disabled individuals. For example, a joint 7-year study of 10,000 young people conducted by the Harvard School of Public Health, the New England Medical Center, and the Harvard Medical School found that overweight women were more likely to be unmarried, have lower incomes, and have higher rates of household poverty than those women who were not obese. In contrast, a difference between obese and non-obese men was only noted in the likelihood of marriage (Frisk and Hernicz 1996).

Current American society tends to condemn obese or overweight individuals. Rarely are they seen as role models, and when they are given public attention through the media it is often in the form of self-deprecating comedy. More than likely this stigmatism is a result of America's obsession with health and physical fitness. Obesity is often seen as a voluntary condition and one that suggests lack of self-control. Laziness, carelessness, indifference, incompetence, weakness, and slovenliness are all elements of the American stereotype of obese people. This perception easily contributes to discrimination in the workplace, social settings, and certainly the criminal justice system.

Further focus on these disabilities as well as others, including blindness, mobility impairment, and HIV are presented in the following discussion. Each disability is examined in terms of the impact on criminal justice, whether it be in the area of employment, victimization, or criminality. We begin with a look at employment of disabled persons.

Employment   The ADA's goal of preventing discrimination in hiring against disabled people is a noble one. However, neither the ADA nor the subsequent regulations of the EEOC addressed the peculiar and unique circumstances of law enforcement, specifically the mobility, physical strength, and vision standards that are minimally required to do police work effectively. Thus, law enforcement may very well be faced with the situation of legally having to hire individuals who are not in fact qualified for police work and who could subsequently endanger the public (Martin 1998).

Disability rights advocates suggest putting disabled individuals on "light" duty. This, however, may be undesirable because it results in someone performing the duties of essentially a clerical worker while receiving the pay scale of a full duty officer. Additionally, it eliminates an available position that could be filled by a non-disabled officer able to perform all of the required tasks. This further endangers the public by limiting the number of officers performing patrol work (Martin 1998).

While these arguments for a law enforcement exemption are indeed compelling, there is always the possibility that they could be used to open the door for agencies to eliminate able individuals from job pursuit based on antiquated, stereotyped presumptions (Martin 1998), which is exactly what the ADA was designed to prevent. This does not mean that law enforcement or other criminal justice agencies must abandon their missions of security in an effort to accommodate disabled individuals.

In tracing the legislative history of the ADA, it can be determined that Congress did not intend to mandate jeopardizing public safety, or destroying the structure of law enforcement departments by forcing agencies to hire officers who could not be relied upon to perform their jobs in emergency or life-threatening situations. However, it is also evident that Congress did not find it necessary to grant such agencies total discretion to presume that all persons with a particular disability were unable to perform the essential functions of the job (Martin 1998). The ADA was not specific in determining how agencies would solve such dichotomies. Therefore, remedies have come about through litigation.

The courts have examined cases of police officers or sworn rescue personnel who were placed on limited duty, medically retired, or retained on the force but denied promotions based on: diabetes, heart disease, lung impairment, cerebral palsy, hemophilia, HIV infection, lost use of an arm, impaired or missing leg, impaired ankle, impaired foot, missing or impaired hand, degenerative joint disease, arthritis, head injury, back injury, neck injury, blindness, impaired vision, deafness in one ear, abdominal ruptures and vein ligations, mental disabilities, depression, drug addition, paraplegia, inability to stand, stress, chronic fatigue syndrome, alcoholism, obesity, and sleep disorder (Martin 1998).

In one particular case directly related to police and fire departments, it was ruled in *Davis v. Meese* (1989), that blanket exclusion of persons with insulin-dependent diabetes from becoming FBI agents was lawful. The court argued that the physical requirement was directly related to legitimate safety and job performance (Martin 1998). A blanket exclusion is any rule or standard that categorically excludes potential applicants on the basis of a certain condition. The crux is that a blanket exclusion is unlawful if there is a possibility that someone suffering from the precluded condition could perform the essential job functions. In other words, across the board exclusion cannot be based on a *probability* that someone with a disabling condition could not adjust to the job requirements.

The major question concerning blanket exclusions under the ADA is where to draw the line. How, for example, can it be argued that blind applicants should be accepted as full-duty police officers? Generally the courts have determined that the answer to this question is based on determining when the condition itself defines the inevitable results of individual testing. Conversely, if a disability varies substantially from one individual to the next, then individual testing is mandated by the ADA. The logic here is that police and fire departments should not have to repeatedly test individuals with identical conditions when an inevitable and obvious conclusion will be reached. For example, no blind person can conduct surveillance of a suspect, or see an unconscious victim; no paraplegic can chase a suspect over a fence; and no deaf person can hear a cry for help (Martin 1998).

The public is entitled to the best police protection it can afford. The capabilities of sworn emergency personnel, such a police officers and firefighters, could easily determine life, death, or serious injury to those in need of rescue. As para-military organizations, police and fire departments rely upon the transferability of their sworn personnel. Any sworn member may be called upon to perform the duties of another (Martin 1998). Therefore, even able-bodied policemen and firefighters will be affected by the physical condition of their fellow officers. An officer's inability to perform in an emergency situation could very well cause the death of another officer. Additionally, persons with disabilities who perform as officers on "light duty" force other officers to compensate for the services that are not equally being met. While such conditions may be uncommon, disability advocates should consider that strict application of the ADA to public safety agencies that results in harm will quickly create fear and hostility toward the Act and those it was designed to protect (Martin 1998).

The ADA only protects individuals from discrimination if they can perform the fundamental functions of the job. It is acceptable for a criminal justice agency to select applicants based on their ability to perform required tasks. Fundamental functions under the ADA are those that are essential. They can be considered as such if the employees are required to perform them and when the elimination of them would fundamentally alter the job. Functions not falling into these two categories are considered marginal and therefore not reasonable grounds to disqualify someone with a disability. Frequency of performing the essential tasks is irrelevant. For example, it is fairly rare that a police officer is required to make a forcible arrest, yet this can be established as an essential function if the department can demonstrate serious consequences of an officer's inability to do so (Rubin 1994).

The ADA does not prevent criminal justice agencies from establishing qualifying standards. Some standards may be considered job-related but yet may not fall under the category of essential function. For example, a standard requirement for both police officers and corrections officers may be that they have a valid driver's license. Such a requirement is fundamental to the patrol duties of a police officer and therefore could be used as a justification for screening out someone who does not hold a valid license. However, corrections officers usually do not need to drive in order to perform their duties, so screening out on the basis of a valid driver's license would not meet the essential function test (Rubin 1994).

The ADA requires that applicants be made a conditional offer of employment before being required to submit to medical tests or providing medical information. Courts have ruled, however, that testing for illegal drug use and physical agility may be given at any point in the application process since they do not qualify as medical examinations. On the other hand, questions that would require the disclosure of a disability by an applicant can be construed as a medical exam (Rubin 1994).

Prior to the enactment of the ADA, criminal justice agencies routinely required applicants to pass written exams, polygraph exams, background checks, medical exams, and psychological exams. The ADA however prohibits disability-related inquiry prior to making a conditional offer of employment, so many of these test are now postponed until an offer is made. Agility tests, however, are lawful at any point during the application process as long as it can be demonstrated that they are consistent with business necessity (Rubin 1994).

In the following discussion some of the problems associated with dealing with applicants or hiring employees in criminal justice agencies who are in some way physically or mentally impaired are examined. In some cases, a person may become disabled after being hired by an agency. Regardless of the circumstances, disabled employees can seek relief under the ADA in the form of reasonable accommodations. In the course of the discussion, we will determine exactly what constitutes such an accommodation for criminal justice personnel.

Mental Impairment   As with physically disabled individuals, mentally disabled applicants for criminal justice positions must be able to perform the essential functions of the position. Agencies should perform assessments on individuals, and be prepared to demonstrate that excluded applicants were disqualified because a reasonable accommodation could not be made that would allow the disabled person to perform the essential job-related functions. Blanket exclusions based on mental illnesses, whether controlled by medication or not, are probably in violation of the ADA (Rubin and Campbell 1995). Therefore, criminal justice agencies must document the presence of mental impairment in an applicant or employee, and show that the impairment will prevent necessary job performance. A fine line exists between the double perils of excluding someone because of a mental impairment or retaining him or her despite the impairment. There is tremendous liability associated with not referring suspected mentally disabled employees for evaluation. If such an employee is unfit and, through their actions or inactions causes harm to an arrestee, inmate, or other employee, the agency may be liable. In the event that a criminal justice employee acquires a mental illness, an evaluation should be conducted to determine if a reasonable accommodation can be made. Temporary mental states, like temporary medical impairments, may not necessarily be covered by the ADA (Rubin and Campbell).

Mobility Impairment   Missing and dysfunctional limbs or appendages may constitute a mobility impairment in some cases and therefore fall under the domain of the ADA. Consider the hypothetical case of a police officer that is missing a hand. His department argues that two hands are needed for both arrests and weapons use. The officer makes the argument that through the use of a prosthesis he is able to perform all of the physical restraint moves and use a weapon. The department's response here is that since the prosthesis is removable, it may startle people by coming off during a struggle. What is actually the appropriate action for the department under the ADA? Part of the problem is that the department has taken for granted that its policy would be viewed as "common sense." However, the legal arguments for its policy may not be supportable given that a prosthesis might qualify as a reasonable accommodation. In this case, the department's best move would be to evaluate the particular individual on the use of his prosthesis through required tasks. This would allow for determination of the likelihood of the prosthesis becoming dis-engaged and therefore leaving the officer one-handed. The department would more than likely not be successful in arguing that the loss of the prosthesis might startle people. In fact, in an arrest situation this might even prove to be an asset. The issue should be the probability of the officer becoming limited to the use of one hand (Martin 1999).

Issues concerning the employment of mobility-impaired individuals are not limited to law enforcement agencies. In the case of *Allison v. Department of Corrections* (1996), it was argued that the discharge of a correctional officer who was unable to adequately per-form the defensive tactics needed to control, restrain, or subdue inmates, was permissible. The issue was both safety of the individual correctional officer as well as other officers and the inmates (Martin 1999).

Visual Impairment   Consider another hypothetical scenario: a police officer has only one eye and has been employed in a small jurisdiction for less than a year. He uses this pre-vious employment as evidence that he is qualified for a position with a major metropolitan police department. The department must first determine what the essential job functions are. If an eye test is required, is it possible that someone with monocular vision could pass the test? Would all individuals with such a physical condition be eliminated prior to taking the eye test? What do experts say about monocular vision? The result of monocular vision would be a limited visual field. The department should determine the minimal visual field required to perform the essential duties of the job. In the case of *Doane v. City of Omaha* (1997), expert testimony was offered that a person with limited field of vision would be a danger to himself, fellow officers, and the public because his reaction time would be lowered. The court however, ruled that the plaintiff had proved his ability to perform essen-tial job functions by working as a police officer for 9 years during which time he made adjustments to compensate for his limited peripheral vision. Martin (1998, 130) argues against the courts ruling in this case:

> How can it be argued that acuity of vision, particularly peripheral vision and depth perception, is not as important for a police officer as they are for a pilot? An officer's ability to visually observe the surrounding area is crucial in aspects of police work ranging from surveillance to a "shoot out." An officer's inability to see danger from one angle in a split second, while turning to focus on another, might well mean the difference between life and death in the midst of gunshots. This applicant's inability to see someone pointing a gun from his "blind side" may cost the life of the officer himself, a fellow officer, or a member of the public. In a less dramatic scenario, a full range of vision may be crucial in observing suspected criminals to detect crimes and to prevent escapes. This is particularly true in a modern urban setting. In consideration of these job duties, having a "full" rather than limited range of vision may well be an essential function of the job.

In a case involving the correctional system, a juvenile corrections officer was injured in the line of duty resulting in blindness in one eye. His doctors indicated that if he was hit in the head or eye area again, he would lose sight in his other eye. The officer requested to wear a protective helmet in order to protect himself as a reasonable accommodation. The department of corrections objected, stating that the helmet would make the officer an easy target for attack. Since the original injury was result of just such an attack, the department may be correct in determining that returning him to his previous position would pose a threat to him and others. The helmet may very well serve as a sign to inmates as to where he is most vulnerable, therefore making him a more likely target. Since the department specifically provides for medical retirements in these types of situations, the DOC may be correct in refusing to accommodate this officer (Martin 1998).

Obesity   In 1997, the National Association to Aid Fat Americans (NAAFA) conducted a survey in which they found that the heavier a respondent, the more likely that he or she had experienced job discrimination (Frisk and Hernicz 1996). Under the *Rehabilitation Act of 1973*, an obese person who has experienced workplace related discrimination has legal recourse, although no federal statute explicitly prohibits such discrimination. In terms of state statutes, only Michigan has a specific clause in its civil rights law concerning obesity. Legislatures in both New York and Texas have specifically refused to enact such a law. Many courts have refused basic human rights protection against discrimination based on obesity, while others have found that it can qualify as a protected disability in limited circumstances. The most successful cases have involved women filing claims under Title VII of the *Civil Rights Act of 1964* against employers' policies that singled them out or disproportionately affected them (Frisk and Hernicz 1996). Given that some protection of obese individuals has occurred under previous federal acts, it is reasonable to conclude that those same protections, at minimum, would be available under the ADA.

A requirement of the ADA is that an obese or otherwise disabled person be able to perform the essential functions of the job without endangering the safety of themselves or others. In the case of *McDonald v. State of Kansas Department of Corrections* (1995), a correctional officer filed suit for obesity discrimination. At the time of his hire, McDonald weighed 400 lbs. Over time, he gained more weight that resulted in physician prescribed restrictions on the use of stairs, walking more than 100 feet, standing more than 15 minutes, bending, squatting, or lifting heavy objects. The Kansas DOC reassigned him to temporary light duty, but terminated him when the doctor reimposed the working restrictions indefinitely. The court did not uphold this claim because the employee was not able to perform the essential functions of the correctional officer position, with or without accommodation (Frisk and Hernicz 1996).

In the case of *Smaw v. Commonwealth of Virginia Department of State Police* (1994), a morbidly obese officer was demoted to the position of dispatcher after failing a monitored weight control program. The dispatcher position had no fitness or weight limitations. For the previous nine years, the officer had been on full duty as a trooper despite surpassing the maximum weight limitations for most of that time. The officer subsequently filed a discrimination suit. The court, however, ruled that obesity failed to meet the definition of an individual whose disability substantially impaired a major life activity (Frisk and Hernicz 1996). Similarly, in *Andrews v. State of Ohio* (1997). The court dismissed overweight police officers' claims of job discrimination because they failed to show that they were disabled as a result of their obesity.

HIV and AIDS   Consider a third hypothetical case: A police officer graduates at the top of her class from the Police Academy. She is HIV positive, but did not reveal this prior to her hiring and training. Without question she is capable of performing all of the duties she was trained to perform in an emergency situation. However, can she perform those duties without posing a direct threat to the health and safety of others? Since the threat is only real if her blood comes in contact with bloodstream of another person, the question is really how high is the risk of contagion? Is that risk high enough to constitute a "direct threat" under the mandate of the ADA? Although statistically improbable, the courts have refused to accept any chance of the transmission of HIV even if such a chance is "infinitesimally small." Additionally, the police department that hires this officer knowing about her potentially life endangering condition, would be liable were the transmission of the virus ever to occur. Given that dangerous situations involving blood shed on the part of the officer, suspect, and/or victim are a possibility, the police agency would more than likely be justified under the ADA in refusing to hire this officer (Martin 1999).

HIV seems to pose little threat in the field of corrections. According to the National Institute of Justice, there has never been a single case of a correctional officer becoming infected with HIV as a result of his occupational duties. Despite this, correctional officers routinely fear that they will become infected by being bitten or spat upon by an infected prisoner; receiving a needle prick, or coming in contact with infected blood while breaking up a fight (Blumberg and Laster 1999).

The previous discussion is merely a sample of the types of issues facing disabled applicants and employees in the criminal justice system. There are, of course, many more related subjects on this topic including, for instance, employment of wheelchair-bound and deaf individuals. However, it is impossible to cover all such related categories in one discussion. We will now move on to the problems faced by crime victims who are also disabled.

VICTIMS

Disabled victims pose particularly delicate issues for criminal justice agencies. However, the most significant issue may be one of benign neglect. Many victims with disabilities have never participated in the criminal justice process, even if they have suffered repeated and brutal victimization. Crimes against disabled people often go unreported, and those that lead to an investigation and arrest are rarely prosecuted. During the criminal justice process, very few disabled victims come in contact with a victims' advocate (Tyiska 2001).

Because underreporting of crimes against people with disabilities is such a problem there is very little research that details how many individuals with a disability become crime victims or how many are disabled by the criminal attacks themselves. However, some studies suggest that persons who are developmentally disabled are 4 to 10 times more likely to become a crime victim than persons who are not disabled. Disabled children are twice as likely as nondisabled children to be physically or sexually abused. Additionally, crimes against the disabled are often extremely violent, and deliberately intended to injure, control or humiliate the victim. Anywhere from 68% to 83% of developmentally disabled women are sexually assaulted in their lifetime; a rate that is 50% above that of the general population. These same victims are more likely to be re-victimized by the offender, and more than half never receive legal or treatment services (Tyiska 2001).

There are many social and legal problems that may affect whether or not the appropriate criminal justice agencies become aware of victimization involving a disabled person. Pervasive isolation serves to insulate people with disabilities so that they may be unaware of available services and resources, or their rights as a victim. Many who experience chronic victimization often do not even know that such conduct is prohibited or that there are means to address the predatory behavior. Accessibility can be limited by both physical and attitudinal barriers. Architectural barriers may prevent disabled crime victims from visiting the appropriate criminal justice agencies or victim assistance programs. Attitudinal barriers may prevent free flow of information that can be further detrimental to the victim.

For example, in California a woman became a paraplegic as a result of being stabbed during a robbery attempt. Neither the police nor hospital personnel informed her of victim assistance or independent living services. The assailant was never apprehended, so the prosecutor-based victim assistance programs did not provide her any services. Eventually her anger and depression overwhelmed her to the point of attempting suicide. As noted earlier, underreporting of crime involving the disabled is a problem. When a crime is reported often times the agency fails to note that the victim is disabled. This is particularly true if the crime is reported by someone other than the victim. If the case progresses, the victim may later be subjected to prejudices and stereotypes about the reliability of their testimony (Tyiska 2001).

Many times a crime that would be devastating to an able-bodied person, is doubly so for a disabled victim. Existing problems can be compounded by lack of accessibility to basic social services, poverty, institutionalization, and other barriers to equal rights. For many victims, there is the added insult that the crime its self is was caused the disability. Disabled persons are often times particularly vulnerable to being victimized because of their inability to fight, flee, notify others, or testify about the crime. A person with a disability may also be more physically frail, and at risk of having the victimization exacerbate existing health or mental problems (Tyiska 2001).

Some offenders are particularly motivated to target disabled individuals because they desire to control their victims. The perception that the victim is unable to defend themselves, identify the suspect, or call for help may heightened the disabled persons likelihood of being targeted. Sadly, these offenders may be performing the service of health professional or caregiver. Similar to pedophiles that seek jobs working with children, some control-motivated offenders will be attracted to jobs in the social services. One survey found that 48% of offenders who sexually abused disabled people gained access to the victim through some sort of disability services. In addition, disabled victims may have magnified reactions to their victimization because they may already have low self-esteem and feel stigmatized from social attitudes. It is not uncommon for them to engage in self-blame, experience confusion, vulnerability, and loss of trust, as well as develop an increase sense of negativity of their physical circumstances (Tyiska 2001).

Criminal justice agencies should note several issues and distinctions when dealing with disabled crime victims. First, because they are more likely in general to be victimized, have a greater risk of being revictimized, and are often times victimized by a caregiver or family member, it should be noted that they may fear retaliation and thus may not report the crime. Second, someone who becomes disabled as a result of the crime may not have the mental or physical ability to withstand many of the typical delays and hurdles of the criminal justice system. Third, if it is a case of domestic violence involving a disabled parent, child custody issues may be particularly complicated. Many courts have awarded custody to the batterer on the assumption that the disabled parent would not be a good caretaker (Tyiska 2001).

A common reaction to the idea of a disabled person being victimized is one of sympathy and outrage. As an offshoot of this, it is hard for us to imagine that people who could be so easily victimized could also become offenders. The following discussion addresses the topic of the disabled person as a suspect, offender, and defendant.

SUSPECTS, OFFENDERS, AND DEFENDANTS

Disabled individuals, including those with mental retardation, learning disabilities, emotional disorders, and hearing impairments are disproportionately arrested compared to their numbers in the general population. This, along with the high rate of victimization for the disabled, may be explained by the presence of the following factors: 1) poor self-esteem, 2) gullibility, 3) difficulty in understanding concepts concerning crime, and 4) the location of many disabled individuals in high-crime neighborhoods. Furthermore, research has shown that interaction between police and disabled persons occurs regularly and often results in negative consequences for both the officers and the disabled person. Contributing to this problem is the fact that law enforcement, court personnel, and correctional staff do not receive intensive training on dealing with individuals who are disabled. Thirty-six states require some instruction on disabled persons as part of police training. An additional four states provide some sort of training but do not require it. Most academies provide training on mental illness, but few incorporate learning disabilities, mental retardation, or physical impairments as part of the curriculum (McAffee and Musso 1995).

The disabled suspect, offender, or defendant is at a distinct disadvantage when encountering the criminal justice system. They are particularly susceptible to having their civil rights violated for a number of reasons including an inability to understand legal concepts or to communicate effectively with various criminal justice personnel. Such problems are illustrated in the following discussion the issues posed by particular types of disabled suspects, offenders, and defendants.

Mental Impairment

The criminal justice system must be aware that mental illness alone is not a crime. Prosecution and incarceration as responses to mental illness are inappropriate. Law enforcement in particular has a duty to distinguish conduct that is the result of mental illness but lacks criminal intent from true criminal behavior (Rubin and Campbell 1995). For example, because of coordination difficulties, individuals with learning disabilities might be perceived as being drunk by police officers. They may appear uncooperative and belligerent during interrogation thus increasing the officer's suspicion and likelihood that they will be arrested. Even if an officer does recognize that the suspect has an impairment, it will not necessarily mean that the officer will respond appropriately. A poorly trained officer may choose to automatically and unfairly dismiss the statements of someone that appears to be mentally retarded. The suspect himself may contribute to the problem by naively divulging self-incriminating information as a result of not understanding the

Miranda warnings. One suggestion to improve police officers' interactions with mentally disabled individuals, is to involve specially trained mental health workers who could be on call for local law enforcement. They would be available to come to arrest sites to assist the officers. This approach however would require sufficient training for the police officers to recognize and respond appropriately to individuals with mental impairments (Rubin and Campbell 1995).

Confusion by law enforcement over the presence of a disability can in fact be deadly. In one instance police officers inadvertently suffocated a man suffering from severe mental retardation. The police were summoned by the man's mother who asked for assistance when he became abusive to her. The police resorted to restraints when he did not obey the orders they had given. The man's sister later stated that he had a vocabulary of only a few words and could not have understood what the police were demanding (McAfee and Russo 1995).

Some may find it difficult to understand how mentally disabled individuals become offenders. On the other hand, there is a stereotype subscribed to by many that mentally disabled people are inherently dangerous. In understanding this issue, it should be noted that mentally impaired individuals are not necessarily lacking in intelligence. While their intelligence may be average or even above average, some offender's lack the ability to fully understand their actions due to a failure in recognizing key elements in certain circumstances. Individuals who do suffer from mental retardation are more likely to be impulsive and due to their poor reasoning abilities can be easily led by others. Their lack of comprehension and need to be accepted may impede their understanding of the implication of their actions. An example of this is an incident where leaders of a shoplifting ring coerced mentally retarded individuals into returning stolen merchandise to a store for cash. The culpability of the retarded persons in this situation can certainly be called into question (Wertlieb 1991).

Once a suspect is detained, the recognition of mental retardation is the responsibility of the defendant's lawyer. There are no formal programs designed to diagnose mental retardation upon an offender's initial entry to the criminal justice system. Unfortunately very few lawyers receive training in the field of disabilities. As a result, many defendants with mild or moderate degrees of mental impairment may go undiagnosed (Wertlieb 1991).

The diagnosis of mental impairment is particularly crucial because of the issue of legal competency. It is not unusual for the public to decry the finding of incompetence in a mentally disabled offender, because of the increasing abuse of the "insanity" defense. However, sometimes the results of being found incompetent are far from being the same as an acquittal. In the landmark case of *Jackson v. Indiana* (1972) a deaf and cognitively impaired person accused of robbery was declared incompetent to stand trial. The state court committed the defendant to a mental institution until such time as he was competent to proceed with the legal hearings. The U.S. Supreme Court, however, intervened and declared that such an action ultimately resulted in a life sentence for someone who had not yet been convicted of a crime. The Court stated that commitment should only be for a period of time needed to determine the probability of obtaining competency. If this is a remote probability, then the court must either release the individual or initiate civil commitment proceedings (Wertlieb 1991).

Some agencies have taken steps to address the problems associated with mentally impaired defendants. For instance, the State of Florida has established the Mentally

Retarded Defendant Program to aid with incompetence determination. If a defendant is found to be competent but lacking in the knowledge to proceed they are given special training on the adjudication process. At the end of such training the individual is reevaluated for competency including a series of psychological, educational, and physical tests. Pretrial diversion programs, such as those offered in cases of many first-time, non-violent offenses, are increasingly becoming a popular method for dealing with offenders who are mentally incompetent to stand trial. In these programs, an offender avoids the entire formal trial process and instead participates in treatment such as job training, drug treatment, family counseling, rehabilitation. An added bonus to this is the avoidance of a criminal record and the resulting stigmatization (Wertlieb 1991).

A doctrine of diminished capacity is another method of dealing with mentally impaired defendants, but one more oriented toward satisfying the public as well as helping the offender. One would be hard-pressed to justify categorically exonerating individuals with mental retardation or learning disabilities such as would be the case in finding them legally insane. Therefore the prospect of a doctrine of diminished capacity is particularly appealing. In the case of an individual pleading diminished capacity, assessment of intent and premeditation is the focus rather than the understanding of criminal actions. This is becoming a popular alternative, however specific criteria for such a plea are not uniform across the nation and in many jurisdictions is unavailable altogether (Wertlieb 1991).

Mobility Impairment

Police may encounter a wide range of problems associated with individuals who have some form of mobility impairment. Not the least of these problems is incorrectly identifying the presence of a disability. Consider the following case: Roland Jackson was arrested for driving under the influence of drugs or alcohol after a motor vehicle accident. The problem however was that Mr. Jackson was not intoxicated, but was exhibiting physical difficulties related to a stroke suffered several years before. The police mistakenly interpreted his slurred speech and partial paralysis of the right side as indicators of substance use. Mr. Jackson explained his physical condition to the officers but was arrested and taken to the police station anyway. He was detained there for two hours while police administered an alcohol sobriety test and drug influence evaluation before they determined that he was not under the influence of any intoxicating substance (Johnson 1998).

Some confusion may exist when it comes to a reasonable accommodation involving a mobility impaired suspect. In the case of *Gorman v. Bartch* (1997), Gorman was a paraplegic who was asked to leave a Kansas City bar. He did so but remained on the sidewalk outside of the bar during which time he stopped two police officers and requested their assistance. The officers subsequently arrested him for trespassing and called for a police van in order to transport Gorman to the police station. This van was not equipped for wheelchair use and lacked a lift and the necessary restraints. Gorman made two requests to the police officers: to be allowed to use the restroom in order to empty his urostomy bag, and that a properly equipped van be secured for his transportation. The police denied both requests. They removed Gorman from his chair and placed him on the bench inside the van. Since Gorman was unable to support himself, one of the officers used Gorman's belt to tie him to the wire mesh behind the bench. His wheelchair was left unsecured in the van. During the ride to the police station, Gorman's belt broke and he was thrown to the floor sustaining injuries to his back and shoulders. In addition, his urostomy bag broke, soaking him in urine, and his wheelchair sustained damage. Gorman filed suit under the ADA, but was denied relief by the court. The Eighth Circuit ruled that arrestees were not protected by the ADA because they were not "qualified individuals with a disability." While the court did not indicate specifically so, it seemed to imply that services provided by police departments, including arrests of individuals, are not covered under the *Rehabilitation Act* or the ADA (Johnson 1998). Unfortunately, such a ruling very well may open the door for sanctioned abuse of disabled suspects by denying them accommodations that would ensure their safety and/or dignity.

Visual Impairment

One significant issue of dealing with visually impaired suspects is the confusion or fear that an arrest scenario may induce in the individual. In one instance, a blind man sought $200,000 in damages for a beating that he received from police after refusing to surrender his white cane. He claims that the officers did not identify themselves as law enforcement (McAfee and Musso 1995).

Hearing Impairment

The problems faced by suspects, offenders, and defendants who are deaf are vast and profound. Communication skills are often minimal, if existent at all, which makes navigating the criminal justice system a nightmare. For example, a man who was prelingually deaf and had a second grade reading comprehension level was interrogated by the police through written notes. He was not provided with a sign language interpreter or legal counsel. He was convicted on the basis of a confession that was later ruled involuntary. Another deaf man spent two days in jail on a misdemeanor charge because he was unaware of his right to counsel and his right to post bail. He was arraigned without an interpreter. In Arizona, a deaf man was allowed to plead guilty when he had no understanding of his Constitutional rights or the consequences of his plea. In New Mexico, a deaf man was determined to be incompetent to stand trial due to his limited language skills. Even though he suffered from no mental illness of any kind, he was committed to a state mental hospital until he was "cured." A deaf man involved in a fight with a hearing individual was charged with battery after the police relied solely on the hearing fighter's version of events. A North Carolina man was ruled incompetent to stand trial due to his deafness, so he spent 67 years in a state hospital even though he was not mentally ill (McAlister 1994).

For the deaf suspect, encounters with the criminal justice system may result in serious injury if communication is impossible. In one such instance, a deaf man brandishing a metal bar died in a struggle with police. According to witnesses, he not able to communicate while being held down that he was suffocating (McAfee and Musso 1995). If police officers, judges, attorney, and psychologists are unaware of the problems faced by deaf suspects, then evidence obtained as a result of the suspect waiving the Miranda rights may be inadmissible. Such legal pitfalls can be avoided by using sign language interpreters, videotaping the interrogation, determining the deaf defendant's reading level and communication capacity, understanding the limitations of lip-reading, and other psycholinguistic factors (Vernon et al. 1996).

In order to ensure the preservation of Constitutional rights for deaf suspects, law enforcement personnel should be adequately trained to do the following:

- Specifically note the presence of hearing aids or non-standard forms of communication.
- Inquire, either verbally or in writing, into whether the suspect needs an interpreter.
- If a sign language interpreter is required, determine whether the suspect needs ASL, PSE, or SE.
- If accommodation is declined by the suspect, use open-ended questions (not "yes or no" questions) to evaluate the ability of the suspect to comprehend the conversation.
- If an interpreter is used, they should have at least ½ hour with the suspect prior to interrogation in order to evaluate the needs of the suspect and to assure that the interpreter has the skill to meet those needs.
- If an interpreter is required, but not immediately available, refrain from continuing the interrogation.
- Use open-ended questions to determine if the suspect understood the Miranda warnings.
- Video tape the interpreter and suspect throughout the interrogation.
- If the suspect is to remain incarcerated, staff must be informed and necessary steps taken to adequately communicate with him/her (McAlister 1994).

While interpreters are often necessary when deaf offenders enter the criminal justice system, caution should be exercised concerning their use. Given that the interpreter is often the first person the deaf suspect is able to communicate with, it is not unusual for them, out of relief, to make incriminating statements without understanding their rights. For this reason, arguments have been made that communications between an interpreter and the deaf person should be given the same protection as the attorney–client privilege. Some states have refused to extend such a privilege and have required the interpreter to testify concerning such statements (McAlister 1994). The questionable confidentiality status between interpreter and defendant alone may also interfere with free communication of defendants with their counsel, which further interferes with appropriate representation (Wertlieb 1991).

Crimes committed by deaf individuals may be just as disturbing as those committed by non-impaired offenders. For example, there has been an increase in the prosecution of deaf persons for pedophilia as well as increased reporting and sentencing of pedophiles that prey on deaf children. This is primarily due to legislation that mandates the reporting of pedophilia, increased litigation, and media attention (Vernon and Rich 1997).

Vernon and Rich (1997) conducted a study of 22 known deaf pedophiles, two of which were women. These offenders by and large had some sort of relationship with the victim either as teachers, residence hall counselors, family members, friends, or fellow students. It was found that the generally held belief that pedophiles have a history of being victimized by sexual abuse was also true among deaf pedophiles. Of the 20 males in this study, there was a clear history of abuse in 12, a strong suspicion of it in 2, and no data on the remaining 6. It was also found that the deaf offenders tended to choose victims that met the same demographics (age range, etc.) as they did at the time of their own first victimization. Multiple forms of pedophilia were found to exist among the 20 case studies, including incestuous, sadistic, homosexual, heterosexual, and bisexual.

One of the female pedophiles, a relative rarity, was prelingually and profoundly deaf. She attended regular public schools but was abused by the other children for being both deaf and overweight. She was equally harassed by the other deaf or disabled children. It was determined that she was gang raped on several occasions by boys at her school, used regularly by them sexually, and sexually abused by an older man. She reacted passively and failed to communicate any of the incidents to her family. She tried to resist going to school, but was forced to attend by her parents, who were unaware of the circumstances. On at least one occasion, her father beat her for refusing to get on the school bus. It was later determined that she had also been sexually abused by her father. She began attending Gallaudet University, but by then was heavily into substance abuse as a form of self-medication. As a result of the abuse, she had developed a phobic aversion to taking a shower or brushing her teeth. She dropped out of Gallaudet and secured employment in a laboratory as an animal caretaker. However her poor anger and impulse control led to her dismissal after she killed a puppy that nipped her. In addition to low self-esteem, rage, significantly flawed judgment, a perception of people and the environment as threatening, and paranoia, she is sexually attracted to children and has a desire to inflict pain on them (Vernon and Rich 1997).

As defendants, deaf individuals are entitled to the same Constitutional protections as hearing defendants. They have the right to be informed of the accusation against them, to remain silent, to confront witnesses, to have assistance of counsel, and to have due process of law. It must be ensured that any waiver of these rights is done knowingly and voluntarily (McAlister 1994). The entering of a guilty plea can be one of the most difficult tasks for the sign language interpreter. The guilty plea litany contains many legal concepts that have no equivalent signs in ASL. In fact, ASL contains very few signs to express any legal concepts. For example, the term "subpoena" does not have a corresponding sign. The interpreter would have to convey the concept in signs that equal the English words "paper require you show-up court later." It is not enough that a deaf defendant understands only one of the consequences of a plea. The court must ensure that they understand all of the consequences such as the charge and the rights that are surrendered including the right to appeal (McAlister 1994).

A common misconception is that providing an interpreter will automatically cure any communication problems between the deaf defendant and the criminal justice system. This is not the case for individuals who have minimal language skills and are not fluent in any form of sign language. Often these individuals not only do not have the verbal skills to convey the legal concepts, they may also lack the conceptual framework to understand the legal concepts. If a defendant is fluent in English, then one accommodation option is real-time captioning which links the court reporter's machine to a computer and displays the words on screen as they are spoken. One drawback is that there is an 8 to 10 second delay between the spoken word and its appearance on screen. If an individual is not fluent in English, but is able to use ASL, then a sign language interpreter can be assigned to communicate with the defendant (McAlister 1994). In *People v. Reets* (1993), the New York Supreme Court dismissed the case of a deaf defendant who could only communicate with his immediate family through self-created gestures consisting of pantomime, drama and gestures. Since the defendant could not attain an effective level communication within a reasonable time, the court ruled that no "judgment could be arrived at fairly" if the defendant went to trial (McAlister 1994).

The issue of competency in deaf individuals can extend beyond the difficulties of communication. The occurrence of psychiatric difficulties is roughly the same rate in deaf individuals as it is in hearing individuals. However, diagnostic techniques and treatment for the deaf and mentally disabled individual are far less sophisticated than for hearing persons. Additionally, there are very few individuals trained in this type of psychiatric method. A medical or psychological degree by itself does not qualify an individual to provide valid testimony on the psychiatric condition of a deaf defendant. This may be a particularly crucial difference when a deaf defendant is being evaluated in preparation for a possible insanity defense. Even if a mental health professional employs the services of an interpreter when dealing with a deaf client, the diagnosis and evaluation may be significantly flawed unless the evaluator has an understanding of the differences in cognition, language, and culture between deaf and hearing patients (McAlister 1994). In one case, deaf defendant Donald Lang was declared by the court to be mentally ill so that he could be given a civil commitment. Lang, however, was not mentally ill but rather was devoid of knowledge of sign language and had virtually no communication skills. Lang was committed based on circumstantial evidence of dangerousness and the court's belief that there was no other solution for someone like Lang (Wertlieb 1991).

Courts routinely sentence deaf individuals to exactly the same punishment as hearing defendants without considering that a deaf inmate has a much harsher experience in prison than the hearing inmate (McAlister 1994).

Obesity

Scant research is available on the subject of obese offenders. However, Wertlieb (1991, 332) noted, "A person's physical appearance can potentially have a profound effect on the police officer's course of action. Studies have indicated that unattractive individuals are typically perceived as more aggressive, antisocial, and dishonest than those considered attractive." In such cases, an obese individual may fail to receive the benefit of the doubt that police may ordinarily extend to others.

INMATES

The ADA has put even the best-intentioned correctional administrators and staff in a difficult position because, while it mandates services for disabled inmates, it does not provide funding to cover the subsequent costs (Vernon 1995). This problem is quite significant given the many architectural barriers that are commonly present in facilities that were built prior to the passage of the ADA. While the ADA does allow for leniency in terms of some architectural modification (such as not requiring modification that would significantly alter or damage facilities of historical significance, or modifications that would impose a true economic hardship), for the most part prison officials must bring their facilities into compliance. Removing architectural barriers is only part of that process. Providing reasonable access and special accommodations in terms of services of programs is also something to be addressed by prison administration. Extra funding for such modification becomes a necessity, but such a request is not often well received by lawmakers. It is their view that funding priorities should be given to relieve prison overcrowding or to build new facilities to provide additional places to incarcerate convicted criminals. The public, likewise, is rarely willing to provide additional tax money for what they view to be "luxury" items for prisoners.

Another omission of the ADA is its failure to specifically address the issues facing inmates or state and federal correctional facilities. The consequence of this is that inmates have a right to the same legal remedies provided to other qualified persons with disabilities who have experienced discrimination until the courts determine otherwise. Historically, the courts have permitted prisoner claims under the federal civil rights statutes. For example many disabled prisoners sought legal recourse under the *Rehabilitation Act* (1973), a forerunner of the ADA. In *Bonner v. Lewis* (1988) the Ninth Circuit ruled that the *Rehabilitation Act* did apply to state inmates who were disabled. Other federal courts have continued to cite this opinion in similar cases (Walvoord 1996). For the most part, courts have ruled on the applicability of the ADA to correctional institutions. However, there have been findings that protect prison officials form monetary liability under inmates' disability discrimination claims. This immunity has not extended to prison officials who fail to provide accommodations for an inmate's disability (Walvoord 1986).

In order to avoid liability, correctional agencies should evaluate their compliance with the mandates of the ADA by examining the following three areas: policies and procedures, architectural barriers, and communications (Rubin and Campbell 1995). Some of the requirements falling in these areas are that correctional facilities must have a minimum of 3% of their cells fully accessible. There must be one accessible cell for each level of security as well as one of each type of specialty cell (e.g. protective custody, disciplinary detention, detoxification, medical isolation, etc.) (Gardner 1994). Some states have created centralized facilities for disabled prisoner in an effort to limit the costs of treatment and accommodation (Robbins 1996).

A disabled inmate is not entitled to accessibility to all areas of a correctional facility, even newly constructed ones. For example, an accessible route is not required for second tier cells that would ordinarily be accessed by stairs. However, common use areas such as exercise yards, workshops, and areas of instruction must be accessible. Areas that serve the public, such as waiting or visiting areas, are also required to be accessible (Gardner 1994). Correctional officials have often justified the denial of services or aids to disabled inmates by suggesting that prison conditions are part of the penalty for a criminal offense and are intended to be restrictive and even harsh (Gardner 1994). Prison administrations must be careful to avoid this trap because, while it may have the support under public sentiment, it does not grant immunity from civil suit under the ADA.

Traditionally corrections officials have been reluctant to make any accommodations that may increase a prisoner's mobility. In their view, an inmate who cannot move freely is less of a security risk. Additionally, there is some concern for safety and security in the provision of equipment and accommodations. Finally, accommodating or rehabilitating a disabled inmate can cause an economic hardship to some correctional facilities (Gardner 1994). Due process is violated when an inmate with a disability is disciplined for not obeying orders or rules that, as a result of his disability, was unable to hear, had not been informed, or could not understand (Gardner 1994). Often times physically disabled inmates are placed in special subunits not specifically designed to accommodate their disability. For example, they may be a place in infirmaries or protective custody with "victim prone" inmates such as the mentally ill, mentally retarded or whose crimes make them vulnerable. In a majority of institutions, this means that the disabled inmates are completely excluded from programs such as vocational education and fro recreation, housing, and work assignments. They also experience restricted academic education and visitation (Gardner 1994).

Due to the increasing number of mandatory life sentences, and the aging of the general inmate population, issues concerning inmates with disabilities will continue grow (Walvoord 1996). As of 2001, the number of disabled inmates in state general prison populations is unknown. However, the California Department of Corrections stated that its prison system contained "345 inmates in wheel chairs, 650 inmates with lower extremity disabilities requiring prosthetics or a walker, 141 inmates who are hearing-impaired, and 219 inmates who are blind" (Carnahan 1999, 292). In addition to the physically disabled, a significant but definitively unknown proportion of the inmate population suffers from severe mental disorders (Carnahan 1999). Assuming that such proportions are representative of the U.S. corrections system as a whole, the continued aging of an ever-growing prison population may bring issues related to disabilities to a crisis level. One way to prepare for this potential crisis is increase the prisons' interactions with public agencies. For example, correctional health and public health are intertwined and therefore correctional facilities should be in collaboration with community based health care and social service organizations to treat the thousands of former inmates who return to the community each month (Hammett et al. 1999).

Another method of preparation is to recognize the distinct differences between disabled and non-disabled inmates, particularly in terms of problems faced by the latter. Most Americans are not aware of the way in which the American courts augment punishment handed down to disabled defendants, stripping them of human dignity in prison (Robbins 1996). Disabled inmates suffer more during incarceration than do non-disabled inmates. In addition to the sentence itself, the disabled inmate will experience a more intense loss of independence and personal difficulty. They may face barriers to rehabilitative, educational, and work programs, as well as have their safety endangered by architectural hazards that may prevent evacuation in the event of an emergency (Gardner 1994). Inmates who are disabled must not only cope with the endemic problems of being incarcerated, but must also deal with the inherent limitations of their disabilities (Robbins 1996). Additionally, it is generally accepted that inmates who have or are perceived to have contributed to their own disability do not receive the same level of sympathy as other disabled inmates. Such may be the case for prisoners who were paralyzed in gunfights, acquired AIDS from intravenous drug use, or who otherwise contributed to health problems through obesity, smoking, or drinking (Gardner 1994).

A third form of preparation for the future of the disabled inmate population is to consider alternatives for their incarceration. The best prospect for relief of disabled prisoners is some form of early-release or compassionate-parole structure. Texas has established a statutory "special needs parole" option that may be exercised for the elderly, physically handicapped, mentally ill, terminally ill, or mentally retarded. Much of the public's support for early releases is aimed at terminally ill prisoners (Robbins 1996). An alternative to early release is to accelerate the practice of transferring disabled inmates to appropriate medical facilities. This practice is relatively common in prisons where there is inadequate treatment for a specific medical problem (Robbins 1996).

Mental Impairment

According to Rubin and Campbell (1995) the prevalence of mental disabilities among inmates is high. It is estimated that 10 million individuals are detained in U.S. jails annually and that 6.4% of these detainees have a severe mental disability. Some experts have estimated this proportion to be as high as 8%, and female detainees with a severe mental disability may be as high as 13%. This means that American jails must accommodate 640,000 to 800,000 mentally disabled detainees each year. Given these numbers, addressing the needs of mentally disabled inmates becomes a priority for corrections officials. Valid approaches to accommodating the needs of mentally disabled inmates include specialized housing units for inmates who pose a direct threat to the health and safety of others, treatment for inmates housed in the general population, and transference to other institutions and services. None of the accommodations, however, may exclude an otherwise eligible mentally disabled inmate from programs and services that are available to the rest of the inmate population (Rubin and Campbell 1995).

There is no jurisdictional uniformity for incarceration of mentally retarded inmates. Some jurisdictions place them in general populations of inmates whereas others implement formal or informal segregation into special units. Finally, some jurisdictions place mentally retarded individuals in psychiatric or mental health facilities (Wertlieb 1991). Regardless of jurisdictional practice, correctional institutions should have policies for screening all inmates for mental disabilities. Those inmates identified as such should then be evaluated by qualified mental health officials. These inmates should also have access to crisis intervention, treatment, and discharge planning services. Such an approach will require the cooperative efforts of corrections, mental health, and medical officials. A facilities deliberate indifference to an inmate's mental disability is looked upon by the courts in the same manner as indifference to an inmate's medical condition (Rubin and Campbell 1995).

The correctional setting (i.e. jail or prison) will determine how a correctional facility accommodates mentally disabled inmates. Diversion to other facilities, special units to house inmates who pose a direct threat to the safety of others, and treatment for those in general population are all valid approaches as long as they do not exclude any eligible inmate for participating in programs and services (Rubin and Campbell 1995). Mentally disabled individuals in local jails may present particularly significant problems for officials because the detainees are coping with both mentally illness and the additional trauma of being arrested (Rubin and Campbell 1995). Prisons on the other hand are faced with the unique situation of accommodating mentally disabled inmates long-term. This may include inmates who have an acute mental illness that is unlikely to improve, as well as inmates who develop mental illness during their confinement (Rubin and Campbell 1995).

Prisons must confront a variety of issues when receiving and housing a mentally impaired inmate. The issues can result in strain on the staff, the administration and the inmate. Of central concern is the resident suspicion with which the prisons staff tends to regard mental-disability claims. This is the result of three blanket sets of circumstances. First, the presence of a mentally impaired inmate produces complications in the system, which is not well received in prison environments that are increasingly understaffed and more demanding. Time and patience is a requirement to address the mental-disability and this, along with improper training, may frustrate prison officials. The treatment needed is considerably different for that provided to inmates with physical disabilities and this may result in the involvement of a state mental health hospital as a third party. Prisoners who are sent briefly to such a hospital for treatment or transference for an extended period pending recovery, present issues of due process protocol which adds to complexity of the existing situation (Robbins 1996).

A second issue is the often-made assumption that mental illness and mental retardation are the same thing. This may result in inappropriate segregation or treatment of both groups. In many cases the problems of mentally retarded prison inmates may be more difficult to solve because, unlike certain mental illnesses, medication is generally not useful for their condition. A third source of frustration for prison officials is the ever-increasing numbers of mentally disabled inmates and the litigation over prison conditions that often accompanies them. Correctional facilities have experienced extreme difficulty in finding placement and treatment for these inmates, which can push the mentally impaired prisoner to extreme heights of disorientation, that when left unmonitored may result in successful suicide attempts (Robbins 1996).

Maximum-security facilities seem to be the most detrimental to the mentally retarded inmate. Such persons are often found "to vegetate" as a result of the lack of human and physical resources. Additionally, adjustment problems are likely to be intensified because the mentally retarded inmate lacks appropriate role models and experiences rejection. Mentally retarded inmates who are placed alongside nondisabled inmates are also often subject to exploitation. They can become easy scapegoats and targets for the venting of resentment and hostility. They are more easily led and manipulated and therefore may develop habits that lead to recidivism. They are also at greater risk of being coerced into homosexual relationships as a means of protection from other inmates. Segregation into solitary confinement or another unit for the mentally ill may be an answer, but these arrangements will fail if the staff do not have the training or expertise to manage special needs offenders (Wertlieb 1991).

Mentally impaired inmates are more likely to be subjected to long, indeterminate sentences. This results from several factors: (a) they are at an automatic disadvantage because they do not always understand prison rules and are therefore likely to incur violations which in turn affects their "good time" standing, (b) alternative sentencing is not generally seen has a good option because these individuals have trouble finding and maintaining steady employment, and (c) the combination of the two previous factors puts the mentally retarded inmate at a great disadvantage when trying to sway a parole board (Wertlieb 1991). An inmate's behavior may also impact their eligibility for certain programs. Accessibility to programs for mentally disabled inmates who are housed with the general inmate population should be readily available. If an inmate requires the use of psychotropic medication, they may still be eligible as long as their behavior is stable enough for general population environments. However, blanket policies such as excluding all inmates on psychotropic inmates from participation in programs and services may be a violation of the ADA. It is not a violation however to require that an inmate's behavior be stable before being eligible to participate (Rubin and Campbell 1995).

The death penalty is a hotly debated topic when it is applied to mentally retarded inmates. The controversies surrounding executions increase when the death row inmate is mentally retarded. Thus far the Supreme Court has not ruled that such executions are cruel and unusual punishment and therefore in violation of the Eighth Amendment. Mental retardation is allowed to be introduced as a mitigating circumstance to juries considering a death sentence, but the mentally retarded inmate is just as likely to be misunderstood by jurors and become a target for overzealous prosecutors, especially if the defense counsel is mediocre (Robbins 1996).

Mobility Impairment

Inmates who suffer from some sort of mobility impairment may have a particularly harsh environment to deal with inside prison. Not only are they easy prey for other inmates because of their inability to defend themselves, they are also potential victims for abuse by corrections officers. The following scenarios illustrate these difficulties.

Douglas Hausmann was a paraplegic inmate who was put in segregation for nine days. Prior to his entering the cell, it was determined that the door would not accommodate the wheelchair. He was left for over 45 minutes outside the cell door, during which time he requested the use of a toilet, but he defecated on his clothing before the correctional officers were able to move him. The officers demanded that he remove his clothes, and then placed him on the toilet within the cell anyway. He was left there for 1½ hours before he finally crawled onto the floor. He was able to pull a mattress off the bed where he lay naked for another hour before a nurse was sent to cleanse him. For the next six days he remained on the bed before he was allowed to shower. During the subsequent three days he was left on the bed, during which time he fell six times and defecated on himself three times. During one of his falls he sprained his arm and hit his head hard enough to require x-rays. His repeated requests for help were ignored (Robbins 1996).

Three inmates at Shawangunk Correctional Facility in New York filed a lawsuit over "an increasingly standard list of complaints" such as inaccessible toilet and shower facilities, denial of catheters and leg bags, etc. One of the inmates additionally was forced to use an inappropriately sized wheelchair, was medicated erratically for spasms, denied physiotherapy, and forced to endure a so-called security restraint known as "the black box." His description of this restraint was that when used on paraplegics who were prone to spasms, it "became a medieval instrument of torture." Life for two of the three inmates had been reduced to a combination of increasing verbal and physical abuse by corrections officers, as well as the enduring of severe medical pains and infection.

Partially paralyzed inmates in a Texas prison were reportedly denied access to their wheelchairs and were left to crawl in their cells. Additionally they were not permitted to use their wheelchairs for the purpose of going to dining halls or other communal locations (Wertlieb 1991).

Reportedly, a wheelchair-bound inmate was not allowed to use his chair and therefore was forced to crawl while in his cell. Another inmate who was sentenced to life in prison was also denied the use of a wheelchair because the cell door was not wide enough to accommodate it. The inmate was virtually bedridden and developed severe ulcers on his body due to the lengthy periods of time he was forced to spend lying in bed. The case of Larry Noland, however, is probably the worst example of discrimination against immobile inmates. Noland was not only confined to a wheelchair, but also used colostomy and urostomy bags for removal of bodily waste. Noland was being kept in a padded cell that lacked a bed, running water, or any means of disposal except for a drain in the floor. Noland needed to wash his hands after emptying the bags, but was denied soap and water, and was only allowed to shower occasionally. The result was that Noland often ate meals with hands that were contaminated with human waste (Carnahan 1999). Confounding Noland's circumstances was the fact that the cell was not well ventilated or temperature regulated, which contributed to the strong odor coming from the open drain in the floor. Furthermore, Noland was constantly on camera and therefore denied any privacy, and consistently had his medication administered late or not at all (Gardner 1994).

Visual Impairment

The ADA does require the provision of auxiliary aids and services for visually impaired inmates. These aids might include mobility aids, including canes; magnifiers, large print materials, brailed materials, talking book cassettes, special tape players, tactile and brailed signage, and special audio programs for the description of videotapes. The services might encompass: institutional orientation materials in an accessible format, orientation to their surroundings, education of correctional personnel on guide techniques, verbal identification, provision of qualified readers, assistance in completing forms, and assistance in the cafeteria. This regulation does pose some problems in that aids such as canes could be used as weapons, batteries for tape recorders could be used to manufacture explosives, and the tape recorders themselves could be used to hide contraband (Gardner 1994). Not all prisons have ignored the needs of blind inmates. New York State has developed a "sensorially disabled unit," where prisoners who are visually impaired are placed. This unit is off-limits to the general inmate population, but the blind inmates are not prevented from accessing the general population if they so choose (Wertlieb 1991).

Hearing Impairment

There are more deaf individuals per capita in the prison population than in America as a nation (McAlister 1994). It is estimated that anywhere from 35% to 40% of inmates have diminished hearing. In 13% to 20% of all inmates this loss is substantial (Vernon 1995). These inmates have a particularly difficult time adjusting to prison environments. Even though their disability is not immediately observable, their isolation from surrounding events is similar to that of the wheelchair-bound inmate. Because corrections officers or other inmates cannot see the disability, the deaf inmate may become a target of hostility for failing to react to being directly addressed. They are not able to hear commands, announcements, nor footsteps that may indicate a potential attack. Many are poorly educated and lack sufficient skills in ASL. Furthermore, they are dependent upon corrections officers, as well as other inmates, in many situations ranging from casual encounters to disciplinary hearing. There is virtually no way to ensure that such assistance or translations will not deliberately sabotaged or at best simply inaccurate (Robbins 1996).

Understanding the deaf culture will allow correctional employees to better understand a hearing impaired inmate's behavior. For example, most will probably want to be housed with other deaf inmates; some will want to avoid other deaf inmates; and still others will want to be isolated from all inmates (Vernon 1995). Providing deaf inmates the option of living with other deaf inmates is one way that prisons can alleviate their isolation. Additionally, quality services would be more feasible and cost effective if deaf inmates are centralized in one location (Vernon 1995).

Like blind and wheelchair bound inmates, deaf prisoners are entitled to accommodations. Prisons would need to make arrangements to provide for emergency coverage of deaf communications 24 hours per day. Some prisons may choose to employ full-time interpreters to handle both the emergency scenarios as well as the routine business between staff and deaf inmates (Vernon 1995). Telecommunication devices for the deaf (TDDs) should be available on the same basis as telephones are available for hearing inmates. Captioned television, strobe lights, and flashing alarm clocks are other accommodations that should be considered (Vernon 1995).

Obesity

One of the few cases to address the issue of obesity as a physical impairment in a correctional setting was *Torcasio v. Murray* (1995). Anthony Torcasio was an inmate in Virginia's Keen Mountain Correctional Center. At 5'7", Torcasio weighed 460 pounds and described his life of morbid obesity as one of "misery and heartache." As a result of his weight, he was unable to stand, walk, or lie down for extended periods. He was also susceptible to losing his balance.

Torcasio requested that the Virginia Department of Corrections (VDOC) provide accommodations by making certain changes to his cell, bathroom facilities, recreational areas, and certain activities. Initially, the VDOC had placed Torcasio in the infirmary upon his arrival at Keen Mountain. Such an arrangement did provide some accommodations for disabled inmates, but it also resulted in more restrictions and fewer privileges. Torcasio subsequently requested to be placed in the general inmate population, after which he requested special accommodations to be made for his physical conditions. "Specifically, he claimed that the prison's shower, toilet, tables, cell doors, building lobby, dining hall, commissary window and pill line, cells, and infirmary, and its recreational programming, medical transportation, and personal aid all failed to accommodate his obesity reasonably" (Walvoord 1996, 1219).

Prison officials responded to his request by providing a private cell, hospital bed, reinforced chairs, and handrails and slip mats for the shower. Torcasio then sued the VDOC under Title II of the ADA for failing to provide reasonable accommodations. The United States Court of Appeals found that the ADA did not clearly establish morbid obesity as a disability and that a reasonable prison administrator may fail to view an inmate suffering from this condition as disabled. Since the ADA did not define the extent of affirmative duties to a morbidly obese inmate, the officials at the VDOC were not in violation.

HIV and AIDS

AIDS is the leading cause of death in American prisons. The following statements concerning demographics of inmates with HIV or AIDS demonstrates how critical this issue has become for corrections officials. A significant portion of the disabled inmate population is HIV positive. As of 1995, 6.3% of state prison inmates were HIV positive.

Of those, 21% were exhibiting symptoms of AIDS (Carnahan 1999). As of 1997, the proportion of known state and federal prison inmates infected with HIV was 2.1%. Of the 23,548 HIV positive inmates, 6,184 were confirmed AIDS cases. Between 1996 and 1997 the number of AIDS related inmate deaths in State prisons dropped from 907 to 538. Between 1991 and 1997, the general prison population grew at a rate of 49%, while the rate of HIV positive prisoners grew at 34%. In 1997, female prisoners had a higher rate of HIV (3.5%), than male state prisoners (2.2%). The rate of HIV cases in prison was more than 5 times that of the U.S. population (Maruschak 1999).

Not only are persons with AIDS considered disabled under the definition of the ADA, but also the courts have ruled that asymptomatic inmates who are HIV positive may also be considered disabled (Carnahan 1999). Because HIV positive inmates are controversial, often targets of inmate violence, and require special medical care that is often cost prohibitive, they can be among the most difficult of disability issues for correctional officials. Infected inmates have claimed both a right to be integrated with the general population and a right to be protected from inmate violence. The uninfected inmates who either through ignorance, prejudice, or legitimate concern are fearful of contracting the virus, have demanded that HIV positive inmates be kept segregated. The results are conflicting issues concerning policy and due process (Robbins 1996). Some of the most complex of these: a) mandatory HIV testing, b) segregation of infected inmates, c) content of educational programs designed to reduce "high-risk" behavior, and d) condom distribution (Blumberg and Laster 1999).

Like the general public, the ignorance-based fear of AIDS is rampant in the prison population. Many inmates believe that AIDS can be transmitted through causal contact such as toilet seats, showers, or even by having their closed washed by HIV positive prisoners. Unlike the general population, however, prisoners reject official explanations of HIV transmittal as being a part of a conspiracy by corrections officials to disguise an AIDS epidemic. This combination of fear and suspicion leads prisoners to be unnecessarily fearful of AIDS and overzealous in their own avoidance of its transmission. Prisoners in Tallahassee, Florida, almost rioted when they were ordered by prison guards to remove a mattress that had been used by a prisoner with AIDS. Prisoners in New Jersey brought their own utensils to meals for fear of contracting AIDS from dirty dishes. A riot resulting in a 10-day lockdown occurred at Stillwater prison in Minnesota after the warden announced that a new inmate was HIV positive and beginning to show symptoms of AIDS (Pappas 1988).

Given the rate of sexual assault in prisons, the risk of transmission of HIV is considerable. The argument thus becomes one of the equal protection and prisoners' rights versus special needs and deference to prison authorities (Robbins 1996). The most comprehensive study conducted on the risk of HIV transmission in prison determined that only .3% of non-infected inmates had tested positive for the virus after 1 year of incarceration. However, if an inmate is serving a sentence of 20 years, this translates to an infection rate of 6%. Most cases of HIV/AIDS in U.S. prisons have been among inmates with a history of intravenous drug use prior to their incarceration. Due to the "war on drugs," the number of high-risk inmates has increased significantly in recent years with as much as $\frac{1}{4}$ of the state inmate population having a history of intravenous drug use (Blumberg and Laster 1999).

The issue of mandatory testing has been raised by some who recognize that inmates are generally individuals who have demonstrated a capacity to engage in antisocial behavior, and homosexual activity. Individuals in support of mass mandatory screening suggest: a) it is the best way to identify HIV positive inmates, b) such a policy would allow corrections officials an opportunity to target education and prevention programs, c) infected inmates could be intensely supervised in order to prevent the transmission of the virus to others, d) it would allow for a more accurate projection of the number of future AIDS cases therefore allowing officials to plan more effectively for funding needs, and e) it will insure that infected inmates received appropriate medical treatment (Blumberg and Laster 1999).

Opponents of mandatory testing believe that educational and prevention programs should be aimed at all inmates, regardless of the presence of the virus. They also criticize segregation programs because such methods might encourage a false sense of security and therefore "high-risk" behavior among non-infected inmates. Even critics of mandatory testing realize the importance of early detection of the virus. However, they argue that inmates who have engaged in high-risk behavior will have a medical incentive to be tested voluntarily. At least two studies have supported this by demonstrating that the majority of detections of HIV among inmates have come through voluntary testing (Blumberg and Laster 1999).

Another fear of mandatory testing is that it will promote fear and prejudice, resulting in the ostracizing of infected inmates. Additionally these inmates may experience discrimination, harassment, and violence, not to mention difficulties concerning employment and housing after release (Blumberg and Laster 1999). Despite this risk, a joint study by the Centers for Disease Control (CDC) and the National Institute of Justice, indicated that the Federal Bureau of Prisons as well as 16 state correctional systems have implemented mandatory screening for HIV (Blumberg and Laster 1999).

Segregation of seropositive inmates is a complex issue for prison officials, and there is no standard for its solution. In one case, prison policy required that HIV positive inmates be segregated into one of two HIV wards. This policy resulted in a "blanket exclusion of HIV-positive inmates from the general prison population housing, educational, employment, community placement and other programs . . . The inmates were categorically separated from virtually all aspects of general population institutional life, e.g. housing assignments, education, employment, recreation, dining, law library use, religious services, family visitation, transportation, sick call, and canteen" (in Carnahan 1999, 295). Individuals who support the idea of segregation of infected inmates argue that the prevalence of high-risk behaviors in prison requires such a practice to prevent the transmission of the virus. They base their arguments on research findings that show: homosexual activity does occur in prison; other sexually transmitted diseases can be passed through this type of contact; tattooing, though generally prohibited, is a very common in prison and there have been documented cases of HIV transmission through this practice; illicit drug use is present in many prisons; and some individuals are sexually assaulted while incarcerated (Blumberg and Laster 1999).

Opponents of segregation argue that since HIV is not passed through casual contact, special housing is unnecessary. Any other practice may contribute to the myth that HIV can be caught through behaviors other than high-risk ones. There is also some concern that segregated inmates are subjected to substandard housing units, denied certain work assignments, and access to rehabilitation and recreation programs. They may also be ineligible for work release or unable to participate in other prison programs causing them to miss the opportunity for "good time" credits. In jurisdictions that contain large numbers of infected inmates, such as the northeastern prison systems, segregation would essentially require the establishment of a second corrections system. This is virtually impossible given the already strained financial situations of most prison systems in America. There is also the possibility that inmates may refuse volunteer testing if they believe the outcome will result in segregation (Blumberg and Laster 1999).

As an alternative to segregation, corrections officials could aim to reduce high-risk behavior through increased supervision, employing more officers, providing intensive education programs, and imposing harsh penalties for sexual assault. The classification process could be used as well for a method of identifying potentially sexually aggressive inmates and those who are likely to become victims. Some suggestion has been made that prisons should distribute or make condoms available to inmates to decrease the transmission of the virus. Few have done so, however, for fear that it will seem to condone homosexual behavior in the prison. There has also been concern that condoms could be used to hide contraband or make weapons. Six jurisdictions in the U.S. allow inmates access to condoms, and there have been few reported problems. There has been a trend toward desegregation of HIV positive inmates. In 1985, there were 38 state systems that still continued the practice, but presently only Mississippi and Alabama engage in separating infected inmates (Blumberg and Laster 1999).

The use of protease inhibitors for HIV treatment has now become the standard for care. Prisons and jails are at a great disadvantage however, given that the annual cost of treatment ($12,000–$16,000 for one person) could quickly consume their entire health care budget. Despite the cost, there is an ethical obligation to treat the HIV infected inmate. The courts however, have left unclear the issue of legal obligation. In the case of *Estell v. Gamble* (1976), the court ruled that inmates had the right of "unqualified access to health care." Lower courts have failed, however, to interpret this as meaning that inmates had a right to the best available care (Blumberg and Laster 1999).

Few lawsuits brought by either infected or uninfected inmates have been successful. Most suits by HIV positive inmates have concerned denial of privileges or disparate treatment. The courts have upheld the right of corrections facilities to implement mandatory HIV testing, as well as segregate infected inmates from the general population. Courts have also supported the singling out of one inmate for testing after the discovery of high-risk behavior, as well as a policy of not testing inmates after such occurrences. Inmates who have challenged the unauthorized disclosure of their medical records under their Constitutional right to privacy have been denied relief by the courts, who have maintained that such a principle does not apply to incarcerated individuals. Equally unsuccessful have been lawsuits filed by uninfected inmates or correctional staff who sought to require institutions to test for HIV in order to reduce the risk of transmission (Blumberg and Laster 1999).

In the case of *Harris v. Thigpen* (1991), maintained that individual inmates who were HIV positive qualified as "handicapped" under the standard of the *Rehabilitation Act.* However, the courts have generally upheld that security and medical concerns outweigh such rights and therefore segregation and disparate treatment is justified (Robbins 1996). In the case of *Gates v. Rowland* (1994) the United States Court of Appeals recognized that other courts were willing to consider the irrational fears of guards and inmates as legitimate interests. Traditionally, accommodation of prejudice and ungrounded fear is not permitted in the courts. However, the Ninth Circuit ruled that in the case of a prison, heightened security concerns and a volatile inmate population allowed for such recognition (Robbins 1996).

CONCLUSION

The community of disabled persons poses unique problems for the criminal justice system. In addition to the myriad issues that can result in the marginalization of a disabled individual, the disability itself may serve as a compounding factor in other aspects that also contribute to discrimination. For example, someone who is already a member of another traditionally marginalized group, such as a racial or ethnic minority, is not precluded from also being disabled. Therefore the population of disabled employees, victims, offenders, and inmates may very well incur intensified experiences of discrimination as they progress through the criminal justice system. It is of utmost importance that criminal justice professionals recognize the individualized needs of the disabled community to avoid further confounding the already weak ability of the system to meet the needs of these individuals. This theme of multiple marginalization factors is continued in Chapter 10 with a discussion of the Elderly in the Criminal Justice system. Readers will find that there are a number of similarities and overlapping issues between the disabled and the elderly when it comes to their experiences within the various roles of the criminal justice arena.

REFERENCES

ATLAS, R. (1992). *Is accessibility a disability? The impact of ADA on jails.* Unpublished manuscript. Obtained from the National Institute of Corrections. Author.

BLUMBERG, M., AND J. D. LASTER. (1999). The impact of HIV/AIDS on corrections. In *The Dilemmas of Corrections*, ed. K. C. Haas and G. P. Alpert. Prospect Heights, IL: Waveland.

BOSARGE, B. B. (1991). Implementing ADA expected to cost law enforcement millions in litigation fees. *Crime Control Digest, 25*(50), 1, 4–8.

CARNAHAN, S. J. (1999). The Americans with Disabilities Act in state correctional institutions. *Capital University Law Review, 27*, 291–316.

FRISK, A. M., and C. B. HERNICZ (1996). Obesity as a disability: An actual or perceived problem? *Army Lawyer*, May, 3–19.

GARDNER, E. (1994). The legal rights of inmates with physical disabilities. *Saint Louis University Public Law Review, 14*, 175–216.

HAMMETT, T. M., P. HARMON, AND L. M. MARUSCHAK (1999). *1996–1997 Update: HIV/AIDS, STDs, and TB in correctional facilities* [NCJ 176344]. Washington, DC: National Institute of Justice.

JOHNSON, J. D. (1998). Does the Americans with Disabilities Act apply to the conduct of law enforcement officers pursuant to arrests? A survey of Gorman v. Bartch. *Georgia State University Law Review, 14*, 901–23.

LONG, L. M., AND A. D. SAPP. (1992). Programs and facilities for physically disabled inmates in state prisons. *Journal of Offender Rehabilitation, 18*(1/2), 191–204.

MARTIN, D. V. (1998/1999). How will police and fire departments respond to public safety needs and the Americans With Disabilities Act? *New York University School of Law Journal of Legislation and Public Policy, 2*, 39–141.

MARUSCHAK, L. M. (1999). HIV in prisons 1997. *Bureau of Justice Statistics Bulletin* [NCJ 178284]. Washington, DC: U.S. Department of Justice.

MCAFEE, J. K., AND S. L. MUSSO. (1995). Training police officers about persons with disabilities. *Remedial and Special Education, 16*(1), 53–64.

MCALISTER, J. (1994). Deaf and hard-of-hearing criminal defendants: How you gonna get justice if you can't talk to the judge? *Arizona State Law Journal, 26*, 163–200.

PAPPAS, V. P. (1988). In prison with AIDS: The constitutionality of mass screening and segregation policies. *University of Illinois Law Review*,1000, 151–90.

ROBBINS, I. P. (1996). George Bush's America meets Dante's Inferno: The Americans with Disabilities Act in prison. *Yale Law and Public Policy Review, 15*, 49–112.

RUBIN, P. N. (1993). *The Americans with Disabilities Act and criminal justice: An Overview* (DOJ Report No. NCJ 140567). Washington, DC: U. S. Department of Justice, National Institute of Justice.

RUBIN, P. N., AND S. CAMPBELL. (1995). *The Americans with Disabilities Act and criminal justice: Mental disabilities.* Washington, DC: National Institute of Justice.

RUBIN, P. N., AND T. DUNNE. (1994). *The Americans with Disabilities Act: Emergency response systems and telecommunication devices for the deaf.* Washington, DC: National Institute of Justice.

SCHNEID, T. D., AND L. K. GAINES. (1991). The Americans with Disabilities Act: Implications for police administrators. *American Journal of Police, 10*(1), 47–58.

SMITH, M. R., AND G. P. ALPERT. (1993). Law enforcement: The police and the Americans With Disabilities Act-who is being discriminated against? *Criminal Law Bulletin, 29*(6), 516–28.

TYISKA, C. G. (2001). *Working with victims of crime with disabilities* [NCJ 172838]. Washington, DC: Office for the Victims of Crime, U.S. Department of Justice.

VERNON, M. (1995). New rights for inmates with hearing loss. *Corrections Today, 57*(2), 140–44.

VERNON, M., AND S. RICH. (1997). *Pedophilia and deafness.* Washington, DC: American Annals of the Deaf.

VERNON, M., L. J. RAIFMAN, AND S. F. GREENBERG. (1996). The Miranda warnings and the deaf suspect. *Behavioral Sciences and the Law, 14*(1), 121–35.

WALVOORD, L. E. (1996). Comment: A critique of Torcasio v. Murray and the use of the clear statement rule to interpret the Americans with Disabilities Act. *Minnesota Law Review, 80*, 1183.

WERTLIEB, E. C. (1991). Individuals with disabilities in the criminal justice system. *Criminal Justice and Behavior, 18*(3), 332–51.

WOOD, E. F. (1990). Toward a barrier-free courthouse: Equal access to justice for persons with physical disabilities. *Clearinghouse Review*, December, 557–59.

10

The Elderly in the Criminal Justice System

Reid C. Toth

❖

INTRODUCTION

Unlike the other status groups discussed in this text, the elderly as a group are difficult to define. With a few exceptions, it is relatively easy to determine the characteristics that define membership in major racial or ethnic groups, along with other marginalized groups such as the disabled, homosexual, and religious orders. The elderly are much more difficult to define as a group because determining identifiable characteristics that are consistent with all members is virtually impossible. Age alone is not always enough to classify someone as elderly, older, or geriatric. Most gerontologists do not accept a strict chronological definition of what constitutes "elderly." Rather, they rely on factors such as limited physical function, employment status, life activities, and self-perception (Goodwin 1992). For the purposes of this discussion, we will rely on a variety of ages, defined as elderly by the context of the discussion. For example, a generic baseline for elderly individuals is age 65. However, when discussing inmates, the age of 50 is more appropriate due to the differences in physical characteristics between inmates and their counterparts in the general population. Given such variations, the authors in this chapter interchangeably use the terms "elderly," "geriatric," "older," and "senior citizen" to describe anyone who falls into a category of special needs based on conditions related to advanced age. When a specific chronological age is relevant to the discussion, it is so noted.

The elderly form a significant and growing segment of society. As of 1995, they constituted 12.8% (33.5 million) of the United States population (Mandino, 2000). The American Association of Retired Persons (AARP) estimates that persons aged 65 years and older will total 66 million Americans by the year 2030. This is an increase from 31 million in 1989 (Kohl et al. 1995). Such a significant growth, as a result of the aging baby boomer population, has been referred to by many as "the graying of America." The impact of such growth will not be limited to white, middle class America. By the year 2050, there will be a 160% increase in elderly African-Americans, 294% increase in elderly Native Americans, 570% increase in elderly Hispanics, and a 643% increase in elderly Asian/Pacific Islanders (Seymour et al. 2000). In terms of geography, America's elderly are concentrated in, and will therefore most significantly impact, the eight states of Florida, California, New York, Pennsylvania, Texas, Ohio, Michigan, and West Virginia (Bourns 2000).

Such multi-ethnic growth in the elderly population will be an important variable for the criminal justice system and its delivery of services. The variation of cultures between ethnic groups can have a significant impact on how an elderly person copes with their role in the criminal justice system, as well as impacting how service providers respond to the elderly. For example, beliefs concerning nutrition, doctors, family, and medication may determine what services an elderly victim will accept. Because beliefs systems vary among ethnic groups, a "one size fits all" approach to service provision cannot be assumed.

Ethnicity can also have an impact on previous living conditions which in turn impacts the future health of the elderly person. Financial solubility can be directly tied to previous work experience. As a result of the elderly person's ethnic culture, they may have been employed in seasonal, temporary, or part-time jobs. This work history not only relates to how much an individual was able to save for their future financial independence, but also determines what type of benefits they will receive from social security. The following discussion focuses on such service delivery problems and on the elderly as clients of the criminal justice system.

THE ELDERLY AS CRIMINAL JUSTICE EMPLOYEES

Empirical research, or for that matter even qualitative discussion, on the elderly and their role as employees in the criminal justice system is extremely limited. Presumably this shortage in the literature is a reflection of the small numbers of older persons who are employed on a salaried basis by criminal justice agencies. While the *Age Discrimination in Employment Act* (29 U.S.C. 623) prohibits unequal treatment of applicants or employees based on their age specifically in regard to hiring, firing, receiving benefits, and other conditions of employment, it does not require that an agency provide positions for those individuals who are incapable of carrying out the basic requirements of the job (See Chapter 9: The Disabled and Physically Challenged in the Criminal Justice System in this text for a discussion of the *Americans With Disabilities Act*). However, in cases involving criminal justice employees, such limitations must be determined on an individual basis, and not simply assumed to be present based on the age of the employee or applicant. For example, the U.S. Supreme Court has rejected mandatory retirement plans for municipal firefighters and police officers, stating that such judgments should be made on an individual's ability to perform the tasks of the position (Peak 2001). As such, many elderly persons due to physical or mental impairment are no longer appropriately suited for the physical demands required of a law enforcement or correctional officer. Even more importantly, the elderly are employed in a limited capacity in any occupation simply due to their eligibility for retirement. Rather than a reflection of discrimination, low numbers of elderly employees simply demonstrates a choice that is normal for aging Americans.

Legal limitations have not, however, resulted in the total absence of elderly representation in the service area of criminal justice agencies. While the elderly might not be eligible for the salaried components of agency work, their effectiveness as volunteers has been well documented. The AARP conducted a nationwide survey of municipal police departments and sheriffs' offices on the issue of using older persons as volunteers within the agencies. Of those agencies that were already utilizing older volunteers, the majority indicated that the work of the older volunteer rated higher than other volunteers' work, and 69% indicated that the quality of work for older volunteers was excellent. Ninety-eight percent of the participating agencies said that they would recommend the use of older volunteers to other agencies. Some of the reasons for using elderly volunteers included:

- Stability, reliability, dependability
- experience or knowledge
- Wisdom, maturity, leadership

- Reduction of work burden on paid employees
- Pleasant to be around
- Better work ethic
- Not motivated by paycheck
- Free labor
- Calming influence
- Relate well to the community (AARP 1994).

While most agencies find the contributions of such volunteers to be invaluable, some still do not. Agencies that did not utilize older volunteers expressed the following concerns about incorporating the elderly into a law enforcement agency:

- Difficulty in training new procedures
- Safety or liability for the volunteer
- Detrimental effects due to the emotional stress of the law enforcement environment
- Ability to withstand and pass a background check
- Mental capacity
- Transportation
- Being disruptive or in the way
- Architectural accessibility (AARP 1994).

Seniors volunteering to assist law enforcement agencies often contribute in the form of routine office work such as filing and typing which relieves officers to concentrate on law enforcement activities. Other variations include neighborhood watches that rely on observations of retired individuals who are at home most of the day and are aware of unusual activity in the area. The elderly also can perform services such as community patrol, traffic control, search and rescue, and home safety educational programs (Bourns 2000). For example, the San Diego Police Department established the Reserve Senior Volunteer Program (RSVP) where workers are used for data processing in the Crime Analysis Unit. Hundreds of volunteers have served through the RSVP program to date. Most senior volunteers are not interested in being police officers, they are interested only in offering support. They often do so through non-arrest positions in neighborhood crime prevention programs (Bourns 2000).

The state of Florida provides an example of a program incorporating elderly volunteers into crime prevention programs. Originating from the attorney general's office, "Seniors vs. Crimes" is a statewide program involving 1,000 elderly volunteers who help law enforcement investigate fraudulent acts such as telemarketing schemes, prescription medicine fraud and other crimes that traditionally victimize those 55 and older. When the project first began in 1989, the "Senior Sleuths" mostly focused on crime prevention education, but has since evolved into an undercover operation that has played a significant role in several high profile cases. One instance involved a five-year investigation into the billing practices of Eckerd drug stores. Senior sleuths were asked to count their pills regularly to see if they were given the full amount. Eckerd was eventually ordered to pay $1.7 million in fines for overbilling the government for Medicaid prescriptions. In other cases, the elderly sleuths play the role of the unwitting victim while con artists pitch schemes such as

$2,000 water treatment systems. Unbeknownst to the con artist, law enforcement have the entire interaction under surveillance (Bloodsworth 2002).

Senior Police Academies are also becoming more common. One of the oldest is at the St. James Parish Sheriff's Department in Convent, Louisiana. The academy program spans one week and covers topics such as personal safety, medical alerts, crime reporting by neighborhood watches, the role of law enforcement, senior victimization, serving on a grand jury, and safe-proofing one's home. The instruction is conducted by sheriff's deputies. Other senior academies are operational in Duncanville, Texas; Monroe, North Carolina (which includes a senior ride-along program); Tulsa, Oklahoma; and Oklahoma City, Oklahoma. In areas where senior academies are not available, some sheriff's departments offer citizen academies where adults of mixed ages can participate (Bourns 2000).

One of the largest and most organized programs involving senior citizens and the police is TRIAD. Begun in 1988 as a formal agreement between AARP, the International chiefs of Police (IACP), and the National Sheriff's Association (NSA), its primary purpose is to provide senior safety and crime prevention information through displays, meetings, and in-service training. TRIAD is permanently located at the NSA office in Washington, DC. Regionally it is composed of over 350 state and local advisory councils known as Seniors and Law Enforcement Together (SALT). Each SALT is comprised of 10 to 15 adult senior leaders from the community as well as the county sheriff and local police chief. The seniors are representatives of AARP, RSVP, Senior Citizen Centers, health care agencies, service organizations, teachers' organizations, religious institutions, and other local agencies that work with the elderly (Bourns 2000).

Unfortunately, when one thinks of the role played by the elderly citizen in the criminal justice system, it is rarely as the good Samaritan volunteer. More often it is as a victim, witness, or offender that older persons find themselves maneuvering the complicated and unforgiving paths through law enforcement agencies, court rooms, and even prisons. The remainder of this chapter examines each of these potential roles in detail, giving particular attention to the special issues posed for the respective agencies when an elderly individual is the client.

THE ELDERLY AS VICTIMS

Fear of Crime

Society's portrayal of the elderly often is that of victims and highly vulnerable people. After reviewing the research literature, Lindquist (1987) came to several conclusions concerning elderly victimization. First, while the elderly suffer low victimization rates in most crime categories, there are some in which they are victimized at a higher rate. Second, different age groups experience variations in victimization according to locale within the United States. Third, overall, the elderly are victimized proportionally less than other age groups. The final observation was that while the heightened sense of fear among the elderly may be irrational, it is based on fairly realistic and accurate interpretations of the likelihood of victimization for certain crimes.

Some people advocate that the elderly are justified in their heightened sense of fear of victimization. These advocates make three primary arguments in defense of this conviction.

First, they suggest that the elderly are primarily most afraid of crimes in which they are more likely to be victimized such as purse-snatching and pocket-picking (Lindquist 1987). National statistics show that individuals 65 or older are less likely than other groups to become victims of all forms of household crime with the exception of personal larceny (purse snatching or pick pocketing) in which case they are equally likely to be victimized as other age groups. The elderly appear to be particularly vulnerable to crime involving economic gain. For example, robbery constitutes 38% of the violent crime committed against the elderly, but only 20% of violent crime committed against those under 65 (BJS 1994). Therefore, their fear is in fact rational and accurate as an assessment of their risk (Lindquist 1987).

Second, the elderly may have a heightened fear of crime because they realize that they are less capable of recovering from a physical assault then their younger counterparts. This is also rational, according to advocates, because studies consistently show that elderly victims of violent crime are more likely to be injured and are less likely to recover (Lindquist 1987). For example, in a 1992 case, a Baltimore, Maryland, man who was 88-years-old was on a daily round of sales calls when he was mugged and robbed of his wallet. In his attempt to resist his attacker, he suffered a fatal heart attack and died before reaching the hospital. He became the city's 287th homicide victim of the year (Bachman 1993). More than 20% of elderly victims of violence sustain similar or other types of injuries during the course of a crime (Klaus 1999). Additionally, elderly victims of violent crime are slightly more likely to face an armed offender, particularly an offender armed with a gun, and they are less likely than other victims to take self defensive measures during the commission of a crime. These victims acted in their own defense 53% of the time, compared to 75% of the younger victims. When the elderly do protect themselves, it is usually a non-physical action such as arguing, screaming, or running away (BJS 1994).

The third argument is that while the elderly are not entirely justified in their victimization fear, those who live in high-crime areas are more frequently victimized and therefore have an appropriate level of fear (Lindquist 1987). The elderly are twice as likely to be raped, robbed or assaulted at or near their home than those in other age groups. One half of elderly victims are victimized near their home compared to one quarter of younger victims. In addition, perpetrators are more likely to be strangers in cases of elderly victimization than in cases where the victim is younger (BJS 1994).

Opponents suggest that the fear of crime among the elderly is unjustified. Some suggest that the elderly do not in fact fear crime but rather fear what they perceive as the "typical" criminal: a young, black, male stranger. These opponents argue that this is not rational because someone fitting this physical description may be totally innocent. Second, it is argued that the elderly do not suffer significantly higher levels of financial loss and physical injury than other groups. The fear in this case comes from an erroneous comparison to the age groups closest to the elderly person. It is true that the elderly are victimized more than middle aged adults, but they are victimized less than younger adults. However the elderly person considers potential for victimization in comparison with the former more so than the latter. Given these circumstantial restrictions, the heightened sense of fear is irrational (Lindquist 1987).

The elderly experienced victimization at lower rates than any other age groups for all crime for the years 1992–97. They were 5 times less likely to be victims of robbery and 12 times less likely to be victims of assault (Klaus 1999). Individuals falling in the

12–24 age range have the highest victimization rates, while those over 64 have the lowest (BJS 1994). According to FBI statistics for 1992, those aged 65 or older, comprised 5% of homicide victims (BJS 1994). For the time period 1992–97, the population of persons over 64 in the population was 31.3 million. These individuals were victims of property and violent crimes 2.7 million times. There were 2.5 million property crimes which included 46,000 purse snatchings or pick pocketings and 165,000 nonlethal violent crimes such as rape, robbery, and assault. There were also 1,000 murders with elderly victims. The elderly were disproportionately victimized by property crimes with 90% of crimes falling in this category. This is compared to 40% for persons aged 12–24. Overall, the elderly made up 15% of the population over age 12, but accounted for 7% of criminal victimizations (Klaus 1999). For the time period 1976–2000, the BJS found that non-fatal violence rates for those aged 50 and older fluctuated only slightly. In cases of homicide for the same age groups, the rates dropped approximately 50% (Klaus and Rennison 2002). Individuals older than age 50 constitute 30% of the population, 12% of murder victims, and 7% of violent crime victims (Seymour et al. 2000). Of elderly victims, white women have the lowest violent crime rates, while black women have the lowest personal theft rates (BJS 1994).

Studies demonstrate that senior citizens are not a homogeneous category and do not fear crime equally. Previous studies show that fear of crime is highest among the elderly for females, blacks, urban residents, the disabled, and the socially isolated. These studies have failed to make a distinction between what are relative and what are absolute levels of fear. For instance, while the elderly may have a higher overall level of fear than younger people, it does not mean that their fear is pronounced or significant. In fact, a 1986 study showed that only 6% of the elderly reported being "very fearful" of becoming a victim. The elderly have a tendency to develop "formless fear" where they express concern of being victimized by crime in general, but they exhibit very little "concrete fear," or fear of specific acts in specific locations such as their home (McCoy et al. 1996).

In some cases, it may be difficult to determine exactly how irrational, or rational, the rate of fear is among the elderly. The statistics discussed in this chapter thus far provide a picture only of known crime rates involving the elderly. Some of these numbers may not be entirely accurate, however, because an elderly person may not always notify someone that they have been victimized. An elderly person's decision to report a crime will most often be based on the amount of money involved, who the perpetrator was, and their confidence that an arrest will be made. They tend not to report crime if they perceive that the police cannot or will not do anything or if they feel the crime is not worth reporting (Goodwin 1992). Those elderly who are victims of personal theft and robbery are more likely to report the crime than younger victims (BJS 1994). If much of the crime against the elderly goes unreported then the missing data or "dark figure of crime" may in fact explain higher rates of fear when quantitative evidence does not.

Types of Victimization

Elder Abuse Much like child abuse, elder abuse is a sinister crime in which people with some sort of control over another person, be it physical, emotional, financial, or otherwise, exploit the vulnerabilities of the person in their care. This may take place in the elderly person's own home, the home of a relative, or even a nursing home. Elder abuse is a relatively recent discovery in terms of research. The first studies on the topic came in the late 1970s. Block and Sinnott published *The Battered Elder Syndrome: An Exploratory Study* in 1979 and, while it was exploratory in nature, it is recognized as one of the early landmark studies. They contacted 24 agencies in Maryland and conducted a survey that included 427 professionals and 443 elders. Their results indicated 26 cases of elder abuse. Another significant study, published in 1988, was conducted by Pillemer and Finkelhor on 2,020 elders in Boston. These individuals were 65 or older and lived either on their own or with their families. They found that 3.2% had been abused. Other subsequent studies have shown even higher rates, between 4% and 10%. Some researchers believe the number to be significantly higher, citing that only one in six elders report the abuse (Wallace, Roberson, and Steckler, 1995).

As a result of the National Elder Abuse Incidence study, it was determined that in 1996 there were at least 1.5 million elderly individuals who experienced abuse, neglect, and self neglect in a domestic setting. For every one of these incidences reported, it is estimated that five go unreported (Seymour et al. 2000). The true extent of elder abuse is difficult to determine because of such unreported incidences. Even more difficult is determining whether such crimes are increasing or decreasing. One survey of state human service agencies reported a 50% increase in elder abuse cases between 1980 and 1990 (Kohl et al. 1995), however it is possible that the only change during this time was in the rate of reporting, not the rate of crime commission.

As mentioned previously, the elderly do not form a homogeneous group. There have been studies documenting the differences in abuse among ethnic groups. For instance, it was found that black victims were more likely to be female than white victims, they were more likely to experience serious abuse, they were not more likely to experience financial or physical abuse than whites, and they tended to be older than victims of other types of abuse. Blacks were also more likely to report abuse to the police than any other ethnic group (Brownell 1998).

Older studies of elder abuse victims suggested that women were more likely to become victims of elder abuse than men. This was partially explained by factors such as the higher proportion of women in the population, the lack of physical ability to resist abuse, and the opportunity for sexual molestation. However, more recent studies have suggested that the majority of elder abuse victims are men. Reasons cited included that such men tended to be more impaired than their female counterparts, that they were often victimized by abusers who felt they were avenging childhood abuse at the hands of the elderly person, and that the elderly male was more likely to engage in excessive behaviors such as drinking that heightened their vulnerability to abuse (Baumhover and Beall 1996).

It has also been determined that the older a person is, the greater their chances of becoming a victim of elder abuse. The oldest of the nation's elderly, those 80 years and older, are abused or neglected at a rate two to three times their proportion of the elderly population (Seymour et al. 2000). Presumably this may be attributed to two factors: as a person becomes older they exhibit more physical and mental vulnerabilities which in turn make them easier targets for abuse; and the longer one is dependent on another, the greater the opportunities for abuse.

Elder abuse can occur in virtually any setting. Nursing homes or assisted care facilities have been featured in the media as breeding grounds for physical and sexual exploitation of the elderly. One explanation for this is simply that the sheer number of potential victims provides fodder for offenders drawn to this type of crime. For the year 1995, 4% (1.4 million) of persons over the age of 64 lived in nursing homes or other long-term care facilities (Klaus 1999). While caregivers are frequently involved in the victimization of an elderly person, workers in facilities providing elder services may also be culprits. In some instances, parolees or probationers are employed by boarding or elder care facilities at the urging of the person's parole officer. In some states, background checks, high level skills, or licenses are not a requirement for employment in elder care facilities. Therefore, individuals who are very vulnerable are often being cared for by past offenders (Mandino 2000). Compounding the problem is the failure of many such institutions to take adequate precautions to protect their clients, or to respond in a responsible manner after an incident. A Senate Special Committee on Aging presented findings to Congress that showed that nursing homes rarely call police for attacks that would have brought an instant response in any other environment (Margasak 2002).

Many elderly individuals are equally unsafe in their own homes or the homes of relatives. As with many other types of crime spanning across age groups, the elderly are more likely to be victimized by someone they know, usually a close acquaintance or relative rather than a stranger. The Pillemer and Finkelhor study, referred to earlier in this discussion, made another significant finding: that elders were more likely to be abused by their spouses than by their children. However, they offered the explanation that elders were more likely to be living with spouses than adult children, therefore skewing the results toward the former. They also found that both males and females were victims, but that husbands tended to inflict more severe abuse. The overall conclusion was that elders are more likely to be abused by people that they live with (Wallace, Roberson, and Steckler, 1995).

Defining abuse can also contribute to the complex issue of reporting and tracking this type of crime. In many cases, caretakers nor the elderly victims interpret actions to be abusive. If confronted with the consequences of the behavior, either party may be surprised that the action was interpreted as abusive. Roberson and Wallace (2001) provide three interesting examples of interactions between the elderly and their caretakers. The question becomes, "is it abuse or is it support?" A 90 year old woman lives with her 55-year-old son. The woman has wandered away from the house several times. The son therefore has taken to locking her in her room from 7:00 pm until the next morning. The room does not have a bathroom. In the second case, a 20-year-old granddaughter frequently visits her 85-year-old grandmother. During these visits the granddaughter combs the grandmother's hair. Afterwards, she takes $40 from the grandmother's purse as payment. The grandmother does not protest because she is afraid the granddaughter will cease to visit. A third case is that of a husband and wife who have taken in the wife's 85-year-old mother. The husband requires that his mother-in-law shower each evening while he stands in the bathroom watching her.

Abuse of the elderly can manifest itself in many ways. Physical abuse occurs when physical force or pain is inflicted upon the victim. Given that fragility often occurs with increased age, physical abuse can be particularly dangerous for the elderly victim. Psychological or mental torment is another form of elder abuse. This may encompass actions such as verbal assaults, intimidation, humiliation, isolation, and threats. Neglect is the most common form of abuse among elderly victims. It occurs when the caregiver fails to provide the basic necessities of life. This may include deliberate denial of food, clothing, shelter, or health care. Financial exploitation as a form of abuse may occur when the caretaker or other influential person mismanages funds, property or other resources.

This may result in loss of independence and freedom for the elderly person if their home or income is lost. Restriction of personal freedom is another form of abuse. The elderly victim may have their right to personal space and freedom of movement curtailed by a caregiver. In extreme cases this means being restrained to a bed, or placed in a closet or small room. A final form of abuse is that inflicted by the victim upon themselves. This may involve intentional or unintentional neglect, or infliction of injury or pain. (Mandino 2000). The National Center on Elder Abuse in 1994 determined that proportions for specific types of elder abuse were (Seymour et al. 2000):

- Physical abuse – 15.7%
- Sexual abuse – 0.04%
- Emotional abuse – 7.3%
- Neglect – 58.5%
- Financial exploitation – 12.3%
- All other types – 5.1%
- Unknown – 0.06%

The most common form of abuse, neglect, essentially comes in two forms. Passive neglect occurs when the caregiver is not able to provide adequate care. This may occur when a middle aged couple cannot afford nursing home care, so they take an elderly relative into their home. Their intentions may be benign, but the resulting care is inadequate. Consider the case of a middle aged couple who take in the husband's elderly mother after she has had several strokes. The couple eventually decides to retire. Shortly after the retirement, the mother has another stroke which leaves her mentally alert but physically unable to communicate or care for herself. Unable to afford nursing home care on their fixed income, the couple continues to care for the elderly mother on their own. Within a year, the husband has a heart attack and dies. His wife continues to care for her ailing mother-in-law but she becomes increasing depressed and isolated from friends and relatives. A family member pays a visit after a year or so and finds the mother-in-law crying in her bed while lying in her own waste. The room is littered with spoiled food and roaches. The daughter-in-law offers the explanation that she could no longer care for the elderly relative but had no means of getting help (Meadows 1998).

Active neglect is another form of abuse. In this case the caregiver intentionally denies food, water, medication, nutrition, shelter, or medical treatment to the elderly victim. The motivation here lies in some gain by the caregiver for denying adequate care to the victim. For instance, a son takes in his elderly father who does not have health insurance but who needs several medications daily. The son gradually convinces the father that he no longer needs the medicine. The son also talks the father into buying a substantial life insurance policy for whom the son is the beneficiary. As the father's health deteriorates, he is hospitalized. Upon release, the son continues to deny medicine and refuses to take his father for medical care. The father is eventually admitted to a veterans' hospital (Meadows 1998).

Approximately one million elderly victims suffer from physical or mental abuse annually. Motivation for such crimes is often centered in stress experienced by the caregiver. Families where there is a history of violence may be more at risk for elder abuse, particularly if the caregiver sees an opportunity for retribution against a formerly abusive parent or older person. Additional factors contributing to elder abuse may be strained family ties, substance abuse, or psychiatric issues. A significant problem in breaking the cycle of abuse is rooted in the reluctance of an elderly victim to report the crime. Often times this reluctance may be due to fear of being placed in an elder care facility, fear of retaliation by the offender, or shame over the victimization (Mandino 2000).

Baumhover and Beall (1996) discussed five theories that are most commonly used to explain elder abuse and neglect. First is the issue of possible psychopathology of the abuser in which case mental illness impacts their behavior. Second is the presence of trans-generational violence where elder abuse is a manifestation of learned violent behavior that has become cyclical. The third, social exchange theory, involves interactions where rewards and punishments are traded between people. Individuals seek to maximize rewards while minimizing punishments. Abusers may rationalize punishment on the grounds that they are not receiving personal rewards that outweigh the costs incurred in maintaining the relationship. The abuse continues as long as the abuser feels that he or she is capitalizing on it. Vulnerability/impairment of the older person is the fourth theory. In this case the defenseless condition of the elderly person provides for opportunities that result in abuse. The final theory, excessive situational demands suggests that certain con-textual variables may act as mediators or aggravators to transform a caregiver's reaction to the circumstances of the elderly person.

Brownell (1998) discussed two further theories on the etiology of elder abuse. The first, proposed by psychologist and domestic violence expert Suzanne Steinmetz suggests that caretaker stress is a primary cause of elder abuse. Known as "social breakdown theory," Steinmetz's explanation is that abuse occurs in situations where the needs of the elderly relative overwhelm the caregiver. The caregiver then reacts to the frustration in abusive ways. Unfortunately, this may become a self-perpetuating cycle. For example, an elderly woman lives with her middle aged daughter who is single and under stress to provide for two teen-aged sons. The daughter, who works during the day, restricts her mother's activities so that she does not fall and injure herself as has happened in the past. She also chooses the mother's meals and clothing. The mother then becomes resentful, bored, and more passive. This, in turn, places more stress on the daughter. The cycle con-tinues to escalate until finally abuse in the form of pushing, shoving, or threats of nursing home placement occur (Brownell 1998).

The second theory, proposed by sociologist Karl Pillemer, states that the elderly relative may be at risk of abuse because they are the caregiver of a dependent adult child. The adult child finds their role socially unacceptable and attempts to gain power over the parent. Pillemer found that in these cases, the most likely victim was not the advanced elderly, but rather those in the 60–74 age range. The elderly victim is usually unimpaired, but may be dealing with an adult dependent child who is impaired. For example, a 70-year-old man lives with his 30-year-old son. The father provides shelter, food, and financial support to the son who is unemployed and suffers from alcoholism. Despite this support, the son is verbally abusive, and often steals money from his father to buy alcohol (Brownell 1998).

Research on successful approaches to eliminating elder abuse is scarce. However, the results of one study on the subject were surprising. Robert Davis of the Vera Institute of Justice in New York City and Juanjo Medina-Ariza of the University of Manchester, England, conducted a study of 403 elder abuse victims in New York housing projects who had received different types of follow-up interventions. They found that in cases where both home visits and public education campaigns had been implemented, new incidents of abuse were actually *more* frequent. This included cases of new calls to the police and increased reports of abuse to researchers who were interviewing the victims. There are three possible explanations for such an increase. The first is that persons who received both types of interventions did not actually suffer from more abuse, but had become more sensitized to such behavior. Second, individuals receiving both interventions may have been more willing to report the abuse. Third, the combination of the two interventions caused more abuse (Study suggests 2002). It is clear that further research on this topic is necessary in order to stem the tide of elder abuse. Until this crime becomes rare, it is the responsibility of criminal justice agencies to recognize the symptoms, respond in a compassionate and efficient manner, and make efforts to meet the specific needs of the elderly victims.

Other Types of Victimization

Crime may be particularly devastating to an elderly person. For instance, an elderly person may be more likely to be physically injured during an interpersonal crime and, due to their age, may not recover with the same agility as a younger person. A broken hip or leg could potentially develop into a problem with life-long implications. Financial loss in the case of a scam or fraud may mean the difference between living comfortably and being deprived of food, medicine, or heat. Victimization may also cause the elderly person to resist becoming financially or emotionally dependent on family members. Elderly victims may even become reclusive because they are embarrassed, distressed, and deprived of self-confidence. Isolation may also be a result for the elderly who have not been victimized, but who have read or heard about crimes involving other elderly people. Fear of crime itself may prevent the individual from attending church, socializing, shopping, or participating in the community (National Institute of Justice 1993).

While all age groups experience crime, there are some specific criminal acts that are more likely to be aimed at the elderly. For example, frauds, scams, cons, purse snatching, theft of checks form the mail, and abuse in long-term care facilities. Age itself does play a factor in predisposing this demographic group to certain types of crime. With age comes some mental and physical factors that make the elderly particularly vulnerable:

- *Loneliness:* an elderly person who does not have the opportunity for much socialization may be too receptive to the conversation of a scam artist.
- *Grief:* if the elderly individual has recently lost a friend or loved one they may be in need of companionship. This need places them at risk for fraud.
- *Loss:* the elderly person may have recently been deprived of employment, family, or friends. As a result, depression may develop causing the older person not to use sound judgment when dealing with swindlers.
- *Sensory Impairment:* Impaired vision or hearing may allow con artists to trick the elderly person into signing contracts with small print or some other manner of commitment.
- *Illness:* Chronic pain or illness predisposes some elderly individuals to being swindled on false medical cures and promises.

- *Vanity:* people who are driven to resist the aging process may be taken on schemes for restoring beauty or reversing other age related characteristics.
- *Limited Income:* Because of fixed incomes, an older person may be tempted by offers at apparently easy money or investments.
- *Mistrust of Banks:* Due to post-Depression era fears of bank failure, the elderly person may tend to keep large amounts of cash at home. This places them at risk for serious financial loss in the case of a burglary or robbery.
- *Isolation:* An elderly person may be easily swindled or exploited on home and car repairs if family members are not available to advise them (National Institute of Justice 1993).

Financial and Property Crimes Frequent crimes committed against older persons are purse-snatching, scams, or other financially motivated acts. As a group, the elderly have more than $1 trillion in assets, making them an irresistible target for offenders looking for financial gain (Mandino 2000). They are such easy targets that the term "crib job" is street lingo for robbing an elderly person because it is considered to be as easy as "taking candy from a baby."

Elderly victims constitute 30% of all fraud cases. Popular methods of defrauding older people include mailings indicating that the individual has won a prize or is potentially the winner of a prize. In many cases, the requirement for retrieving the prize is for the "winner" to send payment for shipping or some other fee. In other cases, the con artist scans the obituary columns and makes contacts with widows/widowers. They then claim that the deceased spouse owed them money either for "specially ordered" products or some other false fee. Perpetrators have a particularly easy time with telemarketing schemes because many elderly individuals are reluctant to terminate the call for fear of being rude or, in some cases where the victims live alone, out of sheer loneliness (Mandino 2000).

Another specific type of financial crime against the elderly is referred to as "the bank embezzler." In this crime, an offender impersonating a bank officer enlists the elderly victim to help him catch an employee who is embezzling money. The victim is encouraged to withdraw all of their money from a bank account and take it home. The next day the phony bank official phones the victim and thanks them for their help in catching the employee. As a gesture of appreciation, the offender offers to come by the victim's home to pick up the money and redeposit it, saving them an extra trip to the bank. Of course, the victim never sees the money again. Tax fraud is another scheme used against the elderly population. A person impersonating an Internal Revenue Service agent contacts the victim and tells them that they are delinquent on their taxes and a cash payment is needed immediately. An address is provided where the offender will retrieve the money. Phony home improvement scams are the most common form of consumer fraud, but other frequent attempts include medical fraud, real estate fraud, mortgage fraud, health and nutrition fraud, investment fraud, and funeral chasing. In the latter crime, an offender gets personal information from an obituary before contacting the bereaved. They indicate to the victim that their deceased loved one made an initial deposit for a service or item and additional payment is now due (Forst 2000).

Financial fraud and abuse against the elderly is most often committed by coercion, misrepresentation, or other means that prey on the elderly person's incompetencies or vulnerabilities. Most often the perpetrator is someone who already has a financial relationship with the older person and who takes or uses the money or property in a manner that is not part of their trust or duty. The victims are usually unmarried and frequently do not report the victimization to police. They may be individuals who are not under the care of social service agencies, may exhibit eccentric behavior, are unable to leave the abusive situation, and have an inability to provide credible evidence in court. The abusers tend to be the older person's caregiver, a person who is most frequently male, younger than the victim with a history of alcohol or drug abuse, mental illness, or serious medical problems. Additionally, the abuser is more than likely financially dependent on the elderly victim (Heisler and Tewksbury 1991).

There are a variety of risk factors associated with fiduciary abuse. Vulnerability is the most common. The elderly are easily identifiable. They often respond to special financial incentives for seniors and otherwise demonstrate their vulnerabilities through physical aids such as canes and walkers. Naiveté is another risk factor. Many elderly persons may be unsophisticated and inexperienced in financial issues particularly if their assets were purchased many years earlier or if such matters have traditionally been handled by someone else. They are often slow to recognize their own victimization or react to signs of exploitation. Even when they are aware of the abuse, a third risk factor of failure to disclose such actions may occur. Often they feel guilty, embarrassed, or responsible. If the offender is a relative, the elderly victim may rationalize the behavior on the grounds that the offender would have received the asset eventually anyway (Heisler and Tewksbury 1991).

Other types of property crimes such as purse-snatching, pick-pocketing, and burglary often result in victimization of the elderly. Elderly victims of burglary tend to suffer more sentimental grief and suffering from the loss of their stolen possessions. The financial impact may also be extreme. A larceny of even a small amount of money may mean that an elderly victim goes without food or medication due to their fixed income status (Seymour 2000).

Crimes of Violence   The elderly are unlikely to be injured while being victimized. However, when such injuries do occur, they are more likely to be serious. For the years 1987–92, the elderly were more than twice as likely as any other group to be seriously injured and require hospitalization after becoming victimized. Perpetrators of such violent crimes are often known to the victim. In cases where homicide victims were over the age of 60, 1994 statistics show that their children were the perpetrators in 42% of the cases, and spouses were the perpetrators in 24% of the cases (Seymour et al. 2000).

Given their vulnerable physical state, many elderly victims have been targets of offenders looking to commit sex crimes. The U.S. Department of Justice has estimated that persons over the age of 64 constitute 1% of sexual assault victims (Seymour et al. 2000). Sexual assault may be particularly difficult for the elderly woman. Today's elderly generation of women were raised during a time when it was not appropriate to discuss sexual matters, therefore many elderly victims of sexual assault are embarrassed to discuss it. To disclose it to their children or in public may be unthinkable. Some are ashamed and discussing the case or submitting to the necessary medical exams seems unbearable. Others are further humiliated by having been forced to participate in specific sexual acts for the first time. Just as with other violent crimes, elderly victims of sexual assault are more likely to sustain serious injuries than younger victims. Because of hormonal changes, the vaginal walls may not be as elastic as in a younger woman and may be more likely to have infections, bruises, or tears that are slow to heal. In addition, the bones of the hip and pelvis may be more brittle in elderly women, particularly if osteoporosis is present, and they may actually be crushed by the weight of the rapist (Wallace, Roberson, and Steckler, 1995).

A 1992 study by Muram, Miller, and Cutler showed that elderly victims of sexual assault were more likely to sustain a genital injury during the assault. These victims experienced such injuries in 50% of the cases and required surgical repair in 15%. This can be compared to the need for surgical reparation in only 6% of the control group. Most of the assaults took place in the victim's home and were committed by a stranger. It is likely that many of these assaults occurred after the perpetrator entered the home in the course of a robbery attempt. Such characteristics differ from younger victims who were more often assaulted away from their home and by someone who was familiar to them (Muram et al. 1992).

Programs for Elderly Victims

Police interaction with elderly victims can be difficult. The unlikelihood of the victim reporting the crime may mean that in the event that the crime comes to the attention of the police, the victim may be an unwilling participant in an investigation. Moreover, police in many cases have not been well trained to deal with the specific needs of the elderly victim and therefore have difficulty communicating successfully with such victims. Some states have taken steps to improve police and community relations with elderly victims. A 1978 study of urban elderly residents revealed that as their contact with police increased, their positive perception of police service decreased. In reaction to the elderly population's perception of police, the Milwaukee, Wisconsin, police department established a special senior citizen unit. Unofficially known as "the Gray Squad," police personnel receive sensitivity training in interviewing and interrogating the elderly. Their primary responsibility lies in investigating and preventing crimes such as assaults, robberies, personal larcenies, and confidence crimes (Zevitz et al. 1991). The state of Massachusetts established the Elder Protection Project in an effort to train law enforcement officers on issues concerning the elderly population. Topics included the changing demographics of the elderly community, methods for communicating effectively, sensitivity when dealing with the elderly, and methods for intervening, reporting, and investigating elder abuse (Kohl et al. 1995).

In addition to improving police–citizen relations, some states and the federal government have established special units for the specific purpose of preventing crimes against the elderly. The Elder Fraud Prevention Team Project (EFPT) is a pilot program developed by Attorney General Janet Reno through the Fraud Prevention Initiative. It is intended to improve the federal government's effectiveness in fraud prevention and involves a collaborative effort of the AARP and law enforcement agencies. EFPT teams conduct on site presentation on types of fraud in metropolitan areas of the country (Seymour et al. 2000). The *Senior Citizens Against Marketing Scams Act of 1993* (SCAMS) was legislation that resulted from congressional concerns of increased fraud activity against the elderly. Such concerns were raised by a two-year Federal Bureau of Investigation undercover operation on telemarketing fraud in Salt Lake City, Utah in 1993. SCAMS proposed new federal statutes criminalizing telemarketing fraud and enhancing penalties when senior citizens were targeted as victims. It also called for the United States

Sentencing Commission to review and report fraud offenses involving elderly victims to Congress (United States Sentencing Commission 1995).

Operation Fraudstop is a campaign by the National Sheriff's Association designed to make it more difficult for con artists and swindlers to be successful over the telephone. It provides education and assistance to telemarketing fraud victims and collaborates with other existing groups such as TRIAD. It also employs additional resources such as the media, publications, and private corporations such as Radio Shack and Wal-Mart (Seymour et al. 2000). TRIAD refers to a joint effort among law enforcement and the community to provide criminal justice and victim's services to the elderly. The concept originated in 1988 when the AARP, IACP, and the NSA came together in a cooperative agreement to address the crime-related needs of the elderly. A Triad is generally comprised of the chief of police, the sheriff, and older leaders in a community. Their primary purpose it to develop, improve, expand, and implement crime prevention and education programs for the elderly. Generally the activities are focused either on pre-victimization/prevention or post-victimization/victim assistance (National Institute of Justice 1993).

Other agencies have been established for the purposes of assisting elderly victims through the process. Adult Protective Services (APS) is a program that serves as a gate-keeper for vulnerable adults who are physically or mentally disabled to an extent that makes them particularly susceptible to abuse, neglect, or exploitation. All states have an APS agency which is authorized to receive reports or referrals, conduct assessments, and develop service plans (Seymour et al. 2000). The American Bar Association (ABA) has established the Commission on Legal Problems of the Elderly to help victim advocates to locate direct services for victims of elder abuse. It is developing a model interdisciplinary curriculum on elder abuse for such service providers (Seymour et al. 2000). Area Agencies on Aging (AAA) serve as coordinating bodies for elderly services and advocacy at the county or regional levels. They receive state, federal, and local funds for a variety of services. They often can provide an up-to-date resource directory of victim services as well as serve as partners in efforts to reach vulnerable elders (Seymour et al. 2000).

THE ELDERLY AS OFFENDERS

It is a bit unusual to think of the elderly as part of the criminal element. The general public does not, under ordinary circumstances, view the elderly population as threatening or dangerous. This stereotype is not unfounded. One of the most widely accepted tenets of criminology is the "inverse age–crime relationship." Ethnographic studies, aggregate arrest statistics, self-report surveys, and analyses of arrest histories all indicate that offenders reduce or terminate their criminal activities as they age (Shover 1985).

Research has shown that both criminal behavior and criminal propensity tends to decline after age 30. However, a small minority of the elderly population does in fact commit crime. Some studies have shown that while the elderly account for only a small proportion of serious crime offenses, in some categories their criminal activity increase at a rate higher than that of the general population (Shichor 1984). It is this latter group that will be the focus of the following discussion.

One difficulty in explaining criminal behavior among the elderly is that it is a typical behavior. The elderly are less likely to be deviant than other age groups, thereby limiting data available on their motivation (Fattah and Sacco 1989). Feinberg (1984) describes the concept of an "elderly delinquent" in which he notes the similarities between some elderly criminals and their juvenile counterparts. Such similarities include: exemption from work responsibilities, basically unstructured schedules, freedom from life planning, low prestige in status, low financial independence, few family responsibilities, emphasis on consumption rather than production, and emphasis on play and leisure as a dominant lifestyle.

Crime among the elderly tends to fluctuate. For the years 1971–92, there was a drop in arrest rates for persons over the age of 50, despite an increase of that age group in the general population. One explanation for this is offered by Merianos and Marquart (1997) who suggest that decriminalization of offenses such as vagrancy, public drunkenness, and loitering may partially explain the overall drop. This is supported by the fact that for the ten-year range of 1972–92, violent crimes among the elderly increased by 84%. Property crime among the elderly increased 107% during the same time frame. One explanation for such an increase in property offenses was that they were the result of older persons who were living on fixed incomes during the late 1970s and early 1980s when the country experienced very high rates of inflation. Approximately 300,000 people aged 55 years or older are arrested annually, with 17% of those involving serious felonies (Aday 1994b).

Like other offenders, elderly criminals can be divided into two categories: first time offenders and repeat/habitual offenders. In 1988, Fry identified specific patterns for the first time elderly offender: (1) violent offenders sentenced for a crime that involved a family member; (2) white-collar property offenders, likely sentenced for fraud after years of successful business experience; (3) drug offenders, more likely to be sentenced for the sale of drugs with no record of prior or current drug use; and (4) alcohol offenders, most likely sentenced to prison for vehicular manslaughter (Aday 1994b). Researchers suggest that first time elderly offenders may be suffering from problems of coping with new conditions in their lives. Often times the elderly person is faced with the simultaneous death of a spouse, loss of employment, reduced income, and loss of status. They are struggling to deal with loneliness, isolation, boredom, poverty, physical infirmity, and restriction of freedom (Fattah and Sacco 1989). Habitual or career offenders who are elderly differ in several aspects from the elderly offender who is arrested for the first time. For instance, 37% of arrests of habitual elderly criminals were for violent crimes compared to 7.5% for new elderly offenders. The offenders who are arrested for the first time after the age of 55 are more likely to have committed a minor offense, whereas career or habitual criminals are more likely to have committed violent or property crimes (Cavan 1987).

Types of Offenses

In a study conducted on a county level criminal justice system, Lindquist et al. (1987) noted that elderly offenders were typically more violent than younger offenders. Crimes for which they were arrested were equally divided between violent and nonviolent offenses, while younger arrestees were much more likely to have committed nonviolent crimes. Statistically, only one-quarter of the younger, but almost one-half of the elderly were arrested and charged with a violent crime. Approximately 80% of crimes involving elderly offenders are property crimes (e.g. shoplifting). However, those elderly offenders who serve prison sentences are most often incarcerated for violent offenses and are likely to have a previous criminal record (James 1992). Violent acts committed by elderly offenders are typically a form of expression and rarely utilitarian; that is, it rarely is used to accomplish other ends such as monetary gain, sexual satisfaction, etc. Elderly offenders are more likely than other age groups to use a firearm in the commission of a violent crime. The gun may serve as an "equalizer" to the physical differences between the offender and a younger victim. Assault is the most common violent offense committed by the elderly. Robbery is one of the least common violent offenses. An elderly person in need of or desiring money will choose other illegal means to obtain it rather than methods that require challenge to the victim (Fattah and Sacco 1989).

Alcohol Related Crime   Alcohol offenses account for the most common reasons for the arrest and detention of elderly offenders (Akers and Le Greca 1988). In cases where alcohol use can be associated with a criminal act committed by an elderly person, it is rare that the individual is a first time offender, or that their alcohol use is infrequent. In most of these situations, the elderly offender is a male with a history of long term chronic alcohol abuse as well as long histories of criminal behavior in relation to the alcohol use (Meyers 1984).

Alcohol-related crimes include driving under the influence, disorderly conduct, or public drunkenness. Most crimes committed by the elderly are misdemeanors, but felonies such as assault, murder, sex offenses, burglary, and robbery do occur. Violent crimes in the elderly are often immediately preceded by alcohol use (Cavan 1987). A significant proportion of arrests involving elderly perpetrators are for driving while under the influence of an impairing substance. The most likely elderly offenders in this category are men who have a history of long-term substance abuse problems. In some cases the social isolation, loneliness, and physical limitations of aging may increase the likelihood of substance abuse. It should be noted however that elderly arrests for DWI account for less than 5% of total arrests in this category (Mandino 2000).

Sex Offenses   Individuals who are elderly at their first arrest have often committed sex offenses. In general, people commit fewer crimes as they age. However, sex offenders tend to remain constant in their activities throughout a lifetime. Therefore someone who was molesting children at a younger age is likely to continue such activities even after they become elderly (Mandino 2000). The rate of sex offenses among the elderly is difficult to determine due to the "dark figure" or number of unreported crimes. Elderly offenders are unlikely to use overt violence or physical force on a victim, and often the offenses are incestuous in nature thereby limiting the chances that the crime will be reported (Fattah and Sacco 1989).

The most common sex offense among the elderly is child molestation. However, this is not to say that one is more likely to develop pedophilia in old age. Rather, the elderly child molester may seek out children as part of a routine activities approach to crime. In other words, children are not preferred sexual targets, but are more accessible and easily controlled than other would-be victims. They pose little physical threat to the elderly offender, are available, are easier to coerce or bribe, and are less likely to report the incident. For the elderly person, this may seem to be a suitable alternative to the rejection expected from enticing another adult. Further, a child's trustful nature, respect for the elderly, craving for affection, and desire to please contribute to the elderly sex offender's ability to perpetrate the crime (Fattah and Sacco 1989).

Homicide   Homicide by the elderly is usually an offense committed by males, most often in the home and against a family member (frequently a spouse) and is overwhelmingly intraracial (Kratcoski and Walker 1988). Homicide by the elderly typically involves an intimate relationship. Stranger on stranger homicide or assault by the elderly is very rare (Fattah and Sacco 1989). Elderly homicide offenders are rarely perpetrators of acts with multiple victims. This can most likely be explained by the circumstances surrounding most multiple victim homicides. Usually these crimes are felony murders, or murders that have occurred while the offender was in the process of committing a felony such as armed robbery or drug dealing. Since the elderly are less likely to be involved in these types of felony activities, they are also less likely to be involved in multiple victim homicides (Wilbanks and Murphy 1984).

Domestic relationships account for a disproportionate number of homicides committed by elderly offenders. Compared to younger offenders, elderly homicide offenders are much less likely to be involved in stranger-on-stranger murders (Wilbanks and Murphy 1984). Elderly perpetrators of homicide are most likely to be African American males (19.25%). Elderly Anglo females are the least likely to commit homicides, accounting for only 0.1% of all murders. Overall, the elderly commit less than 1% of homicides, and in many cases these deaths are an expression of euthanasia for an incapacitated spouse (Mandino 2000).

A Massachusetts study conducted in 1984 found that spouses in that state reacted to each other more violently later in life. Kratcoski (1990) conducted a study on intentional homicides by the elderly and found that in $\frac{1}{4}$ of the cases, the victim was killed by her spouse. In this particular study, 100% of the time the victim was the wife and the offender was the husband. Kratcoski also noted that the circumstances immediately preceding the homicide usually involved an argument or quarrel between the victim and offender. In 44% of the cases, the offender was under the influence of alcohol, and in 40% of the cases, both the offender and victim had been drinking. He also found that a firearm was the weapon of choice in 86% of the cases and that in 9% of the incidents, the assailant committed suicide after the offense. One explanation for the high correlation of spousal relationship with elderly homicide is that older persons are more likely to have withdrawn from a social network, and therefore center much of their activity in the home. The couple, especially in retirement, spends unaccustomed amounts of time in each other's presence. Increased contact within the home is likely to magnify existing tensions and sometimes the result is domestic homicide (Kratcoski 1990).

Annually, more than 500 murder-suicides occur among the elderly resulting in over 1,000 deaths. The elderly are twice as likely as their younger counterparts to commit such acts. In almost every case (99%), a husband kills his wife and then himself. More often than not, he is an elderly man caring for a sick wife. In some cases both spouses are sick and dependent on each other for care. In either case, the male spouse is facing an unwanted change in the relationship. Contrary to popular belief, the wife is rarely a willing or knowing participant. In most instances, there had been a history of marital problems or domestic violence in the relationship. In the overwhelming majority of cases the preferred weapon is a gun—often an old service revolver— and the victims are killed in their sleep (Vann 2002). The following account serves as an example of such crimes. In August 2001, a 68-year-old resident of Winston-Salem, North Carolina, murdered his wife and then committed suicide. One week before the crimes, the man went to a Senior Services center and pleaded for help for him and his wife. He told officials at the center that he and his wife had very little food, that he took insulin for diabetes but did not have a way to monitor his blood-sugar levels, and that he was unable to shop because the tags and state-inspection sticker on his car had expired. Officials arranged for food and medical supplies to be sent to the home, and referred them to a budget-counseling service. Additionally, the center checked into having a wheel-chair ramp built at the home so that the wife could get in and out of the house. However, one day before the killings, the man told neighbors that he was worried over the medical bills stemming from his wife's stroke two years prior, and that he was contemplating suicide. The next day he stabbed his wife to death, and then took his on life with a kitchen knife (Man got help 2001).

Shoplifting   Of the FBI's Type 1 Index Offenses, larceny is the most commonly committed crime by elderly offenders, usually coming in the form of shoplifting (Fattah and Sacco 1989). This crime can be particularly difficult for police, because it is not only common, but difficult to detect while it is occurring. Many times merchants feel sympathy for the elderly offender and are unwilling to report the crime or press charges. Like shoplifters of other ages, the elderly commit this crime for a variety of reasons, including financial hardship that prevents them from buying necessities, boredom, and although rare, kleptomania or a compulsion to steal.

Some states have implemented innovative programs to deal with the issue of elder shoplifters. Florida is one such state. Since 1979, Broward County has operated a nonsectarian program known as the Broward Senior Intervention and Education Program (BSIE) through Jewish Community Centers for elderly shoplifters referred by the Broward County Court. In order for the offender to be eligible they must be at least 60 years old; be charged with no more than one count of misdemeanant shoplifting; have pleaded guilty; be a first time offender; and volunteer to complete the program. The judge withholds judgment, thereby avoiding a criminal record, if the defendant is referred to BSIE. The program is rehabilitative in context and has three primary dimensions: counseling, social activities, and participation with community service organizations. The goal is to reduce recidivism among elderly shoplifters. It has apparently been successful—of the first 1,000 cases handled through the program, there were only 9 cases of recidivism (Feinberg 1984).

Organized and White Collar Crime   One area where the elderly are consistently more criminal than youth is in organized crime syndicates. These groups tend to be age-stratified with the important operational decisions being made by the older leaders. Such decisions may range from legitimate business transactions to violent crimes such as murder. The younger members can be viewed more as "employees" or "soldiers," carrying out the orders of the older members. Examples of organized crime figures who were active well into old age include Charles "Lucky" Luciano, who was influential until his death at age 65; Meyer Lansky, who was still on the run from the law at age 81; Frank Costello, who was active until his death at age 80 and even testified before Congress at age 85; and Vito Genovese, who was still in command from his prison cell at age 71 (Newman 1984).

Elderly members of organized crime may fall into one of several categories. There are those who:

- are still active in both the social and economic aspects of the organization.
- are active in the economic aspects but have little contact with the social or family base. These individuals generally serve as leaders or expert consultants in the "corporation."

- are active only in the family system, as the patriarchal figure, and are less active in the economic area.

- never rose to an important position in the organization and remain small time hustlers or run smaller business aspects of the corporation. These individuals rarely accumulated any wealth and are supported by the organization as if on a retirement pension.

- are absentee owners who are content to reap the profits while refraining from active involvement (Amir 1989).

Elder members of organized crime rarely leave the "profession" by retiring. They are more likely to be pushed out, killed, or arrested (Amir 1989). Like many organized crime figures, white collar criminals are often older individuals who are in the upper-echelon of businesses and professions, and by their seniority in a position to be trusted. An elderly con man's age may, in fact, contribute to the success of his crime simply because people are less likely to suspect they are being victimized by someone who does not fit the stereotype of the "criminal youth" (Newman 1984).

The Police and Elderly Criminals

Dealing with elderly criminals, particularly arrestees, can be a most unrewarding experience for law enforcement officers. Many limitations face the police officer who is confronted with this type of offender. Most crime control procedures used by police are designed for younger, stronger criminals who are a threat and require restraint. Elderly offenders rarely qualify for either of these conditions (Newman et al. 1984). Statutory restrictions place limited control on police officers who are dealing with elderly offenders. In many cases it is immediately suspected by the officer that the offender is mentally ill and that immediate diversion to family care or social services would be the most appropriate action. However, statutory requirements prevent such discretionary decisions on the part of the officer. Compounding the issue is the perception by a sympathetic public that elderly arrestees are not being treated humanely, and the civil liability issues associated with restrictive arrests (Fyfe 1984). Police face a dilemma when arresting elderly offenders because the arrest and processing is more likely to invoke sympathy for the arrestee and lead to the perception that the officer acted unreasonably (Fattah and Sacco 1989).

Police must also be aware that well-intentioned actions on their part may be perceived as threatening by an elderly person who is suffering from diminished mental capacity. Elderly people suffering from senility or dementia may often harbor a fear of victimization bordering on paranoia. Such perception may cause the elderly person to act in a provoked, protective, or otherwise criminal manner (Fyfe 1984).

To avoid such complications, some of the criminological literature suggests that offenders over a certain age be given a special status much like juvenile offenders or mentally ill offenders are awarded. This would involve the establishment of an entire system, much like the juvenile justice system, just for the processing of elderly criminals. There would need to be special elderly offender institutions, modified arrest procedures, geriatric courts, officers with gerontological training, etc. Proponents of such a system argue that it would be designed to protect elderly criminals who suffered from some social, psychological, or physical limitation that would mitigate their responsibility for their own criminal activity (Cavan 1987).

THE ELDERLY IN COURT

Victims and Witnesses

When the elderly appear in court it is most often in the role of victim. It is rare that the elderly appear in criminal court as the accused. Even when this does occur, it is often a case of white-collar offenses, in which other colleagues have shifted to blame to the unsuspecting elder associate. The elderly often become victims of robbery because their physical infirmity impairs their ability to resist their attacker. In the courtroom, unless another eyewitness can be located, these victims are many times the only source of identification against their attacker. The victim is frequently further victimized by the legal system because of their difficulty in testifying effectively (Forer 1991).

The AARP examined 20 different issues facing victims through the judicial process. Each of these issues may have peculiar implications if the victim is elderly, yet only two of them include a resolution specific to the victim's age. The following provide some examples of the issues facing elderly victims and witnesses:

- While offering procedural safeguards, the Bill of Rights is also intended to provide protections to victims of crime. No specific legislation has addressed the issue of protection for victims or witnesses in a specific age group.
- Victims often are in need of assistance in the recovery from their injuries and coping with the judicial process. Older victims are not singled out for special treatment, but rather are grouped with other victims based on the type of crime.
- Compensation programs have been established to provide funds to assist victims in recovery. These are particularly important when restitution from the offender is not available. Some states do actually offer higher compensation payments when the victim is older. Other states specify that victims of certain crimes, such as sexual assault, may receive higher payments. In some cases, victims are exempt from meeting a "financial means test" if they have reached a certain age.
- Restitution programs provide procedures for holding those convicted of crimes financially responsible for assisting their victims. Some states offer special considerations for restitution payments to older victims. For example, in the case of certain crimes, elderly victims may be entitled to payment for counseling services in addition to medical treatment.
- Pre-sentence reports may be incomplete if victim impact statements are not included. Currently there are no provisions that take age into consideration when requiring or permitting victim impact statements.
- Participation by victims can have a significant impact at key points of the judicial process such as bail, continuances, plea bargains, charging decision, and sentencing. No legislation makes specific provisions for including older victims.

- While protection from intimidation and harassment is important for victims and witnesses, not legislation addressing the specific needs of the elderly in these circumstances (AARP 1990).

In addition to the above examples, the AARP also examined amendments to bail laws, restriction of victims' address information, confidentiality of victim counseling, funding for treatment of victims of sexual assault, admissibility of hearsay testimony, speedy disposition/trial, notification to victims of court schedule changes, secure waiting areas in court settings, victim attendance at trial, employer/creditor intercession, return of property, victim participation in parole hearings, and prohibitions on profits from criminal activity. None of these issues has been resolved in such a manner that the victim's age was a consideration (AARP 1990).

Some states have taken action on specific elderly victim legislation. For example, California gives trial-date preference to victims who are 70 or older. Massachusetts and New Hampshire provide speedy trials in efforts to reduce trauma when the victims are 65 or older. In South Carolina, the state victims' bill of rights requires that elderly, children, and handicapped victims be treated "sensitively." South Carolina also waives the $100 compensable loss minimum in its victim compensation measure when the victim is over 65. New York allows for compensation funds to pay for counseling for an elderly or disabled victim even when a physical injury has not occurred (Hunzeker 1990).

Competence is a key concern for elderly persons involved in litigation. Assuming they are found to be mentally competent by the court in question, they are subject to the same rights, protections, substantive laws, and rules of procedure as other individuals. If the elderly person is deemed to be incompetent, then they may be denied control over their own property or even their persons. However, the issue of competence is far from black and white. The law itself may fail to recognize the difference in mental capacity of an octogenarian and a middle aged adult. Between the two legal extremes of competence and incompetence falls a group of aging individuals that find the testimonial requirements of courtrooms to be frustrating and even frightening. These individuals are intelligent and competent but their aging body and mental processes may be slower than the average person. Memory may be less clear, preventing them from recalling precise details. Many times these details can only be recalled in context, and therefore dependent on the elderly person's ability to tell a story in a particular way. While their reasoning remains unimpaired, some elderly may lack the ability to quickly and concisely describe events. They may have a tendency to ramble or branch off on legally irrelevant tangents. Interruptions by counsel and the rigid question and answer process in a courtroom may disrupt this process and frustrate the ability to recall information accurately. Often times courtroom attorneys find it difficult to direct the attention of an elderly witness toward the desired specifics (Forer 1991).

The theoretical and empirical research does suggest that aging has an impact on eyewitness recall and recognition. However, this research also indicates that the elderly are not necessarily incapable of providing valid, convincing, and accurate testimony as eyewitnesses. One conclusion drawn from the literature is that the aging process can adversely affect the senses of hearing and sight. For example, a person's vision may change with age. The elderly often lose their ability to focus on nearby objects and may find it more difficult to discriminate between certain colors. They are more affected by glare and therefore may have difficulty seeing objects in bright sunlight or have difficulty adjusting to oncoming headlights while driving. Hearing limitations also occur with age and are generally most dramatic in the ability to hear high frequencies. Another conclusion evident in the literature is the impact of age on speed and completeness of recall. The aged may suffer from a lesser ability to retrieve memories and it may take them longer to recall specific details of memories. Despite these limitations, the empirical research demonstrates that recognition is much less impaired in the elderly than recall. It has also been shown that the elderly have an acute sense of whether or not they know a specific fact (Timm 1985).

A third conclusion drawn from the empirical research is that certain factors often considered by jurors in the assessment of a witnesses credibility may unfairly prejudice them against an elderly witness. For example, it has been shown that while younger subjects are better able to verbally recall an incident than elderly subjects, they are not better equipped to recognize the assailant or the victim. However, the confidence level of the elderly in their recognition ability is lower despite the fact that the accuracy of recognition is about the same as that of younger individuals. This is important in terms of eyewitness testimony because studies suggest that jurors are often persuaded by the degree of confidence displayed by a witness. Other factors influencing jurors include likeability, forcefulness of speech, and obvious motivation to lie. Due to recall issues, the elderly witness may take longer to respond to memory questions, be more cautions about their accuracy, less forceful in their speech, and focus upon the central details of the incident. Because jurors may respond to negative stereotypes of the elderly, a greater burden is placed on elderly witnesses to demonstrate the reliability of their testimony. As a result, even when the elderly witness is entirely accurate in their testimony, they may not easily persuade a jury (Timm 1985).

Elderly eyewitnesses are often perceived as honest but inaccurate. In a trial where the witness's integrity or honesty is a central element, the elderly witness is perceived well by the jury. However, in cases where the witness's ability to recall events and provide accurate verbal descriptions is of primary concern, then they may be viewed as less credible than a younger person. In general, the elderly are not inherently perceived as lacking in credibility (Bornstein 1995).

Defendants

In examining the nature of elderly defendants, Feinberg (1988) noted that such defendants rarely take advantage of three Constitutionally guaranteed rights of due process: (a) the right to plead not guilty; (b) the right to counsel; and (c) the right to trial by jury. Feinberg noted that these rights could be used in characterizing a defendant's process through adjudication as adversarial. In 92% of the cases he studied, elderly defendants avoided the adversarial nature of adjudication by refusing to invoke these rights. They routinely pleaded guilty (92%) and refused to be represented by counsel (93%), and rarely requested jury trials (14%). These figures were compared with the same measures of younger defendants, and it was noted that elderly defendants are more likely to deliberately avoid being adversarial. Such responses may be explained by compounding variables such as:

- Fear of being further embarrassed
- Feeling powerless

- Fear of increased sanctions
- Desire for quick resolution
- Inadequate coping skills

The failure of laws and rules to take the elderly person's condition into account often results in a traumatic and difficult experience based on a legally sanctioned denial of equal protection (Forer 1991).

Lindquist et al. (1987) examined the processing of elderly arrestees compared with persons under 55. They found that the elderly arrestees were less likely to be prosecuted, and were $\frac{1}{3}$ more likely to have prosecutors reject their case. The elderly were twice as likely to not to be true-billed by a grand jury than their under 55 counterparts. However, once indicted, there was very little difference found for dismissals between the two groups. In fact, non-elderly individuals had an 8% greater chance of having their cases dismissed than elderly arrestees. Overall, Lindquist, White, and Chambers found that the elderly were less likely to be prosecuted, but that the elderly and non-elderly groups were both more likely to be found guilty than not guilty if they went to trial.

Lindquist et al. (1987) also found that elderly defendants who were convicted generally received shorter sentences than their non-elderly counterparts. However, there was not a statistically significant difference found between the elderly and non-elderly groups on type of sentence received. Each group was as likely as the other to be assigned to incarceration or probation. Other studies conducted concerning the severity of sentencing of elderly defendants are conflicting. For example, Professor Dean Champion examined federal sentences of the elderly prior to the implementation of federal sentencing guidelines, and concluded that the elderly received less severe penalties than younger offenders (James 1992). Conversely, Dr. William Wilbanks (1988) conducted a study of California court sentencing of elderly defendants and determined that while, in general, the elderly were sentenced less severely, there were some crimes for which they were sentenced more harshly than their younger counterparts. Specifically, defendants aged 60 and above were more likely to be incarcerated than younger defendants for the crimes of molestation, disturbing the peace, fraud, vehicular manslaughter, aggravated assault, and motor vehicle theft. More recent studies have concluded that older offenders are slightly less likely to be incarcerated than younger offenders, and that their terms of imprisonment tend to be shorter. Steffensmeier et al. (1995) suggest that this treatment is not a direct correlation with age so much as it is a reflection of judges' consideration of three pertinent issues: degree of dangerousness, propensity for crime, and ability to serve time in prison.

In regards to federal sentencing guidelines, the Federal Sentencing Commission issued a policy statement concerning age consideration. It was the Commission's position that age is not ordinarily a relevant consideration for assigning a sentence outside of the federal guidelines. However, it may become a mitigating factor when the person is infirm do to age and a form of punishment such as home confinement would be less costly and equally effective as incarceration. Additionally, age may be a relevant consideration in determining the length and conditions of supervised probation or parole (James 1992). If a person is charged with a capital offense and was elderly at the time of the offense, then they are guaranteed to have their age considered as part of individualized sentencing under the Eighth and Fourteenth Amendments. This precedent was established in the U.S. Supreme Court case of *Lockett v. Ohio* (1978), when the court held that a death sentence was invalid because of statutory limitations placed on the sentencing judge when considering mitigating factors such as age.

Cohen (1985) suggests four different theoretical approaches to sentencing of the elderly. The first approach, which has not been given serious legal consideration, is to hold the elderly defendant to a higher criminal standard, and thus a more severe punishment, than younger criminals. The rationale is that older defendants are "older and wiser" and therefore more culpable than their younger counterparts. A second approach involves less severe punishment for the elderly than younger criminals. The legal argument is that the elderly defendant can show that because of age, he or she suffers from a diminished capacity to cope with ordinary life stressors. The third approach is to avoid sentencing the elderly defendant at all, arguing that the culpability level of the very old is similar to that of the very young or insane. The fourth approach is to practice age neutrality in sentencing which means that age in and of itself is not a factor, but does allow for consideration of other mitigating factors such as functional impairments associated with old age.

THE ELDERLY AS INMATES

Characteristics

Elderly inmates pose myriad problems for correctional workers. While the term "elderly" is generally reserved for those over age 65 in the general population, it can often be applied to inmates as young as age 50. Inmates often appear at least 10 years older and have health issues usually associated with older citizens (Curran 2000). Keeping this in mind, there are three types of elderly inmates: (a) those who are elderly and are being incarcerated for the first time; (b) those who are career criminals and have been in and out of prison most of their lives; and (c) those who are serving long prison sentences and have become elderly while being incarcerated. The combination of these three types of elderly inmates partially explains the recent growth in the elderly inmate population.

The Council of State Governments surveyed 16 southern states concerning the elderly inmate population growth between 1985 and 1997. The overall increase of inmates over the age of 50 was 480%, or from 4,490 to 26,404. North Carolina showed the most significant increase of individual states at 1,140%. Arkansas showed the least growth at 48%. It is important to note that during the same time frame, the general inmate population in these states only increased 147% (Edwards 1998). The current growth of elderly inmates is not necessarily attributable to a crime wave by older persons. Rather, researchers suggest that recent mandatory sentencing laws such as "Three Strikes" and "Truth in Sentencing" have resulted in the incarceration of a greater proportion of offenders regardless of age. Combine this result with the growth of the aged population in general and the effect is an increase in the elderly inmate population (Edwards 1998).

In terms of personal characteristics, elderly inmates have lower IQ's and higher divorce rates than the average inmate. They often have a history of part-time or unemployment and have experienced alcohol abuse within the family. These characteristics combined increase the chances that the elderly person will engage in criminal activity. Those who commit violent crimes are usually nonwhite single males in a low income bracket (Florida House of Representatives 1999). Approximately half of elderly inmates are first-time offenders, the majority of whom went to prison when they were 60 or older (Aday 1994b).

The older inmate who is a first time offender may have more difficulty adjusting to prison life because they are more likely than other first time offenders to define themselves as a lifelong law abiding citizen. Generally they have been successful at social relationships including marriage, have a higher social status, a positive outlook toward life, and committed religious views (Rubenstein 1984). Aday (1994b, 79) found that an elderly inmate's initial reaction to late-in-life incarceration "was often characterized by family conflict, depression, thoughts of suicide, and a fear of dying in prison." Ironically, many elderly inmates report prison as a positive experience. They are relieved from heavy labor, isolated from alcohol, fed well, have access to medical care, and are able to rest frequently (Florida House of Representatives 1999).

Elderly inmates are least likely to be recidivists. Studies report that fewer than 3.2% of inmates over 55 commit another crime upon release, compared to 45% of those age 18–29 (Florida House of Representatives 1999). Older inmates are less likely to be a security risk than they are a victimization risk. The risks of being victimized by other inmates increases as an inmate ages. Therefore it is important to protect elderly inmates from younger, stronger, more aggressive prisoners (Edwards 1998).

There are significant differences between elderly male and female inmates. Women are more likely to live longer, come from a poor background, be single, and outlive their support systems. They are usually considered to be less of a risk upon release. However, lack of community resources, negative stereotyping, lack of vocational training and educational skills combine to create an economic hardship on elderly female inmates once they are released by into society (Florida House of Representatives 1999).

Classification

As mentioned at the beginning of this discussion on elderly inmates one difficulty in classifying inmates is defining what constitutes elderly. Even in the field of gerontological research there is disagreement on the exact age that a person is considered to be elderly. Some define the category as "65 and older" while other use ages of 60, 55, or even 50. An inmate's physical age may be deceiving to the staff. In some cases a 50-year-old inmate may be less able bodied than a 70-year-old inmate (Edwards 1998).The American Correctional Association (ACA) suggests the implementation of a classification system that addresses levels of physical impairment rather than chronological age when determining medical care needs, programming, and housing (Neeley et al. 1997).

Vito and Wilson (1985, 18) categorize the problems and needs of elderly inmates into five groups: "1) adjustment to imprisonment, 2) vulnerability to victimization, 3) adaptation to physical conditions, 4) lack of suitable programs, and 5) diversity of the elderly inmate population." All elderly offenders can be classified into one of three offender categories: first time offenders, recidivists, and aging offenders. Each of these categories represents a unique set of issues for the inmate as well as the prison staff. Security, programming, and supervision are all impacted by the differences between the groups. Complicating the issue is the stereotyped view held by many prison officials that elderly inmates adjust and conform well to institutional requirements. This assumption may result in problems if plans are not already in place for dealing with a difficult or non-standard older prisoner (Florida House of Representatives 1999). Most prisons have been built with the purpose of housing and securing young, healthy and potentially aggressive inmates. In many cases, these same facilities are not conducive to the mobility or accessibility needs of older inmates. In cases where special housing does exist, physical or mental ability rather than age is generally the criteria for placing an inmate there (Edwards 1998).

First-time offenders constitute the largest single category of older inmates. It has been estimated that over 50% of elderly prisoners were sent to prison for the first time when they were age 60 or older. The most common offenses for this group were crimes of passion. This may be explained by the intensity of primary relationships among the aged. As a person grows older, their range of social interaction is narrowed, therefore there is more opportunity for conflict within the remaining relationships. Often these offenses are spontaneous, with the result that the offender does not consider himself or herself to be a criminal. Other causes of crime may be related to physiological conse-quences of aging. For example, chronic brain syndrome can result in a loss of inhibitions which in turn contributes to inappropriate or illegal sexual behavior. As a result, sexual offenses against children are common among elderly inmates. In some prisons, as much as $1/3$ of the geriatric inmates have been incarcerated for sex offenses. Physiological changes may also cause rigidity, suspiciousness, and quarrelsomeness that can manifest as aggressive behavior. In addition to physiological bases actions, white-collar property crimes, sale of drugs, and vehicular manslaughter as a result of being intoxicated are frequent offense of first time elderly offenders. Unique circumstances associated with first time elderly offenders include dealing with someone who is maladjusted to society and poor at adapting to change. They often have a volatile personality; may be at risk for suicide, commit violent acts against other inmates, have poor mental health, be generally withdrawn from society, and be at higher risk for victimization by other inmates. One positive is that these new offenders are more likely to maintain some ties with the community and are therefore easier to place when released (Florida House of Representatives 1999).

Inmates who are recidivists may have long histories of criminal activity or a series of repeat incarcerations. Because of the career nature of their criminal activity, they are the most likely to become geriatric inmates. Usually they pose few problems for prison officials because they are already well-adjusted to prison life. These offenders often have substance abuse or other chronic problems that pre-dispose them to a criminal lifestyle. More often than not they serve consecutive short sentences for lesser crimes and are not a physical threat to others (Florida House of Representatives 1999).

Aging prisoners are those who are serving a long-term sentence and are literally growing old behind bars. They are the least volatile category of inmates. A problem facing prison administrators is the difficulty in placing these inmates upon release. Due to their lengthy sentences they often have few ties to the community, a limited work history, and may be afraid of leaving the familiarity of the institution (Florida House of Representatives 1999).

Johnson (1988) discussed three popular approaches for elderly prisoner care. The Humanitarian approach encourages compassion for the inmates, particularly concern-ing a reduction in miseries related to bureaucratic indifference, poor nutrition, medical neglect, and unhealthy living conditions. Of particular concern for the humanitarian caregiver is the effect of shock from sudden confinement on the first time elderly offender. Because of this concern, the humanitarian approach sometimes overlooks the needs of elderly inmates who are already institutionalized and are not necessarily vulnerable personalities. The second form, therapeutic care, is focused on improving the inmates capacity to cope with their own personal or social problems. While this form of care is sensitive to the inmates' feelings, "avoidance of pain is secondary to stimulating behavioral change deemed essential to solving the client's difficulties" (Johnson 1988, 160). Priority is given to correcting the attitudes, aptitudes and capacities that are at the root of the undesirable behavior. The third form, custodial care, concentrates on merely meeting the basic needs of the inmate. It "centers attention on the obligation of the management of domiciliary institutions to meet ordinary needs of their residents as physical organisms and human beings" (Johnson 1988, 161). It is the duty of correctional leaders to balance security and productivity with the objectives of humanitarian and therapeutic approaches.

State correctional systems have generally adopted three strategies in managing elderly inmate populations: (a) housing elderly inmates in separate facilities; (b) providing hybrid units where elderly inmates are still within the general inmate population but are provided with secure areas; or (c) mainstreaming elderly inmates into the general inmate population. Benefits of separate housing include increased self-respect, reduction of loneliness, increased social interaction, and development of treatment programs for older inmates. On the other hand, segregated inmates may not have access to work assignments or other programs provided to younger inmates. Additionally, not all elderly inmates identify with or relate well to other older inmates (Falter 1999).

Health care

It is a fallacy to assume that health care issues for elderly inmates would be the same as health care issues for the elderly in general society. Traditionally inmates have medical and social backgrounds that predispose them more frequently for illness and disease. There is a greater probability among inmates of risky health behaviors and statistically they are more likely to be HIV-positive and have sexually transmitted or other infectious diseases. Other health issues include the higher instances of regular tobacco, alcohol, and drug use. Given these factors, noted correctional health care researcher B. Jaye Anno, Ph.D. suggested that an inmate's physical age could on average be considered 11.5 years older than their literal chronological age (Edwards 1998). In addition, Rubenstien (1984) noted that the physical and mental condition of elderly inmates deteriorates rapidly once they begin their prison terms.

The difference in cost of incarcerating elderly inmates when compared to other inmates was illustrated in a study by California's Center on Juvenile and Criminal Justice. They found that the average cost of incarcerating a younger inmate was $21,000 on a yearly basis. Comparatively, the cost of incarcerating an inmate over the age of 60 averaged $60,000. The difference in cost was attributed primarily to the health care needs of older inmates. Privatization is one possibility for reducing health care costs. Many state departments of corrections in the South have already begun to contract out a portion of health services. The states of North Carolina, Georgia, Virginia, and Alabama have entirely privatized prison health care (Edwards 1998).

Falter (1999) reported on two studies concerning heath problems of inmates. In a Michigan study of 41 male inmates aged 50–80, it was found that over 80% suffered from at least one chronic health problem and 50% have at least three or more chronic health problems. Another study of 119 male inmates over the age of 50 in Iowa revealed that 40% suffered from hypertension, 19% from myocardial infarction, 18% from emphysema, 97% were missing teeth, 42% had gross physical functional impairments, and 70% were smokers.

Due to such widespread health issues among the elderly inmate population, prison staff must be trained to recognize symptoms specific to aging and to distinguish between normal aging and disease (Florida House of Representatives 1999). The medical attention and special care required for aging inmates demands patience and essential skills that many correctional employees may be lacking (Curran 2000). For example, many elderly inmates may be in need of prosthetic equipment or corrective aids such as eyeglasses, hearing aids, ambulatory equipment, and hearing aids. It is up to the correctional staff to assist the inmate in their day-to-day activities when such devices limit the ability to perform certain tasks. Some other diseases such as Alzheimer's require separate housing units in order to provide adequate care (Curran 2000).

Elderly inmates may have different nutritional needs than the average inmate of the general population. Additionally, they may need special diets or require longer periods of time for eating. As a result, corrections officials may have to consider offering separate diet or eating plans for their geriatric population. This is a wise investment given that a correctly balanced diet can reduce the occurrences of costly future illnesses (Edwards 1998). Nutritional requirements become a concern with elderly inmates because in addition to having less muscle mass, some medications prevent effective vitamin and mineral absorption (Curran 2000).

Older inmates are more likely to suffer from mental problems than younger inmates. It has been estimated that as much as 25% of elderly prisoners suffer from some sort of mental illness. While depression is the most common condition, others include senile dementia (including Alzheimer's disease), organic brain disease, personality disorder, functional psychosis, and paranoid schizophrenia. Substance and alcohol abuse, especially beginning in early life and progressing in severity, is also a significant issue (Florida House of Representatives 1999). Elderly inmates are significantly more likely to experience serious depression than other inmates. This is, in part, due to the bitterness and resentment that can result from the physical, intellectual and emotional deterioration that accompany long term incarceration (Edwards 1998).

Housing

Given the special characteristics and health care needs of elderly inmates, the question of where to house them is a frequent one for prison administrators. Approximately 12 states have provided separate units for medically ailing older inmates (Curran 2000); others house the elderly along with the general inmate population.

Moving elderly inmates into special units can provide secure spaces in traditional areas for violent inmates (Neeley et al. 1997). Elderly inmates may become victim to the "wolf-prey" syndrome in which threats are made against them in exchange for favors. Segregating older inmates on separate tiers or floors is one way to ensure their physical well-being (Curran 2000).

According to the U.S. Department of Justice (Kratcoski and Pownell 1989, 33) a geriatric unit must address the following needs:

- Special diets and nutrition monitoring
- Special exercise needs for prevention of bone deterioration etc.
- Personal hygiene issues (i.e., problems of incontinence)
- Decline in sight, hearing and memory impairment
- Slowing of physical and mental responses
- Modified work and leisure programming
- Monitoring for special problems (i.e., cardiovascular diseases, diabetics, digestive ailments, etc.)
- Modification of physical environment to facilitate walkers, wheelchairs, and other physical aids
- Ultimately, constant bed care and intensive medical supervision.

Additionally, units for the elderly should include smoke alarms, fire alarms, and sprinkler systems. Helping them stay involved in the work force, giving them responsibility for their lives, and keeping them in touch with family is crucial to strengthening their hold on reality (Neeley et al. 1997).

Space in separate geriatric facilities may be limited resulting in a waiting list for older inmates. There are also ethical concerns with the "principle of least eligibility" whereby providing heart surgery or a kidney transplant for inmates does not fair well with the public when members of society are unable to receive the same level of care. As a result of lack of space, ethical concerns, or costs, elderly inmates often do not benefit from specialized programming (Aday 1994a).

Another problem with specialized housing is that there often are not enough elderly inmates to justify the expense. This is the case in Vermont, North Dakota, South Dakota, Hawaii, and Maine, where the states have had little choice but to mainstream older inmates. This is particularly true for elderly female inmates where South Carolina is the only state to provide special housing (Aday 1994a). Some opponents to segregated housing for the elderly argue that individuals who would not ordinarily be incarcerated will be sentenced to prison just because there is a special facility available in which to house them (Florida House of Representatives 1999).

One growing concern for prison staff is the increasing number of terminally ill inmates that result from more AIDS cases and the imposition of long sentences. Not all elderly or terminally ill inmates are deemed eligible for release, so other methods of coping with the circumstances must be found. Many prisons are establishing formal hospice programs which focus on managing pain rather than curing the illness, and providing the best quality of life for the terminally ill inmate (Florida House of Representatives 1999).

The cost of housing geriatric offenders may be impacted by necessary architectural changes, health care needs, and specialized training for prison personnel (Curran 2000). In some ways, transferring elderly prisoners to separate geriatric units can reduce security costs. In North Carolina, the elderly are housed at McCain Correctional Hospital where savings are significant because of the reduction in the required number of security personnel. The reduction is based on the unlikely event that such inmates will escape or become violent.

Programs for Elderly Inmates

In most states, programming for the elderly inmates lags behind that for other inmates. Most physical activities are geared toward younger inmates. Vocational training is not popular with the older inmates because of their unlikelihood of returning to the workforce. Counseling, too, is directed toward rehabilitation in younger inmates rather than coping issues such as chronic illness. Elderly inmates are in need of wellness programs rather than programs that prepare an inmate for reentry to society (Aday 1994a).

Programs for elderly offenders who are granted parole or who reach the end of their sentences are sorely lacking. Elderly offenders who are released back into the community, particularly those who have been incarcerated for long periods of time may need financial assistance as well as help in finding housing. They need help in getting social security reinstated and determining their eligibility for Medicaid. Parole reviews must be set reasonable intervals taking into account the physical ability of the inmate to keep such appointments (Aday 1994a). Early release may be difficult for elderly inmates to achieve. In many cases a stipulation of parole or probation is the securing of a full-time job outside of prison. Due to their advanced physical state, many elderly inmates have difficulty locating work. In some cases this may mean that the elderly inmate is unable to sustain his or herself outside of prison (Edwards 1998).

The Project for Older Prisoners (POPS) was started in 1989 by a Tulane law school professor. The groups goal is to reduce overcrowding by identifying low-risk, high-cost offenders for early release. Law students volunteer to study cases involving older inmates. Their standards are quite restrictive: the inmate must be at least 55, have served at least the average time for the offense, been evaluated as unlikely to commit future crimes upon release, and must not have committed a sex offense or homicide. In addition, the victim or the victim's family must agree to the early release. The program has been extremely successful in that no prisoner released through POPS has ever been returned to prison for committing another crime (Florida House of Representatives 1999).

The Pacific Region of Correctional Service of Canada has developed the Reintegration Effort for Long-term Infirm and Elderly Federal Offender (RELIEF) program, which includes four self-contained, six-bedroom houses where clients and caregivers live together. The intention is to provide a more home-like and less institutional setting for the elderly and infirm offenders who are approved for conditional release. They are provided with supervision, general and medical care by workers trained in hospice and specialized community medical services. The offenders are regularly assessed to determine the level of care required and are assigned to one of the houses based on the care level (e.g. high, medium, low). The "high" level residents require 24-hour caregiver availability with the residents typically reliant on wheelchairs, walkers, etc. A second house is for medium level residents who require 14- to 16-hour caregiver availability due to reduced physical capacities. They do not require the same level of care as the high level residents because they are more ambulatory. They do still have a need for assistance with bathing, personal care, and access. The third house accommodates "low" level residents who require 8 to 10 hours of caregiver availability. Unlike the other two houses, the residents in the low category are able to participate and take partial responsibility for cooking, cleaning, and laundry. The fourth house is set aside for a caregivers' residence. In addition to health care and living assistance, these offenders are provided with training in self-sufficiency, living skills, and programs targeted for the elderly (Stewart 2000).

In cases where inmates are expected to serve the remainder of their natural life in prison, other programs can be helpful. For example, the National Prison Hospice Association provides hospice care for inmates who are terminally ill but who do not qualify for medical parole (Curran 2000).

Most housing, health care, and programming for elderly inmates lags far behind that of the general inmate population, and grossly behind that of society. Table 1 summarizes a self-evaluation completed by each state concerning their most pressing need in relation to elderly inmates and what special accommodation or programs are already in place.

CONCLUSION

The elderly pose significant problems, require special assistance, and need an understanding of their unique position in society. Such issues must be addressed by criminal justice personnel in all branches of the system whether it is a situation of law enforcement handling a victim, or a correctional officer dealing with the aging process of an inmate. Some of these issues have been addressed in this chapter. Other issues have been addressed in other chapters of this text such as Chapter 9: The Disabled and Physically Challenged in the Criminal Justice System with whom the elderly share common traits. It is not possible to cover every possible unique situation posed by the elderly criminal justice client in a book. It is therefore up to each criminal justice agency to evaluate its own effectiveness in dealing with these special clients and to continue to develop improved methods for coping with such individuals and their situations.

REFERENCES

AARP 1990. American Association of Retired Persons. (1990). Issues Affecting Crime Victims: Background, Current Status, and Implications for Older Persons. Washington, DC: AARP

AARP, 1994. American Association of Retired Persons. (1994). *A report on the 1994 study of the use of volunteers in police agencies*. Washington, DC: AARP

29 U.S.C. § 792. *Architectural and Transportation Barriers Compliance Board*.

ADAY, R. H. (1994a). Golden years behind bars: Special programs and facilities for elderly inmates. *Federal Probation, 58*(2), 47–54.

ADAY, R. H. (1994b). Aging in prison: A case study of new elderly offenders. *International Journal of Offender Therapy and Comparative Criminology, 38*(1), 79–91.

AKERS, R. L., AND A. J. LA GRECA. (1988). Alcohol, contact with the legal system, and illegal behavior among the elderly. In *Older offenders: Perspectives in criminology and criminal justice*, ed. B. McCarthy and R. Langworthy, 50–61. New York: Praeger.

AMIR, M. (1989). Aging and aged in organized crime. *Journal of Offender Counseling, Services and Rehabilitation, 13*(2), 61–85.

BACHMAN, R. (1993). Double edged sword of violent victimization against the elderly: Patterns of family and stranger perpetration. *Journal of Elder Abuse and Neglect, 5*(4), 59–76.

BAUMHOVER, L. A., AND S. C. BEALL. (1996). *Abuse, neglect, and exploitation of older persons: Strategies for assessment and intervention*. Baltimore: Health Professions Press.

BLOODSWORTH, D. (2002). Senior enlisted in fraud crackdown. *Wilmington Morning Star*. March 14.

BORNSTEIN, B. H. (1995). Memory processes in elderly eyewitnesses: What we know and what we don't know. *Behavioral Sciences and the Law, 13*, 337–48.

BOURNS, W. F. (2000). Police gerontology services for the elderly: A policy guide. *The Justice Professional, 13*, 179–92.

BROWNELL, P. J. (1998). *Family crimes against the elderly: Elder abuse and the criminal justice system*. New York: Garland.

Bureau of Justice Statistics. (1994). *Murder in families*. Washington, DC: U.S. Department of Justice.

CAVAN, R. S. (1987). Is special treatment needed for elderly offenders? *Criminal Justice Policy Review, 2*(3), 213–24.

COHEN, F. (1985). Old age as a criminal defense. *Criminal Law Bulletin, 5*(1), 11–17.

CURRAN, N. (2000). Blue hairs in the bighouse: The rise in the elderly inmate populations, its effect on the overcrowding dilemma and solutions to correct it. *New England Journal on Criminal and Civil Confinement, 26*(2), 225–64.

EDWARDS, T. (1998). *The aging inmate populations: A special series report of the Southern Legislative Conference*. Atlanta: Council of State Governments.

FALTER, R. G. (1999). Selected predictor of health services needs of inmates over age 50. *Journal of Correctional Health Care, 6*(2), 149–75.

FATTAH, E. A., AND V. F. SACCO. (1989). *Crime and victimization of the elderly*. New York: Springer-Verlag.

FEINBERG, G. (1984). Profile of the elderly shoplifter. In *Elderly criminals*, ed. E. S. Newman, D. J. Newman, and M. L. Gewirtz, 35–50. Cambridge, MA: Oelgeschlager, Gunn, & Hain.

FEINBERG, G. (1988). The role of the elderly defendant in the criminal court: Full-dress adversary or reluctant penitent? In *Older offenders: Perspectives in criminology and criminal justice*, ed. B. McCarthy and R. Langworthy, 123–42. New York: Praeger.

Florida House of Representatives Committee on Corrections and Florida Corrections Commission. (1999). *An examination of elder inmate services: An aging crisis*. Tallahassee: Author.

FORER, L. G. (1991). *Unequal protection: Women, children and the elderly in court*. New York: W.W. Norton.

FORST, L. S., ed. (2000). *The aging of America: A handbook for police officers*. Springfield, IL: Charles C. Thomas.

FYFE, J. J. (1984). Police dilemmas in process elderly offenders. In *Elderly criminals*, ed. E. S. Newman, D. J. Newman, and M. L. Gewirtz, 97–112. Cambridge, MA: Oelgeschlager, Gunn, & Hain.

GOODWIN, D. W. (1992). Police services and the elderly. *Law and Order*, June, 68–71.

HEISLER, C. J., & TEWKSBURY, J. E. (1991). Fiduciary abuse of the elderly: A prosecutor's perspective. *Journal of Elder Abuse & Neglect, 3*(4), 23.

HUNZEKER, D. (1990). *State legislative response to crimes against the elderly*. Washington, DC: National Conference of State Legislatures.

JAMES, M. F. (1992). Sentencing elderly criminals. *American Criminal Law Review, 29*, 1025–44.

JOHNSON, E. H. (1988). Homicide among the elderly: Analysis of the victim/assailant relationship. In *Older offenders: Perspectives in criminology and criminal justice* ed. B. McCarthy and R. Langworthy, 156–63. New York: Praeger.

KLAUS, P. A. (1999). *Crimes against persons age 65 or older, 1992–1997* [NCJ 176352]. Washington, DC: Bureau of Justice Statistics.

KLAUS, P., & RENNISON, C. M. (2002). *Age patterns in violent victimization: 1976–2000*. Washington, DC: Bureau of Justice Statistics.

KOHL, R., D. BRENSILBER, AND W. HOLMES. (1995). *Elderly protection project: Final project report*. Washington, DC: U.S. Department of Justice.

KRATCOSKI, P. C. (1990). Circumstances surrounding homicides by older offenders. *Criminal Justice and Behavior, 17*(4), 420–30.

KRATCOSKI, P. C., AND D. B. WALKER. (1988). Homicide among the elderly: Analysis of the victim/assailant relationship. In *Older offenders: Perspectives in criminology and criminal justice*, ed. B. McCarthy and R. Langworthy, 62–75. New York: Praeger.

LINDQUIST, J. H. (1987). Issues in the criminal victimization of the elderly. In *The elderly: Victims and deviants*, ed. C. D. Chambers, J. H. Lindquist, O. Z. White, and M. T. Harter, 142–60. Athens, OH: Ohio University Press.

LINDQUIST, J. H., O. Z. WHITE, AND C. D. CHAMBERS. (1987). Elderly felons: Dispositions of arrests. In *The elderly: Victims and deviants*, ed. C. D. Chambers, J. H. Lindquist, O. Z. White, and M. T. Harter, 161–76. Athens, OH: Ohio University Press.

Lockett v. Ohio, 438 U.S. 586, 597 (1978)

Man got help days before killings. (2001). *Wilmington Morning Star*. August 16.

MANDINO, C. (2000). Old enough to know better? Aging and criminal justice. In *Investigating difference: Human cultural relations in criminal justice*, ed. Criminal Justice Collective of Northern Arizona University, 161–70. Boston: Allyn & Bacon.

MARGASAK, L. (2002). Nursing home crimes often unreported, probe finds. *Wilmington Morning Star*. March 4.

McCOY, V. H., J. D. WOOLDREDGE, F. T. CULLEN, P. J. DUBECK, AND S. L. BROWNING. (1996). Lifestyles of the old and not so fearful: Life situation and older persons' fear of crime. *Journal of Criminal Justice, 24*(3), 191–205.

MEADOWS, R. J. (1998). *Understanding violence and victimization*. Upper Saddle River, NJ: Prentice Hall.

MERIANOS, D. E., AND J. W. MARQUART. (1997). From the outside in: Using public health data to make inferences about older inmates. *Crime and Delinquency, 43*(3), 298–314.

MEYERS, A. R. (1984). Drinking, problem drinking, and alcohol-related crime among older people. In *Elderly criminals*, ed. E. S. Newman, D. J. Newman, and M. L. Gewirtz, 51–66. Cambridge, MA: Oelgeschlager, Gunn, & Hain.

MURAM, D., K. MILLER, AND A. CUTLER. (1992). Sexual assault of the elderly victim. *Journal of Interpersonal Violence, 7*(1), 71–76.

National Institute of Justice. (1993). *TRIAD reducing crime against the elderly: An implementation handbook*. Washington, DC: U.S. Department of Justice.

NEELEY, C. L., L. ADDISON, AND D. CRAIG-MORELAND. (1997). Addressing the needs of elderly offenders. *Corrections Today, 59*(5), 120–24.

NEWMAN, D. J. (1984). Elderly criminals and American crime patterns. In *Elderly criminals*, ed. E. S. Newman, D. J. Newman, and M. L. Gewirtz, 3–15. Cambridge, MA: Oelgeschlager, Gunn, & Hain.

NEWMAN, E. S., D. J. NEWMAN, AND M. L. GEWIRTZ. (1984). *Elderly criminals*. Cambridge, MA: Oelgeschlager, Gunn, & Hain.

PEAK, K. J. (2001). *Justice administration: Police, courts, and corrections management*. 3rd ed. Upper Saddle River, NJ: Prentice Hall.

RUBENSTEIN, D. (1984). The elderly in prison: A review of the literature. In *Elderly criminals*, ed. E. S. Newman, D. J. Newman, and M. L. Gewirtz, 153–75). Cambridge, MA: Oelgeschlager, Gunn, & Hain.

SEYMOUR, A., M. MURRAY, J. SIGMON, M. HOOK, C. EDMUNDS, M. GABOURY, AND G. COLEMAN. (2000). *National victim assistance academy*. Washington, DC: Office for Victims of Crime, Office of Justice Programs, U.S. Department of Justice.

SHICOR, D. (1984). An exploratory study of elderly probationers. *International Journal of Offender Therapy and Comparative Criminology, 32*(2), 163–74.

SHOVER, N. (1985). *Aging criminals*. Beverly Hills, CA: Sage.

STEFFENSMEIER, D., J. KRAMER, AND J. ULMER. (1995). Age differences in sentencing. *Justice Quarterly, 12*(3), 583–602.

STEWART, J. (2000). Reintegration Effort for Long-term Infirm and Elderly Federal Offenders (RELIEF) program. *Forum on Corrections Research, 12*(3), 35–38.

Study suggest intervention increases elder abuse. (2002). *Criminal Justice Newsletter, 31*(24), 6–7.

TIMM, H. W. (1985). Eyewitness recall and recognition by the elderly. *Victimology: An International Journal, 10*(1–4), 425–40.

United States Sentencing Commission. (1995). *Report to Congress: Adequacy of penalties for fraud offenses involving elderly victims*. Washington, DC: U.S. Government Printing Office.

VANN, K. (2002). Murder-suicides no always mutual. *Wilmington Morning Star*. March 5.

VITO, G. F., AND D. G. WILSON. (1985). Forgotten people: Elderly inmates. *Federal Probation, 49*(1), 18–24.

WILBANKS, W. (1988). Are elderly felons treated more leniently by the criminal justice system? *International Journal of Aging and Human Development, 26*(4), 275–88.

WILBANKS, W., AND D. D. MURPHY. (1984). In *Elderly criminals*. ed. E. S. Newman, D. J. Newman, and M. L. Gewirtz, 79–91. Cambridge, MA: Oelgeschlager, Gunn, & Hain.

ZEVITZ, R. G., D. CRIM, AND A. M. GURNACK. (1991). Factors related to elderly crime victims' satisfaction with police service: The impact of Milwaukee's Gray Squad. *Gerontologist, 31*(1), 92–101.

11

Hate, Pride, Fear, and Religious Intolerance

Gordon A. Crews

❖

CHAPTER OUTLINE

INTRODUCTION

People are knowingly and unknowingly drawn into *Hate, Nationalist, Heritage, Religious,* and *Patriot* groups through many avenues. The two most popular, at least since the late twentieth century, appear to be pathways laid by carefully developed and strategically placed fear propaganda disseminated most often over the Internet and through underground music and media. This combined with socioeconomic factors, including growing economic pressures, has played a major part in making many people, particularly those in the working and lower-middle class, susceptible to messages of hate, fear, and intolerance.

There are myriad indicators reflecting these possible catalytic socioeconomic pressures, most of which have increased dramatically since the 1970s. Changing demographic trends, decreasing wages, increasing child poverty, diminishing opportunities for the less educated, and high rates of both juvenile arrests and adult incarceration, often are at the summit of these factors. Moreover, recent examinations (Crews and West 2006) seem to reflect the rise of *ethnic nationalism* with young people of all races more willing than they have been in past decades to blame others for their ills and to accept the idea of *separation of the races.*

Some argue (Crews and West 2006) that income inequality between social classes is a factor that can generate more social resentment than actual economic losses. Unfortunately, income inequality has reached levels unprecedented since the Great Depression. Since the 1960s (U.S. Department of Commerce 2005), these disparities have reached a level where the total after-tax income of the top 1% of American households exceeds that of the bottom 20%. The gap in accumulated wealth between the upper class and the lower class is even greater, with the wealthiest 20% of households owning nearly 85% of the nation's total wealth.

In addition to economic fear, there are other concerns of many in the United States. Some time shortly after 2050, the white majority that has long dominated American society will more than likely disappear, with whites becoming a minority. While the percentage of blacks in the population is expected to remain fairly steady, the number of Hispanics is growing rapidly (U.S. Department of Commerce 2005). As of 2007, Hispanics are the nation's largest minority group. These demographic changes are used frequently by various groups in the United States to "strike fear into whites' hearts" and to argue that America is not the country it once was, thus insinuating that action must be taken to avoid such a future.

The idea of religious persecution conflicts drastically with the positive role religion generally plays in communities across the United States, but this fear often brings out this behavior and feelings in people as well. For many of those involved, membership in a religious group provides a sense of identity and creates unified communities for followers of a particular faith. Quite often, in the more religious societies, the people's identity is actually centered on their religious beliefs. Many Americans have begun to question, "what if this identity simply centers around one's race, nationality, or religious beliefs?"

Many religious belief systems are complex and often difficult for non-group members to grasp or understand. For the most part, it can be argued that the majority of religions support and promote the well being of all human beings. Most religious teachings support and promote peace and unity of all people in the world. Although religion can provide a spiritual basis for human rights, it also has often become the basis for denying individuals or a group these basic rights. After World War II, in which human rights of various groups were violated through the Holocaust, the nations of the world decided to create a *Universal Declaration of Human Rights* (2006) that included the right of freedom of religion (echoing those protections of the United States' Constitution). An attempt at genocide is one issue, but what about the simple day to day interactions of those of different races, religions, and nationalities? This is where the issues of *hate, fear, pride*, and *religion* become of paramount concern to United States' citizens.

CONTEMPORARY HISTORY AND DEVELOPMENT OF INTOLERANCE IN AMERICA

Amid huge social changes since the mid to late twentieth century, a group of white suburban youths emerged that could impact the future of racially-, nationally-, and religiously-based hate groups and hate crime in the United States. An underclass of white youths, in many cases impacted by extreme change and dislocation, has altered the state of American views of hate. Although, it must be remembered that many people come to white supremacist movements through no particular hardship and that it would be a mistake to describe all racist youth as coming from deprived circumstances. Many are alienated middle-class youth who are led to neo-Nazism and other types of philosophies through Internet sites or various types of propaganda. However a far larger, and apparently growing, number of white anti-social youth in general have developed from American socioeconomic discontent (Crews and Montgomery 2001).

Many American youth are being raised in extremely desolate environments. They could be described as living on the edge of the country and of the nation's economy. Some state (Schafer and Navarro 2003, p.3) that these youth face a "depressing suburban world of aging strip malls and fast food restaurants." In such a world, most are simply surrounded by individuals, including their parents, who are trying to maintain their position in the lower middle class or to survive from day to day. Many of the children of these families have experienced racial conflicts in their schools and in racially changing neighborhoods. The result is that most have the fear that the modern economy, and the world, is leaving them behind (Crews and Montgomery 2001). When feelings such as these emerge, it is very easy for one to seek another on which to place the blame for their own misfortune.

While child poverty overall (Crews and Montgomery 2001) has been declining in inner city and rural areas, it still remains a significant problem in many suburban areas. As mentioned previously, income inequality has grown to levels not seen since the 1930s. Another unfortunate devolution that America continues to experience is in the family structure and the inherent support it provides children. The U.S. divorce rate has doubled since 1960, with half of all marriages ending in divorce. There is also the continued problem of lack of support in two parent families due the need for two income households. Lack of such structure obviously allows children to seek direction from someone other than a parent or guardian. It should not be surprising then that they will seek out alternative groups in which to join for guidance and structure.

While overall drug use has been declining in the United States, the use of methamphetamine and hallucinogens seems to be growing among lower- to middle-class Whites. Many believe that this has helped draw increasing numbers of youths into crime and delinquency and, in many cases, the eventual incarceration. Once there, many of those who had no former affiliations join racist gangs for survival (Wooden 1995).

High rates of child poverty, juvenile arrests, child deaths, and teenage birth rates are among the factors used to document the problems facing American youth. Young whites are becoming more and more susceptible to these issues. They often begin as children seeking an alternative family in a street gang (very often racist in nature) and are drawn into crime through the drug culture and associated music. When they go to prison, as many do, they typically join racist prison gangs, either predominantly criminal groups like the Nazi Low Riders or more overtly political ones like the Hammerskin Nation. Once back on the streets, these individuals, then viewed as older heroes by many younger members, recruit more youths into street affiliates of the prison gangs (Crews and Montgomery 2001).

HATE, FEAR, AND IGNORANCE

It is an old adage that *ignorance* leads to *fear*, and fear leads to *hate*. Generally, humans fear what they do not understand and they, in turn, very often hate what they fear. Obviously, this can (and most often does) lead to conflict between individuals of different races, creeds, and national origins. Unfortunately, many do not take the time to learn of other cultures or belief systems which are different from their own. Instead they often look to another to simply "tell" them what they should and should not think and believe about others. This other person may be a parent, a religious leader, or an individual with a private agenda.

Hate groups know this to be true; they know that most people are inherently paranoid and often times apathetic (especially when it comes to trying to understand new events). They know that many want someone to pull together what they supposedly need to know in a nice tight package that they can digest quickly and easily. Hate groups, and others of alternative belief systems, obviously, are happy and ready to be the ones to offer the package.

Extent of Hate Groups in America

As would be expected, it is virtually impossible to determine the true extent of hate, nationalist, heritage, religious, and so-called patriot groups in the United States. The only manner in which to obtain an estimate of the problem is to examine the number of active groups in the United States. There are fortunately a number of organizations (Gerstenfeld et al. 2003) in the country that help monitor the activities of groups that can be identified and to evaluate new groups as they emerge. The Internet has allowed extensive dissemination of information from and about these groups, and does offer some indication about the extent of these groups. The problem becomes in trying to determine whether a group is actually as large as portrayed, or is just one individual trying to represent a few (or one) as many.

Active Hate Groups in the U.S. in the Twenty-First Century

According to the Southern Poverty Law Center (SPLC) (2006), there were approximately 457 active hate groups operating in the United States as the country moved into the new millennium. This was based on information gathered by their Intelligence Project from various groups' publications, citizens' reports, law enforcement agencies, field sources, and news reports. This monitoring is conducted each year by this operation to identify organizations known to be active. Active was defined by the SPLC as any group that held marches, rallies, speeches, or meetings, conducted leafleting, published literature, or committed criminal acts. As mentioned earlier, the problem is with the number of entities that are found only on the Internet, it is very difficult to ascertain whether such a posting truly represents a group or simply one individual.

The center categorizes groups by the following headings: *Klan, Neo-Nazi, Skinhead, Christian Identity, Black Separatist,* and *Other.* As would be expected, many of these groups are migratory in nature and not affiliated with a primary national group, so estimates are difficult to maintain. The Center points out that Skinheads are such an organization. Christian Identity describes a religion that is fundamentally racist and anti-Semitic. Black Separatist groups are organizations whose ideologies include tenets of racially based hatred. The "Other" category includes groups and publishing houses endorsing myriad hate doctrines (Intelligence Report 2000a).

Official Definitions of Hate Crimes

Typical hate crime legislation criminalizes the use of force or the threat of force, against a person because they are a member of a specific, protected group. Four definitions of the term *hate crime* are:

- *Hate Crimes Statistics Act* (Bureau of Justice Statistics 2001): crimes that manifest evidence of prejudice based on race, religion, sexual orientation, or ethnicity, including where appropriate the crimes of murder, non-negligent manslaughter, forcible rape, aggravated assault, simple assault, intimidation, arson, and destruction, damage or vandalism of property.
- Bureau of Justice Administration (Boeckmann and Turpin-Petrosino 2002): offenses motivated by hatred against a victim based on his or her race, religion, sexual orientation, ethnicity, or national origin.
- Anti-Defamation League (Boeckmann and Turpin-Petrosino 2002): crime committed because of the victim's actual or perceived race, color, religion, ancestry, national origin, disability, gender (male or female) or sexual orientation.
- National Education Association (Boeckmann and Turpin-Petrosino 2002): offenses motivated by hatred against a victim based on his or her beliefs or mental or physical characteristics, including race, ethnicity, and sexual orientation.

The term *perceived* is important in these and other definitions because many assaults are based in error on the incorrect belief that the victim is Jewish, gay, or a member of some other group that the perpetrator hates. Traditional hate crime legislation protects persons because of "race, color, religion or national origin." Most state laws include additional protected groups. Some laws are restrictive and only protect a member of a group if she/he is involved in specific activities.

A criminal act is considered a hate crime if the perpetrator of a crime is motivated by hate of a group to which the victim belongs. However, existing federal legislation does not recognize as hate crimes those criminal acts which specifically target women, the disabled, and homosexuals (Shively 2005).

Some Facts about Hate Crimes

The following is a list of findings that are commonly held by researchers in the area of hate crimes (Shively 2005):

- Whereas people generally commit ordinary crimes with which the victims are familiar, strangers overwhelmingly commit hate crimes and acts of violence.
- Most perpetrators of hate crimes are under the age of 20.
- Most hate crime incidents are not reported to the police.
- Many law enforcement agencies still do not transfer their hate crime statistics to the FBI.

- It appears that attacks against gays tend to be more severe than those against other minority groups.
- Most anti-gay hate crime perpetrators perceive gay bashing to be socially sanctioned and, therefore, acceptable behavior.
- The total annual number of hate crimes in the U.S. reported to the FBI continues to grow in the United States; this increase may be mainly due to more thorough reporting of data in recent years.
- A gradually increasing percentage of hate crimes are based on sexual orientation. The other classifications are either stable or decreasing as a percentage of the total.

Arguments Pro and Con about Hate Crime Legislation

The following is a brief listing (Shively 2005) of many of the arguments relating to the pros and cons of hate crime legislation in the United States.

Con

- The legislation is not needed in that every crime they cover is already illegal under existing state and local laws.
- They are unfair in that American justice is based on the principle that everyone is treated identically. If hate crimes legislation is passed, then the perpetrators of two identical crimes would receive different sentences, depending upon some characteristic of the victim.
- Many feel that they are a political vehicle for homosexual activists.
- Federal hate crime legislation would increase federal government participation in law enforcement.
- Hate Crime legislation would grant unfair special privileges to gays and lesbians because it would identify them as a protected class.

Pro

- The legislation is needed in that protecting a group under hate crime legislation will make the public aware that the group is vulnerable, has been extensively victimized in the past, and is in need of protection.
- They are fair in that a hate crime is more serious than a conventional crime because it abuses more than the immediate victim.
- Homosexuals, and in fact all groups that are targeted by hate crimes, are in need of protection, but the law would protect more groups than gays and lesbians.
- Increased federal involvement in hate crime prosecution would be beneficial in that sometimes local prejudice prevents individuals who target specific groups from receiving a proper trial and sentence.
- Homosexuals would not be given special privileges in that no law mentions gays, lesbians, or homosexuals.

Creation of the Universal Declaration of Human Rights

To many (Anti-Defamation League 1999) the Holocaust demonstrated how people could be deprived of their most fundamental rights. Therefore, in 1948, the United Nations established the *Universal Declaration of Human Rights*. This document has served to provide a clear and uniform definition of fundamental human rights. When this document was signed, the United Nations had 25 state members. Any state that wished to become a member to the United Nations since that time has had to agree to follow the principals of this Declaration.

Below are excerpts from the 30 Articles of the Universal Declaration of Human Rights (2006):

- *All human beings are born free and equal in dignity and rights. They are endowed with reason and conscience.* (Article 1)
- *Everyone has the right to life, liberty and security of person.* (Article 3)
- *No one shall be subjected to torture or to cruel, inhuman or degrading treatment or punishment.* (Article 5)
- *No one shall be subjected to arbitrary arrest, detention or exile.* (Article 9)
- *Everyone is entitled in full equality to a fair and public hearing by an independent and impartial tribunal, in the determination of his rights and obligations and of any criminal charge against him.* (Article 10)
- *No one shall be subjected to arbitrary interference with privacy, family, home or correspondence, or to attacks upon his honor and reputation. Everyone has the right to the protection of the law against such interference or attacks.* (Article 12)
- *Everyone has the right to freedom of thought, conscience and religion; this right includes freedom to change his religion or belief, and freedom, either alone or in community with others and in public or private, to manifest his religion or belief in teaching, practice, worship and observance.* (Article 18)
- *Everyone has the right to freedom of opinion and expression.* (Article 19)
- *Everyone has the right to freedom of peaceful assembly and association.* (Article 20)

RACISM

Racism and its myriad forms and nuances, is the primary culprit behind most of the racial and religious conflicts across the country and world. The history of racism in the United States is actually quite fascinating, albeit frightening and saddening as well (see Chapter 1). A recurring question that seems to appear time and time again is whether humans are born with "racist tendencies," or is it a learned behavior and thought pattern. Whether it is natural or learned, there are many who seek as many ways as possible to spread such feelings to others.

Racist Literature

The expression of hate and intolerance comes in all shapes, sizes, and colors. People are exposed to it through home radios, televisions, and computers. It appears to many youths in their bedrooms through their families' Internet connections. Still, it is most available in the oldest form known, the printed word. The American "hate movement" has long relied on the power of the printed word to proclaim the superiority of one race or group of people over another. From glossy full-color magazines to crude homemade tabloids, "hate literature" has played an important role in recruitment, movement building and the wide dissemination of conspiracy theories.

The following is a brief list of the most prominent periodicals of leading hate groups. This list has been compiled and is maintained by the Intelligence Report Project of the Southern Poverty Law Center in Montgomery, Alabama (2006).

- *WAR* is the official mechanism of White Aryan Resistance (WAR), based in Fallbrook, California.
- *Calling Our Nation* is the primary publication of the Aryan Nations/Church of Jesus Christ Christian, based in Hayden Lake, Idaho.
- *The Struggle*, a monthly offering from the World Church of the Creator, is a relative newcomer to the world of literature and is markedly different from many other such publications.
- *National Alliance Bulletin*, by William Pierce, the former physics professor who headed the prominent neo-Nazi National Alliance, strives to appeal to a higher class of individuals: articulate, educated, and polished.
- *American Renaissance* is a monthly journal with an academic tone that is the venue for Jared Taylor, who has written books and articles arguing that blacks are genetically inferior to whites.

Racism in Corrections

In jails and prisons around the country (Montgomery and Crews 1998), allegations of racist and sometimes violent guards continue to plague the American corrections industry. It has been alleged that there are growing numbers of correctional officers who invoke the Klan or white supremacist ideology to intimidate or punish inmates. It has also been reported that sometimes such intimidation is directed towards other staff and even correctional administrators.

To many it is not surprising to hear that there are a large number of correctional staff who promote violence and racial animosity. Instead of trying to contain the potential problems that threaten the security of each and every prison, some correctional staff may actually conspire to make the problems worse. The Southern Poverty Law Center (2006) reported that since 2000 in at least six states, guards have appeared in mock Klan attire, and have been accused of race-based threats, beatings, and even shootings in 10 states. In addition, they report that suits have been filed in at least 13 states by black guards alleging racist harassment or violence from their own colleagues. There is also much discussion about the uncounted settlements reached in civil cases filed by guards or inmates where damages are sealed by court order. Obviously this makes an understanding of the true dimensions of this problem difficult to ascertain.

Race-based gangs like the Aryan Brotherhood, the Aryan Circle, the Bloods, the Crips, and the Mexican Mafia remain active in American prisons and jails of the twenty-first century. These groups make for an interesting co-existence in correctional facilities. Obviously these groups do differ in their history, make up, and motives. The

Aryan Brotherhood, for instance, originated in the prisons as a violent and white supremacist gang, while Crips and Bloods trace their roots to economically motivated black street gangs on the "outside." Some groups are essentially organized crime families, while others concentrate simply on racist ideology. It is apparent that they all contribute to a prison world that is divided by race and largely ruled by violence. Even for a new inmate uninterested in racist ideology, it is often a matter of survival to join up with one or another gang. If that is not possible or desired, many weaker inmates fall prey to rape, extortion and violence from those around them (Intelligence Report 2000c).

Any examination of the history of corrections in the United States (Montgomery and Crews 1998) will demonstrate the changes that occurred during the second half of the twentieth century. Many who have worked in corrections in the past would argue that there was an unwritten correctional code that allowed order to be maintained between correctional officers and inmates. And, that there was an inmate code, that is, a sense of solidarity among inmates which gave much structure and control to inmate behavior. It appears that this code has disappeared in the twenty-first century. Most would argue that younger inmates are solely "out for themselves" and will take advantage of any opportunity that presents itself to cause a disturbance. Also, they have subdivided the prison population along very distinct racial lines (Intelligence Report 2000c). A frightening discovery that is being realized in the twenty-first century is that some guards actually help the gangs thrive by favoring one or another group. It is increasingly being reported that staff, either through commission or omission, are supporting some racist and gang activity.

It must be pointed out that most correctional officers and officials do the best they can to maintain order in the correctional environment. Even though they are faced with the constant potential for violence and rioting, they are able to maintain a reasonably safe environment. However, there are those who become embroiled in the battles they see around them, and a certain number wage brutal offensives of their own. In some cases, correctional officers take matters into their own hands, rather than dele-gating violence to prisoners. Some of these "guard gangs" actually organize around themes of physical strength and a shared animosity to prisoners (Montgomery and Crews 1998).

With the number of inmates of jails and prisons quadrupling to about 2 million dur-ing the 1980s and 1990s, a growing number of prisons have been built in rural, largely white areas of the country. Many of those sent to these prisons are black and Latino, while the employees are typically mostly white. As a result, the guard-inmate relationships that develop are often fraught with tension (Montgomery and Crews 1998).

Racism of guards is most often very subtle. Certain black guards, for instance, might avert their eyes to violence from Bloods and Crips, and some even favor gang members with extra food and other rewards. In the same way, some white guards may favor Aryan Brotherhood members. Prison officials faced with openly racist employees must act or face potentially expensive court disputes. In most cases where prison guards have been fired for their White Supremacist activities, the courts have sided with the prison administration. Despite this fact, many accusations of prison officials turning a "blind eye" to such activities among their staffs still occur. Whether prison officials do so because they are too timid to act, hope the problem will go away, or are secretly sympathetic to the racist cause, they run the risk not only of creating an explosive situation among the inmate population, but also of claims of a "hostile work environment" by other prison employees (Intelligence Report 2000c).

Racism on University Campuses

At institutions of higher learning, including many of America's leading universities, "hate" and "fear" are becoming more and more evident. Across the nation, colleges and universities are experiencing hate activities and crimes. In an environment that historically has been considered a place of the "best and brightest" and those that are the most "tolerant and open-minded," it is hard for many to believe that hate groups and racism still thrive. Any examination of higher education in America will reveal that violent racism and homophobia are becoming frighteningly commonplace.

The Federal Bureau of Investigation (Bureau of Justice Statistics 2006), reported approximately 250 campus incidents of hate in 2004. Most experts agree that this number is almost certainly a vast underrepresentation of the real level of campus hate crimes. Perhaps more startling than the absolute number is the fact that such crimes, along with hate crimes committed on other school campuses, represent 9% of the total number of hate crimes nationwide. Far more common than hate crimes are campus *bias incidents*. These are defined as incidents that do not rise to the level of prosecutable offenses but that may nevertheless posed the threat of instigating additional race based violence on a college campus.

For many students (Thomas and Weise 1999), the diversity found on most American university campuses allows them to experience different cultures and viewpoints. For some however, many of whom grew up in racially homogenous suburbs, it has the exact opposite effect. America has discovered expressions of diversity can trigger hate and bias incidents on campus. Gay Pride or Black History Month posters, for instance, often become message boards for hateful graffiti artists. Affirmative action and expressions of identity politics, Black Studies programs, or gay rights organizations, for example, also play a part in fostering resentment.

As many students (Thomas and Weise 1999) react negatively to encounters with others who are different, so do some people who are not connected to the campus. College campuses are often starkly different demographically from than the communities that surround them. Seeing people unlike themselves in college and bound for success, some off-campus individuals react violently. In fact, they are responsible for some of the worst violence against students.

Another interesting side note is that at many American universities and colleges, a growing number of professors are endorsing Holocaust denial, race-based IQ theories, and eugenics. Although most of these theories are not embraced by other academics, they are becoming more and more influential on college students. Some college students may react negatively to campus diversity, particularly if they perceive that "political correctness" is being forced upon them. They may use this to justify an intellectual basis for their feelings of racism and homophobia (Crews and Montgomery 1996).

A BRIEF EXAMINATION OF PRIMARY GROUPS

A complete examination of all hate groups and other potentially violent organizations operating in the United States is beyond the scope of this text. Instead, the following is a brief overview of the primary groups operating in the United States as of the early twenty-first century.

Ku Klux Klan

The status, influence, and danger of the Ku Klux Klan in the twenty-first century is debatable (Gerstend et al. 2003). Some argue that the organization is alive and well, though it may be operating much more covertly than ever before. Others believe that due to devastating lawsuits and public attention, the group is essentially non-existent. A few offer that remaining members have left the organization for other types of hate groups.

The plan (Gerstend et al. 2003) to "rebuild" the South by Northerners in 1865 at the end of the Civil War was known as "Reconstruction." This effort brought great resentment from most Southern Whites. These feelings, combined with anger over the new social and political status of former slaves, caused a group of ex-Confederate soldiers to form a secret society called the Ku Klux Klan (KKK) (from the Greek word *kuklos*, meaning circle, and the Scottish word *clan*). Their dress included the robes and hoods which would come to symbolize the group.

The original purpose (Gerstend et al. 2003) of the KKK was to assist the widows and children of fallen Confederate soldiers and to resist Reconstruction. The founder, General Nathan Bedford Forrest, left the group in 1869 due to its membership's increasing violence in its efforts to terrorize blacks and those whites seen as sympathizers. The "Klan Acts" of 1871 made this group illegal and condemned their activities. By 1877, as Northerners abandoned their efforts to "rebuild" the South, the group essentially disappeared.

Since this time, the KKK has re-emerged during times of racially-based national turmoil. The U.S. Supreme Court's ruling in the 1954 case of *Brown v. Board of Education* and the eventual upheaval of the 1960s and 1970s gave new purpose and strength to the Klan.

It appears that the KKK has essentially served as the grandfather of sorts to the more modern hate groups. The larger groups fragmented starting in the late 1960s and crippling lawsuits of the 1980s and 1990s essentially drove the group's membership underground. While the group's summit may have passed, its views, tactics, and message are still carried forward by younger members in newer groups.

Aryan Nations

The Aryan Nations (*Intelligence Report* 2000a) emerged in the White Supremacist movement in the mid-1970s at a time when many felt the KKK's influence was disappearing. The group's advocacy of a "White Power Revolution" and its mantra for a "Whites Only" homeland in the Pacific Northwest made it distinctive from other existing groups. Richard Butler, an alleged avid follower of the arguably racist, anti-Semitic Christian Identity Faith, preached a reportedly racist doctrine at his Church of Jesus Christ Christian on the Aryan Nations compound. Identity, he reportedly informed those in attendance, granted Whites "divine permission to hate." Butler immersing himself with the symbolism of the Nazi movement, and many would argue that by the end of the twentieth century he presided over a sphere of influence that included some of the organized hate movement's most radical members (e.g., ex-Texas Grand Dragon Louis Beam, National Alliance leader William Pierce, Klansman Glenn Miller, and White Aryan Resistance founder Tom Metzger).

During the mid-1990s, Butler reportedly developed an Aryan World Congress that met each year upon his compound. Many argue (Hoover and Johnson 2004) that this became an event that symbolized the group's greatest strength, its ability to provide common ground for a wide range of potential extremists. Since the late 1990s, there have been a number of reports that Klansmen, militant tax protesters, neo-Nazis, and Identity believers have gathered at such meetings and have operated under Aryan Nations' guidance.

Since this time, it has been reported that the Aryan Nations have became determined to reinvent their organization with a range of new tactics and ventures designed primarily to capitalize on the growing neo-Nazi Skinhead movement in the United States. To these ends, it is reported that Butler began hosting annual youth festivals for Skinheads at his compound featuring bands playing White Power music. At the same time, it is reported that the Aryan Nations began actively pursuing news coverage, particularly those media outlets with young audiences. As a result of its media efforts, Aryan Nations received attention from such media outlets as SPIN Magazine, the British Broadcasting Corporation (BBC), *Redbook*, the *New York Times*, NBC's *Inside Edition*, and Ted Turner's CNN (Teague 1999).

In the twenty-first century, as with many other types of groups, the Aryan Nations returned to one of their older recruiting methods, sending "ambassadors at large" on aggressive "diplomacy tours." Their missions were generally to bring other White Supremacist groups under Aryan Nations' control and guidance. It is reported that many groups joined the Aryan Nations as a result of such recruiting activities, taking an oath to the Aryan Nations group while retaining their own organization's name and membership (*Intelligence Report* 2000a).

New Black Panthers

In stark contrast to the original Black Panther leaders of the 1960 and 1970s, leaders of the New Black Panther Party reportedly speak of "White Devils" and "Bloodsucking Jews." One of the first times America was exposed to this new movement was when approximately 50 black men carrying assault rifles and shotguns and wearing fatigues and berets appeared in Jasper, Texas, in 1998. They were there, they announced, to protect fellow blacks against attacks following the murder of James Byrd, Jr., and to confront the KKK. This announcement also caused a large number of KKK members to appear to protect whites in the same aftermath (Wassmuth and Bryant 2002).

Many argue (Intelligence Report 2000e) that this event introduced the nation to a group that few Americans had heard of at that time, the New Black Panther Party. Some offer that this group was simply trading on the name of a group of Black militants famous in the 1960s and 1970s; the "new" Panthers portrayed themselves as "the only men bold enough to take on the violent racism of the KKK and other White Supremacists." Instead of working for efforts such as the health clinics and free breakfast programs of the original Panthers, allegedly the new group's leaders focused their efforts almost exclusively on hate rhetoric about Jews and whites.

It is reported that this group did not have a national office, a publication, or even an Internet site, and seemed to be disorganized. Despite this perception, the new Panthers have managed to sustain themselves through several incarnations since their beginnings in the early 1990s. In 2000, the Panthers appeared publicly in Atlanta, Dallas, Detroit, Houston, New York, Norfolk, Virginia, and Washington, D.C. In 2001, it was reported that the party appeared to be a federation of as many as 35 chapters in at least 13 cities with informal but important links to certain Black Muslims and other small black groups. The party's overall ideology continues to be difficult to assess. It appears that some local leaders seem far less radical and less given to anti-Semitism and hatred of white people than their national spokesmen (Intelligence Report 2000e).

Religious Intolerance

While debatable, organized religions each tend to teach that their beliefs are true, and that other religions are, to various degrees, essentially wrong. These beliefs can sometimes lead to prejudice against other faith groups. However, most major religions also teach an *ethic of reciprocity* (i.e., respect for one's fellow man). Most teach the importance of treating others as one wishes to be treated. One implication of such an ethic is that others should be granted religious freedom, thus being allowed to freely follow their own, different, spiritual paths as a fundamental human right.The problem becomes that many do not wish to take the ethic to that point. If religious groups were to stress this belief contained within their religious texts, then religious prejudice would, in theory, disappear.

Religious prejudice results in acts such as discrimination, ridicule, oppression, advocating restrictions on human rights, economic attack, physical attack, etc. In some areas of the world, it continues to involve imprisonment and assassination (Hill et al. 1998).

In addition, research studies have found various trends that seem to continue from decade to decade and generation to generation (Crews and Montgomery 2001):

- Americans are generally prejudiced against non-Judeo-Christian religions.
- Churchgoers are more prejudiced than are non-Christians.
- Born-again Christians are more prejudiced than are all churchgoers.
- Prejudice against homosexuals has dropped significantly since the 1980s.
- Prejudice against Atheists has dropped slightly, but remains very high.

Inquisition and Persecution

Religious persecution (Ostendort 2002) has been defined as the persecution of individuals within a group in their efforts to maintain their religious identity, or the abuse of power by an individual or organization that causes members of a religious group to suffer. This can manifest itself in myriad ways, but there are several basic pathways along which most of this intolerance is manifested.

The Issue of "Power"

Religious persecution often involves the abuse of "power." For example, the Holocaust illustrates how Adolf Hitler and the Nazis abused their power in efforts to exterminate the Jewish people. Power sometimes falls into the hands of benevolent individuals who use it to contribute to societies in positive ways. Other times power is given to individuals who use it to benefit only themselves or to fulfill their personal ambitions. However, sometimes the exercise of power by one group can have severe consequences for another group (Hill et al. 1998).

Ultra-Conservative Christian Views of Non-Christian Religions

Many Ultra-Conservative Christians vary greatly in their beliefs towards non-Christian religions. They generally accept that their religion is the only fully valid faith. It alone is based upon the Word of God, as expressed in the Bible. Some believe that an individual will be sent to Hell when she/he dies if she/he has not first been "saved" by trusting Jesus as Lord and Savior while on earth. This would include essentially all members of non-Christian churches. They may view other world religions as one of the following (Roberts and Winter 1997):

- only partially true, or
- mostly worthless, or
- influenced by Satan or
- actually controlled by Satan, or
- a variety of Satanism.

In addition, many conservative Christians do not recognize other denominations as being truly Christian. This is seen in their local ministerial associations that are frequently separate from the mainline/liberal Christian ministerial group in the same city. Some conservative Christians believe that the Gods and Goddesses of other religions are actually demons. Thus, they see little difference among Hinduism, Buddhism, Satanism, Neopaganism, and all other non-Christian religions. They believe that while members of these religions think that they are worshiping deities, they are really interacting with evil spirits or with Satan himself (Roberts and Winter 1997). This sets the stage for extensive conflict and potential violence.

Liberal Christian Views of Non-Christian Religions

Most Liberal Christians tend to view the major religions of the world as different attempts to understand deity, humanity, and the rest of the universe. They generally view the all-evil quasi-deity, Satan, as being a concept of profound evil, and not as a living entity with supernatural powers. They believe that this concept is associated mainly with Christianity and Islam. They see the Gods and Goddesses of non-Christian religions as being unrelated to Satan, although some of those deities may have both good and evil aspects. They view all of the major religions as inspiring many of their members to lead more moral and spiritual lives. They welcome and value religious diversity (Robert and Winter 1997). Ironically, this is almost the opposite of what detractors would offer about the liberal perspective.

Anti-Abortion Violence

Since the late 1990s (Clarkson 1998), experts state the number of nonviolent clinic "blockaders" has decreased, largely as acts of terrorism have alienated many in the larger anti-abortion movement. At the same time, those who have always advocated some violence have become increasingly revolutionary, seeing themselves as fighting a "Holy War" to recreate society in a religious mold. It appears that those in the most militant wing of the anti-abortion movement are more and more willing to kill.

Although nonviolent forms of protest are the preferred methods for most who oppose abortion, violence and threats of violence have been part of the anti-abortion movement since the Supreme Court's *Roe v. Wade* decision legalized abortion. Between 1972 and 1995, anti-abortion terrorists have been responsible for six murders and fifteen attempted murders, according to the National Abortion Federation (Clarkson 1998). They have also been reportedly behind some 200 bombings and arsons, 72 attempted arsons, 750 death and bomb threats and hundreds of acts of vandalism, intimidation, stalking, and burglary during this same period. While most people involved in clinic protests are clearly not involved in or necessarily supportive of violence, these protests remain the common ground of expression for abortion opponents of both nonviolent and violent persuasions.

IDENTITY GROUPS

Since the late 1940s, the theology of Identity has circulated through groups such as the KKK, neo-Nazis, the Posse Comitatus, and racist Skinheads. The twentieth century found that it apparently reached beyond traditional White Supremacists to an expanding network of anti-government extremists. Modern America has seen a growing problem with the Patriot Movement involving paranoid theories of government conspiracies and Biblical justifications for violence (Berlet 2004).

Identity members subscribe to the so-called "Israel Message." They believe that white people are the true Israelites and that Jews and people of color are subhuman "Children of Satan." who, along with the American government, are to be destroyed in an apocalyptic battle. Their hatred of the federal government is the cornerstone of all efforts. It appears that the single most dangerous element in the Militia Movement is the expanding network of Identity followers (Ostendort 2002).

Identity groups such as The Covenant, Sword and Arm of The Lord (CSA), the White Patriot Party, the Posse Comitatus, Aryan Nations, and the Order, have been responsible for the racist right's most violent episodes since the early 1990s. Identity's apocalyptic theology is rooted in British-Israelism, a view of mid-Victorian England that maintained that the Anglo-Saxons were the true "Lost Tribes of Israel." In America these beliefs were transformed into a fiercely anti-Semitic, racist theology by a small group of extreme right-wing leaders (Poisoning the Web 2001).

The American Identity doctrine continues to maintain that whites will be pitted against evil non-white satanic forces in an apocalyptic battle. Identity professes that Adam was a white man, the product of a Second Creation. In Identity's system, God's first creation produced people of color, "the beasts of the field," or "mud people." Jews, according to Identity, are literally the Children of Satan, the descendants of a union between Eve and the Serpent. These individuals mated with the "beasts" to produce the Edomites, mongrel people who are the embodiment of Satan and the source of the entire world's evil (Crews and Montgomery 1996).

Identity is a post-millennial religion, meaning that in order for the "Second Coming" to occur, God's law on Earth must first be established through a great battle known as Armageddon. In this battle, the forces of good (the White "Israelites") will be pitted against the armies of Satan, represented as the Jewish-controlled federal government. Identity followers will wage war against ZOG (the Zionist Occupation Government), "race traitors," and anyone else they view as enemies (Ostendort 2002). Because their theology envisions an "end of time" battle in the near future, Identity adherents advocate keeping a well-stocked arsenal and survival gear readily accessible. All are fiercely anti-gun control. Many live in armed compounds or "covenant communities" (Berlet 2004).

Identity followers believe that America is the New Jerusalem and that the U.S. Constitution was given to their ancestors, the white Christian founding fathers, by God. They believe the authentic Constitution consists of only the Articles of Confederation and the first Ten Amendments of the Constitution (the Bill of Rights). Under their ideology, only white Christian men are "true sovereign citizens" of the Republic. Other Americans are merely Fourteenth Amendment "state citizens," the illegal creation of an illegitimate "de facto" government. The Fourteenth Amendment, ratified in 1868, extends citizenship rights to all persons born or naturalized in the United States and guarantees equal protection of laws to all persons (Crews and Montgomery 1996).

Identity believers contend that modern American government is illegitimate, a view they share with non-Identity Patriots and tax protesters. Identity followers believe the Internal Revenue Service, civil rights legislation, and abortion rights are unlawful. Their vision of a violent battle against the forces of an illegitimate American government makes the widening Identity network an increasing threat (Ostendort 2002).

Identity's "Israel Message," with its anti-democratic interpretation of the Constitution and its theories of an "international Jewish banking" conspiracy, has steadily spread throughout the United States, England, Canada, Australia, and South Africa. Adherents have actively promoted Identity's anti-Semitic paranoia and hatred through a variety of methods including books, newsletters, audio cassettes, videos, short-wave and AM radio, satellite and cable television, the Internet, camp meetings, far-right Patriot rallies, and church congregations. Identity followers have also promoted the sect through a series of strategic alliances with other extremists (Poisoning the Web 2001).

Westboro Baptist Church

In October 1998, at the funeral of gay murder victim Matthew Shepard, members of the Westboro Baptist Church of Topeka, Kansas, made international news when they held up signs reading "No Fags in Heaven" and "God Hates Fags." This group believes that "God's hatred is one of His holy attributes." Incorporated in 1967 as a not-for-profit organization, the virulently homophobic Westboro Baptist Church considers itself an "Old School" Baptist Church. The Church is led by Reverend Fred Waldron Phelps, Sr., and many WBC congregants are related to Phelps by blood. His wife, several of his children, and dozens of his grandchildren frequent the church (Koch Crime Institute 2000).

While the WBC has picketed the gay community at hundreds of events nationwide, most of the individuals protested by the Church are not homosexual. In fact, WBC most often targets people it mistakenly claims are gay or those it believes to be encouraging homosexuality. Many church fliers emphasize the race or religion of these individuals, suggesting that their intolerance spreads beyond its abhorrence of homosexuality. What appears to be anti-gay rhetoric is often a vehicle for anti-Semitism, hatred of other Christians, and even racism (Koch Crime Institute 2000).

Trained as a lawyer, Fred Phelps was disbarred in 1979 by the Kansas Supreme Court, which asserted that he had "little regard for the ethics of his profession." The formal complaint against Phelps charged that he misrepresented the truth in a motion for a new trial in a case he had brought, and that he held the defendant in the case up to "unnecessary public ridicule for which there is no basis in fact." Following his disbarrment from Kansas State courts, Phelps continued to practice law in Federal courts. In 1985, nine Federal court judges filed a disciplinary complaint charging him and six of his family members, all attorneys, with making false accusations against them (the Phelps' unsuccessfully fought the complaint). In 1989, Fred Phelps agreed to surrender his license to practice law in Federal court in exchange for the Federal judges allowing the other members of his family to continue practicing in Federal court (Koch Crime Institute 2000).

In 1991, the WBC staged its first public demonstration, targeting a park in Topeka, Kansas, allegedly frequented by gays. Thousands of protests have followed as evidenced by their website. In addition to speeches on the picket lines, the Church spreads its message via faxed fliers and "News Releases." These faxed documents also appear at WBC's web site, godhatesfags.com, along with photos of Church pickets and a schedule of upcoming demonstrations. A second WBC Web site, godhatesamerica.com, contends that the United States is "doomed" because it supports gays. According to Fred Phelps, "God invented the Internet for us to preach on" (Koch Crime Institute 2000).

The Creativity Movement (Formerly the World Church of the Creator)

This group is known by various names: The Creativity Movement, Church of the Creator, and The Christian Identity Movement. The founder was reportedly Ben Klassen, but the leader as of the late twentieth century was Matt Hale. The group has been described as White Supremacist in nature, and is a whites-only atheist "religion." Women are to be wives and their husbands' entertainment, and have a great number of children. Some state the group wants to exterminate all others, including other White Supremacists, and make an all-white planet ruled by the one leader of the church who has absolute power. It is also reported by some that they also want to "cull out the misfits," by sterilizing deformed or retarded whites. They also feel Adolf Hitler, Friedrich Nietzsche, and Ben Klassen were the three greatest persons in history (Gerstenfeld et al. 2003).

Past members report that the group controls where, how, and with whom the member lives and associates; what clothes, hairstyles the person wears; what food the person eats, drinks, adopts, and rejects (a "raw" food diet as described in their holy book *Salubrious Living*). Members are expected to be able to commit any act of terrorism when and if the leader demands, although the only time this is allowed, according to Klassen, was when they think their Constitutional or religious rights are in any way being hampered. Many members have been jailed for acts they supposedly did on their own without the leaders' approval or order. Some report that spying on other members and former members is clearly encouraged by leader Matt Hale (as of 2006 serving a forty-year sentence for conspiring to have a judge killed). Betraying or leaving the group is seen as treachery or treacherous apathy to the white race, and Ben Klassen (who died of suicide in 1993) requires the severest punishment for those who betray them (Gerstenfeld et al. 2003).

Nation of Islam

The Honorable Minister Louis Gene Walcott Farrakhan and the Nation of Islam (NOI) continue to be the center of much debate in the United States. Some even argue that he is not a Muslim, nor is his doctrine Islam. Farrakhan is the leader of a group many feel is a black racist cult-type organization called the Nation of Islam (NOI) (founded in Detroit, Michigan, in the 1930s). Many feel that even though the group calls its followers Muslims, in reality, they have very little to do with the faith of Islam. Islam believes in the total transcendence of almighty God (called, in Arabic, Allah); the NOI teaches that black people are angelic gods. Islam maintains universal brotherhood; the NOI apparently states that Islam is for blacks alone. Islam teaches that prophethood ended with Muhammad ibn Abdullah, more than 1,400 years ago. The NOI teaches that Farrakhan's teacher, Elijah Muhammad, is the last prophet. Islam teaches principles of spiritual and moral decorum such as prayer, fasting, charity, and pilgrimage. Many believe that Elijah Muhammad cast these out or altered them beyond recognition (American Defense League 1998).

The roots of the NOI can be traced back to the early part of the part of the twentieth century with the emergence of black militant groups. For the most part, NOI surfaced as a social movement. It was a large organized group of people committed to collective goals and ideals to preserve or change the existing political economic structure and human relationships in a society. The NOI is a unique type of movement because it not only is designed at winning black converts but also focuses on black socioeconomic issues. In this sense, the NOI can be seen as much a movement for temporal change as it is one of religious enlightenment. Movements such as this arise during periods of social change, and the time period of the NOI's formation, circa 1930, was a crucially dynamic period in the United States. The aftermath of World War I combined with the Great Depression created social conditions that provoked discontent among blacks. Following the migration of southern blacks to northern cities such as Chicago, New York, and Detroit, blacks experienced a period of prosperity and expected their status to continue to improve. However, when the converse occurred and their status dropped after World War II, frustration, anxiety, and discontent arose (American Defense League 1998).

The NOI deviates considerably from the teachings of orthodox Islam. Their idea of blacks as racially superior and whites as evil is contradictory to the teachings of racial equality found in orthodox Islam. Although the name of this group seems to imply that they are part of the orthodox Islamic religion, this is not the case. There are significant differences ranging from interpretation of the Five Pillars to the perception that the members of the NOI have in regards to their diverse culture. The NOI is much more inclusive and politically radical than orthodox Muslims. Two of the Black Muslims' doctrines are at the heart of the controversy: their insistence that blacks must separate themselves from the abhorrent and doomed white race and their belief that it is the manifest destiny of the black nation to inherent the earth. These doctrines are in flagrant contrast to orthodox Islamic ideals of an all-embracing unity of mankind (Gerstenfeld et al. 2003).

However controversial Farrakhan may be, to contemporary blacks the social and economic message he preaches may be appealing. Through his messages, he has given many urban Blacks a sense of hope and blamed their social and economic condition on the "system," and the larger racist white society. Louis Farrakhan is most notably known for outspokenness and leading of the black community and his inflammatory statements about Jews. Farrakhan has received more press coverage than any other African American, with the exception of Rev. Jesse Jackson. The coverage of his statements and beliefs, however anti-Semitic and anti-white they may be, have ironically made him more sympathetic to blacks (American Defense League 1998).

Farrakhan and the NOI in general, have had a profound impact on the black youth. Many feel that no leader has had more of an impact on the younger black generation than he. Few leaders and organizations make themselves as accessible to the youth. In addition, youth appear to be drawn to Farrakhan because like their predecessors, they too face economic hardships and Farrakhan's message of economic empowerment via economic separation is a welcome remedy to their financial problems (American Defense League 1998).

NATIONALISM, PATRIOTISM, AND PERSONAL PRIDE

It appears to be impossible for an individual in the United States to draw attention to their own pride in their race, religion, heritage, or nationality, without risking stigmatizing others. One's personal pride is very often at the center of their conflict with others.

Patriot Periodicals

The following is a brief overview of some of the associated Patriot literature that can be found in the United States. From theories about black helicopters and secret concentration camps to proposals for "untaxing" oneself, the publications of the Patriot movement offer a glimpse into the bizarre and conspiratorial thinking of the extreme right in the United States. Because militias, "common-law courts," and other Patriot groups make wide use of the Internet, radio, and even television programming, their motives and plans become easier to evaluate. Advertisements in all these periodicals help the movement to create a network that offers the reader a radically alternative lifestyle (Intelligence Report 2000f).

- *The American's Bulletin*, published by Robert Kelly in Central Point, Oregon, proclaims the tabloid as "America's Source for the Uncensored Truth."
- *Center for Action S.P.I.K.E.* is a mixture of articles on paramilitary training, which is called SPIKE, short for "**S**pecially **P**repared **I**ndividuals for **K**ey **E**vents."
- *Media Bypass*, published by Tree Top Communications in Evansville, Indiana, carries a mix of articles ranging from those written by well-known conservative columnists to those involved in the sovereignty and antigovernment movement.
- *The Patriot Report*, published by The Present Truth in Sallisaw, Oklahoma, features a listing of conspiracy theories.
- *The Spotlight*, a tabloid published by the anti-Semitic Liberty Lobby in Washington, D.C., is reported by some to be America's best-read conspiracist publication.
- *Taking Aim*, the publication of the Militia of Montana (MOM), debuted in 1994; the Noxon, Montana-based newsletter, became one of the first Patriot periodicals of substance.

Straight Edge

Unfortunately, even philosophies which have very positive messages at their core can sometimes lead to violence and intolerance. "Straight Edge" refers to a philosophy whose most basic tenets promote a drug-free lifestyle. It is said to have developed as an offshoot of the punk rock/hardcore scenes of the early 1980s when the term itself was believed to have been coined by Ian Mackaye while he was the singer of the band Minor Threat. Mackaye avoided the nihilistic tendencies of punk rock, instead promoting the simple philosophy of "don't drink/don't smoke/don't fuck" (Straight Edge 2006).

In the years since the demise of Minor Threat in the 1990s (Straight Edge 2006), many believed that these views have transformed the belief systems of many teenagers worldwide. Increasingly disenchanted with societal problems, some young people have adopted the Straight Edge doctrine supposedly as a blueprint to better first themselves, and then the world in which they live. While the original definition of Straight Edge only included the rejection of mind-altering substances and promiscuous sex, late twentieth century interpretations included a vegetarian (or vegan) diet and an increasing involvement and awareness of environmental and political issues (Crews and Montgomery 2001).

In that Straight Edge (Straight Edge 2006) evolved out of the punk rock/hardcore scene, it is not surprising that music continues to play an important role. The Teen Idles, an early 1980s Washington, D.C., band, and predecessor to Minor Threat, can arguably be called the first Straight Edge band. Since that time there have been many bands that have so labeled themselves. In the mid to late 1980s, Straight Edge hardcore reached a zenith, especially in New York City. While the bands of this period did much to popularize Straight Edge, it can be argued that they also contributed to its close-minded and antagonistic aspects. The attitude between Straight Edge and the rest of the world often took on adversarial tones during this time, largely becoming "The positive youth crew versus people who drink, smoke, and/or do drugs." Many people dislike Straight Edge and its adherents because of such intolerant views (Straight Edge 2006).

It can be argued that the espousing of a drug-free lifestyle probably has left its positive impact on many American youth. Perhaps such ideals are more pertinent than ever in the twenty-first century as the focus continues to reach beyond affecting merely oneself to altering and improving one's society and environment. Unfortunately, as with almost all philosophies, the problems arise when members take their beliefs to the extreme. There have been a number of documented incidents where Straight Edge members have used physical violence to attack those not practicing their beliefs. Members of this movement in many cities have reportedly attacked interracial and homosexual couples across the country (Straight Edge 2006).

Militias

By the end of the twentieth century, the number of militia-type groups decreased by half, possibly marking the demise of a movement that peaked in the mid-1990s. On January 1, 1994, the Militia of Montana, the nation's first major militia group, was officially inaugurated in Noxon, Montana, beginning a movement that would grow immensely over the next few years. Although, by 2000, the antigovernment "Patriot" movement of which militias were the most prominent part appeared to be declining. Many would argue that the movement had been drastically impacted by arrests, the defection of hundreds of soft-core supporters, and the drift of hard-liners into racist hate groups or the always unidentifiably mysterious underground. In many ways, some would argue, the end of the millennium symbolized the pivot point of the Patriot movement (Militia Watchdog 2006).

During this time, the Intelligence Project (2006) identified a total of 217 Patriot groups, generally defined as radical antigovernment groups that oppose the "New World Order" and subscribe to a variety of conspiracy theories that were popular in the late 1990s. This number represented half of the 1998 total of 435 Patriot groups and a decline of more than 75% from the 858 groups at the movement's peak during 1996. Militias were apparently becoming much less active at the turn of the century. However, it also appeared that radical right extremists were increasingly joining race-based hate groups or taking up "lone wolf"-type terrorist activity (Berlet 2004).

By the close of the twentieth century, public anger over gun control, the growing power of the federal government, and standoffs with law enforcement during incidents at Ruby Ridge, Idaho, and Waco, Texas, led many to join Patriot groups, particularly militias. Thousands more appeared in "common-law" courts (vigilante courts set up by people who believed they could "asseverate" themselves from government and not be liable for taxes). Publishing houses specializing in the conspiracism that typified Patriot groups expanded around the country. Largely because Patriot groups presented themselves as non-racist, even though most Patriot ideology derives directly from White Supremacist groups of the 1980s, they were for a time remarkably successful at recruiting (Militia Watchdog 2006).

Even the 1995 Oklahoma City bombing, with the ideological ties of its perpetrators to the Militia movement, apparently did not contribute to a decline in Patriot growth. Within weeks of the attack, Patriots were working to deny even ideological connections between the Militia movement and the bombing. Instead, they portrayed the attack as having been carried out by the federal government, possibly using suspect Timothy McVeigh as an unwitting "patsy" in part of its plot. The idea, Patriot conspiracists argued, was to frighten good Americans so that they would accept passage of draconian anti-terrorism laws (Militia Watchdog 2006).

The apparent decline of the Patriot movement was also symbolized in the millennial date change. During 1999, Patriots had predicted all manner of mayhem, from the beginning of the Biblical end-times, to the collapse of Western civilization due to the Y2K "computer bug," to imposition of martial law. However, essentially none of these events came to pass, angering many who had been urged repeatedly to prepare for such catastrophes (Militia Watchdog 2006).

Patriot Groups

The Intelligence Project of the Southern Poverty Law Center (2000a) identified 217 "Patriot" groups that were active at the close of the twentieth century. Of these groups, 68 were militias, four were "common-law courts," and the remainder fit into a variety of categories such as publishers, ministries, citizens' groups, and others. The SPLC pointed out that generally, Patriot groups define themselves as opposed to the "New World Order" or adhere to extreme antigovernment doctrines. They also stated that being listed in such a manner does not necessarily imply that the groups themselves advocated or engaged in violence or other criminal activities, or were racist. Their lists were generally compiled from field reports, Patriot publications, the Internet, law enforcement sources, and news reports. When known, groups are identified by the city, town or county where they are located. Within states, groups are listed alphabetically by place of origin.

Posse Comitatus/Freeman Movements

While the roots of the purported Christian Patriot movement and the Posse Comitatus can be traced back to the nineteenth century, the movement as it exists in the early twenty-first century appears to have received its start in the early 1970s. William Potter Gale originally founded the Posse Comitatus, which is Latin for "power of the county," in 1970. But these efforts did not gain significant momentum until Gale was able to join his Christian Identity beliefs (i.e., a theology identifying Jews as the literal progeny of Satan and blacks as sub-human) with the growing anti-tax movement in the early 1990s (Berlet 2004).

There have been tax protesters and anti-federal government individuals in the United States since before the Declaration of Independence. However most would argue that the right-wing tax protest movement did not actually take hold until the 1930s, largely as a conservative reaction to President Franklin D. Roosevelt and the Democrats. Many would also argue that it was a movement that was buoyed by anti-Semitism and unfounded beliefs about Jewish banking conspiracies. These fears combined with the philosophy behind the Christian Identity movement in the early 1990s and gave the impetus for more action in the United States (Levitas 2002).

Posse Comitatus published their first manifesto in 1971, recommending the organization of local Posse groups throughout the United States and declaring that the county sheriff was the only legal law enforcement officer who had any authority over U.S. Citizens. They pioneered a so-called "common-law court" methodology by "indicting" people in Oregon, Idaho, and elsewhere using "citizens' grand juries." The first known case of a citizens' grand jury issuing a written threat was in 1972, in a conflict between a tax protester named George Kindred and state revenue authorities in Ingham County, Michigan. A Posse group there issued a notice threatening the local sheriff and law enforcement authorities for their enforcement of a state tax order (Poisoning the Web 2001).

When the militias (Levitas 2002) first began to appear, one of the principal issues they used to recruit followers was gun control. Right-wing Christian Patriot activists, many of whom had originated from the Posse movement, initiated the first meetings of some militia groups in Montana. They used issues like gun control to hold public meetings, which attracted many concerned individuals, along with themes like environmental regulation and concerns about the United Nations and United States sovereignty.

Many would (Levitas 2002) argue that the movement has become more militant and the amount of associated violence has increased. Opponents would offer evidence that these types of groups are very willing to confront agents of the U.S. federal government. Many would also add that previously there was a clearer division between the "patriotic" Posse Comitatus and the more violent and revolutionary movements. Since the later part of the twentieth century, there is great debate as to whether this distinction has faded. One of the most dangerous reported trends being seen is the transformation of the Posse movement into something that is more willing to embrace an armed and violent revolutionary philosophy (Poisoning the Web 2001).

National Alliance

The Neo-Nazi organization that some argue may have inspired the bombing of the Murrah Federal Building in Oklahoma City continues to flourish in the United States. The West Virginia-based National Alliance, founded by William Pierce, has reportedly grown at unprecedented levels since its inception in the early 1990s. During the early years Pierce aggressively used the Internet and the airwaves to formulate a massive recruitment campaign, among them reportedly followers of the anti-government patriot movement and even members of the nation's armed forces. Some would argue that in attempts to expand his organization, Pierce capitalized on the publicity of the Oklahoma City bombing of 1995. Timothy McVeigh, put to death for his involvement in the bombing, was a zealous advocate of Pierce's 1978 race war novel, *The Turner Diaries*. The book depicts a truck bombing remarkably similar to the Oklahoma City incident (Crews et al. 1996).

Some feel that the organization's growing influence among Patriots and members of the U.S. military, combined with its ideological connections to the Oklahoma City bombing, establish it as one of the most dangerous groups operating in North America in the twenty-first century. Reportedly, since the late 1990s, National Alliance's membership has drastically increased. Prior to his death, Pierce stated (National Alliance 2006) that his long-range goal was to ignite a worldwide race war and establish an Aryan utopia in North America (i.e., a fascist society free of Jews, blacks, other racial minorities, and other "traitors" to the white race).

Pierce is viewed still by many as the White Supremacist movement's undisputed master of propaganda. Thousands of copies of the National Alliance's pamphlet, "Who Rules America," have been distributed throughout the country since the late 1990s. Pierce (National Alliance 2006) also marketed his own two novels, *Hunter*, published in 1989, and his most widely known work, *The Turner Diaries*, the infamous race war novel first published in 1978. Pierce also sold another work, *Serpent's Walk*, published in 1991 with the false name of Randolph D. Calverhall listed as its author.

It has been reported (National Alliance 2006) that in the fall of 1995, Pierce turned his attention to the Patriot movement, announcing an effort he called the "Militia Project." His aim was to develop contact with and exert influence over the hundreds of Patriot militia organizations that operated in all 50 states. A month before Pierce began this effort; the National Alliance began disseminating its propaganda to a global audience through a sophisticated, well-designed site on the Internet. In October 1995, two months later, Pierce reported that more than 500 users were accessing the Alliance's Internet page each day. In 1996, he said that figure had more than tripled to an average of 1,764 users daily.

The site still contains a membership application form, policy and position statements, essays from the group's erratically-published magazine, National Vanguard, transcripts and audio files of the National Alliance's radio show "American Dissident Voices" and articles from Free Speech, a newsletter for the group's radio listeners (National Alliance 2006).

HERITAGE AND ATAVISM

Heritage and atavism are also interesting causes of conflict between individuals. Much like national pride and love of one's god, love of one's personal heritage appears to be a matter which is better left unspoken and private. While many groups have the luxury of being able to enjoy the freedom to be proud of their race and minority heritage, it appears that Whites, while debatable, cannot without the fear of being labeled as racist. And, as it is natural in human nature, there are those who are not concerned with possibly receiving this label, some actually reveling in such distinction.

Neo-Confederate Movement

A neo-Confederate movement (Intelligence Report 2000f), many would argue, involving White Supremacists and a racist ideology continues to grow across the United States. In South Carolina in January 2000, Americans were given the opportunity to observe a new social movement. This involved a group of approximately 8,000 people gathered on the steps of the South Carolina Statehouse to oppose the removing of the Confederate Flag from atop the Statehouse. Many were dressed in Confederate soldiers' gray, clothed in the stars and bars of the Confederacy or simply wearing street clothes. Alone among the Southern states, South Carolina still flew the flag above the dome of its Statehouse. This group was unsuccessful in trying to get the state office to refuse to surrender the flag in response to a NAACP boycott.

By June of that year, the issue had been settled in what many neo-Confederates viewed as a loss. In a compromise, the flag was removed from the Statehouse to a nearby spot on the Capitol grounds. Apparently this defeat did not hurt the movement, but instead gave the group more momentum to continue. Sine this time they have continued to stage more flag rallies and developed a political action committee to back flag supporters, and even, through a new political party, promoting various slates of candidates across the Southern states (*Intelligence Report* 2000f).

The ideological core of the neo-Confederate comes mainly from the League of the South (LOS), a group with a reported 9,000 members that has been growing steadily since its formation in 1994 and, to a lesser extent, the Council of Conservative Citizens (CCC), with about 15,000 members. Some would argue that the influence of these two organizations has also impacted many people in relatively apolitical, longstanding groups like the Sons of Confederate Veterans (SCV) and the United Daughters of the Confederacy (UDC).

The bonds between many of these groups are reportedly strong ones. Most of the key ideologues in the movement are members of more than one group, typically LOS and CCC, but also many of the more "mainstream" neo-Confederate groups. A few reportedly have links to militias and other antigovernment Patriot groups. The central theme for all of these groups is seen (whether founded or not) by many as a deep dislike and hatred for black people (*Intelligence Report* 2000f).

The appearance of a modern neo-Confederate movement, of course, is not the first time in recent history that reactionary groups have arisen to "defend the Southern cause." In the 1950s and 1960s, the White Citizens' Councils (WCC) arose to defend segregation and Jim Crow laws. By the 1970s, these groups were disappearing, but were replaced by the Councils of Conservative Citizens (CCC), a group that held similar views. It was in this period that a contemporary version of the neo-Confederate movement began to build. The CCC, in particular, led the attack on such things as school busing, non-white immigration and affirmative action (*Intelligence Report* 2000f).

The contemporary neo-Confederate movement did not gain national attention until the League of the South was founded in 1994. The group began as a respectable, non-racist organization led mainly by academics and was able to grow very rapidly. The group reported 4,000 members by 1998 and offered that they have doubled their number by 2000. It appeared to many that the group mixed clearly racial themes, while opposing non-white immigration, busing, and interracial marriage. Unlike the CCC, the LOS considered the removal of the Confederate flag from the South Carolina statehouse to be a primary issue (*Intelligence Report* 2000f).

While extremely controversial, many feel the racism in this movement to be undeniable. The spread of racist ideology in the neo-Confederate movement is apparent to many by the number of cross-memberships that activists hold in different groups. Members including many leaders of the LOS and CCC, in particular, also belong to other organizations such as the SCV. With these cross-memberships, explicit racism has sometimes risen to the movement's surface in speeches, on postings on the Internet and in neo-Confederate publications (*Intelligence Report* 2000f).

Many groups have taken the perceived lead of LOS in seeing the South as being fundamentally "Anglo-Celtic" (i.e., disregarding contributions made by blacks, Native Americans, Jews, and others to Southern culture). By exposing these and similar themes, the neo-Confederate movement has grown substantially (whether intentionally or not) by providing a home for thousands of people with racist feelings who nonetheless who may seek the cover of groups that present themselves as mainstream (*Intelligence Report* 2000f).

Ultimately, an unfortunate situation continues. While very controversial, it must still be pointed out that this in no way is to state that all southern whites who show pride in their Southern heritage or interest in the history of the Confederacy are racists or White Supremacists. Instead, strong pride in one's heritage may simply be nothing more than personal honor, with no inherent attack against others intended.

American Nazi Party

Many argue (Glass 1999) that German National Socialism has been revamped by some over the decades since World War II in order to keep up with the changing times and to continue to be attractive to a new generation of White Supremacists in Europe and the United States. It is difficult for many to believe that Nazism could still be a vibrant philosophy even after over 50 years since World War II. Although this philosophy has undergone many changes over the decades, the basic tenants have not changed. It is being packaged and presented differently to a new breed of potentially disenchanted individuals. An interesting side note is that it is not returning with the expected symbolism of the swastikas and storm trooper uniforms, but instead it appears to be manifesting itself through a youth rebellion and an "outlaw" mentality. Modern Nazism (Crews 2003) has become a broader-based movement more connected to the youth culture than ever before. Many groups are attaching this philosophy to music, literature, and occult venues. Those doing so realize that this has always been one of the best ways to attract young people. Other groups are attaching the philosophy to religious and conservative political views that are already a foundation in American society.

One of the groups (Glass 1999) that may have been most successful in such efforts was the American Nazi Party (ANP). George Lincoln Rockwell, founder of the ANP and assassinated in 1967 by a disgruntled follower, was the first to take critical steps in the revamping and updating of fascist ideology. He is credited with coining the term "White Power" and broadening its definition from the narrow German concept of the Aryan race, which excluded Slavs, Poles, Italians, Greeks, and others. This philosophy was very popular because it told white working-class immigrants for the first time that they were part of the "master race." Youth who were emotionally insecure, living in impoverished neighborhoods, and who could not see a bright future were (and would continue to be) very susceptible to such ideologies (Glass 1999).

Rockwell was reportedly also responsible for the Holocaust Denial myth that has developed as one of the major tenets of modern National Socialists. He felt that for the movement to grow, it had to separate itself from the murder of millions of Jews and others during World War II. He also felt he needed to separate the movement from atheism and attach it to a religious foundation. Since Rockwell's death, the Neo-Nazi movement has continued to draw a parallel and association with the Christian Identity movement (Jones 1999).

Many argue (Jones 1999) that neo-Nazis also have embraced and expanded the mysticism and occultism that is associated with fascist ideologies. They would also state that the growing New Age phenomenon in the United States is quite possibly being exploited, deformed, and manipulated to promote racist and fascist ideas. As discussed in other areas of this chapter, the music of choice is changing as well. National Socialist Black Metal and White Power Music have taken the forefront in popularity with many young American followers. This music has also developed in to a very popular recruiting tool for such groups. A final issue that is drawing much concern is that "National Socialism" is becoming much less national and instead more international in scope.

Impact of Modern Music and Culture

Since the mid-1970s (Crews 2003), "Heavy Metal" music has been linked to Satanism and the occult by many across the United States. Since this time, some would argue that musicians and actors intent on reviving declining careers through any means necessary(especially through controversy) promoted this image. In the twenty-first century, it can be argued that what was once done for shock value and to sell records has evolved into an actual conscious attempt by some to spread hate, fear, intolerance, and violent ideologies among the youth of most countries.

Metal Music, like all music, is constantly evolving and being reinvented by those who are responsible for its production. New generations generally build on the past, most often pushing the levels of what is acceptable and adding new twists to the music and its message. The newest generation of Metal Bands, known as the Black Metal Underground (Crews and West 2006), is so extreme in many cases that some would argue that it makes more traditional Heavy Metal performers like Ozzy Osborne and Marilyn Manson appear passive. For those who may want to turn the ever existing teenage angst into hatred, this metal scene is a natural target. Like Heavy Metal, most of those involved in Black Metal (term coined by the group Venom in the 1980s) are white and suburban. It has been said that Black Metal got its name because it performers and fans embrace the concepts of darkness and evil. Many of its fans believe they have not been accepted or have been alienated by traditional Christianity. Thus they reject this religion and believe those who are accepted are hypocrites and deserve whatever ills await them (Koch Crime Institute 2000).

The music and its increasing identification with violence and belief systems is important. While many adults find it difficult to imagine being swayed to the point of violence by the lyrics of a song, the fact is that for many youths music does play just such a role. Many of those who have left this music scene have argued that teenagers who listen to the songs repeatedly actually are affected by the words. With such lyrics echoing in their heads, a certain percentage of these still-forming youths may actually be transformed into full-fledged haters (Crews and Montgomery 2001).

The majority of Black Metal fans (Crews and West 2006), of course, as with most music fans in general, are not threatening to burn down their neighborhood church and are not active hate group participants. Most are into it for the music, the style, and the nihilism that seems so attractive to many rebellious and alienated teenagers. Unfortunately, "openly hidden" within this scene are those who are hoping to take advantage of the Black Metal fan's possible penchant for the dark side to spread neofascist and other racial ideology. In addition to the concerts held in both Europe and the United States, these ideologues are using the Internet to build connections and solidarity within this potentially violent scene, a development that is deeply troubling to many because of the popularity of Metal Music among American small town youths.

National Socialist and Black Metal

Since the mid-1970s (Crews and West 2006), Metal music has evolved and diversified from Blues Music and Rock and Roll into Speed Metal, Death Metal, Grindcore, and Black Metal. Some Metal bands were offshoots of Punk Rock and promoted independent thought and action, while others appealed to the dark side, increasing the controversial nature of their lyrics, performances, and lifestyles. It appeared to many that Black Metal had fully embraced this new "dark side" of human nature.

Black Metal emerged in the early 1980s (Moynihan and Soderlind 2003), when the English band Venom reportedly coined the term. Many would argue that the band's songs of Satan and evil actually inspired a generation. Musically, Black Metal has been called by some a teenage soundtrack to the battle between good and evil. The music has an atonal quality, blazing fast guitar riffs, violent nihilistic lyrics that are growled instead of sung, and ambient keyboard and synthesizer sounds. In appearance, the genre's musicians have not strayed far from the traditional Heavy Metal style with long hair and metal-studded leather jackets, although there is one new addition, "corpse paint," in which the musicians and fans cover their faces with white face paint and use black makeup to darken their eyes and mouths (popularized, among other places, in the movie *The Crow*). Some actually wear Viking attire, complete with robes, swords, and other medieval pieces.

Most participants (Baddeley 2006) agree that by definition, Black Metal bands are vehemently anti-Christian. Some follow this line because of their belief in Satan as a deity, while others see themselves as independent thinkers opposed to the supposed "sheep-like mentality" of Christianity. Others adhere to pre-Christian theologies like Odinism, Asatrú, and other polytheistic pagan faiths and feel that it is their atavistic duty to fight back against Christianity and other dominant religions. Many in the "scene" are extremely well read and intelligent. Most have attended or are in college, and often quote people such as Heidegger, Shakespeare, and Nietzsche. Some argue that it is the combination of the "will to power" philosophy of Nietzsche and the ethnic nationalism that is often associated with the worship of pagan gods that first pointed some in the scene toward violent racism and anti-Semitism.

Since the early 1980s, Black Metal (Baddeley 2006) has grown exponentially in the United States and in other countries. Many are arguing that neo-Nazism, White Power, and hatred of Jews and people of color is building in the Black Metal scene in the twenty-first century and forging alliances outside of Metal. They would argue that Black Metal music has evolved from a rebellious adolescent genre to a scene increasingly affiliated with neo-Nazism and murder. When the first Black Metal bands started releasing recordings in the early 1990s with Satanic lyrics and began adopting the Black Metal moniker, a youthful subculture grew around the music. Youth were quite possibly enchanted by the shocking anti-Christian themes and the dark concert displays of skulls, capes, and devilish make-up. By the 1990s, a more political offshoot had also evolved out of the Black Metal scene, "National Socialist Back Metal" (NSBM). This type of music combines Satanism with pagan and neo-fascist themes (Intelligence Report 2000d).

As Black Metal bands (Baddeley 2006) emerged across Europe in the 1980s and 1990s, Scandinavia, especially Norway, emerged as the scene's epicenter. The band Mayhem was formed in 1984 by Norwegian Øystein Aarseth. Reportedly dubbing himself and his followers the "Black Circle," Aarseth successfully merged the Satanist and neo-Pagan theologies. Christianity, he would argue, should be violently expelled from Norway and replaced with his cultish mix. It has been argued (Moynihan and Soderlind 2003) that this effort led directly to church burnings that have occurred across Europe and Scandinavia since the mid to late 1990s.

Skinheads

The Skinhead phenomenon (Crews and Montgomery 2001) originated in England where gangs of menacing-looking, shaven-headed, and tattooed youths in combat boots began to be seen in the streets in the early 1970s. According to participants, their style was meant to symbolize tough, patriotic, working-class attitudes in contrast to the supposedly skittish, pacifist, middle-class views of the hippies of the time.

Many argue that the racist and chauvinist attitudes that prevailed at that time among many Skinheads later evolved into a crude form of Nazism. From the start, Skins drew public notice for their bigotry and taste for violence, exemplified by their frequent assaults on Asian immigrants, attacks that came to be known as "Paki-bashing." In the years that followed, the Skinhead movement spread from England to the United States and beyond. Racist Skinheads in the twenty-first century are found in almost every industrialized country whose majority population is of European decent. It appears that those attracted to the movement are white youths between the ages of 13 and 25, with males outnumbering females. While Skins retain the mythology of the movement's working-class origins, in reality they come from a broad range of socio-economic backgrounds. The look favored by male Skinheads is instantly recognizable, a shaved head or closely cropped hair, jeans, thin suspenders or braces, combat boots, a bomber jacket, sometimes emblazoned with Nazi insignia, and tattoos of Nazi symbols and slogans. For security reasons, Skinheads sometimes adopt a less conspicuous look, by, for example, letting their hair grow out (Crews et al. 2006).

Most Skinhead gangs range in size from fewer than ten to several dozen members. To those devoted to the movement, being a Skinhead is a full-time way of life and not simply adherence to a fashion. Skinhead activities dominate the social and domestic life of gang members. They often live in communal "crash pads" and stick to themselves when out in public. They generally only have relationships with other Skins (Crews and Montgomery 2001).

Many argue that neo-Nazi ideology combined with the gang lifestyle provides Skinheads with a seductive sense of strength, group belonging, and perceived superiority over others. It could also be said that invocation of Viking imagery offers the Skinhead a perception of himself as a racial warrior. Many Skinheads glorify Adolf Hitler and aspire to create his vision of a worldwide, pan-Aryan Reich. These strands, a sense of power, of belonging, of destiny, combine to create the appeal the Skinhead movement holds for disaffected youngsters. It appears that Skinhead violence differs little from one country to the next. Those violent factions seem to simply seek out members of their identified (hated) groups and attack them. While their means of attack varies, Skinheads take special pride in using their boots as weapons. Vandalism is another Skinhead specialty, scrawling racist graffiti and desecration of Jewish synagogues, cemeteries and memorials to the Holocaust (Anti-Defamation League 1995).

While some Skinheads (Crews 2001) have been known to use drugs, many consume alcohol. Heavy beer consumption often precedes incidents of Skinhead violence. A major aspect of Skinhead life is their devotion to bands that play White Power "Oi" music, a loud and abrasive type of music whose lyrics generally espouse messages of bigotry and violence. Music appears to be the Skinhead movement's main propaganda weapon and its chief means of attracting young recruits. Skins maintain universal ties through their music, distributing recordings internationally and organizing concert tours and music fests that feature both domestic and foreign bands (Crews and Montgomery 2001).

Record labels devoted to White Power music produce and market recordings, with informal networks of enthusiasts exchanging bootleg or homemade cassette tapes. The artwork on the jackets of Skinhead recordings are characteristically devoted to racist and violent images. Concerts range from performances in local hangouts to international festivals that attract Skinheads from neighboring countries. At these festivals, swastika-emblazoned banners decorate the bandstands while Skinheads, arms outstretched, shout slogans like "Sieg Heil" and "White Power." In whatever context the bands play, the event often degenerates into a free-for-all of slam dancing and scattered fistfights (Crews and Montgomery 2001).

Also central to the Skinhead scene are their magazines (commonly called *skinzines* or *zines*), usually crudely written newsletters that focus on Skinhead bands and their recordings. The zines promote Skinhead ideology and advertise services popular among Skins such as tattoo parlors, clothing stores that sell Skin fashions, and Oi music distributors. In addition, they announce concerts and other events of interest to Skinheads. Zines are published sporadically, and it is not unusual for some to go out of business after a few issues and for new ones to emerge. The zines serve as a vital link between Skinheads in different countries. The publications generally maintain friendly relations internationally, carrying favorable reviews of foreign bands and detailing the exploits of their counterparts abroad (Crews and Montgomery 2001).

Hammerskin Nation

A harder, more disciplined, and more international group (Hammerskin Nation 2006) has emerged from what began in the 1990s as a small Dallas, Texas, Skinhead organization. In the 1980 animated film adaptation of *The Wall*, the rock group Pink Floyd's rock anthem for angry youth, a little fascist character struts across a stage and rouses his followers to violence against minorities. The fans are portrayed in the film as a mass of marching twin claw hammers. Since the late 1990s, these crossed hammers signify what many would argue are the best organized, most widely dispersed and most dangerous Skinhead group known, the Hammerskin Nation (HN).

Prior to the 1990s, the American conventional view of Skinheads by law enforcement, monitoring organizations, and even some White Supremacists, was that they were little more than drunken street gangs. They were seen as dysfunctional youth in and out of jails and given to fighting among themselves, simply brawlers who could not be organized or controlled. It was believed that these individuals were not interested in organizing around a platform of any sort. For them, it was far more satisfying to discharge violent acts not only on minorities, gays and anti-racists, but on each other as well. This uncontrolled behavior, combined with their shaved heads, steel-toed boots, and bodies most often covered with racist tattoos, made Skinheads easy targets for law enforcement (Hammerskin Nation 2006).

The American Hammerskins (Crews et al. 1996) first appeared in the late 1980s as the Dallas-based Confederate Hammerskins and spread to Georgia, Tennessee, and Florida. During this period, more namesakes followed such as the Northern Hammerskins in the Great Lakes region, the Eastern Hammerskins in Pennsylvania and New Jersey, and the Western Hammerskins in Arizona and California. By 1989, the Hammerskins emerged as the unifying organization for these dispersed groups. Within a few years, Hammerskins had become global, moving from North America across the Atlantic to the east and the Pacific to the west. By 2000, Hammerskins had viable chapters in Australia, the Czech Republic, France, Germany, Great Britain, the Netherlands, New Zealand, Poland, Serbia, Slovenia, and Russia. Like outlaw motorcycle gangs such as the Hell's Angels, Hammerskins had a strict recruitment policy that required not only "face-time" with prospective members but a three-month probationary period.

Joining the Hammerskins was not like joining most White Supremacy organizations, which typically asked for little more than mailing in a cursory application along with a modest membership fee to a post office box. Unlike criminal street gangs, Hammerskins had a focused and relatively sophisticated political philosophy. Loyalty to Hammerskins was paramount. Hammerskins were permitted to also join neo-Nazi groups like the National Alliance or Aryan Nations, but are Hammerskins first and always (Hammerskin Nation 2006).

As with other traditional Skinhead organizations, the main recruiting tool for the Hammerskin Nation remains the White Power rock concert. Since the late 1990s,

Hammerskins have sponsored numerous concerts each year in Florida, Georgia, Kansas, Nevada, Pennsylvania, Texas, and Budapest, Hungary (Hammerskin Nation 2006).

Many argue (Crews and West 2006) that arising out of Hammerskin Nation is a new generation of leaders on the White Nationalist Revolutionary Front. Many of these leaders have experienced the American prison system and have returned to their neighborhoods more hardened, better disciplined and better educated than their predecessors on the racist right, most of whom have done essentially nothing more criminal than marching down the street with a swastika on their sleeve. The Internet and inexpensive airfares have drawn the Hammerskins into a transnational movement that has become increasingly uniformed and connected. With maybe the exceptions of White Aryan Resistance's Tom Metzger and the National Alliance's William Pierce, the previous neo-Nazi leadership has little relevance to this newer generation of racist revolutionaries. Some would argue that the elders of organized White Supremacy are giving way to a leaner, meaner, and smarter species of neo-Nazi, one that follows not the banner of the Third Reich but the twin claw hammers of the new pan-Aryan movement.

FACTORS COMMONLY FOUND IN DESTRUCTIVE DOOMSDAY TYPE GROUPS

There is no objective, precise checklist of danger signs to warn one against becoming involved with a destructive or doomsday type of religious-based or other type of group. However, some individuals and organizations have written guidelines that give a general idea of the degree of manipulation and danger found in religious and other groups (Crews and Montgomery 1996).

Each of the following approaches the problem from a different perspective. They list some symptoms that are found to some degree in most perfectly legitimate religious groups. It is when the symptoms become extreme that one should become concerned (Crews and Montgomery 1996):

- *Apocalyptic Beliefs:* The leader's preaching concentrates heavily on the impending end of the world, often at a great battle (e.g. War of Armageddon). In addition the leader preaches that through group suicide at a particular instant, they will all be transported to a wonderful place and escape the devastation that is about to come to the earth. The group is expected to play a major, elite role at the end time.
- *Charismatic Leadership:* A single male charismatic leader leads them. The leader dominates the membership, closely controlling them physically, sexually and emotionally.
- *Social Encapsulation:* They are a small religious group, not an established denomination. The group (or at least the core members) lives together in an intentional community that is isolated from the rest of society. There is often extreme paranoia within the group; they believe that they are in danger and that they are being closely monitored and heavily persecuted by governments or people outside the group. People on "the outside" are demonized. Information and contacts from outside the cult are severely curtailed.

- *Other Factors:* The group leadership assembles an impressive array of guns, rifles, other murder weapons, poison, or weapons of mass destruction. They may prepare defensive structures. They follow a form of Christian theology (or a blend of Christianity with another religion), with major and unique deviations from traditional beliefs in the area.

Some religious groups are destructive, but are a hazard more to the public than their own membership. They disseminate hatred and fear against minorities, typically non-Whites, communists, homosexuals, and Jews. They do not usually call for direct and immediate violence against these minorities. However, they often inspire some of their less mentally-stable members to target minorities randomly. The Christian Identity movement and World Church of the Creator are typical. Their members have been responsible for dozens of assaults and random murders in the United States (Crews and Montgomery 2001).

CONCLUSION

It is clear that hate and fear still work. They bring people together, they sell merchandise, they can develop a subculture, and they can push along a struggling movement or ideology. It should then be no wonder why they are so popular in American society. It has been said that love brings people together, but others argue that it is actually hatred of a common enemy which brings them together the closest. Hate and Patriot groups have known this fact for a long time and have used it to their advantage. It appears that the youth of America could very well be the pawns in the "perceived" racial war that so many groups are proposing will someday occur. Unfortunately, the youth are those that appear to be most susceptible to being said pawns. Only with a concentrated effort on all fronts can America attempt to stop this perceived tide of hatred across the country.

Americans have also discovered that religious persecution is often not simply the persecution of a group because of their faith; rather it can take myriad forms and manifestations. As has been seen in many examples, religious persecution can be the result of the abuse of power, the means to a political end, or the struggle of a group to maintain its religious identity. Unfortunately, there are those in the world who appear to work daily to threaten the future of religious tolerance in the United States. Many argue that this should be a warning to anyone concerned about religious freedom, religious tolerance, and social stability in the United States (and the world). During periods of major social stress, some might exploit low opinions of minority religions. Such stress may be induced by a serious economic recession, or rapid changes in ethical norms. The world has seen this occur in many regions where long-standing religious frictions were manipulated by a small number of political and religious leaders, and used to fuel atrocities, crimes against humanity, and genocide.

In reality there should be no issue of right or wrong as far as belief is concerned. Faith groups naturally have entirely different views of the nature of their own and other "religions." It is actually a difference in definition, whether one's understanding of religious truth includes or excludes the beliefs of other faith groups. Unfortunately, excluding other religions can lead to misunderstandings and conflict. The problem comes when groups try to practice exclusivism (the idea that there can only be one true faith). The same individuals who make this suggestion usually accuse any faith or Christian denomination other than their own of being anti-Christian or Satanic. Most groups are not anti-Christian, but simply different. Problems can occur when individuals convert their beliefs into practice.

It can be argued that religious minorities in the United States have been heavily discriminated against. Anti-Semitism is believed to be responsible for the largest number of serious religious attacks in the country at any given time. However, those who are open with their faith have probably suffered the greatest on a per-capita basis. There have been incidents of lynching, attempted mass murder by stoning, shooting, assaults, firebombing, and other criminal acts.

It appears that the only answer to these mounting problems may be actually quite simple. Many state that only through understanding, tolerance, and acceptance can this hope to change. Unfortunately, it appears that this need for tolerance and understanding will have to wait. The efforts in 2006 to tighten the boarders of the United States and decrease the amount of illegal immigration appear to be rejuvenating many existing groups and feelings as well as serving as the impetus for new groups to develop whose message and purpose may at first not be totally clear. In 2006, a group calling itself the New Minutemen emerged to lead a national effort to support the U.S. government's efforts to establish increasingly harsh anti-immigration legislation. In an eerie echo of the past, the group's motto is that they are a vigilant group, not a vigilante group—as with all things, only time will tell.

REFERENCES

American Defense League. (2001). *Recurring hate: Matt Hale and the World Church of the Creator*. New York: Anti-Defamation League.

American Defense League. (1998). *The other face of Farrakhan: The hate-filled prelude to the Million-Man March*. New York: Anti-Defamation League.

Anti-Defamation League. (1995). *The Skinhead international: A worldwide survey of Neo-Nazi Skinheads*. New York: Anti-Defamation League.

Anti-Defamation League. (1999). *Report sites Neo-Nazi National Alliance as most dangerous organized hate group in America*. New York: Anti-Defamation League.

BADDELEY, G. (2006). *Lucifer rising: Sin, devil worship, and rock n roll*. London: Plexus Publishing.

BERLET, C. (2004). Christian identity: The apocalyptic style, political religion, palingenesis and neo-fascism. *Totalitarian Movements and Political Religions, 5*(3).

BOECKMANN, R., AND C. TURPIN-PETROSINO. (2002). Understanding the harm of hate crime. *Journal of Social Issues, 38*(2), 207–55.

Bureau of Justice Statistics. (2006). *Improving the quality and accuracy of bias crime statistics nationally*. Washington, DC: U.S. Department of Justice.

CLARKSON, F. (1998). Anti-abortion extremism. *Intelligence Report*. Montgomery, AL: Southern Poverty Law Center.

CREWS, G. A. (2001). Shadows in the streets: Policing, crime prevention, and street gangs. In *Policing and Crime Prevention*, ed. D. Robinson, pp.127–36. Upper Saddle River, NJ: Prentice Hall.

CREWS, G. A. (2003). Everyday is Halloween: A goth primer for law enforcement. *Forum: Law Enforcement Executive Journal, 3*(3), 165–82.

CREWS, G. A., AND R. H. MONTGOMERY, JR. (2001). *Chasing shadows: Confronting juvenile violence in America*. Upper Saddle River, NJ: Prentice Hall.

CREWS, G. A., R. H. MONTGOMERY, AND W. R. GARRIS. (1996). *Faces of violence in America.* Needham Heights, MA: Simon and Schuster.

CREWS, G. A., J. PURVIS, AND M. HJELM. (2006). The emerging problem of preppie gangs in America. In *Handbook of juvenile justice: Theory and practice*, ed. B. Sims and P. Preston. Marcel Dekker pp. 193–217., New York, NY.

CREWS, G. A., AND A. D. WEST. (forthcoming, 2006). Preppie gangs in America. In (Ed.), *Encyclopedia of public administration and public policy*, ed. J. Rabin. Marcel Dekker, New York, NY.

GERSTENFELD, P., D. GRANT, AND C. CHIANG. (2003). Hate online: A content analysis of extremist internet sites. *Analysis of social issues and public policy, 3*(1), 29–44.

GLASS, A. J. (1999). New tools coming to help parents protect kids on Internet. *State Newspaper, Columbia, SC.* May 6.

Hammerskin Nation. (2006). Retrieved from www.hsn.com

HILL, B., P. KNITTER, AND W. MADGES. (1998). *Faith, religion and theology.* Mystic, CT: Twenty-Third Publications.

HOOVER, K. R., AND V. D. JOHNSON. (2004). Identity-driven violence: Reclaiming civil society. *Journal of Hate Studies, 3*, 83–94.

Intelligence report. (2000a). Aryans without a nation. Montgomery, AL: Southern Poverty Law Center.

Intelligence report. (2000b). At the crossroads. Montgomery, AL: Southern Poverty Law Center.

Intelligence report. (2000c). Behind the wire. Montgomery, AL: Southern Poverty Law Center.

Intelligence report. (2000d). From Satan to Hitler. Montgomery, AL: Southern Poverty Law Center.

Intelligence report. (2000e). Snarling at the white man. Montgomery, AL: Southern Poverty Law Center.

Intelligence report. (2000f). Rebels with a cause. Montgomery, AL: Southern Poverty Law Center.

JONES, V. M. (1999). *Youth Crime Watch of America.* Washington, DC: Office of Juvenile Justice and Delinquency Prevention.

Koch Crime Institute. (2000). *The changing threat of gangs, cults, and the occult.* Topeka: KCI Seminars.

LEVITAS, D. (2002). The radical right after 9/11. *The Nation*, 56–72.

MONTGOMERY, R. H., JR., AND G. A. CREWS. (1998). *A history of correctional violence in America.* Lanham, MD: American Correctional Association.

MOYNIHAN, M., AND D. SODERLIND. (2003). *Lords of chaos: The bloody rise of the satanic metal underground.* Los Angeles: Feral House.

OSTENDORT, D. (2002). Christian identity: An American heresy. *Journal of Hate Studies, 1*(1), 23–55.

Poisoning the web. (2001). *Christian identity movement and Posse Comitatus groups.* Englewood Cliffs, NJ: Prentice-Hall.

ROBERTS, J., AND T. WINTER. (1997). *The best of human events: Fifty years of conservative thought and action.* New York: Huntington House Publishers.

SCHAFER, M., AND M. NAVARRO. (2003). The seven stage hate model: The psychopathology of hate groups. *FBI Law Enforcement Bulletin*, 19–23.

SHIVELY, M. (2005). *Study of literature and legislation on hate crime in America: Final report.* Washington, DC: National Institute of Justice

Southern Poverty Law Center. (2006). Retrieved from www.splcenter.org.

Straight Edge. (2006). Retrieved from www.straight-edge.org.

TEAGUE, M. (1999). *The Aryan Nations Home Page.* Aryan Nations Youth Corps. Retrieved from www.nidlink.com/~aryanvic/youthcorps.html.

The Militia Watchdog. (2006). Retrieved from www.milita-watchdog.org.

The National Alliance. (2006). Retrieved from www.natall.com.

THOMAS, K., AND E. WEISE. (1999). Hate groups share youths with Web games. *USA Today*. July 8..

U.S. Department of Commerce, Bureau of the Census. (2000). *Statistical abstracts of the United States*. Washington, DC: U.S. Government Printing Office.

WASSMUTH, B., AND M. BRYANT. (2002). Not in our world: A perspective of community organizing against hate. *Journal of Hate Studies, 1*(1), 109–31.

WOODEN, W. S. (1995). *Renegade kids, suburban outlaws*. New York: Wadsworth Publishing.

WOOLF, L., AND M. HULSIZER. (2003). Intra- and inter-religious hate and violence: A psychosocial model. *Journal of Hate Studies, 2*(5), 5–25. *Universal Declaration of Human Rights*. (2006). Retrieved from www.un.org.

12

The Criminal Justice System's Response to Minorities

John Falconer

❖

CHAPTER OUTLINE

INTRODUCTION

This book has given depth to the topic of special populations and the criminal justice system by dealing with each group in separate chapters. Scholars and professionals, likewise, tend to focus their attention on the specific parts of criminal justice system, but it is important for the observer to understand that no component of the criminal justice system exists in a vacuum anymore than a racial or ethnic group lives in isolation from other people. To understand a given part of the system, we must understand how it relates to the internal and external environment.

Social organizations like the criminal justice system are often perceived as machines comprised of parts that do predictable tasks, much like a watch. This can be a deceptive convenience for policymakers, managers, and critics if they are prone to the notion that decision-makers are in control of the organization and can solve problems by fixing broken parts: In Chapter 11, Gordon Crews discussed instances where prison guards would align with certain hate groups. A mechanistic resolution would be to change the hiring practices and supervision of guards. Likewise, if a district court is unable to communicate with an immigrant population, we can hire translators; if a neighborhood is experiencing a high crime rate, we can increase patrols in the area. This view ignores the nature of organizations, which are more accurately understood as living, dynamic systems.

Clancy and Webber (1995) described organizations as self-adaptive systems, which respond to stimuli from within and without the organization in ways that are not always anticipated or controlled. Continuing the watch metaphor, a technician can replace a gear to change the speed of the hands and all the other parts will work predictably. By contrast, if a local police department perceives that alcohol use by minors is a problem, the solution is not so easy. An increase in traffic stops may increase the issuance of citations, but it could also result in negative reactions from the public, uneven fate in courts depending on individual legal representation, or it could prompt students to go to other jurisdictions for social activities.

While the ability of organizations to adapt is a strength when it comes to responding to unforeseen events like disasters, it also makes change implementation difficult because of the complexity of the system. The criminal justice system has both complexity of detail (many parts) and dynamic complexity (many relationships between parts). Consider that in any town in the country, there are local, county, state, and federal law enforcement agencies; layers of state and federal court systems; and state and federal prisons. These are guided by policy and law from the local, county, and state level, which are driven by local, state, and federal forces in politics, demographics, economics, and technology.

The experience of each minority group is unique, but the preceding chapters identify some parallels in how the criminal justice system interacts with them. These patterns include majority world views, challenges in communication, and individual acts of discrimination among others. These patterns suggest that there is some organizational consistency in dealing with members of special populations, which begs continued macro analysis. It is also clear that change in one area has implications for other areas of the system.

This chapter will explore how the three components of the judicial system—law enforcement, courts, and prison systems—have affected and been changed by minority group issues, providing context for the reader to tie together the information in the preceding chapters.

LAW ENFORCEMENT

The interaction between law enforcement and racial groups is heavily influenced by the status of certain groups as minority populations. That is, it may be less important to the relationship that a person is of African American descent, gay, or Muslim than the fact that they are not of the "majority" in the community. In Chapter 2, Catherine Burton touched on the history of the U.S. legal system serving as a vehicle for enforcing the will of White people on African Americans. This situation dates to the colonial era when law enforcement supported slave ownership, and continues through the present with the current debate over racial profiling. For hundreds of years, minority groups have viewed police as agents of the majority perspective, which frames the relationship between the criminal justice system and members of special populations.

Some scholars and law enforcement professionals argue that race is not a primary factor defining interaction with an individual or a group. Police, like all humans, use their prior experience to understand situations, so an individual's characteristics may bring police scrutiny, affect interrogations, or prompt a decision to use force. Officers may be responding to cues from location, income, or age. But if race is perceived to be an issue by the public, it becomes a reality affecting how the public interacts with the police. This section will explore some of those perceptions, then go on to discuss racial profiling and policing strategies.

The cliché that perception is reality in human relations holds true in law enforcement. If a group of individuals believe that they are being treated differently by police officers, they are going to respond to the police department as if they are being discriminated against. Black youths tell of being stopped by police consistently when driving through predominantly white neighborhoods, violating notions that define where people of certain races "ought" to be (Bass 2001). This creates a perception, whether real or not, that police are enforcing the will of the majority. For their part, minority group members perceive stricter enforcement of laws, harassment, greater use of force, and a lower level of service when police interact with members of minority groups (Sigler and Johnson 2002). Because members of minority groups do not expect good service from police departments, they become less likely to report crimes even though they are no less tolerant of criminal acts (Sigler and Johnson 2002). By contrast, whites generally hold a higher opinion of police and are perceived as being more supportive of law enforcement (Weitzer and Tuch 2004).

And likewise, if police believe that members of certain groups are less prone to constructive interaction, their communication with people in those groups can be influenced. "Police see these minority groups as less supportive of law and order than majority groups," according to Sigler and Johnson (2002, 274), who went on to write that "Relations between the police and racial minority groups . . . are strained at best." With poor relations in the background, there is a lack of social capital between the police and minority groups that would allow trust and a willingness to cooperate with each other.

As relations between police departments and minority groups deteriorate, a frequent response is to try building better communications. This flows from the idea that the more people understand each other, the less likely it is that there will be misperceptions that exaggerate problems. In Aurora, Colorado, there is a strong perception among the African American community that the police department is targeting people by race and responding in overly aggressive ways (Meyer 2005). The perception can be seen in a few simple facts: Aurora's population is 14.5% African American, but 44.6% of the people hit with taser guns in 2004 were African-American, and only 3.7% of the police force is African American (Meyer 2005). This fosters a feeling among African Americans that the police department is less representative of their community and more aggressive in dealing with blacks than they are with white suspects. While Police Chief Terry Jones argues that "perceptions aren't fact," the department acknowledged that there are problems (Meyer 2005). The department has initiated regular communications with the Denver chapter of the NAACP, as well as a group of ministers, a volunteer citizen group, and the city's Human Relations Commission. A different example comes from Lynne Snowden, who wrote in Chapter 3 that the Latino population tends to be isolated from mainstream news. Latinos get most of their information from Spanish language outlets and by word of mouth. Effective outreach plans would recognize this reality, considering how the target audience gets its news.

One of the most highly charged issues in law enforcement is the use—and perceived use—of racial profiling. Broadly, profiling is the use of various indicators by law enforcement personnel to identify potential violators of the law. While this approach does not create individual violations, it does shape the pool of people who will enter the criminal justice system by giving disproportionate police scrutiny to certain racial groups. In law enforcement increased scrutiny equals increased arrests, so the technique has strong potential to bring selected groups into the justice system. Profiling came into use along major transportation routes in response to the growing use of crack cocaine and the "drug war" begun the 1980s (Ramirez et al. 2003). This was an adaptation of the criminal justice system in response to changes on the street as well as at the national policy level, prompting police to look for successful indicators associated with drug possession and trafficking. African American motorists perceived that they were being targeted for traffic stops based on race, and data support them. In an often-cited study completed in the late 1990s, "13.2% of drivers on the New Jersey turnpike were black, and that blacks and whites violated the traffic code at roughly the same rates . . ." but 73.2% of the people arrested were black (Bass 2001; data from Harris 1999). State legislatures have advanced measures to prohibit or monitor the use of profiling, but it will remain a problem because perceptions will persist.

Profiling raises civil rights issues that can be unpalatable to society, but such tactics are highly connected to the external environment. In World War II, mainstream society was willing to sacrifice the liberties of Japanese Americans to mitigate a perceived threat to the country. In contemporary America, the use of racial profiling has been accepted as a response to terrorism following the tragedies of September 11, 2001 (Ramirez et al. 2003). This suggests a familiar pattern whereby society weighs threats and considers the value of law enforcement responses. The majority group appears exempt from profiling, but it has on occasion been willing to impinge on the rights of minorities to increase identification of law breakers.

While profiling represents a tactical change in law enforcement, the major strategic change in the last 25 years has been the use of community policing (Zhao et al. 2003). Community policing changes the organizational priority of police departments away from crime control to an increased emphasis on maintaining order and delivering services tailored to the needs of a given community (Zhao et al. 2003). This is meant to indirectly but more effectively reduce crime. In an area where there are problems in the relationship between a minority group and a police department, more regular and casual interaction between residents and officers is thought to build understanding and cooperation.

An alternative to this approach is the Zero Tolerance Policy implemented in New York City in the 1990s. Growing from the "Broken Windows" strategy that emphasized the maintenance of order in areas that were visibly unkempt, Mayor Giuliani and Police Chief Bratton discarded community policing in favor of a strategy of enforcing laws that improved the "quality of life" in neighborhoods. These included crackdowns on littering, graffiti, prostitutes, and minor drug-related crimes, which disproportionately affected members of racial minority groups. While the crime rate fell in New York City, research has not demonstrated that the Zero Tolerance Policing strategy is the cause.

Law enforcement responds to changes in the social environment, like all organizations. These changes can come from local communities, as when part of the constituency engages in a public debate about police harassment or discrimination; they can come from the national level as in the cases of the Drug War and the War on Terrorism; and they can come internally as we saw in the changing emphasis on crime-enforcement, order preservation, and service delivery. It is a certainty that law enforcement agencies will continually need to find ways of adapting to changing circumstances, but the challenge of pursuing their mission while treating minority groups with fairness will endure.

THE COURT SYSTEM

People charged with crimes are tried in court to determine their guilt and assess a punishment. The Sixth Amendment to the U.S. Constitution provides this right, as well as the right to an attorney and a trial by a jury of their peers. The court system is meant to provide a rational, fair, and fact-based process for adjudicating criminal charges, but as suggested at the beginning of this chapter, organizations are not machines. Subtle, consistent pressure from many small parts can affect the entire nature of the system. A common cultural experience can create just such a pressure.

There is substantial research indicating that members of minority groups do not, statistically, meet with the same results as white people in the judicial system (Engen et al. 2003). This is not to say there is purposeful discrimination, but there are points in the processes of courts where culture and experience create advantages and disadvantages. One way of explaining this is by considering the courts a majority institution, or what Christine Cruz (2005) refers to as a "white space." Courts are derived from European legal tradition, and the attorneys, judges, and prosecutors are educated from a white perspective. Law schools and the majoritarian culture train attorneys to focus on certain factors and to remove race from their analysis in all but a few cases (Pearce 2005). Race is not an issue to white people, so the argument goes, thus it is not part of legal analysis.

But race and other demographic characteristics frequently define the context for events that come before a court. When attorneys bypass racial issues in their defense strategy in favor of other defenses, they are enabling a system that includes discriminatory elements while neglecting relevant factors that may benefit a client's case. Cruz (2005) argues that race provides essential context for an individual, and thus his or her actions. If the attorney representing an individual does not understand that context, their ability to represent the client is impaired. "Racial and cultural issues imbedded in a legal problem emerge more clearly in the context of a community; and understanding the community can help the lawyer understand the client much better" (Cruz 2005, 2143). This can be highly relevant in cases of harassment, police brutality, discrimination, and public disorder complaints.

As race can alter the ability of the attorney to represent the client, it also affects the analysis of the judge. Because judges tend to be white and male, the judiciary holds built-in biases based on the common experiences and perceptions of that demographic. The pattern of how this homogeneity affects the system can be seen in "Kevin Lyles' 1997 study [that] revealed that eighty-three percent of Caucasian Judges believed African American litigants were treated fairly by the criminal justice system, whereas only eighteen percent of African-American Judges held this same belief" (Wynn and Mazur 2004, 783). The pattern of wealthy white men ruling on cases affecting lower-income members of minority groups suggests a disconnect with population subgroups in the system. In Lebanon, Tennessee, a judge told a Mexican woman she would risk losing custody of her daughter if she didn't improve her English (Nation in Brief 2005). And in Sarpy County, Nebraska, a judge ordered a Mexican American man to refrain from speaking "Hispanic" around his five-year-old daughter, or his visitation rights would be curtailed (Fears 2003). When the judiciary is not even able to respond effectively to language issues, less obvious differences are sure to subtly affect the juridical process.

The influence of judges is often particularly evident at the sentencing stage where aggravating and mitigating circumstances influence decisions. When judges are less prepared to understand these circumstances, which often contain issues beyond the facts of the offense, they instill a pattern of rulings that has disparate outcomes (Engen et al. 2003). Beyond cultural awareness, personal prejudices can affect sentencing. Reid Toth cited in Chapter 8 an incident where a judge stated he would have trouble sentencing someone to life in prison for killing a prostitute or "queer." As a systemic response, sentencing guidelines were developed to reduce the influence of vague factors on judicial decisions, but Engen et al. (2003) found that the framework for departing from the guidelines still allowed minorities to be disadvantaged. As an alternative, structured sentencing alternatives can provide judges with guidance on how specific factors can influence a sentence, increasing perceived fairness across demographics.

Juries are yet a third component of the court system where the cause and effect of racial issues come into play. Prosecutors and defense attorneys recognize that individual experiences affect how jurors view witnesses, victims, and defendants. In part, this is attributable to the fact that trials at a minimum present two versions of events, and often they provide incomplete information. Jurors draw upon their instincts when analyzing witnesses, and use their perspectives to understand and interpret scenarios put forth by the opposing sides. This often invokes racial issues—as mentioned above—that provide the context for events.

Attorneys anticipate how jurors of various racial and ethnic backgrounds will view their arguments, and seek the most favorable jury possible. "A lawyer with an ounce of resolve and a modicum of planning can easily ensure that no minorities will appear in a jury if he or she believes it strategically advantageous" (Gannaway 2002, 377). In *Batson v. Kentucky* (1986), the U.S. Supreme Court ruled that jurors could not be removed from the pool because of their race, but peremptory strikes allow lawyers to remove jurors for race-neutral but unspecified reasons. Texas courts have taken a consistent stand against peremptory strikes that include a racial component, but elsewhere in the country judges allow removals that include but are not limited to race-neutral reasons.

There are policy models of ensuring that minority group members are present in a jury, such as the Hennepin Model that "requires juries to mirror the racial composition of the community" (Boatright 2003, 342). Another approach is to require that at least three people on a twelve person jury be minority group members, based on the notion that three present a critical mass of resistance that is not easily pressured by the balance of the group (Boatright 2003). The peremptory strike issue and various requirements for representation on a jury are efforts to increase the diversity on juries, acknowledging both that monolithic cultural representation does a disservice to the system and that consistent and fair responses to the problem of jury bias have yet to emerge.

In a clear example of systemic adaptation, courts have responded to the high volume and particular characteristics of drug offenses by creating special "drug courts." Offenders are law breakers, but they also are driven by habits that differ from other types of offenders. Drug courts establish behavioral objectives, require various treatments, and monitor compliance with the threat of incarceration providing an incentive for compliance. When effective, this approach benefits the state by helping to control prison population and reducing related expenses, and replacing punishment with treatment is a more effective method of changing behavior (Cresswell and Deschenes 2001). Because minorities comprise a disproportionate share of drug convictions, it is important to the issue of race and criminal justice to consider the impact of drug courts on minorities. Cresswell and Deschenes (2001) explored this issue, and found that minority group members perceived drug court diversion programs to be more severe than did non-minorities, and that minorities viewed prison to be less severe than did non-minorities. While the authors suggest the confrontational and behavioral control techniques run counter to minority cultures, the effectiveness of the programs suggest they are a valuable development in the system.

The process of self-adaptation can at times be masked behind political battles. Barry Feld (2003) wrote that a series of Supreme Court decisions in the 1950s and 1960s strengthened due process in juvenile courts, disrupting the discriminatory practices common in southern states known as Jim Crow laws. While the state justice systems in the South had developed according to local forces, the federal level responded to bring national values to bear. What appeared to be targeted political battles were in fact part of a larger systemic evolution. This process continued as urban crime rates climbed in the 1960s and 1970s, and conservative politicians used strict law and order messages to appeal to majority group voters with insecurities about minority groups (Feld 2003). Their response came in the form of harsher sentences that were focused on punishment rather than rehabilitation.

Despite the ideal of equality before the law, the judiciary is heavily influenced by internal forces like the demographics of judges, juries, and attorneys, and external forces like history and politics. Diversity in the judiciary, juries, and attorneys can mitigate the impact of cultural backgrounds, but at present the system falls short of that goal.

PRISONS

Racial background is a driving factor in the prison experience. As mentioned in the previous section, African Americans tend to see prison as a less severe experience than whites, but this may be a socioeconomic rather than racial issue. The suggestion is that people who grow up in economically depressed urban settings may be better prepared for prison life than others. That said, the demographic setting in prison can be very different than in mainstream society. For example, minorities are strikingly over-represented in prison: "At midyear 2004 there were 4,919 black male prison and jail inmates per 100,000 black males in the United States, compared to 1,717 Hispanic male inmates per 100,000 Hispanic males and 717 white male inmates per 100,000 white males" (Prison Statistics 2005). In 2003, the annual mid-year prisoner count found that state and federal prisons and local jails held 665,100 white males, 832,400 black males, and 363,900 Hispanic males (Harrison and Karberg 2004). In sum, whites transition from being in the majority on the street to being in the minority in prison.

Over the past 50 years, prison gangs largely defined by race have emerged as the primary organizing force in prison subculture (Hunt et al. 1993). Various factors drive this issue, including competition for resources through the underground economy, the pressures of overcrowding, and affiliation with outside gangs. It is clear that when an individual enters prison race "is the most significant referent even for those prisoners without formal and informal group ties" (Jacobs 1975). This is a new experience for whites to whom race was not a big factor in everyday life, but tremendous pressure comes to bear on people to join a gang. Gordon Crews writes in Chapter 11 that in the first half of the twentieth century, there was an inmate code that defined solidarity against the guards. This has yielded in recent decades to a culture of gangs defined by race.

The emergence of powerful race-based gangs has affected the treatment of individuals, such as white custodians assigning safe or easy jobs to white inmates (Ross and Hawkins 1995). However, the existing research does not offer a definitive answer as to whether there is a systematic effect of bias (Walker et al. 2004). This may be in part due to the fact that state and federal prisons employ African Americans at a rate roughly proportionate to the general population (Walker et al. 2004). Beyond showing racial preferences, it is also clear that prison guards use race and gang affiliation for their own ends. They transfer individuals to certain areas of the prison where they will be beaten, they sell drugs and other contraband to gangs, and they create heightened security environments to control prisoners (Hunt et al. 1993; Ross and Hawkins 1995).

Although an individual ends up in prison as a consequence of their experience with law enforcement and the court system, their race remains an important factor because the transition from an individual in the system to a member of a group within the system. Whether or not a person had a strong racial identity before prison, the culture within prison often pushes individuals to become part of a group.

PUBLIC POLICY

Beyond law enforcement, courts, and prison, lies the public policy arena where elected officials, media, and the general public develop ideas and steer the criminal justice system. However, to argue that politics affect the criminal justice system would address only part of the picture. People respond to emerging issues, and they invoke criminal justice issues and perceptions of crime in pursuit of their own goals. The criminal justice system affects people, and people affect politics. Recalling the opening discussion in this chapter, the criminal justice system and society at large are not machines where clear and predictable relationships exist. A change in one part of the system can cause unforeseen and much larger reactions in other parts of the system.

One problematic example of this was the rapid proliferation of crack cocaine. Politicians saw this as a major social problem, and declared a "war on drugs." Crack was particularly an urban problem, and police in urban areas began use of profiling techniques to identify drug dealers and users. The result was increased scrutiny on African-American males, which led to more arrests of African American males for drug and other offenses. This in turn created a public and political response, as Catherine Burton documented in Chapter 2. As the war on drugs also produced more drug-related criminal charges, the system responded with drug courts.

A more contemporary example is the proliferation of gang violence, which is seen by the middle class as a largely minority-driven issue like crack cocaine was in the 1980s. This provides an opportunity for policymakers to take on an issue with racial and economic undertones, playing to voters who seek more order in society. In May 2005, the U.S. House of Representatives passed a bill entitled *Gang Deterrence and Community Protection Act* that would "greatly expand federal authority to prosecute gang members, even for local activity" (House Overreaches 2005). New definitions of offenses will enable the federal government to prosecute crimes previously dealt with by state governments. The bill has yet to pass the Senate and be signed into law.

The major national criminal justice issue today is terrorism, a direct reaction to the events of September 11, 2001. Congress responded by passing the *USA PATRIOT Act*, which has had many repercussions. Federal law enforcement can now conduct limited "sneak and peek" searches without informing targeted individuals, and in national security instances can obtain search warrants without allowing judges to review the circumstances of the case. The act included other measures, all intended to strengthen the hand of the criminal justice system in the effort to prevent new acts of terrorism. The public accepted this ceding of privacy as a necessary trade-off for a broadly desired policy objective.

Hate crimes offer another example of the intersection between public opinion, politics, racial minorities, and the criminal justice system. In the 1980s, a growing trend in hate-motivated crimes was set against a backdrop of a victims' rights movement. Increased media coverage created a heightened public awareness of hate crimes, and various civil rights groups worked to define hate crimes and focus political attention on responses. States variously passed laws defining hate crimes and creating increased sentences where hate was a factor (Martin 1995).

One of the characteristics of systems is that change is not affected easily. New legislation represents a mechanistic view, where change in one part of the system is intended to solve a cross-cutting problem. While hate crimes legislation established race and bias motivated crimes as a distinct issue, the societal goal cannot be achieved without integrated changes across the system. For example, while hate crimes legislation created a new type of crime, the system still relies on law enforcement to recognize such crimes and record them as such. In jurisdictions where the police force is particularly disconnected from minority group issues, an officer may not be prepared to effectively interview witnesses, record evidence, and document events to establish motivations for a crime. Likewise, the attorneys, judges, and juries in the court system may not be able to understand the social context of the incident. Thus, to make a change as broad as instituting hate-crimes as part of the criminal justice system, legislation must be combined with knowledge and acceptance throughout the different parts of the system. Otherwise, changes may fail or prompt unintended reactions that undermine the policy objective.

CONCLUSION

This book has documented how various groups are unique because of language, collective history, the ways they view others (religious groups), or the ways others view them (gays and lesbians). In each case, the group's characteristics cause them to have different experiences with a criminal justice system dominated by a vague and shifting "mainstream" population. We learned that demographic majorities can use the criminal justice system to enforce a cultural perspective, whether that deals with sexual orientation or ideas about "who" belongs "where." These perspectives might be imposed consciously by individuals, or systematically by homogenous collective experience.

These prejudices can be mitigated by effective research and public discussion, but the system can obstruct this process as well. A vivid example appears in Chapter 3, where Lynne Snowden notes that the FBI's Uniform Crime Report does not recognize "Hispanic" as a demographic category. This makes it difficult to understand how a rapidly growing segment of the population is interacting with the criminal justice system. We cannot learn without the information.

Another fundamental challenge is communication between the criminal justice system and minority communities. When people do not trust the police, they are less likely to report crimes and more likely to perceive injustice. Likewise, when police do not understand the groups they are there to serve, they have difficulty recognizing crimes and understanding behavior.

A third problem is the representation of minorities in police departments, court systems, and in corrections. Diverse populations in each of these stages of the system can increase understanding and communication among all parties, reducing the aggravation of problems. Issues such as profiling, charging, legal representation, sentencing, and the impact of race in prisons are each affected by the cultural composition of criminal justice system employees.

The challenges of the minority experience within the criminal justice system have deep roots in American history. As with most social issues, better information, communication, and inclusion are the principles of improvement. The authors hope this book has advanced the reader's understanding, and thereby contributed to the constructive development of criminal justice in America.

REFERENCES

Bass, S. (2001). Policing space, policing race: Social control imperatives and police discretionary decisions. *Social Justice, 28*, 156–176.

Boatright, R. (2003). Race in the jury box: Affirmative action in jury selection. *Justice System Journal, 24*, 341.

Clancy, D., and R. Webber. (1995). *Roses and rust: Redefining the essence of leadership in a new age*. Sydney: Business & Professional.

Cresswell, L., and E. Deschenes. (2001). Minority and non-minority perceptions of drug court program severity and effectiveness. *Journal of Drug Issues, 31*, 259–292.

CRUZ, C. (2005). Four questions on critical race praxis: Lessons from two young lives in Indian Country. *Fordham Law Review, 73*, 2133–2160.

ENGEN, R., R. GAINEY, R. CRUTCHFIELD, AND J. WEIS. (2003). Discretion and disparity under sentencing guidelines: The role of departures and structured sentencing alternatives. *Criminology, 41*, 99–130.

FEARS, D. (2003). Judge orders Neb. father not to speak "Hispanic." *Washington Post*. October 17.

FELD, B. (2003). The politics of race and juvenile justice: The "due process revolution" and the conservative reaction. *Justice Quarterly, 20*, 765–800.

GANNAWAY, G. (2002). Texas independence: The Lone Star State serves as an example to other jurisdictions as it rejects mixed-motive defenses to Batson challenges. *Review of Litigation, 21*, 375–418. Austin: University of Texas.

HARRIS, D. (1999). The stories, the statistics, and the law: Why driving while Black matters." *Minnesota Law Review, 84*, 265–328.

HARRISION, P., AND J. KARBERG. (2004). Prison and jail inmates at mid-year 2003. *Bureau of Justice Statistics Bulletin*. May. http://www.ojp.usdoj.gov/bjs/pub/pdf/pjim03.pdf. Accessed May 16, 2005.

HUNT, G., S. RIEGEL, T. MORALES, AND D. WALDORF. (1993). Changes in the prison culture: Prison gangs and the case of the Pepsi generation. *Social Problems, 40*, 398–409.

JACOBS, J. (1975). Stratification and conflict among prison inmates. *Journal of Criminal Law and Criminology, 66*, 476–482.

MARTIN, S. (1995). A cross-burning is not just an arson: Police social construction of hate crimes in Baltimore County. *Criminology, 33*, 303–326.

MEYER, J. (2005). African-American, police at odds in Aurora Chief battling "perceptions." *Denver Post*. April 22, 2005.

Nation in Brief. (2005). *Washington Post*. April 19, 2005.

PEARCE, R. (2005). White lawyering: Rethinking race, lawyer identify, and rule of law. *Fordham Law Review, 73*, 2081–2100.

Prison Statistics. (2005). Bureau of Justice Statistics. http://www.ojp.usdoj.gov/bjs/prisons.htm. Accessed May 26, 2005.

RAMIEREZ, D., J. HOOPES, AND T. L. QUINLAN. (2003). Defining racial profiling in a post-September 11 world. *American Criminal Law Review, 40*, 1195–1233.

ROSS, L., AND D. HAWKINS. (1995). Legal and historical views on racial biases in prison. *Corrections Today, 57*, 192–195.

SIGLER, R., AND I. JOHNSON. (2002). Reporting violent acts to the police: A difference by race. *Policing, 25*, 274–293.

The House Overreaches. (2005). *Washington Post* editorial. May 16,

WALKER, S., C. SPOHN, AND M. DELONE. (2004). *The color of justice*. 3rd ed. Belmont, CA: Thomson Wadsworth.

WEITZER, R., AND S. TUCH. (2004). Reforming the police: Racial differences in public support for change. *Criminology, 42*, 391–416.

WYNN, J., AND MAZUR, E. (2004). Judicial Diversity: Where independence and accountability meet (Perspectives: Judicial Elections versus merit selection) . *Albany Law Review, 67*, 775–792.

ZHAO, J., N. HE, AND N. LOVRICH. (2003). Community policing: Did it change the basic functions of policing in the 1990s? A national follow-up study. *Justice Quarterly, 20*, 697–720.

CASES

Batson v. Kentucky (1986), 476 U.S. 79

Index